DUMBARTON OAKS
MEDIEVAL LIBRARY

Jan M. Ziolkowski, General Editor

THE LIFE OF SAINT NEILOS

OF ROSSANO

DOML 47

The Life of Saint Neilos
of Rossano

Edited and Translated by

RAYMOND L. CAPRA

INES A. MURZAKU

DOUGLAS J. MILEWSKI

DUMBARTON OAKS
MEDIEVAL LIBRARY

HARVARD UNIVERSITY PRESS
CAMBRIDGE, MASSACHUSETTS
LONDON, ENGLAND
2018

Copyright © 2018 by the President and Fellows of Harvard College
ALL RIGHTS RESERVED
Printed in the United States of America

Library of Congress Cataloging-in-Publication Data
Names: Capra, Raymond L., 1971– editor, translator. | Murzaku, Ines
Angjeli, editor, translator. | Milewski, Douglas J., editor, translator.
Title: The life of Saint Neilos of Rossano / edited and translated by
Raymond L. Capra, Ines A. Murzaku, Douglas J. Milewski.
Other titles: Bios kai politeia tou hosiou patros håemåon Neilou tou
neou. | Bios kai politeia tou hosiou patros håemåon Neilou tou neou.
English.
Description: Cambridge, Massachusetts : Harvard University Press, 2018. |
    Series: Dumbarton Oaks medieval library ; 47 | Texts in Greek with
English translations on facing pages ; introduction and notes in English. |
    Includes bibliographical references and index.
Identifiers: LCCN 2017018920 | ISBN 9780674977044 (alk. paper)
Subjects: LCSH: Nilus, the Younger, Saint, –1004. | Christian saints—
Italy—Biography. | Christian saints—Byzantine Empire—Biography. |
Christian hagiography.
Classification: LCC BX4700.N355 L5 2017 | DDC 270.3092 [B]—dc23
LC record available at https://lccn.loc.gov/2017018920

Contents

Introduction

The Life of Neilos of Rossano, a saint from Calabria, is generally considered "the masterpiece of Italo-Greek monastic literature."[1] Saint Neilos vividly exemplifies Greek monastic life in tenth-century southern Italy at a time when the region had come under the control of the Byzantine Empire. Italo-Greek monks of this period pursued both the cenobitic and the eremitic forms of monasticism and often moved easily back and forth between the two modes of life, in a manner very similar to their fellow Orthodox monks in Greece and Anatolia. Those living as solitaries greatly revered the rigorous asceticism of the desert fathers of Egypt and Syria, while their cenobitic brethren followed the traditions advocated by Theodore of the Stoudios monastery in Constantinople in the early ninth century and Athanasios at the Great Lavra on Mount Athos in the tenth century. At the same time, Italo-Greek monks were familiar with the Benedictine traditions espoused by their Latin-speaking brethren who lived further north, closer to Rome, and in some cases interacted in a friendly and collegial manner with them. The schism of 1054 that divided the Eastern and Western churches had not yet taken place, although already differences had emerged in liturgical practice and monastic rules.

Biography of Saint Neilos

Neilos of Rossano, who is also known as Neilos the Younger, was born in Rossano, Calabria, circa 910, shortly after the conquest of the region from the Lombards by the Byzantine general Nikephoros Phokas the Elder. Neilos's hagiographer describes him as a "gift from God" granted to his family, which was one of the most illustrious Rossanese families of the time. While Neilos was still young, both of his parents died, and from this point he was raised by his elder sister, who took meticulous care of his education. According to the *Life,* the young Neilos was highly intelligent, witty, and physically attractive to women; he married a local girl and had a daughter. Around 940, at the age of thirty, Neilos abandoned his birthplace, wife, and child to enter monastic life at the monasteries of Merkourion in the nearby Byzantine province (a so-called theme) of Lucania. He then moved to Lombard territory to receive the monastic habit at the monastery of Saint Nazarios, because of threatening letters from the Byzantine governor of Rossano sent to all monasteries of the region that would potentially receive Neilos.[2] Once the situation calmed down around 940/41, Neilos returned to Merkourion, following the guidance of Phantinos the Younger (who was born in Calabria in the late ninth century and died in Thessalonike in the late tenth century) and progressing in monastic life and virtue. After three years in Merkourion, following his great desire for the solitary life and with the permission of his superiors, Neilos took up residence around 943 as a hermit in a cave near the monastery, which had a sanctuary dedicated to the Archangel Michael; here he fought the temptations of the flesh. Two years

later, still leading a solitary life, he received his first disciple, Stephen from Rossano. During the years 952 to 953 Neilos returned to the region near Rossano, where he founded the monastery of Saint Adrian on his family property and remained for twenty-five years.

Neilos fled Calabria around 978 on account of raids from Muslim Sicily. Neilos and his brethren then began their northbound trajectory to the Benedictine monastery of Monte Cassino, where they lived at the dependency of Valleloukion (S. Angelo di Valleluce) for fifteen years, following the Greek rite. During this period the number of brethren increased, all their necessities were provided for in abundance, and the monastery grew in size and fame. However, some of the Greek brethren eventually lapsed from a scrupulous observance of the monastic rule according to which they had originally been tonsured; this caused Neilos to move in 994 to Serperi, near Gaeta, which was humbler and poorer in comparison to Valleloukion. Serperi turned out to be the perfect place to practice asceticism. Here, escaping from the dangers of vainglory, Neilos avoided dealings with the region's powerful magnates with very few exceptions.

After the death in 1003 of his beloved disciple Stephen, Neilos went to Grottaferrata in Tusculum near Rome, where he would die and be buried. The Count of Tusculum, Gregory, despite being known for his cruelties, offered Neilos his house, his territories, and his fortress, where Neilos found his final resting place in Grottaferrata. According to tradition the villa donated by Gregory to Neilos and his brethren was Marcus Tullius Cicero's villa, where he wrote the *Tusculanae Quaestiones*.[3] Neilos died on September 26, 1004, sur-

rounded by his beloved brethren. He begged them not to delay burying his body in the earth, on level ground, so that pilgrims might rest there, for Neilos, too, had been a pilgrim all the days of his life. The *Life* ends with a prayer that, through the intercession of the saint and his saintly brothers, the future generations who hear or read of their deeds may also be deemed worthy to become their associates in the kingdom of heaven.[4]

To sum up, the *Life* presents Neilos as a charismatic monastic leader who attracted disciples wherever he went. He was frequently on the move, disregarding the principle of monastic stability, that is, remaining for life in the monastery where one is first tonsured. He went back and forth between cave hermitages and cenobitic monasteries, but he preferred the solitary life. He imposed strict obedience upon the monks whom he directed, but himself always set an example of humility, hard work, and ascetic behavior. He was a man of many talents, a skilled calligrapher and hymnographer, and bilingual in Greek and Latin.

The Vita of Saint Neilos and Its Author

There is no consensus among scholars about the authorship of *The Life of Saint Neilos*. According to the monastic tradition of Grottaferrata, the *Life* was written by Saint Bartholomew the Younger, otherwise known as Saint Bartholomew of Grottaferrata, third successor of Neilos as abbot.[5] Other scholars disagree with the attribution to Bartholomew. However, there is consensus that Saint Neilos's *Life* was written in Grottaferrata or in a nearby Latin region and the anonymous hagiographer was probably a Calabrian monk,

one of Saint Neilos's early disciples.[6] The unidentified author was an eyewitness of the historic events of the period and a faithful disciple of the saint who practiced firsthand the teaching of his spiritual father and teacher.[7] A phrase in the prologue (chap. 1.1), "these last times of the last centuries," suggests that the *Life* may have been written early in the eleventh century, soon after Neilos's death, as it implies millenarian concerns that were common in this era.[8]

In comparison to the *Lives* of other Italo-Greek saints who were born and active in southern Italy and Sicily, the biography of Saint Neilos not only is documented in the hagiographic text and in the religious hymns dedicated to the saintly monk but can be traced independently in other sources as well. For example, the year of Neilos's death is documented in a Grottaferrata inscription that indicates the year 6513 (1004) according to the Byzantine calculation.[9]

Hagiographic sources that confirm the information in the *Life* of Neilos include the tenth-century *Life of Saint Phantinos*. According to Enrica Follieri, Neilos and Phantinos first met in the region of Merkourion around 939, when Neilos was in his late twenties and Phantinos had concluded his monastic "probation" and had begun the monastic establishments of Merkourion, to which the *Life of Saint Phantinos* (chaps. 17 and 18) makes specific reference.[10] In addition, the *Life of Saint Bartholomew the Younger* also refers to Neilos and the reputation the saint left behind for those who were "lovers of virtue."[11] Neilos is also mentioned in the *Chronicle of Montecassino* and the *Life of Saint Adalbert, Bishop of Prague.*[12] All these sources attest to the historicity of the person named Neilos and the accuracy of factual and historical information presented in the *Life.*[13]

The author writes good quality Greek in a middle level of style, with predominantly biblical allusions, but with occasional quotations from or references to patristic literature as well, such as the orations of Gregory of Nazianzos, the ascetic rules of Basil of Caesarea, and an encomium of John of Damascus. He also reveals familiarity with monastic literature, including the Lives of the Desert Fathers; the Ladder of John Klimax; some hagiographic texts, including the Life of Ambrose in Latin; and the writings of Theodore of Stoudios. Unusually, the vita of Neilos contains no account of posthumous miracles that occurred at his tomb, and there are very few descriptions of miracles performed during his lifetime. Rather, Neilos is described as delegating healing cures to others (chaps. 58–59).

ECCLESIAL-HISTORICAL CONTEXT FOR THE VITA OF NEILOS

In the tenth century, southern Italy was part of the Byzantine Empire, subject to rule by Constantinople. It contained diverse communities of Greek- and Latin-speaking Christians, Jews, and Muslims, alongside pockets of Franks, Bulgarians, Armenians, and people of other ethnicities. The Calabria of Neilos's lifetime was a region caught between the competing ambitions, strategies, politics, and military adventures of its Byzantine overlords to the northeast, the Holy Roman Empire to the north, and Arab emirs in Sicily and North Africa. It was an insecure territory that did not enjoy long periods of tranquility. The vita makes a number of references to Muslim raiders who tried to storm the walls of Rossano (chap. 2) and threatened the security of ru-

ral monasteries; some monks were forced to retreat to the safety of a nearby fortress, while others were captured and carried off to Sicily (chap. 71). Around 978 Neilos decided to leave Calabria for Capua, because he foresaw that the region would be overrun by Muslims (chap. 72.2–3).

The Life of Saint Neilos offers a snapshot of a cultural and ecclesial world that was soon to vanish on account of several decisive events: the schism between the churches of Rome and Constantinople in 1054, the start of the papal Gregorian reforms in the latter half of the eleventh century, which would transform the Western Church and set it further apart from its Eastern counterpart, and the beginning of the age of the Crusades in 1090. Already in the tenth century Latin and Greek Christians had developed some different liturgical and monastic traditions. Thus, the Latins used unleavened bread for the Eucharist, and their priests were clean shaven, while Greek priests used leavened bread and were bearded. In the monastic sphere, Latin monks belonged to a single Benedictine order, and were permitted to eat meat on occasion, whereas each Greek monastery was a separate foundation with its own rule, and the eating of meat was strictly forbidden. An instructive section of the vita of Neilos (chap. 78) features a discussion between Neilos and the Latin monks of Monte Cassino on differing traditions in East and West about fasting on the Sabbath. Nonetheless, while clearly conscious of their distinctiveness, and at times quite contentiously so, the Eastern and Western halves of the Christian world in the tenth century still understood themselves as part of a single religious community. Remarkably, Aligernus, abbot of the Benedictine monastery of Monte Cassino, invited Neilos, who was bilingual, to cel-

ebrate the liturgy in Greek at Monte Cassino. Neilos not only accepted the invitation but composed a Greek hymn in honor of Saint Benedict (chaps. 73.4–74.1).[14] Statesmen from the respective realms at various times sought to extend that sense of spiritual commonality into political reality by linking the two empires through marriage, such as that of the Greek Theophano to Otto II (r. 967–983).[15] The youthful Otto III, Theophano's son, aspired to become more Greek than Saxon and understandably looked up to Neilos as a spiritual father (chaps. 92–93). The Western world at the close of the first millennium was widely open to the spiritual and cultural influences of the Byzantine tradition, as the emergence of a great and confidently Western and Christian civilization in the High Middle ages was two centuries distant in the future. Additionally, in this period the papacy was not the dynamic force it would shortly become. Indeed, Neilos's lifespan overlaps with the nadir of papal history, the tenth century witnessing the See of Rome reduced to a political pawn with several truly notorious occupants.[16]

Saint Neilos's Calabria, therefore, was the westernmost extension of the Byzantine religious, political, and cultural world, at whose core lay the rich and multifaceted experience of Greek monasticism. The consensus of scholars is that the re-Hellenization of Calabria and of Terra d'Otranto (approximately the eighth to the eleventh century) can be attributed mainly to the spread of Greek monasticism, which in certain regions either accompanied or preceded the re-Hellenization process, thus preparing the way for the next phase: the Byzantine domination of the region.[17] Biagio Cappelli maintained that the first ascetic influx in the area followed the armies of the Byzantine general Belisarius

and later those of Narses, who brought to a successful conclusion the sixth-century campaign against the Arian Goths, a war that certainly had religious undertones.[18] However, Cappelli did not specify the precise region of the empire from which these monks emigrated. This first migration of Eastern monks to southern Italy was followed by a second wave of migration, this time from the Balkan Peninsula, which by the end of the sixth century was devastated by the Avar invasions.

Later movements of Greek monks into southern Italy followed the Muslim conquest of Sicily in the ninth century.[19] Francesco Russo, a native Calabrian ecclesiastical historian, provides a general timeline of the ascetic movement in Calabria. He specifies that its origins lie between the end of the sixth century and the first half of the seventh century, and it slowly but definitely advanced to the point of supplanting every other similar Latin form of monasticism during the eighth and ninth centuries.[20] It reached its zenith during the tenth and eleventh centuries, during Neilos's lifetime.[21] While augmented at discrete moments by refugees from political crises, the growth of Greek-speaking monasticism in Calabria was a product of the continuous circulation of peoples in the early medieval Mediterranean.[22]

From the eighth to the twelfth century, southern Italy and especially Calabria became what Paolo Giannini calls the Terra dei Monaci (Land of the Monks), with thousands of monasteries that spread in the mountains and in the vicinities of the great cities and castles. Virtually everywhere the monks could find a peaceful place to dedicate themselves to prayer and the service of God, they erected a monastery.[23] Calabria was considered "the new Thebaid," a land

that provided abundant opportunities for Byzantine monks to establish themselves.[24] However, Cappelli appropriately observed that the great ascetic migrations in southern Italy did not initiate but instead completed what he calls the centuries-old process of Hellenization that southern Italy underwent.[25] Italo-Greek monasticism, which originated in the Christian East, and its wide enculturation in southern Italy testify to monasticism's adaptability. Additionally, Italo-Greek monasticism highlights the southern Italian region and culture, which was a locus of communication and in constant connection and exchange with the surrounding cultures and a suitable habitat that accommodated different monastic lifestyles, including both eremitic and cenobitic monasticism.

The *Lives* of the Italo-Greek monks are indispensable primary sources for the study of the somewhat obscure history of southern Italy, providing precious testimonies to the persons, places, local customs, struggles of daily life, and the quite unique ascetic practices and discipline followed by Italo-Greek monks. In southern Italy, similar to Byzantine society elsewhere, monks played multiple roles: they were spiritual guides and models to be emulated by the locals. Because of their considerable numbers, culture, and influence—economic and otherwise—on the local population, the Italo-Greek monks raised awareness and appreciation of Byzantine civilization in the West. Saint Neilos is one of the most celebrated representatives of this cultural and religious influence of the Italo-Greek monks. It was the monks who helped to form both the rural and the urban people of southern Italy in the ideals of Byzantine civilization, fostering societal and cultural cohesiveness within southern Italy

and giving its population a sense of belonging to the broader Byzantine Empire.[26]

Italo-Greek monasticism was elastic and highly adaptive, while being a tributary to the broad river of the Greek monastic tradition. Traditionally, Italo-Greek monasticism had hosted both solitary hermits and those who were more inclined to a communal lifestyle, an accommodation that was favored by monastic, civil, and ecclesial leaders. The coexistence of these forms of ascetic life in Italy was the result of the ninth-century reforms started by Saint Theodore the Stoudite in Constantinople, which emphasized communal monastic life, as well as of the reaction to these reforms by monks who sought to preserve the opportunity for a life of solitude and spiritual tranquility within the context of cenobitic monasticism.[27] The *Lives* of Italo-Greek saints, including the *Life of Saint Neilos,* point to this integration of cenobitic and eremitic monasticism. According to Neilos's *Life,* the saint preferred a solitary life of spiritual tranquility (chap. 44.2) but also acknowledged the difficult challenges and rigor of cenobitic life (chap. 33.1).

Among the characteristics of Italo-Greek monasticism of the tenth and eleventh centuries was a tendency to expand in a central-north direction within the Italian peninsula. This tendency was sometimes encouraged, as in the case of Neilos, by pressure from Muslim expansion into southern Italy.[28] In addition, the ninth through eleventh centuries saw a constant flow of people, many of them Greek-speaking monks, coming on pilgrimage to Rome. The Italo-Greek monks, like Italo-Greek clergy in general, were spiritually inclined to the Church of Constantinople, while readily granting a primacy of honor to the papacy. The

tombs of the apostles Peter and Paul were places of pilgrimage and prayer for Italo-Greek monks, as they were for Eastern monks on pilgrimage to Rome. Conversely, people from the West were recorded in pilgrimage toward the spiritual, miracle-working elite of Eastern monasticism. These monastic exchanges and dialogue confirm that what Enrico Morini called a mutual ecclesiastical hospitality between two parts of Christendom indeed existed, and the estrangement and doctrinal-theological contentions had not yet entered the people's consciousness.[29] Christendom and the Church were understood as one, undivided, and indivisible, East and West.

Translations of the Vita of Neilos

The first Latin translation of the *Life,* based on Crypt. Gr. B. β. II (430), the original eleventh-century manuscript, was made in 1585 by Cardinal Guglielmo Sirleto (Guglielmus Sirletus) and includes the now missing folios of that manuscript. The second Latin translation by Matthaeus Caryophilus (Matthaios Karyophylles), *Vita Sancti Patris Nili Iunioris,* was published in Rome in 1624. Niccolò Barducci under the auspices of Cardinal Barberini made the first Italian translation in 1628; this was followed by Giovanni Minasi's *S. Nilo di Calabria, monaco basiliano nel decimo secolo* in 1892, Antonio Rocchi's *Vita di San Nilo abate* in 1904, and Germano Giovanelli's *Vita di S. Nilo, fondatore e patrono di Grottaferrata* in 1966. A translation in modern Greek with facing medieval Greek text by Sister Maxime, Ὁ ὅσιος Νεῖλος ὁ Καλαβρός. Ὁ Βίος τοῦ ὁσίου Νείλου τοῦ Νέου (910–1004). Εἰσαγωγὴ -

Κριτικὴ ἔκδοσις τοῦ κειμένου - Μετάφρασις - Σχόλια - Ὑμνογραφικὸ ἔργο τοῦ ὁσίου, was published in 1991.

Ours is the first translation into English. We should note that to add clarity we have frequently inserted proper nouns instead of pronouns and have also added some short explanatory phrases. For biblical citations we have used the English translation of Sir Lancelot Brenton for the Septuagint and the second edition of the Revised Standard Version of the New Testament, occasionally modified as necessary.

A debt of thanks is owed first to Dr. Alice-Mary Talbot, the Byzantine Greek series editor, for sharing her superb knowledge of Greek, for her energy and supreme dedication to this project, and for suggesting innumerable corrections and recommendations during every step in the preparation of the manuscript. Thanks are owed, too, to Professor Alexander Alexakis, for his meticulous review of the translation and his helpful suggestions and corrections, which captured accurately and eloquently the meaning of the Greek original. Professor Charles Barber also made a number of valuable suggestions. While all remaining errors are our own, without these colleagues' great erudition, which they very generously and genially shared, this volume would have not been the same. We are also grateful to two assistants at the Dumbarton Oaks Medieval Library, Nathanael Aschenbrenner and John Zaleski, who helped to prepare the manuscript for publication.

Moreover, we are indebted to the monastic community of the Monastery of Grottaferrata, especially Abbot Emeri-

tus, Archimandrite Fr. Emiliano Fabbricatore O.S.B.I., for his generous suggestions and help in understanding hidden meaning of the text.

Special thanks to the archivists and librarians at the Monastery of the Mother of God of Grottaferrata, without whose help and professionalism this work would not have been possible. Dr. Stefano Parenti, librarian at the monastery of Grottaferrata, provided access to the Greek manuscript and other important primary sources related to the era of Saint Neilos. We express our gratitude to the Monastery of Grottaferrata State Library for providing a digital file of the original manuscript.

Last but not least, sincere thanks to our families, Seton Hall colleagues, and students. They supported and encouraged us all throughout this project.

NOTES

1 See, for example, Hester, *Monasticism and Spirituality*, 200–201 and 201n154. Although many of the detailed studies on Neilos and Calabrian monasticism are in Italian, for this Introduction and the notes to the translation we have used English bibliography wherever possible.

2 The threats may have reflected the antimonastic policy of Romanos I Lekapenos (r. 920–944); see *ODB* 2:1450. Alternatively, Neilos's abandoned family or the local ecclesiastical authorities may have pressured the governor of Calabria in order to prevent Neilos from neglecting his family responsibilities. See chapter 4.3 of the *Life* of Neilos, below.

3 Ermanno Ponti and Filippo Passamonti, *Storia e storie di Grottaferrata* (Rome, 1939), 54–55.

4 For a very detailed English summary of the *Life* of Neilos, see Hester, *Monasticism and Spirituality*, 203–21.

5 Giovanelli, *Βίος καί πολιτεία τοῦ ὁσίου πατρός ἡμῶν Νείλου τοῦ Νέου*, 12–22.

6 Andrea Luzzi, "La vita di San Nilo da Rossano tra genere letterario e

biografia storica," in *Les* Vies des saints *à Byzance. Genre littéraire ou biographie historique? Actes du II' colloque international philologique "EPMHNEIA," Paris, 6–7–8 juin 2002,* ed. Paolo Odorico and Panagiotis A. Agapitos (Paris, 2004), 189.

7 Vera von Falkenhausen, "Gli Ebrei nell'Italia meridionale bizantina (VI–XI secolo)," in *Gli Ebrei nella Calabria medievale: Studi in memoria di Cesare Colafemmina,* ed. Giovanna de Sensi Sestito (Soveria Mannelli, 2013), 30.

8 See Paul Magdalino, "The Year 1000 in Byzantium," in *Byzantium in the Year 1000,* ed. idem (Leiden, 2003), 233–70, esp. 241. Kolbaba dates the vita "within the first two decades after Nilus's death" (Tia Kolbaba, "Latin and Greek Christians," in *The Cambridge History of Christianity,* ed. Thomas F. X. Noble and Julia M. H. Smith [Cambridge, 2008], 3:213–29 at 228).

9 Falkenhausen, "Il percorso geo-biografico di San Nilo di Rossano," 87.

10 Enrica Follieri, ed., *La vita di San Fantino il Giovane: Introduzione, testo greco, traduzione, commentario e indici* (Brussels, 1993), 121.

11 Germano Giovanelli, *S. Bartolomeo juniore, confondatore di Grottaferrata* (Grottaferrata, 1962), 15.

12 Falkenhausen, "Il percorso geo-biografico di San Nilo di Rossano," 87.

13 On the factual reliability of southern Italian hagiography of the tenth century, see Hester, *Monasticism and Spirituality,* 149–50. For an assessment of the *Life* of Neilos as a historical source, see Falkenhausen, "La Vita di S. Nilo come fonte storica per la Calabria bizantina," 271–305.

14 Rousseau, "La visite de Nil de Rossano au Mont-Cassin," 1111–37; Sansterre, "Saint Nil de Rossano et le monachisme latin," 339–86.

15 The interest in forging these dynastic ties began as early as the reign of Charlemagne, when the Byzantine empress Irene arranged for her son Constantine to wed the Frankish king's daughter Rotrud. This would also be a feature of the Ottonian era of Neilos's lifetime. Judith Herrin, *The Formation of Christendom* (Princeton, 1987), 412–13; Friedrich Heer, *The Holy Roman Empire,* trans., Janet Sondheimer (London, 2002), 41–49.

16 Of the twenty-five men who held the title Bishop of Rome during Neilos's lifetime, including two antipopes, seven met violent deaths, at least three of them through the complicity of their successors. All these popes were appointed through the direct involvement of the prevailing civil power of the day. See *ODP* 119–39.

17 Cappelli, *Il monachesimo basiliano,* 15.

18 Ibid.

19 Morini, "Greek Monasticism in Southern Italy," 76–78.

20 In the sixth century the Calabrian bishops did not participate in the Roman synods, and they introduced Greek rites in the liturgy in their dioceses. However, the presence of almost all Calabrian bishops was documented at the seventh-century Council of Rome (679), convened by Pope Agathos at the special request of Emperor Constantine IV to discuss the Monothelite question. There were thirteen bishops from Calabria and Sicily in attendance. In 681 Bishops Abundantius of Tempsa and Giovanni of Reggio participated in the Council of Constantinople. Pauline Allen and Bronwen Neil, eds., *Maximus the Confessor and His Companions: Documents from Exile* (Oxford, 2002), 29.

21 Russo, *Monachesimo greco e cultura in Calabria,* 15.

22 Valerie Ramseyer, *The Transformation of a Religious Landscape: Medieval Southern Italy 850–1150* (Ithaca, N.Y., 2006), 87–88.

23 Paolo Giannini, "Il monachesimo basiliano in Italia," *Bollettino della Badia Greca di Grottaferrata* 41 (1987): 8.

24 Francesco Russo, "I monasteri greci della Calabria nel secolo XV," *Bollettino della Badia Greca di Grottaferrata* 16 (1962): 117. A "new Thebaid" is a reference to the Early Christian monastic complexes in the vicinity of Egyptian Thebes (ancient Luxor), such as the Pachomian monastery at Pbow and Shenoute's White Monastery at Sohag; see *ODB* 3:2031–32.

25 Cappelli, *Il monachesimo basiliano,* 19.

26 On societal cohesion among Christian communities in southern Italy, see Annick Peters-Custot, "*Convivencia* between Christians: the Greek and Latin Communities of Byzantine South Italy (9th–11th centuries)," in *Negotiating Coexistence: Communities, Cultures and* Convivencia *in Byzantine Society,* ed. Barbara Crostini and Sergio La Porta (Trier, 2013), 203–20. See also Hester, *Monasticism and Spirituality,* 148.

27 Morini, "Greek Monasticism in Southern Italy," 85–88; Rosemary Morris, *Monks and Laymen in Byzantium, 843–1118* (Cambridge, 1995), 50.

28 Alex Metcalfe, *The Muslims of Medieval Italy* (Edinburgh, 2009), 35.

29 Enrico Morini, "The Orient and Rome," *Harvard Ukrainian Studies* 12–13 (1988–1989): 850–51.

THE LIFE OF SAINT
NEILOS OF ROSSANO

Βίος καὶ πολιτεία τοῦ ὁσίου πατρὸς ἡμῶν Νείλου τοῦ Νέου

Πάτερ, εὐλόγησον

I

Ἡ χάρις τοῦ Κυρίου ἡμῶν Ἰησοῦ Χριστοῦ καὶ ἡ ἀγάπη τοῦ Θεοῦ καὶ Πατρὸς καὶ ἡ κοινωνία τοῦ Ἁγίου Πνεύματος—καλὸν γὰρ ἐκ Θεοῦ τε ἄρχεσθαι καὶ εἰς Θεὸν καταλήγειν—εἴη μετὰ πάντων τῶν φιλοπόνως ἀκροωμένων καὶ μετὰ τῆς ἐμῆς εὐτελείας καὶ πτωχονοίας, τοῦ μέλλοντος τολμηρῶς διαγγέλλειν περὶ τοῦ βίου τοῦ ὁσίου πατρὸς ἡμῶν Νείλου τοῦ Νέου. Οὐ γὰρ δι᾽ ἀνθρώπου, οὐδὲ δι᾽ ἀνθρωπίνης ὑποβολῆς ἢ παρακλήσεως τὸ τοιοῦτον ἔργον ἐχειρισάμην. Οὐδὲ γάρ εἰσι νῦν ἐν τοῖς ἐσχάτοις καιροῖς τῶν ἐσχάτων τούτων αἰώνων οἱ τὰ τοιαῦτα ζητοῦντές <τε> καὶ πολυπραγμονοῦντες· τοὐναντίον μὲν οὖν, πολλοὶ οἱ μωκίζοντες καὶ πρὸς ταῦτα ἀηδιζόμενοι, οἱ μήτε τοῖς παλαιοῖς διηγήμασι τῶν ἁγίων πιστεύοντες, μήτε τοῖς νεωστὶ τελεσθεῖσι πειθόμενοι, ἀλλὰ διὰ πάντων καὶ ἐν πᾶσιν αὐτοῖς τὰς τῆς ὠφελείας ὁδούς, ὡς εἰπεῖν, ἀποφράξαντες,

The Life and Conduct of Our Holy Father Neilos the Younger

Father, give your blessing!

Chapter 1

Since it is good to begin with God and to end with God, *may the grace of* our *Lord Jesus Christ, and the love of God* the Father *and the fellowship of the Holy Spirit* be *with all* who listen to me conscientiously, and also with my unworthy self, impoverished of understanding, for boldly undertaking to narrate the life of our holy father, Neilos the Younger. For I did not undertake so great a task either through man or at human prompting or urging. For now in these last times of the last centuries there are none who seek out the lives of the saints and actively study them. Rather, on the contrary, there are many who deride and detest them, as they neither believe in the old stories of the saints, nor have confidence in the deeds of the more recent ones. Instead, in every possible way they themselves block off, so to speak, the beneficial paths, and they have established one aim in regard to all

ἕνα σκοπὸν ἐν ἅπασι τίθενται, τὸ πρὸς τὰ ἑαυτῶν μέτρα κρίνειν τὸ πιστὸν ἐν τοῖς λεγομένοις, τὸ δ᾽ ὑπερβαῖνον τὴν ἑαυτῶν δύναμιν, ὡς ἔξω τῆς ἀληθείας, ταῖς τοῦ ψεύδους ὑπονοίαις καθυποβάλλειν.

2 Δι᾽ ὃ τὸν ἀόρατον νοῦν, τὸν Θεόν, φημι, καὶ Πατέρα, καὶ τὸν ἄναρχον καὶ συναΐδιον Λόγον, καὶ τὸ πανάγιον καὶ ὁμοούσιον Πνεῦμα θεμέλιον καὶ ἀρχὴν προθέμενοι τοῦ λόγου, οὕτω τῆς διηγήσεως ἀπαρξόμεθα, εἰ καὶ μή τινι ἄλλῳ γε χρησιμεύσουσαν, ἀλλ᾽ ἡμῖν τοῖς ἐν ταύτῃ ἀσχολουμένοις καὶ μικρόν τι τὸν νοῦν ἐκ τῶν γηΐνων ἀπαγομένοις, οὐ μικρὰν τὴν ὄνησιν καὶ τὸ κέρδος ἐργαζομένην, καθάπερ τοῖς μυρεψοῖς ἡ τῶν ἀρωμάτων ἀναστροφὴ τὴν ἐξ αὐτῶν ἡδύτητα καὶ ἀπόλαυσιν. Δεῖ τοίνυν τὴν ἐνεγκοῦσαν τοῦτον ἡμῖν τὸν ἀοίδιμον Νεῖλον προτάξαι τῷ λόγῳ, ἵνα μηδὲν τῶν δεόντων ἐλλείπῃ τῷ πάντα τὰ κατ᾽ αὐτὸν ἐρευνῶντι.

2

Τὸ Ῥυσιάνον οἶδ᾽ ὅτι πάντες γινώσκουσιν, οὐ μόνον διὰ τὸ προκαθῆσθαι τοῖς τῆς Καλαβρίας τέρμασι, μέγιστόν τε τυγχάνειν ὁμοῦ καὶ ἀνεπιβούλευτον, ἀλλὰ καὶ διὰ τό, πάσης τῆς χώρας ἐρημωθείσης καὶ πασῶν τῶν πόλεων ἔργον γεγενημένων τῆς τῶν Σαρακηνῶν πολυεπηρείας, μόνον διαφυγεῖν μέχρι καὶ νῦν τῆς αὐτῶν ἀπωλείας τὸν νόμον.

things: to *judge by their own standards the reliability of the stories that have been told to them.* So *that which exceeds the limits* of their comprehension they malign as *beyond the bounds of truth, suspecting that it is essentially false.*

For this reason setting forth the invisible mind, I mean 2 God our Father, and the coeternal Word which is without beginning, and the all-holy and consubstantial Spirit as the foundation and the beginning of our discourse, we shall thus begin our narrative. Even if it should not be useful to anyone else, it will be for us monks who study this account, and in some small way it will divert our minds from earthly concerns, since the benefit and the profit to be gained are not small, just as for perfumers the mixing of aromatic spices brings forth their sweetness and pleasure. So then we should begin this narrative with a word about the city that gave birth to our celebrated Neilos, so that nothing essential be lacking for those who wish to know all the details of his life.

Chapter 2

I know that everyone is familiar with Rossano, not only for the city's defensive position on the borders of Calabria, being both large and impregnable, but also as the only city, amid the devastation of the entire region and all the cities that have fallen victim to the great threat of the Saracens, which has up to now escaped the decree of their destruction.

Τοῦτο δὲ οὐκ ἐξ ἀνθρωπίνης σοφίας ἢ βοηθείας συνέβη, ἀλλὰ τῇ δυναστείᾳ καὶ ἀντιλήψει τῆς ἐκεῖ ἐπισκιαζούσης ἐξαιρέτως Δεσποίνης ἡμῶν Θεοτόκου καὶ ἀειπαρθένου Μαρίας, ἥτις πολλάκις τῶν ἀθέων Ἀγαρηνῶν ἐν νυκτὶ προσελθόντων καὶ συλῆσαι τὸ φρούριον βουληθέντων, ἅμα τῷ προσεγγίσαι αὐτοὺς τῷ τείχει ὥστε καὶ κλίμακα ἐπιθεῖναι, λέγεται ἄνωθεν ὡς γυνὴ πορφυροφόρος ἐποφθῆναι αὐτοῖς, λαμπάδας ἐν ταῖς χερσὶν κατέχουσα καὶ ταύταις αὐτοὺς καταβάλλουσα καὶ τοῦ τείχους ἀποδιώκουσα. Καὶ τοῦτο σαφῶς ὡμολόγουν οἱ ἐξ αὐτῶν γενόμενοι πρόσφυγες.

2   Ἐκεῖθεν τοίνυν ὁ ὅσιος πατὴρ Νεῖλος ἀνέτειλεν καὶ ἐκεῖσε τὰς τῆς σωματικῆς ἡλικίας ἀρχὰς κατεβάλετο, δῶρον ἀπὸ Θεοῦ χαρισθεὶς τοῖς γονεῦσιν αὐτοῦ· πρὸς γὰρ ἀδελφῇ ἐτέχθη ἄρρεν αὐτοῖς ἐπιθυμητικῶς. Καὶ δῶρον παρ᾽ αὐτῶν ἐνεχθεὶς καὶ τῷ οἴκῳ τῆς Θεοτόκου εὐθύμως ἀποκληρωθείς, φύσεως δὲ εὐκληρίας τυχὼν καὶ νοὸς ὀξύτητος καὶ φρενῶν ἀστειότητος, πάντας τοὺς συνηλικιώτας αὐτοῦ ὑπερέβαλλεν ἔν τε συνέσει καὶ ταῖς ἀποκρίσεσιν αὐτοῦ καὶ τῇ τῶν Γραφῶν νουνεχεῖ ἀναγνώσει, οὐ μὴν ἀλλὰ καὶ ἐν ταῖς πρὸς τοὺς διδασκάλους ἐρωτήσεσιν, ὥστε θαυμάζειν ἐκείνους, πόθεν τῷ τοιούτῳ βρέφει τὰς Γραφὰς ἐρευνᾶν καὶ ἐπερωτᾶν τὰ τοιαῦτα. Ἠγάπα γὰρ ἀεὶ τοὺς τῶν ἁγίων πατέρων βίους ἐκ νεότητος αὐτοῦ, φημὶ δὴ Ἀντωνίου καὶ Σάββα καὶ Ἱλαρίωνος καὶ τῶν λοιπῶν τῶν γεγραμμένων ἐν τῇ αὐτῇ καθολικῇ ἐκκλησίᾳ, καὶ μετὰ πολλοῦ πόθου καὶ συνέσεως αὐτοὺς ἀεὶ διεξήρχετο. Ὅθεν

This did not happen as a result of human wisdom or assistance, but because of the power and succor of our Lady, the Mother of God, the ever-virgin Mary who especially watches over the city. Often when the godless Hagarenes attacked in the night, intending to plunder the citadel, and were close enough to the wall to place their ladders, it is said that she would appear to them from on high as a woman clothed in purple, brandishing in her hands torches with which she would cast down the Saracens and thus drive them away from the wall. The refugees from the Saracens clearly confirm this account.

From this city, then, the holy father Neilos originated, 2 and there he passed the early years of his earthly life. He was a gift granted by God to his parents, who longed for a son to be born to them in addition to their daughter. Accordingly, they brought him as a gift and eagerly dedicated him to the church of the Mother of God. The boy was well endowed by nature with health and a sharp mind, as well as a nobility of intellect, and he surpassed all his peers in *his understanding and his answers* and in his thoughtful reading of Scriptures, as well as in his questions for his teachers, so that they were astonished by such a child who could investigate such things and examine the Scriptures. From his youth he always loved the lives of the holy fathers; I speak of Anthony, Sabas, Hilarion, and others whose images were painted in the cathedral. He always read through the stories of their lives with

καὶ ὑπῆρξεν αὐτῷ τὸ μισοπόνηρον εἶναι καὶ ἀποστρέφε-
σθαι τὰς ἐν τοῖς οἴκοις τῶν ἀρχόντων διατριβάς, μισεῖν τε
καὶ ἀποβδελύττεσθαι πᾶσαν περιεργίαν καὶ ἐξουθενεῖν τὰ
λεγόμενα φυλακτὰ καὶ τοὺς λεγομένους ἐξορκισμούς,
καίτοι γε οὐδὲ τῶν τοιούτων ἀπορήσας βιβλίων διὰ νοὸς
ὀξύτητα καὶ σπουδὴν τὴν ἐν ἅπασι.

3

Μετ᾽ οὐ πολὺ οὖν, τῶν γονέων αὐτοῦ τὸν βίον ὑπ-
αλλαξάντων καὶ παρὰ τῆς ἀδελφῆς ἀνατρεφομένου καὶ
εὐσεβῶς ἐκπαιδευομένου (ἦν γὰρ καὶ αὐτὴ φιλόθεος πάνυ,
εἰ καὶ τὸν τοῦ βίου ζυγὸν ὑπεισῆλθεν), ἡνίκα δὲ τῆς ἡλικίας
τὸ ἄνθος αὐτῷ προσετέθη, οὐχ ὑπῆρχεν ὁ τῆς νουθεσίας
τὸν χαλινὸν ἐπιθεῖναι τῷ νέῳ σπουδάζων καὶ διὰ συνεχοῦς
διδασκαλίας πρὸς τὰ κρείττονα αὐτὸν ὁδηγήσων, οὐ τῶν
ἐπισκόπων τις, οὐχ ἱερέων, οὔτε ἡγουμένων ἢ μοναζόντων·
σπάνιον γὰρ ἦν ἐν τοῖς χρόνοις ἐκείνοις ἐκεῖσε τὸ τῶν
μοναστῶν σχῆμα, ἵνα μὴ λέγω ὅτι καὶ βδελυκτόν. Στοχα-
σάμενος οὖν ὁ Διάβολος τὸ μέλλον ἐξ αὐτοῦ ἀναφύεσθαι
κέρδος καὶ ὡς ἀντίπαλος αὐτῷ καὶ ἐχθρὸς εὑρεθήσεται
μέγας (δεινὸς γάρ ἐστιν ἐκ τῶν προλαβόντων τεκμη-
ριῶσαι τὸ μέλλον), ἤρξατο κατατοξεύειν τὰς τῶν γυναικῶν
ἀγάμους ἐπὶ τῷ κάλλει τοῦ νέου, οὐ μὴν ἀλλὰ καὶ ἐπὶ
τῇ καλλιφωνίᾳ τῆς ψαλμῳδίας αὐτοῦ καὶ τῇ ἐν ἅπασι

great desire and understanding. This was the source of his hatred of evil and his avoidance of spending time in the houses of the powerful. He both hated and loathed all superstitions, and mocked the so-called amulets and supposed exorcisms, though he himself did not lack knowledge of the books on such subjects, due to his sharpness of mind and eagerness to know everything.

Chapter 3

Not long after, his parents departed this life, and he was raised by his sister and piously educated, for she was wholly God-loving even though she had assumed the yoke of marriage. When he came into the bloom of youth, however, there was no one present to bridle the young man with admonishment, and no one to lead him toward a better path through continual education, no bishop, or priest, or abbot or monk. For in those days the monk's habit was rarely seen in Rossano, and even then, I dare say, when seen it was despised. And so the Devil, foreseeing the good that was to come from Neilos and that he would become a rival and great enemy (for the Devil is clever at divining outcomes from their initial beginnings), began to shoot his arrows at unmarried women, captivating them with the youth's good looks, his sweet singing of the psalms, and his energy and

διεγέρσει καὶ ἐπιτηδειότητι. Διὸ οὔτε ἴσχυσεν ἀποδρᾶσαι τὰς αὐτῶν πολυτρόπους παγίδας, ἀλλά, καθάπερ ἔλαφος πληγεὶς εἰς τὸ ἧπαρ, θηρεύεται ὑπὸ μιᾶς αὐτῶν, ὡραιότητι μὲν καὶ φύσεως κάλλει τὰς ἄλλας ὑπερβαλλούσης, ἐκ γένους δὲ εὐτελοῦς καὶ τοῦ τυχόντος καταγομένης. Ζεύγνυται τοίνυν αὐτῇ καὶ θῆλυ τὸ πρώτως τεχθὲν παιδίον ὑπῆρξεν αὐτοῖς.

2 Ἡ δὲ τοῦ Θεοῦ παντέφορος πρόνοια, καὶ πάντα πρὸ τέλους γινώσκουσα, προϊδοῦσα τὴν μέλλουσαν δι᾽ αὐτοῦ γενήσεσθαι τοῖς ἀνθρώποις μεγίστην ὠφέλειαν καὶ ὅτι πολλοὶ δι᾽ αὐτοῦ τῆς τῶν οὐρανῶν βασιλείας κληρονόμοι γενήσονται, οὐκ εἴασεν αὐτὸν ἐν τῷ βορβόρῳ τοῦ βίου κυλίεσθαι, ἀλλὰ πρῶτον μὲν ἐμφυτεύει ἐν τῇ καρδίᾳ αὐτοῦ τὴν τοῦ θανάτου μνήμην ἀνέκλειπτον καὶ τὴν τῶν μελλόντων κολαστηρίων ἀτελεύτητον βάσανον. Ἔπειτα δὲ φρίκη μεγίστη καὶ πυρετῷ σφοδροτάτῳ ἀεννάως παλαίειν αὐτὸν συνεχώρει, ὡς προβλέπειν καθ᾽ ἡμέραν πρὸ ὀφθαλμῶν αὐτοῦ τὸν ἅρπαγα θάνατον.

4

Ἐν μιᾷ οὖν τῶν ἡμερῶν μηδενὶ εἰρηκώς, μηδὲ θαρρήσας τὸ οἰκεῖον μυστήριον ἀνθρώπῳ τινί, πορεύεται πρός τινας χρεωστοῦντας αὐτῷ ποσὸν ἱκανόν, λέγων πρὸς αὐτούς· "Ἀμπελῶνα κάλλιστον εὕρηκα καὶ ἀνάγκην ἔχω τοῦ

aptitude in all things. Consequently, Neilos was not strong enough to escape their manifold snares, but just like a stag wounded in the heart, he was captured by one of them who surpassed the others in her comeliness and natural beauty, though she was born to a modest and ordinary family. He then entered the yoke of marriage with her, and their first-born child was a girl.

The all-seeing providence of God, which knows all things 2 even before they come to pass, foreseeing the great benefit that he would bring to humankind, and that through him many would inherit the kingdom of heaven, did not allow Neilos to wallow in the filth of life, but first planted in his heart the inescapable memory of death and the unending torment of future punishments. And then God permitted him to struggle with incessant shivering and a violent fever, so that every day Neilos saw before his eyes death, which snatches away humankind.

Chapter 4

One day Neilos, having spoken to no one and not daring to reveal his secret to anyone, went to some people who owed him a large sum of money, and said to them, "I have found a most beautiful vineyard, and I need to buy it."

ἀγοράσαι αὐτόν." Λαβὼν δὲ ἐξ αὐτῶν ὅσον ἂν εὑρέθησαν ἔχοντες, τὸ λεῖπον καταλείψας, ἔξεισι τῶν ἐκεῖσε τῇ νόσῳ βαρέως κατατρυχόμενος. Συνείπετο δὲ αὐτῷ καὶ μοναχός τις Γρηγόριος τῷ ὀνόματι, ποδηγέτης αὐτῷ τῆς πρὸς τὸ μοναστήριον ἀπαγούσης ὁδοῦ γινόμενος. Φθάσας δέ τινα ποταμὸν καὶ εἰσελθὼν τοῦ περάσαι αὐτόν, τότε ἔγνω τὴν τοῦ Θεοῦ ὁδηγοῦσαν αὐτὸν ἀντίληψιν βοηθοῦσαν αὐτῷ καὶ πρὸς τὸ οἰκεῖον ἄγουσαν βούλημα. Τῆς γὰρ νόσου κατὰ τὸ μέσον τοῦ ποταμοῦ, καθάπερ φορτίον βαρύ, ἀφαιρεθείσης ἀπὸ τῶν ὤμων αὐτοῦ, προθύμως τοῦ λοιποῦ τὴν ὁδὸν διήνυε καὶ τερπόμενος ἔψαλλεν· "Ὁδὸν ἐντολῶν Σου ἔδραμον, Κύριε, ὅταν ἐπλάτυνας τὴν καρδίαν μου."

2   Καταλαβὼν δὲ τὰ περὶ τὸ Μερκούριον μοναστήρια καὶ θεασάμενος τοὺς οὐρανίους ἐκείνους καὶ θαυμασίους ἄνδρας—λέγω δὴ Ἰωάννην τὸν μέγαν καὶ Φαντῖνον τὸν περιβόητον, Ζαχαρίαν τε τὸν ἰσάγγελον καὶ τοὺς λοιποὺς ἅπαντας, πράξει καὶ λόγῳ θειότατα διαπρέποντας—καὶ καταπλαγεὶς ἐπί τε τῇ θεωρίᾳ αὐτῶν καὶ τῷ ταπεινῷ σχήματι, πλήρης δακρύων ἐγένετο καὶ πρὸς ἔνθεον ζῆλον σφοδρῶς ἀνεφλέγετο. Καὶ αὐτοὶ δὲ θεασάμενοι παλαιὸν φρόνημα ἐν νεαρῷ σώματι, ἤθους τε πῆξιν καὶ κατάστασιν εὔχρηστον, ἀγασθέντες δὲ ἐπὶ τῇ γλυκύτητι τῆς αὐτοῦ ἀναγνώσεως, καὶ ἐπὶ τῇ τοῦ νοὸς ὀξύτητι, ἔγνωσαν προορατικῷ ὄμματι τὴν ἐπ' αὐτῷ μέλλουσαν πολυπλασιάζεσθαι χάριν τοῦ Πνεύματος καὶ ὡς πολλοὶ δι' αὐτοῦ τῆς τῶν οὐρανῶν βασιλείας κληρονόμοι γενήσονται καὶ εὐλογίαις αὐτὸν κατεπλούτησαν καὶ εὐχαῖς ἐπεστήριξαν.

3   Οὐ πολὺ τὸ ἐν μέσῳ, καὶ γράμματα καταπληκτικὰ καὶ

Taking from them as much as they could find, he forgave them the rest of their debts, and went away from there still grievously afflicted by his illness. He was accompanied by a monk named Gregory who became his guide on the road leading to the monastery. When he arrived at a river and waded in to cross it, he then realized that it was God's assistance that was guiding him and leading him to the place of his desire. For while he was in the middle of the river, the great burden of his illness was lifted from his shoulders, and he enthusiastically completed the journey, joyfully singing, "Lord, *I ran the way of Your commandments when You did enlarge my heart.*"

When he arrived at the monasteries in the region of 2 Mount Merkourion, he saw those heavenly and wondrous men—I speak of the great John, the renowned Phantinos, the angelic Zacharias, and all the others distinguished for their holiness in word and deed—and was awestruck by their appearance and their humble habit. His eyes welled up with tears, and he became greatly enflamed toward the pursuit of divine zeal. When they saw in him the mindset of an older man in a youthful body, his resolute disposition, and helpful character, and admired the sweetness of his recitation and the sharpness of his mind, they knew with a prophetic eye that the grace of the Spirit would increase in him and that many would inherit the kingdom of heaven through him. And they showered blessings upon him and supported him with prayers.

Shortly thereafter, terrifying letters and horrible threats 3

ἀπειλαὶ φρικώδεις παρὰ τοῦ πάσης τῆς χώρας ἐπικρα-
τοῦντος τὰ μοναστήρια κατελάμβανεν, ὡς, εἴ τις τολμήσειε
χεῖρα ἐπιβαλεῖν κληρικῷ τῷ τοιῷδε, τὴν χεῖρα μὲν αὐτοῦ
ἀποκόπτεσθαι, τὸ δὲ μοναστήριον τούτου δημεύεσθαι.
Ὑφ᾽ ὧν καταπλαγέντες οἱ τῶν μοναστηρίων ἐξάρχοντες,
ἐβουλεύσαντο τοῦτον ἐφ᾽ ἕτερον κράτος ἐκπέμψασθαι,
κἀκεῖσε τὸ ἅγιον σχῆμα ἐνδύσασθαι, καὶ ἑαυτοὺς ἀπει-
ράστους φυλάξαι τῆς τῶν κρατούντων ἀγανακτήσεως.

5

Ἄθρει δὴ τότε πάλην ἀγγέλου καὶ Διαβόλου, τοῦ μὲν
ὅπως τὸν ἄνδρα τοῦτον ἀπαλλάξῃ τοῦ ταραχώδους καὶ
σκοτεινοῦ τούτου βίου καὶ πρὸς τὴν γῆν τῆς ἐπαγγελίας,
ἥτις ἐστὶν ὁ βίος τῶν διὰ Κύριον ἀσκουμένων, ἐξάξας τῷ
Θεῷ προσῳκειώσῃ καὶ ἄλλον Μωϋσέα ποιήσῃ, τοῦ δὲ
πᾶσαν μηχανὴν καὶ πάντα λίθον κινοῦντος, ὅπως τὸ τοιοῦτον ἀγαθὸν ἐμποδίσῃ, ὅπερ ἀδύνατον ἀπεδείχθη. Οὐ
γὰρ ἐδύναντο πᾶσαι αἱ βασιλεῖαι τῆς γῆς συναχθῆναι, ἵνα
τὸν Νεῖλον ἐκ τῆς οἰκείας ὁρμῆς ἰσχύσωσιν ἀναστεῖλαι.
Σκέπτεται τοίνυν ὁ τοῦ Θεοῦ ἄνθρωπος καταλαβέσθαι τὸ
τοῦ Ἁγίου Ναζαρίου καλούμενον μοναστήριον κἀκεῖ τὸ
τοῦ πόθου πληρῶσαι ἐπάγγελμα.

2   Ὅπερ νοήσας ὁ πᾶσι τοῖς ἀγαθοῖς ἀνθιστάμενος, προλαμβάνει τὰ ἔμπροσθεν καὶ παγίδας δεινὰς κατὰ τὴν ὁδὸν

from the governor of the whole region reached the monasteries, saying that if anyone should dare to tonsure a cleric of this sort, his hand would be chopped off and that monk's monastery would be confiscated. Stricken with fear by these threats the superiors of the monasteries decided to send him to the land of another ruler where he could be clothed in the monastic habit, and so they might free themselves from the governor's displeasure.

Chapter 5

See then the struggle between the angel and the Devil; while the former strives to free this man from this turbulent and dark life, and to lead him toward the promised land, which is the life of those who practice asceticism for the sake of the Lord, so that he might be united with God, making him a second Moses, the latter uses every device and moves every stone in order to impede this good deed, a task which proved to be impossible. For all the kingdoms of the earth would not be able to join together and be strong enough to deter Neilos from his intended path. Then this man of God decided to go to the monastery named for Saint Nazarios and there carry out his desired vow.

As soon as the Enemy of all that is good learned of this, 2 he went ahead of him and placed terrible snares along the

τίθησιν, οἰῳδήποτε τρόπῳ τὸν δρόμον τοῦ δικαίου ἐγκόψαι βουλόμενος. Καὶ δὴ τὴν ὁδὸν διανύοντι καὶ τῷ Θεῷ προσλαλοῦντι ψαλμοῖς καὶ ὕμνοις καὶ ὁλοψύχοις δεήσεσιν, μέλλοντι πρὸς ἀκτὴν ὑπεξέρχεσθαι καὶ τῷ τῆς θαλάσσης εἴδει καθωραΐζεσθαι, βάρβαρος εἷς τῶν φρυγάνων ἐκπηδήσας, καθάπερ ποτὲ ἡ ἔχιδνα τοῦ Παύλου, τῆς χειρὸς τοῦ ἁγίου ἐδράξατο καὶ ὁμοῦ πρὸς τὰ ἔμπροσθεν οἴχοντο. Οὐ πολὺ τὸ διάστημα, καὶ ἰδοὺ πλῆθος Σαρακηνῶν ἐκ δεξιῶν ἀνακεκλιμένων ὑπὸ τὸ ἄλσος, μελανῶν Αἰθιόπων, ἀγριοφθάλμων, κακοπροσώπων, καὶ πάντων δαιμόνων προσεοικότων· πρὸς δὲ τὸ ἕτερον μέρος, μέγεθος πλοίων πρὸς τῇ γῇ σεσυρμένων τὸν αἴσιον πλοῦν, ὡς εἰκός, ἀπεκδεχομένων.

3   Ταῦτα ἰδὼν ὁ μακάριος Νεῖλος ἀθρόον καὶ τὴν δεινὴν καὶ ἀσυνήθη θέαν ἐκείνην καὶ τὸ ξένον σχῆμα κατανοήσας, οὐ τῆς οἰκείας φρενὸς ὑπεξέστη, οὐδ' ἠλλοιώθη ὅλως τὴν ὄψιν, ἢ τὸν λόγον παρεσαλεύθη, ἀλλ' ἡσυχῇ τὴν χεῖρα βαλὼν ἐν τῷ στήθει καὶ τῷ σημείῳ τοῦ σταυροῦ ἑαυτὸν καθοπλίσας, εὐθάρσως καὶ ἀνδρείως ἀνταπεκρίνετο πρὸς τὰς ἐρωτήσεις· τῶν γὰρ ἄλλων ἁπάντων οἷόν τινι χαλινῷ τῇ τοῦ τῶν ὅλων Θεοῦ προνοίᾳ κατασχεθέντων καί, οἷον εἰπεῖν, ἐν τῷ τόπῳ ἀπον*/ναρκησάντων, μόνος ἐκεῖνος ὁ τοῦτον κρατήσας πρὸς αὐτὸν διελέγετο, τίς εἴη καὶ πόθεν καὶ ὅπη πορεύοιτο καὶ πάντα διερευνώμενος.

road, wishing by some means to interrupt the righteous man's journey. As Neilos traveled along the road, he sang psalms and hymns to God, as well as heartfelt prayers. When he was about to come out onto a coastal headland and enjoy the beauty of the sea, a barbarian leaped out from the underbrush and just like Paul's viper seized the holy man by the hand, and together they proceeded on. A little further along, behold, on his right-hand side there was a crowd of Saracens—black Ethiopians with wild eyes, evil faces, all appearing like demons—reclining beneath a grove of trees. On the other side lay a great number of ships drawn onto the shore awaiting a favorable opportunity to set sail.

As soon as Neilos saw this terrible and unusual spectacle 3 and recognized their foreign clothing, he did not abandon his normal disposition, alter his countenance, or falter in his speech. Rather, calmly placing his hand on his breast and arming himself with the sign of the cross, he cheerfully and boldly responded to their questions. Since all the others were restrained, as if by a bridle, by the providential care of the God of all and were, so to speak, stopped dead in their tracks, only the man who had captured Neilos spoke to him, questioning him about everything: who he was, where he was from, and where he was traveling.

6

Τοῦ δὲ τὴν πατρίδα καὶ τὸ γένος καὶ τὸν σκοπὸν τῆς ὁδοιπορίας ἀληθῶς ἀναγγείλαντος, θαυμάσας ὁ βάρβαρος ἐπί τε τῷ ἄνθει αὐτοῦ τῆς νεότητος—οὔπω γὰρ τῆς ἡλικίας ἐπλήρου χρόνον τὸν τριάκοντα—καὶ ἐπὶ τῷ κάλλει τῶν ἱματίων—ἀκμὴν γὰρ τοῖς ἀπὸ τοῦ κόσμου ἐκέχρητο— οὐ μὴν ἀλλὰ καὶ ἐπὶ τῇ συνέσει καὶ ταῖς ἀποκρίσεσιν αὐτοῦ, φησὶ πρὸς αὐτόν· "Οὐκ ἔδει σε τοιοῦτον νεώτερον ὄντα τοῖς μοναχικοῖς πόνοις ἀπὸ τοῦ νῦν σεαυτὸν κατατῆξαι, ἀλλὰ πρὸς γῆρας, ὅτε οὐδὲν κακὸν δύνῃ ποιῆσαι, τότε ἂν ἐπορεύθης, εἴγε ὅλως ἐβούλου, πρὸς τὸν τοιοῦτον ἀγῶνα." "Οὔ," φησὶ πρὸς αὐτὸν ὁ ἐχέφρων ἀνήρ, "οὐ βούλεται ὁ Θεὸς ἀκουσίως ἡμᾶς εἶναι καλούς. Ἀλλ᾽ οὐδὲ ἰσχύει γέρων ἀρέσαι Θεῷ, ὥσπερ οὐδέ σοι γαμβρὸς ἀσθενής, ἢ βασιλεῖ στρατιώτης νωθρός. Κἀγὼ νῦν ἐν τῇ νεότητι θέλω δουλεῦσαι τῷ Θεῷ, ἵνα ἐν γήρει παρ᾽ αὐτοῦ δοξασθῶ." Ταῦτα ἀκούσας ὁ ἄπιστος ἐκεῖνος Ἀγαρηνὸς καὶ ὥσπερ αἰδεσθεὶς τὴν ἀρετὴν τοῦ ἀνδρός, μᾶλλον δὲ ὑπὸ τῆς ἄνωθεν προνοίας τὴν καρδίαν μεταβληθείς, ἀπέλυσεν αὐτόν, ὑποδείξας αὐτῷ τὴν ὁδόν, μηδὲν σκληρὸν ἢ ἐναντίον ποιῆσας ἢ λέξας αὐτῷ, ἀλλὰ καὶ ἐπευξάμενός φησιν αὐτῷ καὶ προθυμοποιήσας αὐτὸν ἐν λόγοις ἱκανοῖς καὶ προτρεπτικοῖς εἰς ἀρετήν.

2 Ἐπειδὴ τοίνυν διέστησαν ἀλλήλων, καὶ ἡ τοῦ Θεοῦ πρόνοια τὴν πρὸς τὸν ἑαυτῆς θεράποντα σκέπην τε καὶ ἀντίληψιν ἐπεδείξατο *ἐν μέσῳ πυρὸς καμίνου καὶ ἐν μέσῳ*

Chapter 6

While Neilos was truthfully describing his birthplace and his family, and the purpose of his journey, the barbarian marveled at the flower of his youth—for he had not yet reached the age of thirty—and at the beauty of his clothes—for he was still wearing worldly dress. Nor was the Saracen any less amazed *at his understanding and his answers.* He said to Neilos, "Such a fine young man as you should not mortify yourself henceforth with monastic toil. You can do that in your old age, when your potential for wicked behavior diminishes. Then, if you really want, you should embark on that struggle." "No," the prudent man said to him, "God does not wish us to be good against our will. And an old man does not have the strength to please God, just as a feeble son-in-law does not please you, nor does a lazy soldier please the king. I wish to serve God now in my youth, so that in old age I shall be glorified by Him." Hearing this, as if he esteemed the man's virtue, or rather because his heart had been changed by heavenly providence, that infidel Hagarene released him and showed him the right road, all the while neither doing nor saying anything harsh or hostile to him. Rather, he prayed for Neilos and encouraged him with many words of exhortation on the path of virtue.

When they parted ways, divine providence showed His 2 servant protection and support *in the midst of a fiery furnace,*

λεόντων, ἤ, μᾶλλον εἰπεῖν, ὄφεων καὶ σκορπίων καὶ τῆς τοῦ ἐχθροῦ ἁπάσης δυνάμεως ἀβλαβῆ καὶ ἀπήμονα τοῦτον δια-φυλάξασα, ἵνα γνῷ καὶ αὐτὸς τὴν τῆς φύσεως ἀσθένειαν καὶ τὴν τῆς ἀνθρωπίνης δυνάμεως οὐθενότητα, μικρὸν ἑαυτὴν ὑποστείλασα καὶ οἷον αὐτὸν τῆς αὐτῆς ἐνεργείας καταλείψασα, τότε δή, τότε φόβος καὶ τρόμος ἐπιπίπτει αὐτῷ, καὶ δειλία θανάτου περιέσχεν αὐτόν. Ἐννοούμενος γὰρ εἰς οἵων παγίδων ἐμπεπτώκει πληθύν, οὐδὲ τοὺς πόδας πρὸς τὴν ὁδὸν κατευθῦναι ἠδύνατο, ἀλλ᾽ ὅλος δι᾽ ὅλου κλονούμενος, πυκνὰ πρὸς τὰ ὄπισθεν ὑπεβλέπετο, τὴν τοῦ ξίφους τομὴν δολερῶς, ὥσπερ ἔθος αὐτοῖς, παρ᾽ αὐτῶν αὐθωρὸν ἀπεκδεχόμενος. Ὁ δὲ Σαρακηνός, ὡς εἶδεν αὐτὸν μήτε ἄρτον μήτε πήραν ἐπιφερόμενον, μήτε οἴνου παράκλησιν, λαβὼν μεθ᾽ ἑαυτοῦ ἄρτους ξηροὺς καὶ λίαν καθαρούς, ἤρξατο τρέχειν ὀπίσω αὐτοῦ, κράζων αὐτὸν ἀδελφὸν καὶ προσμεῖναι τὴν ἄφιξιν αὐτοῦ ἐκβοῶν.

7

Ὅπερ εἰς μείζονα φόβον καὶ ἀγωνίαν, ὡς εἰκός, αὐτὸν περιέβαλεν. Λογισάμενος ἀληθῆ προϋπειληφέναι ἑαυτόν, καὶ μόνον τὴν ψυχὴν παρετίθετο ταῖς χερσὶ τοῦ Δεσπότου Χριστοῦ. Τοῦτον ἰδὼν δειλανδρίσαντα ὁ Σαρακηνὸς καὶ τῷ δέει τὰς ὄψεις ἀχρωθέντα καθάπερ νεκρόν, ἤρξατο ἐπιπλήττειν σφοδρῶς καὶ τὸ ἄνανδρον ὀνειδίζειν αὐτοῦ.

in the midst of lions or, even better, *of serpents and scorpions,* safeguarding him unharmed and unhurt *from the power of every enemy.* So that Neilos himself might know the weakness of human nature and the worthlessness of human capability, God's providence then receded a little and deprived Neilos of its activity. Then fear and trembling assailed him, and dread of death overcame him. Realizing that he had fallen into a multitude of snares, he was unable to move his feet forward on the path. Instead he frequently looked behind him in a state of total agitation, expecting the sudden and treacherous slash of a sword, as was the barbarian manner. Now since the Saracen had seen Neilos leave carrying *neither bread nor bag* nor even some wine for refreshment, he took some loaves of dry white bread and began to run after Neilos, shouting at him, "brother," and calling out for him to wait so that he could catch up.

Chapter 7

This pursuit and shouting quite reasonably cast Neilos into greater fear and anxiety, and truly believing that his previous suspicions were correct, he could only entrust his soul into the hands of Christ our Master. The Saracen, seeing him cowering and his face white as a corpse with fear, began to berate him severely and to reproach his cowardice. "In

"Ἡμεῖς γάρ," φησίν, "λυπούμεθα περὶ σοῦ, ὅτι οὐδὲν ἔχομεν ἄξιον τῆς σῆς τιμῆς, καὶ σὺ τὰ μὴ πρέποντα λογίζῃ
περὶ ἡμῶν. Δέξαι ταῦτα τὰ μικρά, ἅπερ ἐχορήγησεν ὁ
Θεός, καὶ πορεύου ἐν εἰρήνῃ τὴν σὴν ὁδόν."

2   Δεξάμενος τοίνυν ὁ τοῦ Θεοῦ ἄνθρωπος τοὺς ἄρτους,
ὡς ἐκ Θεοῦ πεμφθέντας αὐτῷ, καὶ καταπλαγεὶς ἐπὶ τῇ
τοσαύτῃ ἀντιλήψει καὶ περιποιήσει τοῦ Θεοῦ περὶ αὐτόν,
οὐδὲ τὸ ὄμμα εἰς οὐρανὸν ἐπᾶραι ἠβούλετο, ἀλλ' ὥσπερ
αἰδούμενος ἀναβλέψαι πρὸς τὸν Θεόν, κάτω δὲ τὸ πρόσωπον μετὰ πολλῆς ταπεινοφροσύνης εἰς τὴν γῆν νενευκώς,
μετὰ δακρύων τὰς τοῦ Δαβὶδ ἠφίει φωνάς· "Τί ἀνταποδώσω
Σοι, Κύριε," λέγων, "περὶ πάντων, ὧν ἀνταπέδωκάς μοι
μεγίστων Σου εὐεργεσιῶν; Σὺ γάρ, Δέσποτα, ἀντελάβου
μου ἐκ γαστρὸς μητρός μου, καὶ οὐ συνέκλεισάς με εἰς χεῖρας
ἐχθρῶν." Μετὰ δὲ ταῦτα κρούων τὸ στῆθος καὶ τὰς πλευρὰς αὐτοῦ, ὡσανεὶ ἐπέπληττε τὴν ἰδίαν ψυχὴν καὶ ἔλεγεν·
"Εὐλόγει, ἡ ψυχή μου, τὸν Κύριον, καὶ πάντα τὰ ἐντός μου
τὸ ὄνομα τὸ ἅγιον αὐτοῦ. Εὐλόγει, ἡ ψυχή μου, τὸν Κύριον,
καὶ μὴ ἐπιλανθάνου πάσας τὰς ἀνταποδόσεις αὐτοῦ."

3   Ἐν τούτοις διανύσαντος τὸ λεῖπον τῆς ὁδοῦ, καὶ λοιπὸν
προσεγγίζοντος τῇ ἤδη προλεχθείσῃ μονῇ, ὑπαντᾷ αὐτῷ
ἐν σχήματι ἱππέως ὁ τῶν δικαίων Ἐχθρὸς καί φησι πρὸς
αὐτόν· "Ποῦ πορεύῃ σύ, κληρικέ; Μὴ μοναχὸς ὑπάγῃς
γενέσθαι ἐν ταύτῃ τῇ μονῇ; Καὶ ἵνα τί οὕτως ἐπλανήθης
κακῶς; Ὄντως κάλλιον ἠδύνασο ἐν τῷ οἴκῳ σου καθεζό-
μενος σῶσαι τὴν σὴν ψυχήν, ἤπερ εἰσερχόμενος μέσον
τῶν ἀγρίων τούτων θηρῶν." Ἤρξατο δὲ κατηγορεῖν τοὺς
μοναχούς, μυρίας λοιδορίας ἐπιχέων τῷ ὀνόματι αὐτῶν,

truth," he said, "we regret that we have nothing worthy with which to honor you, and yet you think the worst of us. Take these small items which God has provided, and continue your journey in peace."

And so the man of God accepted the bread as if it were ₂ sent to him from God, and astonished by such divine support and concern for him, he was not even willing *to lift up his eyes to heaven.* Rather, as if ashamed to look up toward God, he bowed his face down to the ground with much humility and with tears spoke aloud the verses of David, saying, "*What shall I render to* You, Lord, *for all the* great blessings *with which* You have *rewarded me? For You,* Master, *have helped me from my mother's womb, and You did not shut me up into the hands of enemies.*" After this, he beat upon his chest and his sides, as if he were castigating his own soul, and said repeatedly, "*Bless the Lord, O my soul; and all that is within me, bless His holy name. Bless the Lord, O my soul; and forget not all* His gifts."

Reciting such blessings, he completed the rest of his jour- ₃ ney. Not far from the aforementioned monastery he encountered the Enemy of the righteous in the guise of a cavalryman, who said, "Where do you journey, clergyman? Surely you are not going to be a monk in that monastery? For what purpose have you been so badly deceived? Surely you would be better able to save your soul by remaining in your home than by entering into the midst of these wild beasts." Then he began to denounce the monks, pouring forth a myriad of

φιλαργύρους καὶ κενοδόξους καὶ γαστριμάργους ἀπο-
καλῶν καὶ ὅτι· "Εἷς λέβης τοῦ μαγειρίου αὐτῶν ἐχώρησεν
ἄν με σὺν τῷ ἵππῳ τούτῳ σταθῆναι ἐν μέσῳ αὐτοῦ."

4   Μέλλοντος δὲ τοῦ δικαίου ἀποκριθῆναι αὐτῷ καὶ εἰπεῖν,
"Σὺ τίς εἶ ὁ ἀνακρίνων καὶ μεμφόμενος τοὺς δουλεύοντας
τῷ Θεῷ; Ἄξιος γὰρ ὁ ἐργάτης τῆς τροφῆς αὐτοῦ," ἐκεῖνος
βύσας τὰ ὦτα, ὡσεὶ ἀσπὶς δρομαίως ἀνεχώρησεν ἀπ᾽ αὐτοῦ.
Ὁ δὲ ὅσιος κατασφραγισάμενος ἑαυτὸν τῷ σημείῳ τοῦ
σταυροῦ, καὶ δυσωπήσας τὸν Θεὸν σκεπάσαι καὶ διαφυ-
λάξαι αὐτὸν ἀπὸ τοῦ κατακρῖναι τὸν οἰονδήποτε μοναχόν,
εἰσῆλθεν εὐθύμως εἰς τὴν ἁγίαν ἐκείνην μονήν.

8

Καὶ προσκυνήσας τόν τε ἡγούμενον καὶ πάντας τοὺς
ἀδελφοὺς καὶ παρακαλέσας, ἵνα διὰ τὸν Κύριον εὔξονται
ὑπὲρ αὐτοῦ, προσεδέχθη παρ᾽ αὐτῶν ὡς υἱὸς καὶ ἀδελφὸς
ἀγαπητός· ἰδόντες δὲ αὐτὸν κεκοπιακότα λίαν ἐκ τῆς
ὁδοῦ, φιλοφρόνως ἐδεξιώσαντο αὐτὸν ἔν τε ἰχθύσι καὶ
οἴνῳ καὶ τῇ λοιπῇ παρακλήσει τῶν μοναχῶν, καθὼς ἔθος
αὐτοῖς· αὐτὸς δὲ τὰ πολλὰ παριδὼν ὡς ἀνοίκεια ὄντα τοῖς
εἰσαγωγικοῖς καὶ μάλιστα τοῖς σφριγῶσι τῇ τῆς νεότητος
ἀκμῇ καὶ βουλομένοις τὸν τοῦ Χριστοῦ ζυγὸν ὑπελθεῖν,
ἄρτῳ μόνῳ καὶ ὕδατι τὴν χρείαν ἀπεπλήρου τοῦ σώματος,
ἀνάξιον ἑαυτὸν κρατῶν διὰ τὴν ἀγάπην τοῦ Χριστοῦ καὶ

abuses against their name, calling them avaricious and vain-glorious and gluttonous. He added, "There would be room for me and my horse to stand inside one cauldron of their kitchen."

Just as the righteous man was going to respond to him 4 with the words, "Who are you to judge and reproach the servants of God? Even *the laborer deserves his food,*" the Devil ran away from him, *stopping his ears* and slithering away *like an asp.* The holy man sealed himself with the sign of the cross, and begged God to watch over him and keep him from criticizing any monk. He then cheerfully entered within that holy monastery.

Chapter 8

When he knelt down before the superior and all the brethren, and implored them to pray to the Lord on his behalf, Neilos was received by them as a son and beloved brother. When the monks saw that he was exhausted from the journey, they welcomed him hospitably with fish and wine, and other customary monastic refreshments. However, Neilos refused most of it as inappropriate fare for novices and certainly not fitting for those in the vigor of youth who desired to assume the yoke of Christ. He fulfilled his bodily needs with bread and water alone, deeming himself unworthy to partake even of these, because of the love of

τῆς αὐτῶν μεταλήψεως. Εἶτα, μετὰ ταῦτα ἀνατίθησι τῷ
ἡγουμένῳ πάντα τὰ κατ' αὐτὸν καὶ τὸν λογισμὸν τῆς
ἀφίξεως αὐτοῦ, παρακαλῶν τῷ τοιούτῳ σκοπῷ ἐνδῦσαι
αὐτὸν τὸ σχῆμα τῶν μοναχῶν, ὥστε μὴ πλέον τῶν τεσσαράκοντα ἡμερῶν ποιῆσαι ἐν αὐτῇ τῇ μονῇ, ἀλλὰ τῇ
αὐτοῦ βουλῇ καὶ εὐχῇ ὑποστρέψαι αὐτὸν πρὸς τοὺς ἁγίους
πατέρας οἷς ᾠκειώθη ἐν τῇ ἀρχῇ καὶ ἐπήλειψαν αὐτὸν νουθεσίαις καὶ διδασκαλίαις πνευματικαῖς.

2   Πρὸς τούτοις, ὁ μὲν ἀββᾶς ἠβούλετο ἅμα τοῦ καθ-
ιερῶσαι αὐτὸν καὶ ἡγούμενον καταστῆσαι ἐν ἑτέρῳ μοναστηρίῳ αὐτοῦ. Αὐτὸς δὲ ἀκούσας τοῦ τοιούτου λόγου,
τοσοῦτον ἐφάνη αὐτῷ φορτικὸν καὶ ἀπρεπές, ὅτι καὶ δεξιὰς δέδωκε τῷ Θεῷ τοῦ ἀπ' ἐκείνης τῆς ὥρας, εἰ πατριάρχην βουληθείη τις καταστῆσαι αὐτόν, μηδόλως ποτὲ
καταδέξασθαι οἰανδήποτε ἀρχήν, ἀλλ' ἀρκετὸν τυγχάνειν
αὐτῷ τὸ ἐν τῇ τάξει τῶν μοναχῶν εὐαρεστῆσαι Θεῷ καὶ
μὴ ὑπερφρονεῖν, παρ' ὃ δεῖ φρονεῖν, ἀπολλύντα τὸ σωφρο-
νεῖν. Οὐ μόνον δὲ τοῦτο, ἀλλὰ καὶ ἑτέροις τισὶν ὅροις
περιέσφιγξεν ἑαυτόν, ὑφ' ὧν ὡς περιεκτικωτέροις καὶ κε-
φαλαιωδεστέροις τῶν ἀρετῶν συγκρατούμενος, τὰ λοιπὰ
πάντα ἐπαινετὰ καὶ καλὰ τούτοις συνέψονται ὡς ἐν
ἁλύσεσι τὰ ἐχόμενα. Ἔστι δὲ ταῦτα τὸ φυλάξαι τὸ σῶμα
αὐτοῦ ἐν ἁγνείᾳ καὶ καθαρότητι, ὡς προσφορὰν καὶ δῶρον
προσαχθὲν τῷ Χριστῷ, καὶ τὸ ἀπέχεσθαι φιλαργυρίας, τῆς
ῥίζης πάντων τῶν κακῶν, μέχρι καὶ ἑνὸς ὀβολοῦ, καὶ τὸ
μὴ ἐκβαλεῖν μοναχὸν ἢ ἡγούμενον ἀπὸ τῆς ἰδίας μονῆς
ἕνεκεν τῆς παροικίας αὐτοῦ.

Christ. Afterward he explained to the superior all that had happened to him and the reason for his arrival; because of this he begged the superior to clothe him in a monk's habit, so that he should not spend more than forty days in the monastery, but, in accordance with his desire and prayer, return to the holy fathers with whom he had been originally associated and who had prepared him with admonitions and spiritual teachings.

The superior, though, wished for something more than this after his consecration, namely, to establish him as the superior in yet another monastery. When Neilos heard this plan, it appeared to him so onerous and unseemly that he swore to God that from that hour onward, even if someone should want to make him patriarch, he would not accept such a position under any circumstance. Instead it would suffice for him to be well-pleasing to God in the monastic ranks, and *not think of himself more highly than he ought,* and thereby destroy his prudence. In addition, he also restrained himself with some other rules and guided by them as embracing and summarizing the cardinal virtues, he expected that all praiseworthy and good things would follow in sequence like the links of a chain. These were his strictures: to keep his body chaste and pure as a sacrifice and gift offered to Christ; to reject *the love of money, the root of all evils,* to the point of not possessing a single coin; and not to expel a monk or superior from his monastery for the sake of taking his position.

9

Τούτων ἕνεκα τῶν κανονισθέντων καὶ ὁρισθέντων αὐτῷ ὑφ᾽ ἑαυτοῦ ἐν τῇ ἀμφιάσει τοῦ σχήματος τοῦ ἀγγελικοῦ, πολλοὺς καὶ μεγίστους ὑπέμεινε πειρασμούς· πρὸς γὰρ τὸ ἀντιτεῖνον μᾶλλον ἡ μάχη ἀεί, κατὰ τό· "Ἐν ὁδῷ ταύτῃ ᾗ ἐπορευόμην ἔκρυψαν παγίδα μοι." Τῇ δὲ divina ope communitus, ac propria alacritate concertans, haec usque ad extremum vitae spiritum immobiliter servavit. Cum igitur quadraginta dies in sancti ac magni martyris Nazarii monasterio permaneret, ubi et sanctum habitum se induit, per totos hos dies neque panem, neque vinum gustavit, neque aliud ex his quae igni conficiuntur; sed vivebat arborum fructibus et oleribus contentus. Multum autem illi hoc ad male patiendum fuit, homini a deliciosa vita repente ad austeram hanc vivendi formam translato.

2   Neque enim desidia abstinentiae pondus levabat, aut multo somno otium transigebat: sed totam diem in pulchre scribendo conterebat, ut monasterio manuum suarum monumentum relinqueret, neque, quod otiosus panem manducaret, condemnaretur. Noctem autem in oratione, psalmis et genibus flectendis ducebat, tribus certaminibus sibi propositis trinitate munito, duplici continentia, corporis labore et afflictione, cum vigiliis peracta. At ne quis existimet, initia certaminum huiusmodi exstitisse, fines autem minus feliciter peractos; sed quemadmodum principium approbatum, ita et postremum Deo fuit acceptum.

Chapter 9

Because of the rules and limits he placed upon himself once he was garbed in the angelic habit, he endured many great trials; for where there is resistance, there always is the battle. As it is written, *In the very way wherein I was walking, they hid a snare for me.* Fortified by divine assistance as well as striving through his own ardor, he steadfastly preserved these rules until the last breath of his life. Therefore, while Neilos was passing forty days in the monastery of the holy and great martyr Nazarios, where he also donned the holy vestment, he tasted in all that time neither bread nor wine nor any other cooked food. Instead, he lived content with fruits and vegetables. Nonetheless he had to endure much harsh suffering for this, being a man suddenly brought from a luxurious life to this austere manner of living.

Nor did he lighten the burden of abstinence through idle- 2 ness, or spending his leisure time in long naps. Rather, he consumed the whole day in beautiful calligraphy, so that he might leave the monastery a monument from his own hands, and not be denounced as a man who ate bread in idleness. Moreover, he spent the night in prayer, singing the psalms, and in genuflections, and in setting three tests for himself, so as to become strong through the practice of this trinity: a twofold self-restraint, through toil and mortification of the body, complemented by vigils. But let not anyone suppose that although the beginnings of his contests were of this sort, they came to a less happy ending; rather just as the beginning was approved by God, so also the end was

Manifestum autem hoc erit Dei gratia adiuvante et oratione progrediente.

3   Quodam die adiit illum ex familiaribus veteribus quidam, qui cum laudasset eum, quem erga Deum bonum animum prae se tulit, dum in mundo vitam degeret, et rursus in monastica conversatione; cumque beatum illum praedicaret, propterea quod *bonam partem elegit, quae non auferetur ab eo.* At is: "Si bonum," inquit, "est, O frater, quod laudas, quare et tu non aemularis?" "Propterea quod," inquit, "non exsistit mihi amictus, neque lana confecta tunica." Statim autem surgens sanctus vir, dempto sibi, quem gerebat, amictu, novum ac maxime delectabilem, ei dat excusationes importunas fingenti, ac quamprimum zonam dissolvens, studebat sese exuere, ut et tunicam illi daret, "Cape," inquiens, "haec, frater, modo, ne bona parte priveris; de me vero abiecto illius servo Dominus providebit."

4   Cum ille viri magnanimitatem perspexisset, immensamque charitatem atque efferventem zelum, non permisit illum omnino exui, erubescens nudum videre; amictum autem solum capiens ac sibi imponens: "Poenitens," inquit, "credo Domino nostro Jesu Christo, et spero in sanctas tuas orationes, quod ob recordationem huius amictus studebo et ego Deo placere et certamen subire pro meae animae salute." Quibus dictis, discessit attonitus atque hominis virtutem admirans. At sanctus Nilus, cum petiisset a monasterii cellario unius pecudis pellem, hanc manibus conficiens ac benedictionibus variam exornans, suis humeris

pleasing to Him. This will be made manifest by the assistance of God's grace as the narrative proceeds.

One day one of the old household servants approached 3
Neilos. He had praised him as one who displayed goodwill toward God both while he lived in the world and again in monastic life; and he was proclaiming Neilos blessed, because *he chose the good part which shall not be taken from him*. But Neilos responded, "If what you praise is good, brother, then why do you not imitate it as well?" "Because," the servant said, "I have neither a monastic cloak nor a woolen tunic." Immediately the holy man stood up, took off the cloak he was wearing, which was new and most exquisite, and gave it to the man who was making unsuitable excuses. He instantly unfastened his belt and tried to take off his clothes so that he might give him the tunic as well. "Now take these, brother," he said, "so that you will not be deprived of the better portion. As for me, certainly the Lord will provide for His humble servant."

When that man saw Neilos's generosity and immense 4
charity, and also his exuberant zeal, he did not permit him to disrobe completely, ashamed to see him nude. He took only the cloak, put it on himself, and said, "I repent; I believe in our Lord Jesus Christ, and I place hope in your holy prayers. With this cloak as a reminder, I too shall strive to please God and to undertake the contest for the salvation of my soul." With these words, the servant went away astonished, admiring the man's virtue. But after holy Neilos had asked the cellarer of the monastery for a single sheepskin, with his own hands he made this into a garment, adorned the spotted hide with blessings and placed it upon his shoulders,

imposuit, secum cogitans eum qui dixit, *"circumierunt in melotis et pellibus caprinis."*

5   Propositum autem hoc unum illi erat, vitam apostolicam et zelum propheticum in animi promptitudinem suscipere, atque ad illos assidue aspiciens, ex illis formabat interiorem atque exteriorem hominem: caput inopertum habebat, iuxta apostoli praeceptum; una vero tunica omne tempus induebatur, evangelicum dictum sequens; pedesque nudos gerens, propterea quod ita a propheta sunt cum admiratione huiusmodi pedes approbati. Quamvis ab huiusmodi laboribus atque afflictionibus extremae senectutis infirmitas atque imbecillitas illum amovit, tamen ab animi virtutibus ne ipsa quidem mors absterruit, quominus in illis primas principatum haberet, neque illius memoriam futuri aevi delevit oblivio, siquidem iuxta apostolum *manent haec tria: spes, fides et charitas.*

6   At interea ad ea quae coepimus redeamus. Erat regulus quidam, quem comitem vocant in regionibus illis, durus ac nimium inhumanus, nullam suae salutis rationem habens: utens autem tyrannide atque arrogantia, servituti subiecit innocentem animum cuiusdam, qui ad illud monasterium, ubi beatus Nilus versabatur, pertinebat. Quodam igitur die cum ille tyrannus irruisset in monasterium ad explendum proprium ventrem, neque enim ob animae utilitatem; cum esset discessurus, praefectus nihil ausus est ea de re dicere, veritus arrogantiam atque illius impudentiam; advocavit beatum Nilum, in quo admirabilis eloquendi libertas inerat, atque illum adhortatur, ut terribilem illum principem

pondering within himself the man who said, "*They wandered about in sheepskins and goatskins.*"

Then he had this single purpose: to emulate the life of the 5 apostles and the zeal of the prophets in eagerness of mind, and he formed both his interior and exterior person by continually looking toward those men as examples. He kept his head uncovered, in accordance with the rule of the apostle; he wore only one coat in every season, following the words of the Gospel; he walked with bare feet, because in this way his feet were admired by the prophet. Although, eventually, the infirmity of extreme old age and its accompanying weaknesses made him desist from such efforts and rigors, nonetheless not even death deterred him from the virtues of the spirit because he held first rank in exercising them. Nor has oblivion erased the memory of this man in a future age, since indeed, according to the apostle, *there remain these three: hope, faith, and charity.*

Now let us go back to where we were in our narrative. 6 There was a petty king, whom they call a count in those regions, a harsh and exceedingly cruel man who had no concern for his salvation. Through his tyranny and arrogance, he subjected to servitude the innocent soul of a certain domestic servant, who belonged to the monastery where the blessed Neilos was staying. One day that tyrant had rushed into the monastery to fulfill his carnal desire, certainly not to benefit his soul. When he was about to leave, the superior did not dare to say anything to him regarding this matter, in dread of the man's arrogance and impertinence. The superior summoned holy Neilos, who possessed a marvelous facility for fearless speech, and urged him to approach that

aggressus, animae quam iniuste occupaverat, liberationem impetraret.

7 Qui velut a Deo iussus, atque indubitata fide armatus adiit temerarium illum et opere et λόγοις παρακλητικοῖς καὶ νουθεσίαις πνευματικαῖς, ὡς ἐκ τοῦ ἀββᾶ ἀπείληφεν αὐτόν, ὑπομιμνήσκων αὐτὸν καὶ περὶ τῆς ὑποθέσεως τοῦ προκειμένου σκοποῦ. Τοῦ δὲ λίαν ἀντιλέγοντος καὶ ἀνανεύοντος πρὸς τὴν τοιαύτην παράκλησιν, καὶ διομνυμένου ὡς οὔτε οὐρανόθεν ἀγγέλου, οὔτε ἀπὸ γῆθεν ἀνθρώπου πεισθήσεται τοῦ ἀπολῦσαι τὴν τοιαύτην ψυχήν, ὁ θεόπνευστος Νεῖλος τῷ τοῦ θανάτου κέντρῳ ὑπένυσσεν αὐτόν, ὡς ἱκανοῦ ὄντος κατανύξαι καὶ ἀπαλῦναι καὶ λιθίνην ψυχήν.

8 Ὁ δὲ οὐδ' οὕτως ἐκάμπτετο τὴν ψυχήν, κατεχόμενος ἀναισθησίᾳ πολλῇ, ἀλλὰ ἀποκρίνεται μετὰ ἀπονοίας καί φησιν· "Ὕπαγε, καλόγηρε, δέκα ἔτη ὑπάρχουσιν αἱ ἡμέραι μου· ἐν τοῖς ὀκτὼ ἔτεσι πληρώσω τὰ τῆς ψυχῆς μου ἐπιθυμήματα, καὶ τοὺς ἐχθραίνοντάς μοι ὑποτάξω, ὡς θέλω ἐγώ· εἰς δὲ τὰ δύο ἔτη μετανοῶ καὶ προσδέχεταί με ὁ Θεὸς ὡς τὴν πόρνην καὶ τὸν λῃστήν." Τότε ὁ ἀββᾶς Νεῖλος ὑπὸ τοῦ Ἁγίου Πνεύματος ἐμπνευσθεὶς ἀποκρίνεται αὐτῷ καί φησιν· "Πρόσεχε σεαυτῷ, ταπεινὲ ἄνθρωπε· ἃ γὰρ ἐλπίζεις δέκα ἔτη βιῶσαι καὶ τὰ θελήματα τῆς ψυχῆς σου πληρῶσαι, δέκα ἡμέραι τυγχάνουσι μόναι. Μὴ τοίνυν πλανῶ, ἐν ὀνείροις καὶ μαντείαις σεαυτὸν ἀπατῶν."

9 Ταῦτα μετὰ παρρησίας πρὸς αὐτὸν εἰρηκὼς καὶ ὑποστρέψας ἐν τῇ μονῇ, τῷ μὲν ἡγουμένῳ ἀνήγγελλε τὴν ταχίστην ἀπώλειαν τοῦ δεινοῦ, ὁ δὲ σοβαρὸς ἐκεῖνος ἀνὴρ ῥίγει καὶ πυρετῷ παραχρῆμα συσχεθείς, ἔκειτο μέχρι τῆς

terrible ruler and try to obtain the release of the soul whom he had seized.

As if commanded by God and armed with his unshakeable 7 faith, Neilos went to that brazen man. By actions, words of exhortation, and spiritual admonitions, just as if they had come from the superior, Neilos censured him for this crime. However, the count resisted excessively and refused to listen to this entreaty, and swore that neither a heavenly angel nor an earthly human being would persuade him to release that innocent soul. Neilos, inspired by God, prodded him with the goad of death, thinking this sufficient to spur to compunction and soften such a rock-hard soul.

The tyrant, filled with great insensitivity, was not swayed 8 in his soul, but responded with frenzy and said, "Go away, monk, I have ten years remaining in my life. For eight of them I shall fulfill the yearnings of my heart, and subdue my enemies, as I wish. For the last two I shall be penitent, and God will receive me as He has the prostitute and the thief." Then inspired by the Holy Spirit father Neilos replied to him and said, "Take heed, wretched man, for the ten years that you hope to live and fulfill the yearnings of your heart, they are but ten days. Do not therefore be led astray, deceiving yourself with dreams and divinations."

Having said these fearless words to him, Neilos returned 9 to the monastery and reported to the superior the imminent demise of the terrible count. And in fact that haughty man was immediately afflicted with chills and fever. He lay

ἐνάτης ἡμέρας βασανιζόμενος ἀνηκέστως· καὶ τῇ δεκάτῃ
συστάσεως αὐτῷ ἐνεχθείσης παρὰ τῶν οἰκητόρων τῆς
κώμης καὶ πάντων βουλευομένων αὐτὸν ἀποκτεῖναι, αὐτὸς
μαθὼν τοῦτο πρὸς τῆς ὑπ᾽ αὐτοῦ πορνευομένης μαινάδος,
ἐπελάβετο μὲν τῷ θράσει τῆς σπάθης καὶ πάντας αὐτοὺς
διεσκόρπισεν ἐπιφανεὶς καὶ μόνον, τῷ δὲ φόβῳ καὶ τῇ
δειλίᾳ κατασχεθεὶς ἐπὶ πλεῖον καὶ βουληθεὶς τῇ φυγῇ τὴν
σωτηρίαν εὕρασθαι, ὑπὸ τῶν ἰδίων συμποδισθεὶς καὶ
πεσὼν ἁρμάτων τοῦ ζῆν ἀπηλλάγη καὶ οὕτως ὑπὸ τῶν
παρ᾽ αὐτοῦ πολλάκις ἀδικηθέντων τὴν κεφαλὴν ἀπετμήθη
καὶ τοῖς κυσὶ παρεδόθη εἰς βρῶσιν. Καὶ ἐπληρώθη αὐτῷ ἡ
πρόρρησις τοῦ ἁγίου, ὡς οὔτε ἐντός, οὔτε ἐκτός, ἀλλ᾽ ἐν
τῇ δεκάτῃ ἡμέρᾳ.

10   Μετὰ δὲ ταύτας τὰς ἡμέρας ὑπέστρεψεν ὁ ὅσιος πατὴρ
ἡμῶν Νεῖλος πλήρης ὢν Πνεύματος Ἁγίου καὶ πίστεως
πρὸς τοὺς ἁγίους πατέρας τοὺς ἐν τῷ Μερκουρίῳ (καὶ γὰρ
πέφυκε τῷ ὁμοίῳ τὸ ὅμοιον πάντως συνήδεσθαι), καὶ
πάντες ἰδόντες αὐτὸν ἀποστολικὸν καὶ βίον καὶ ζῆλον καὶ
σχῆμα καὶ ἐπιτήδευμα περιβεβλημένον, ἔχοντα δὲ καὶ τὴν
εὐπρεπεστάτην ταπείνωσιν σὺν τῇ αἰδῶ τῷ μετώπῳ προ-
καθημένην, ἠγαλλιάσαντο καὶ εὐφράνθησαν καὶ τῷ Θεῷ
ἐπ᾽ αὐτῷ δόξαν ἀνέπεμψαν.

10

Αὐτὸς δὲ πάντας μὲν ἐσέβετο καὶ ἐδόξαζεν ὡς ἀγγέλους
Κυρίου, ἐξαιρέτως δὲ σχέσιν καὶ ἀγάπην ἐκέκτητο
μεγίστην πρὸς τὸν τίμιον πατέρα Φαντῖνον. Κἀκεῖνος δὲ

for nine days in cruel torment, and on the tenth day there was a rebellion of the inhabitants of the town, all desiring to kill him. Upon learning this from the servant girl who had been seduced by him, the count boldly drew his broadsword and scattered them all solely by his appearance. Nevertheless, he was even more oppressed by fear and dread, and desired to find safety in flight, but he was tripped up by his own armor, fell, and departed this life. Then the people he had so often wronged cut off his head and gave it to the dogs to eat. And so the holy man's prediction was fulfilled, neither before nor after, but precisely on the tenth day.

Afterwards our holy father Neilos, filled with the Holy Spirit, and full of faith, returned to the holy fathers on Mount Merkourion; for it is natural that like always accord with like. When they all saw him clad in the apostolic life and zeal and habit and profession, bearing the most comely humility and respect upon his brow, they rejoiced and were gladdened, and gave glory to God.

Chapter 10

Neilos for his part venerated and glorified them all as angels of the Lord, but he developed an especially close relationship with and great love for the venerable father

πάλιν τὸ αὐτὸ φίλτρον ἢ καὶ πλέον ἐδείκνυεν πρὸς τοῦτον, τὴν τοῦ Πέτρου καὶ Ἰωάννου, ἢ Βασιλείου καὶ Γρηγορίου συζυγίαν καὶ ἀδιάσπαστον γνώμην ἐν ἑαυτοῖς προδηλοῦντες. Συγκαθημένων γὰρ αὐτῶν πολλάκις καὶ τὰς Γραφὰς ἀναγινωσκόντων, συνήγοντο οἱ ἀδελφοὶ πρὸς αὐτοὺς πάντες, παρακαλοῦντες ἀκοῦσαι λόγον ὠφελείας ἐκ τοῦ στόματος αὐτῶν. Καὶ ἀκούοντες τοῦ λόγου τῆς χάριτος τοῦ ἐκπορευομένου διὰ στόματος τοῦ ὁσίου πατρὸς Νείλου, θεωροῦντες δὲ καὶ τὴν ἀστράπτουσαν χάριν ἐπὶ τὸν ἅγιον πατέρα Φαντῖνον, οὐδὲν ἄλλο ὑπελάμβανον τούτους ὑπάρχειν, ἀλλ' ἢ Πέτρον καὶ Παῦλον, ὧν καὶ τὸν βίον ἐζήλουν. Τινὲς οὖν τῶν ἀδελφῶν ἀπελθόντες εἰς προσκύνησιν τοῦ μεγάλου πατρὸς Ἰωάννου, ἤρξαντο ἐπαινεῖν τὸν μακάριον Νεῖλον, ὡς ὠφελείας ὑπόθεσιν παρὰ τοῦ Θεοῦ πεμφθέντα ἐν τοῖς τόποις ἐκείνοις, προστιθέντες καὶ τοῦτο, ὅτι οὔτε ἄρτου, οὔτε οἴνου μεταλαμβάνει, ἄσκησιν διώκων ὑψηλοτάτην. Ἐκέλευσεν οὖν αὐτοῖς ὁ πατὴρ ἀποστεῖλαι αὐτὸν πρὸς αὐτόν.

2   Καὶ τούτου γεγονότος καὶ μετὰ χαρᾶς προσδεχθέντος, κελεύει ὁ μέγας πατὴρ Ἰωάννης δοθῆναι αὐτῷ ποτήριον οἴνου μέγιστον, βουλόμενος ἰδεῖν εἰ κατὰ Θεόν ἐστιν ἡ αὐτοῦ πολιτεία. Λαβὼν δὲ τὸ ποτήριον ὁ ὅσιος Νεῖλος καὶ αἰτησάμενος εὐλογίαν, ἀνυποστόλως αὐτὸ πέπωκεν ἕως τέλους, μήτε τὸ ἀθρόον τῆς βλάβης τοῦ οἴνου καταπτήξας, μήτε τὴν οἰκείαν κρίσιν τῆς τοῦ πατρὸς διακρίσεως κυριωτέραν ἀποδείξας, ἀλλὰ τὴν κοπὴν τοῦ θελήματος εὐλόγου τε καὶ ἀλόγου ὡς σωτηρίας μεγίστην ὑπόθεσιν τῶν λοιπῶν προτιμήσας. Τότε ὁ μέγας ἐκεῖνος θαυμάσας

Phantinos, who in turn showed Neilos the same affection, if not more. They demonstrated a bond between them like that of Peter and John, or Basil and Gregory, displaying an inseparable mind. For often when they were seated together reading the Scriptures, all the brothers would gather around them, requesting a beneficial word from their mouths. Upon hearing the word of grace flowing from the mouth of the holy father Neilos and seeing the radiant grace of the holy father Phantinos, the brethren took them to be nothing less than Peter and Paul, whose lives they emulated. Some of the monks who had gone to pay homage to the great father John began to praise the blessed Neilos, as a bulwark of assistance sent by God into their midst, and they added that he partook of neither bread nor wine, pursuing the highest degree of asceticism. And so the father John ordered them to send Neilos to him.

When this was done and Neilos was joyfully received, the great father John desired to see if his conduct was in accordance with God and ordered that a large cup of wine be given to him. Taking the cup, the holy Neilos requested a blessing, and then without hesitation drank it down; neither did he wince at the force of the wine's effect, nor did he demonstrate his own opinion to be superior to the discernment of father John. He preferred as the greatest foundation of salvation the denial of his own will, whether with good reason or without reason. Then that great father him-

2

καθ᾽ ἑαυτὸν τοῦ ἀνδρὸς τὴν σοφίαν, καὶ τὸ ἀνυπόκριτον
τῆς αὐτοῦ ὑπακοῆς κατὰ πάντα (ἐπείρασε γὰρ αὐτὸν καὶ
ἐν ἄλλοις, μᾶλλον δὲ ἐδίδαξεν οἷα πατὴρ υἱὸν γνήσιον),
ἔφη πρὸς τοὺς παρόντας· "Οὐκ ἔλεγον οἱ πατέρες ὅτι ὁ
ἀββᾶς Νεῖλος οὐ γεύεται οἴνου; Ὡς ἔοικε, ἄλλα ὁρῶσιν οἱ
ἄνθρωποι, καὶ ἕτερα λέγουσιν."

II

Εὐθέως οὖν ἀναστὰς ἐκεῖνος, βάλλει μετάνοιαν λέγων·
"Συγχώρησόν μοι, τίμιε πάτερ, ὅτι οὐδέποτε ἐποίησά τι
ἀγαθὸν ἐνώπιον τοῦ Θεοῦ· ὅμως ἡ ἐγκράτεια, πάτερ, ὡς
καὶ αὐτὸς μᾶλλον ἐπίστασαι, συμβάλλεται πᾶσιν ἐν ἅπασιν, τοῖς μὲν γέρουσιν, ἵν᾽ εἰκὼν καὶ τύπος τοῖς νέοις
γενήσωνται, τοῖς νέοις δ᾽ ἡμῖν καὶ εἰσαγωγικοῖς, ἵν᾽ ὅπως
μὴ τῇ φλογὶ πλείονα ὕλην προσθήσωμεν, ἢ τὸ θηρίον
ἀγριώτερον καὶ δυσκάθεκτον καταστήσωμεν. Τὸ μέντοι
ἐπιτυχεῖν τῆς παναγεστάτης εὐλογίας τῆς σῆς τιμίας
χειρός, εἴτε διὰ πόματος οἴνου, εἴτε διὰ κλάσματος ἄρτου,
πατριαρχικῆς χάριτος ἄξιον, καὶ τῆς αὐτῆς δωρεᾶς ἰσόρρο-
πον."

2   Ταῦτα ἀκούσας ὁ μέγας Ἰωάννης, ὑπομειδιάσας τῷ
προσώπῳ καὶ ἀγαλλιαθεὶς τῷ πνεύματι, πολλῷ πλέον
εὐλογίαις αὐτὸν ἀντημείψατο καὶ εὐχαῖς κατεπλούτησεν.

self was amazed at the man's wisdom and his unfeigned obedience toward all (for he tested him in other ways as well; indeed, he taught him as a father teaches his own son). He said to those present, "Didn't the fathers say that father Neilos drinks no wine? As it seems, men see one thing and say another."

Chapter 11

Then Neilos immediately stood up, and prostrated himself, saying, "Forgive me, venerable father, for I have never done any good before God. As you yourself know better than I, father, temperance profits everyone in all situations: for the elders that they become an image and model for the young, and for us who are young and novices, so that we do not add more fuel to the fire, or allow the wild beast to become fiercer and more unruly. However, to attain a most holy blessing from your venerable hand, whether through a drink of wine or a piece of bread, is worth as much as the grace of a patriarch and equal to the gift itself."

Upon hearing this, a smile came across the great John's 2 face. Rejoicing in his spirit John rewarded him with many more blessings, and enriched him with prayers. He reminded

Ἐνουθέτει δὲ αὐτὸν συμμέτρως ἀσκεῖν, μήπως ὑπὸ νόσου ἢ γήρως πιεσθεὶς μέλλῃ τότε ἐπιζητεῖν τὰ μὴ τῷ σχήματι πρέποντα. Καὶ τότε μὲν κατέσχεν αὐτὸν παρ᾽ ἑαυτῷ, εὐφραινόμενος ἐπὶ τῇ ἡδυτάτῃ ἀναγνώσει αὐτοῦ καὶ τῇ εὐστόχῳ τῶν νοημάτων ἀναπτύξει καὶ διασαφήσει τῶν θείων Γραφῶν. Ἐσχόλαζε γὰρ ὁ μέγας Ἰωάννης ἀεὶ ἐν τοῖς λόγοις τοῦ Ἁγίου Γρηγορίου τοῦ Θεολόγου, ὥστε τῇ πολλῇ πείρᾳ, ἣν ἐξ αὐτῶν ἀνελάβετο, ἄλλον Θεολόγον παρὰ πᾶσι γνωρίζεσθαι.

3   Ἐν μιᾷ δὲ τῶν ἡμερῶν ἀναγινώσκοντος ἐν τῇ αὐτῇ βίβλῳ τοῦ ὁσίου πατρὸς ἡμῶν Νείλου, καὶ τοῦ γέροντος βουληθέντος διευκρινῆσαι ἕν τῶν τῷ ἁγίῳ διδασκάλῳ πονηθέντων δογμάτων, οὐκ ἤρεσε τῷ ἀββᾷ Νείλῳ ἡ τοῦ γέροντος ἑρμηνεία, ὡς μὴ τὸν σκοπὸν τοῦ διδασκάλου ἐν ἀκριβείᾳ καταλαβόντος. Καὶ βουληθέντος τὸ ἴσον τῆς διανοίας ἐν ἑτέρῳ χωρίῳ τῆς αὐτῆς βίβλου σαφέστερον ἀποδεῖξαι καὶ τὴν ὀρθότητα τοῦ δόγματος, καθώς ἐστιν, ἀποφῆναι, ἐπετιμήθη σφοδρῶς παρὰ τοῦ μεγάλου, ὡς οὐκ ἐξὸν αὐτῷ ἐρευνᾶν τὰ τοιαῦτα, νέῳ ὄντι καὶ ἀρχαρίῳ καὶ ἀκμὴν ἐν τοῖς πάθεσι τοῦ βίου ἰλυσπωμένῳ. Αὐτὸς δὲ ἀκούσας, οὐδαμῶς ἐταράχθη, ἢ ὅλως παρεσαλεύθη τῆς πίστεως καὶ ἀγάπης, ἧς ἐκέκτητο πρὸς τὸν γέροντα, ἀλλ᾽ οὕτως ἐδέξατο αὐτοῦ τὰ ὀνείδη, ὡς ὁ διψῶν ὕδατος πεπλησμένον ἀγγεῖον. Καὶ γὰρ εἶχεν αὐτὸν ὡς τὸν Ἅγιον Ἰωάννην τὸν Βαπτιστήν· πολλάκις δὲ οὕτω προσεκύνει τὸν τόπον ὅπου ἵσταντο οἱ πόδες αὐτοῦ ἐν τῇ ἐκκλησίᾳ, ὡς καὶ τὸ ἅγιον βῆμα τοῦ θυσιαστηρίου.

Neilos to practice his asceticism in moderation, so that when he was constrained by sickness or old age he would not then seek after things inappropriate to the monastic habit. Then he kept Neilos by his side, taking pleasure in his most mellifluous recitation, as well as his shrewd explanation of concepts and his interpretation of the divine Scriptures. For the great John was always studying the orations of Saint Gregory the Theologian, so that, as a result of the great experience he had acquired from those texts, he was known to all as a second Theologian.

One day while our holy father Neilos was reading the 3 same book, the elder John wished to explicate one of the doctrines elaborated by the holy teacher. But his interpretation was not satisfactory to father Neilos, as he did not precisely understand the teacher Gregory's point. Neilos wanted to show his intention more clearly by comparison with another passage from the same book, and to demonstrate the correctness of the doctrine just as it was. He was sharply rebuked by the elder since it was not possible for him to investigate such matters, inasmuch as he was still young and a neophyte, still wallowing in the mud of life's passions. At these words, Neilos was not at all taken aback or shaken in the faith and love which he had acquired for the elder. Rather he received the reproaches just as a thirsty man welcomes a container filled with water. For Neilos regarded him as Saint John the Baptist and often venerated the place in the church where the superior placed his feet, as one would do at the holy sanctuary of the altar.

12

Τῆς δὲ ἑσπέρας καταλαβούσης, καὶ πορευθέντος αὐτοῦ ἡσυχάσαι ἐν τῷ ἰδίῳ κελλίῳ, ὑπεισῆλθεν αὐτῷ λογισμὸς ταράσσων καὶ ἐνοχλῶν αὐτὸν σφόδρα, "εἰ ἄρα ὁ μέγας ἐπ' ἀληθείας ἐπέπληξεν αὐτῷ, ὡς κακῶς νενοηκότι τὴν χρῆσιν τοῦ Θεολόγου, μή ποτε καὶ αἴρεσις λογισθείη, ἢ μόνον ταπεινῶσαι βουλόμενος τὴν ἐμὴν ὑψηλοφροσύνην καὶ μεγίστην ἀλαζονίαν." Καὶ ταῦτα διενθυμούμενος, μικρὸν ἀπενύσταξεν. Ὁ δὲ πάντων τῶν δικαίων παρατηρῶν τὰς παρατροπὰς τῶν ἐνθέων διαβημάτων τοῦ ὑποσκελίσαι ἢ κρύψαι παγίδα, βουληθεὶς σινιάσαι καὶ τὸν ὅσιον τοῦτον, φαίνεται αὐτῷ καθ' ὕπαρ ἐν σχήματι δύο πρεσβυτέρων μεγάλων λεγόντων· "Ἡμεῖς ἐσμεν Πέτρος καὶ Παῦλος· ἰδόντες δέ σε," φησίν, "ἀσχάλλοντα περὶ τῶν θείων δογμάτων, ἤλθομεν τοῦ συνετίσαι σε, καὶ διδάξαι τὴν ἀλήθειαν πᾶσαν." Εἶπον τοίνυν αὐτῷ καὶ χρῆσιν ὅσον τὸ τῆς Δεσποτικῆς Εὐχῆς ὕφος, καὶ ἀπέστησαν. Ὁ δὲ εἰς ἑαυτὸν ἐλθὼν (οὐδὲ γὰρ καθεύδων ὑπῆρχεν), ἐφιλοτιμεῖτο μὲν πρὸς τὸ παρὸν ἐπὶ τῷ ἀκαίρως φανέντι καὶ τὴν χρῆσιν ἐπὶ στόματος εἶχεν, τὴν δὲ ἔννοιαν αὐτῆς οὐκ ἠρεύνα, καὶ ταῦτα δι' ὅλου τοῦ ὄρθρου καὶ ἕως πρωΐας.

2 Περὶ δὲ τὸ διάφαυμα ἡσυχίαν ἄγων βαθεῖαν καὶ μέλλων ἐξερευνῆσαι τὸ τῆς ἀποκαλύψεως βάθος, εὗρε τὸ νομιζόμενον μέλι πικρότερον ἀψινθίου καὶ τὴν κρυπτομένην θεολογίαν προδήλως αἵρεσιν δεινοτάτην. Τότε ὁ ὀξύνους ἀνὴρ ἐκεῖνος καὶ ταχὺς εἰς τὸ διακρῖναι τὸ καθαρὸν ἀπὸ

Chapter 12

When evening came and Neilos had gone to pursue spiritual tranquility in his cell, a thought occurred to him that disturbed and troubled him greatly: whether the great John had truly rebuked him for misunderstanding the passage in the Theologian so that he might never have a heretical thought, or "if he only wanted to humble my arrogance and boastfulness." As he pondered these matters, he dozed off for a while. The one who observes the deviations in the divine steps of all righteous people, and looks to trip them up or to hide snares, wished to test this holy man as well. He appeared to him in a waking dream in the guise of two venerable elders who said, "We are Peter and Paul, and seeing that you are troubled about the divine doctrines, we have come to instruct you and to teach you the whole truth." Then they also uttered some words like the text of the Lord's Prayer and departed. Then coming to his senses—for he was not yet sound asleep—Neilos prided himself for the moment on that misleading vision, and he had their words on his lips. Still he had not examined the meaning of the words; and he remained thus throughout the matins service until morning.

Around dawn, while persevering in his deep spiritual tranquility, he began to examine the deeper meaning of the revelation, and found that what he had thought to be honey was bitterer than wormwood, and that the hidden theology was clearly a most terrible heresy. Then that sharp-witted man, who was quick to distinguish the genuine from the

45

τοῦ κιβδήλου, καταμαθὼν τὸν παμμέγιστον δόλον τῶν νοητῶν πολεμίων καὶ τὴν ἄφθαστον πανουργίαν ἐκείνην, προστρέχει τῇ τοῦ Σωτῆρος σταυρώσει, ῥίπτει ἑαυτὸν ἐπ' ἐδάφους ἐν συντετριμμένῃ καὶ ταπεινῇ τῇ καρδίᾳ, αἰτεῖται ἀπάλειψιν ἐκ καρδίας τῆς πονηρᾶς ἐκείνης ἐγγραφῆς καὶ βεβήλου, ἧς καὶ τετύχηκε παραχρῆμα. Ἀναστὰς γὰρ τοῦ τόπου ἐκείνου, οὐδαμῶς οὐδέποτε ἠδυνήθη ἀπ' ἐκείνης τῆς ὥρας εἰπεῖν ἢ κἂν ἐννοῆσαί τι τῆς πονηρᾶς χρησμῳδίας ἐκείνης εἴτε ἀρχήν, εἴτε τέλος. Ἄπεισι δὲ καὶ πρὸς τὸν μέγαν ἐργάτην καὶ βάλλει αὐτῷ μετάνοιαν, ἀπαγγέλλων τὰ πάντα.

13

Ὁ δὲ γέρων μειδιῶντι τῷ προσώπῳ ἐκράτησεν αὐτὸν τῆς χειρὸς καὶ εἶπεν· "Ἀνδρίζου, ὦ τέκνον, ἀνδρίζου καὶ κραταιούσθω ἡ καρδία σου, καὶ ὑπόμεινον πειρασμοὺς τῶν δαιμόνων, ἵνα καὶ σὺ ἐπιστρέψας στηρίξῃς πολλῶν ψυχὰς ἐν τῇ γενεᾷ σου, φῶς καὶ ἅλας ἀναδειχθεὶς ἐν τῷ κόσμῳ τοῖς πλανωμένοις. Καί γε ἐγὼ οἶδα τὴν ἐκ τοῦ Θεοῦ ἀγχίνοιάν σοι δοθεῖσαν καὶ τὴν χάριν τοῦ Λόγου, καὶ ἔγνων ὅτι ὀρθῶς διεκδικεῖς τὸν σκοπὸν τοῦ ἁγίου. Ἀλλά, φοβούμενος μὴ τῷ τῆς οἰήσεως κρημνῷ περιπέσῃς, ὅπερ πολλάκις εἴωθε συμβαίνειν τοῖς κατὰ σὲ ταχυδρόμοις, ἄμεινον κέκρικα εὐφρανθῆναί με ἐν τῷ σὲ ἐξ ἐμοῦ λυπηθῆναι, καθὼς

counterfeit, fully understood the enormous deception of his spiritual enemies, and their incomparable villainy. He ran to the icon of the crucifixion of the Savior, threw himself to the floor, and with a contrite and humbled heart he begged the Lord to erase from his mind that wicked and profane imprint, and immediately it so happened. Arising from that place, from that hour he was never able to speak of, or even to bring to mind, any part of that wicked utterance, neither the beginning nor the end. Then he went to the great worker John and prostrated himself before him, telling him everything he had experienced.

Chapter 13

The elder took him by the hand and with a smile upon his face said, "*Be of good courage,* my child, *be of good courage and let your heart be strengthened and endure* the temptations of demons, so that by repenting you too may support the souls of many in your generation, being revealed as *light* and *salt* to those who go astray in the world. For I know the shrewdness of mind given to you by God, and the grace of the Word. I know as well that you correctly defended the doctrine of the holy author. Yet in my fear that you might fall from the precipice of self-conceit, which often happens to quick thinkers like yourself, I have judged it better for me *to be gladdened by the pain I have caused* you, as the apostle

ὁ ἀπόστολος διδάσκει, ἢ τὸ Ἅγιον Πνεῦμα κατὰ σοῦ λυπηθῆναι ἐν τῷ σὲ οἰήσει καὶ ὑψηλοφροσύνῃ κατενεχθῆναι." Ταῦτα καὶ πλείονα τούτων εἰρηκὼς πρὸς αὐτόν, ἐπευξάμενός τε καὶ εὐλογήσας, ἀπέλυσεν ἐν εἰρήνῃ.

2   Ὁ δὲ ὅσιος πατὴρ ἡμῶν Νεῖλος ἔτι καὶ ἔτι προκόπτων καὶ αὐξανόμενος ταῖς κατὰ Θεὸν ἀναβάσεσι καὶ θεώσεσιν, ἠράσθη καὶ τῆς μητρὸς πασῶν τῶν ἀρετῶν, ἡσυχίας, πλείονα πλοῦτον ἐκ ταύτης ἰσχύων κερδῆσαι καὶ ἄπειρον σοφίαν. Καὶ τοῦτο ἀναθεὶς τοῖς ἁγίοις πατράσι, διὰ τὸ πάντα μετὰ βουλῆς αὐτῶν πράττειν, τῇ αὐτῶν συνέσει καὶ δι᾽ εὐχῶν συνεργείᾳ τὸ βουλευθὲν ἐκυρώθη. Σπήλαιον δέ ἐστιν οὐ μακρὰν τῶν μοναστηρίων, ἐν τῷ ὕψει τοῦ κρημνοῦ διακείμενον, ἔχον ἐν αὐτῷ καὶ θυσιαστήριον ἐπ᾽ ὀνόματι τοῦ ἀρχιστρατήγου Μιχαήλ, πάνυ πρὸς ἡσυχίαν ὂν ἐπιτήδειον τοῖς ἐπιτηδείοις. Ἐν τούτῳ τῷ σπηλαίῳ ὁ ἀνδρεῖος ἐκεῖνος ἀναλαβὼν Ἡλιοῦ τὸν ζῆλον καὶ Ἐλισσαίου τὴν καρτερίαν, τήν τε ὑπομονὴν πάντων τῶν ἁγίων, ἀνέρχεται κατοικήσων μετὰ πλείστης χαρᾶς τε καὶ προθυμίας.

3   Ἐν ᾧ κατὰ μόνας αὐλιζόμενος καὶ τὸν Θεὸν προσδεχόμενος, μᾶλλον δ᾽ ἐνώπιον αὐτοῦ παριστάμενος καὶ τὸν ἀόρατον ὡς ὁρατὸν προορώμενος, πολλοὺς καὶ μεγίστους ἀγῶνας ἀνδρικῶς ἐπεδείξατο, πάντων τῶν προηγωνισμένων ὁσίων τε καὶ δικαίων τὰς ἀρετὰς καὶ τὰ ἆθλα ἀναμάξασθαι σπεύδων· ἅπερ οὐδεὶς ἂν ἰσχύσει ἢ λόγῳ φράσαι, ἢ γραφῇ παραδοῦναι διὰ τὸ ἐν κρυπτῷ μόνῳ τῷ τὰ κρυπτὰ εἰδότι προσαναφέρεσθαι, εἰ μή πού τις ταῦτα ἀπὸ τοῦ τέλους τεκμήραιτο, τουτέστιν τῆς παρὰ τοῦ Θεοῦ

teaches, than to grieve the Holy Spirit on your account if you are carried away by self-conceit and haughty pride." He said this and more to Neilos, and with a prayer and blessing sent him off in peace.

And our holy father Neilos, ever progressing and grow- 2
ing in his ascent toward God and deification, loved spiritual tranquility as the mother of all the virtues, being able to derive from it greater spiritual wealth and boundless wisdom. He brought the following proposal to the holy fathers, since he did everything with their consultation and consent, and through their wisdom and the support of their prayers, and his plan was approved. There is a cave not far from the monastery, situated upon the summit of a steep crag, which had a sanctuary dedicated to the archangel Michael, and was most suited to those pursuing spiritual tranquility. The courageous Neilos, assuming the zeal of Elijah, the perseverance of Elisha, and the patience of all the saints, climbed up to live in that cave with great joy and enthusiasm.

In this cave he lived alone, receiving only God, or, rather, 3
abiding in His presence, and seeing before him the invisible as if it were visible. Bravely he persevered through many great labors, always striving to take on the virtues and the challenges of the holy and just men who had labored before him. Such deeds no one would be able to express in words, or commit to writing, because they were offered in secret to Him alone who sees secret actions, unless somehow someone could have inferred these exploits from their outcome,

δόξης καὶ τῆς πατρικῆς ἀνταποδόσεως. "Ὁ Πατήρ σου," γάρ φησιν, "ὁ βλέπων ἐν τῷ κρυπτῷ, ἀποδώσει σοι ἐν τῷ φανερῷ," καὶ "τοὺς δοξάζοντάς με," φησί, "δοξάσω."

14

Τίς δ᾽ οὕτως ἐδοξάσθη καὶ ἐτιμήθη ἐν τῇ γενεᾷ ταύτῃ, ὡς ὁ μακάριος οὗτος, οὐ μόνον παρὰ πιστῶν βασιλέων καὶ ἀρχόντων, πατριαρχῶν ὁμοῦ καὶ ἀρχιερέων, ὁμοφύλων καὶ ἀλλογλώσσων, ἀλλὰ καὶ παρὰ τῶν ἀπίστων τυράννων, λέγω δὴ τῶν τῶν Σαρακηνῶν φυλαρχούντων, οἵτινες μόνῳ τῷ ὀνόματι αὐτοῦ τιμὴν ἀπεδίδουν, ἐπειδὴ τῆς θέας ἠμοίρουν; Ἐχέγγυα δὲ ἅπαντα ταῦτα τῆς τοῦ ἀνδρὸς πρὸς Θεὸν διαπύρου ἀγάπης καὶ τῆς ὑψοποιοῦ ταπεινο-φροσύνης καὶ τῶν πολλῶν νηστειῶν καὶ ἀγρυπνιῶν καὶ μετανοιῶν καὶ ἀπείρων κακουχιῶν, οὐ μὴν δέ, ἀλλὰ καὶ τῶν ἐμπύρων πειρασμῶν καὶ πολέμων νοητῶν καὶ ὁρατῶν καὶ νοσημάτων σωματικῶν, τῶν παρὰ τῶν πνευμάτων τῆς πονηρίας ἰσχυρῶς αὐτῷ ἐπενεχθέντων διὰ τὸ μέλλειν αὐτὸν ἀναβαίνειν εἰς ὕψος, ὅθεν ἐκεῖνα κατῆλθον.

2   Ἐπειδὴ δὲ ἐκ πολλῶν τῶν ἐκείνου κατορθωμάτων ὀλίγα δεῖ μνημονεῦσαι, ὅσα ἡμῖν τοῖς ἀναξίως αὐτῷ ἐκ καρδίας ἀγαπηθεῖσιν ἡ ἀψευδὴς αὐτοῦ εἴρηκε γλῶσσα προτροπῆς ἕνεκα τῆς ἡμῶν προθυμίας τῆς εἰς τὰ κρείττω κατὰ τοὺς τῶν παλαιστῶν ἢ πολεμιστῶν διδασκάλους, ταῦτα παρα-

that is to say, from God's glory, and His paternal reward. For the Scriptures say, *"Your Father who sees in secret will reward you openly,"* and *"for I will only honor them that honor me."*

Chapter 14

Who has been so glorified and honored in this generation as this blessed man? Not only by faithful kings and rulers, by patriarchs and archbishops alike, by his own people and foreigners, but even by the infidel tyrants, I speak of the Saracen rulers, who gave honor to the mere mention of his name, although they had not seen him. All this was proof of the man's ardent love for God, his exalting humility, his many fasts, vigils, prostrations, and endless mortifications; and no less the fiery temptations, the battles both spiritual and visible, and the bodily illnesses that were fiercely inflicted upon him by the evil spirits because he was about to ascend to the height from which they had fallen.

And we need to mention a few of that man's many accomplishments, as many examples as his truthful tongue told us—we who, although unworthy, were loved in Neilos's heart—for the sake of encouraging our enthusiasm for the good, like the teachers of athletes and warriors. Let us

θῶμεν τῷ λόγῳ τοῖς βουλομένοις ἐκ πάντων ὠφέλειαν καρποῦσθαι, οὐ θαυμάτων μεγίστων ἢ τεραστίων ἀπόδειξιν παριστῶντα, οἷς καταπλήττεται ἡ ἀκοὴ τῶν νηπιωδεστέρων ἢ τῶν ἀπίστων, ἀλλὰ κόπων ἀμέτρων καὶ μόχθων, οἷς τὸν ἀπόστολον ἐγκαυχώμενον οἶδα. Ὅμως καὶ ταῦτα τοῖς μὲν ἀπείροις πολλάκις ἄπιστα δόξουσιν, τοῖς δὲ ποσῶς πεπειραμένοις ζῆλον ἐνθήσουσι καὶ μνήμης ἐμπύρευμα.

15

Ἐκεῖνος ὁ ἔνσαρκος ἄγγελος ὑπέταξε μὲν ψυχὴν καὶ πνεῦμα τῷ νόμῳ τοῦ Πνεύματος, μηδὲν ὅλως ἐάσας τὸν νοῦν φροντίζειν τῶν κάτω καὶ χαμαὶ ἐρχομένων, ἀλλ᾽ ἐξερευνᾶν τὸν νόμον τοῦ Θεοῦ καὶ ἐν ὅλῃ καρδίᾳ ἐκζητεῖν τοῦ πληρῶσαι τὰς ἐντολὰς αὐτοῦ, ὑπέταξε δὲ τὴν σάρκα τῷ πνεύματι, πλεῖστα αὐτῇ νομοθετήσας καὶ σφόδρα δουλαγωγήσας τοῦ εὐπειθῆ καὶ εὐήνιον εἶναι τῷ νεύματι τοῦ Ἐπιστατοῦντος. Ἐδίδαξε μὲν γὰρ αὐτὴν τοῦ διὰ δύο ἡμερῶν ἢ τριῶν ἢ καὶ πέντε λαμβάνειν τῆς τροφῆς τὸ χρειῶδες (καὶ τοῦτο ἀεὶ ἐνδεὲς καὶ οἷον ἂν τύχῃ), τῇ τε τῶν ἡδέων ὀρέξει μηδαμῶς ἐπισπεύδειν, ἀπέχεσθαι οἴνου καὶ παντοίων διὰ πυρὸς ἐδεσμάτων. Ἐμάστιζε δὲ αὐτὴν ἐν ἀγρυπνίᾳ καὶ ψαλμῳδίᾳ, παννύχῳ τε στάσει καὶ τῶν γονυκλισιῶν πλήθει.

2   Ἐπειδὴ δέ ἐστι καὶ ἐν αὐτοῖς τοῖς καλοῖς πανουργία

include these deeds in our narrative for those who wish to reap some benefit from everything, not those deeds which demonstrate his great miracles or portents, the hearing of which astonishes the more simpleminded or the faithless, but rather let us tell of his measureless *labors* and *toils,* by which I know the apostle was made proud. Nevertheless even these deeds may often seem unbelievable to the inexperienced, but for those with some experience they will instill zeal and a *burning desire for recollection.*

Chapter 15

That angel incarnate subjected his soul and spirit to *the law of the Spirit,* in no way allowing his mind to be concerned with base and earthly things, but to seek the law of God, and with all his heart to strive to fulfill His commandments. Neilos made his flesh subject to his spirit, laying down many laws for it and reducing his body nigh to bondage until it was obedient and responsive to the nod of the One who governs. He trained his body to partake of essential nourishment once every two or three days, sometimes even only every five, and even then always a meager meal of whatever was at hand. For in no way did he yield to the desire for more pleasing fare, but abstained from wine and all cooked foods. He also used to flog his flesh with vigils and singing psalms, and his all-night standing vigils were interspersed with numerous genuflections.

Since even in these good works lurks the cunning of ₂

δαιμόνων, πέρα τοῦ μέτρου ἐκτείνεσθαι ὑποβάλλουσα τοῖς ἀπείροις, πάντα ἐκείνῳ μέτρῳ διετελεῖτο, ἵν', εἰ μὲν ἐλλείψει τι τῶν τετυπωμένων, ῥαθυμίας δειχθῇ τὸ λεῖψαν, καὶ ὡς χρεώστην ἑαυτὸν τὴν συνήθειαν ἀπαιτήσῃ, εἰ δέ τι περισσότερον ὁ λογισμὸς ὑποβάλλει, δαιμόνων εἶναι τὸ ἔργον καὶ ἀποφεύγειν τὸν δόλον.

3 Ὅθεν ἀπὸ πρωῒ ἕως τῆς τρίτης ὀξέως ἐκαλλιγράφει, λεπτῷ καὶ πυκνῷ χρώμενος ἰδιοχείρῳ καὶ τετράδιον πληρῶν καθ' ἑκάστην, ἐν τούτῳ πληρῶν τὴν ἐργάζεσθαι κελεύουσαν ἐντολήν. Τὴν δὲ τοῦ Πνεύματος χάριν μετὰ τῶν ἀποστόλων λαμβάνων, ἵστατο μέχρις ἕκτης παρὰ τῷ σταυρῷ τοῦ Δεσπότου μετὰ Μαρίας καὶ Ἰωάννου, τὸ Ψαλτήριον τηρῶν καὶ ποιῶν γονυκλισίας χιλίας, τελειουμένης κἂν τούτῳ τῆς ἀεὶ προσεύχεσθαι ἐντολῆς παρεγγυώσης. Ἀπὸ δὲ ἕκτης ὥρας ἕως ἐνάτης ἐκάθητο ἀναγινώσκων καὶ ἐξερευνῶν τὸν νόμον τοῦ Κυρίου καὶ τὰ ποιήματα τῶν ἁγίων πατέρων καὶ διδασκάλων. Τοῦτο γὰρ ὁ θεῖος ἀπόστολος γράφει, "Πρόσεχε," λέγων, "τῇ ἀναγνώσει." Ἐνάτην δέ γε πληρώσας καὶ ὡς θυμίαμα Θεῷ ἀναπέμπων τὸν ἑσπέριον ὕμνον, ἐξήρχετο ἔξω, ἀναπατῶν καὶ ὡραϊζόμενος καὶ μικρὸν ἀναπαύων τὴν αἴσθησιν κεκμηκυῖαν τῷ μήκει τῆς ἡμέρας, φέρων ὁμοῦ τὸ τοῦ ἀποστόλου ἐπὶ στόματος, ὅτι· "Τὰ ἀόρατα τοῦ Θεοῦ ἀπὸ κτίσεως κόσμου τοῖς ποιήμασι νοούμενα καθορᾶται," καὶ τό· "Ἐκ τῶν δημιουργημάτων τὸν Δημιουργὸν καταλαμβάνοντες."

demons, which urges the inexperienced to extend them-selves in immoderate fashion, Neilos did all things in mod-eration so that, whenever he lapsed in any of the practices prescribed by the monastic rule, the lapse might be attrib-uted to laxity, and, considering himself in debt for the defi-cit, he would compensate for the lapse. If, however, an inap-propriate thought suggested something more excessive, Neilos knew it to be the work of demons and so avoided the trap.

From dawn until the third hour, he would rapidly copy 3 manuscripts, using his own minute and compact handwrit-ing to fill a quire every day. In this activity he fulfilled the prescribed commandment that bids one occupy himself with work. Receiving the grace of the Spirit with the apos-tles he would stand until the sixth hour near the cross of the Lord in the company of Mary and John, reciting the Psalter and making a thousand genuflections. In this he fulfilled the commandment exhorting us to pray constantly. From the sixth hour until the ninth he would sit reading and studying the law of the Lord and the works of the holy fathers and teachers, for the divine apostle wrote, "*Attend to the reading of scripture.*" Having carried out the service of the ninth hour and offered up the vespers hymn *as incense* to God, Neilos would go outside to walk a bit and enjoy the view, and to re-store a little his mind which was wearied by the length of the day. He also carried upon his lips the saying of the apos-tle, "*Ever since the creation of the world* God's *invisible nature has been clearly perceived in the things that have been made,*" and also, "*We comprehend the Creator from His creations.*"

16

Πολλοὺς δὲ καὶ ἀπεστήθιζε λόγους καὶ χρήσεις τοῦ Θεολόγου καὶ τῶν λοιπῶν διδασκάλων, γυμνάζων ἀεὶ τὸν νοῦν ἐν τούτοις καὶ ῥεμβασμοῦ καιρὸν μὴ παρέχων, ἅμα δὲ καὶ τὴν φύσιν τῇ μαθήσει ὀξύνων. Ἡλίου δὲ δύναντος προσερχόμενος τῇ τραπέζῃ ἐκείνῃ—λίθος δὲ ἦν μέγιστος αὕτη καὶ πινάκιον ἐπ᾽ αὐτῆς ἀπόκλασμα κεραμίου—μετελάμβανεν εὐχαρίστως τροφῆς, ἧς μετεῖχεν ἐκεῖνος, ποτὲ μὲν ψιλὸν ἄρτον καὶ ὕδωρ ἐν μέτρῳ, ποτὲ δὲ ὄσπρεον ἐψημένον καὶ μόνον. Ἐν καιρῷ δὲ τοῖς τῶν δένδρων καρποῖς αὐτοῖς ἠρκεῖτο καὶ μόνοις. Ἐπύκτευσεν ὁ ἀνδρεῖος ἀρκεσθῆναι πολλάκις τοῖς αὐτομάτοις δρυὸς κερατίοις, μυρσίνων τε τοῖς καρποῖς καὶ κομάρων καὶ τοῖς ὁμοίοις, ἀλλὰ διὰ τὸ μὴ καταδέχεσθαι τὸν οἰκοδεσπότην γινόμενον ἀληθῶς ὡς ἀσκὸν ἐν τῇ πάχνῃ, ὑπέστρεφε πάλιν ἐν τῇ τοῦ ἄρτου χρήσει.

2 Τί δεῖ πολλὰ λέγειν; Τοσαύτας πολιτείας διῆλθεν, ὅσας παρ᾽ ἑνὸς ἑκάστου τῶν ἀρχαίων πατέρων πραχθείσας ἀνέγνω. Τεσσαράκοντα μὲν ἡμέρας ἄγευστος οὐ διῆλθεν, ὑφορώμενος τὸν ἐν ἐπαίνοις βάσκανον τῶν ἀνθρώπων καὶ τὸ τοῦ τύφου κατακλῶν δεινότατον κέρας· τρὶς εἴκοσι διῆλθεν, δὶς ἐν αὐταῖς γευσάμενος μόνον, παρὰ γυναικὸς φιλοθέου καὶ τοῦτο μαθὼν τελεσθὲν ἐκ τῆς Θεοδωρήτου Πρακτικῆς Ἱστορίας. Διὸ καὶ τῇ πείρᾳ αὐτὸ δοκιμάσας, εὗρεν ἀληθῆ εἶναι τὰ γεγραμμένα.

3 Πεποίηκεν ἕνα ἐνιαυτὸν παρὰ μῆνα μὴ γευσάμενος

Chapter 16

He had learned by heart many of the Theologian's orations and sayings, as well as those of the other teachers, always exercising his mind in their works, so as not to have any opportunity for distraction and also to sharpen his natural abilities through study. When the sun set he went to the table—this was a great stone, and for a plate he used a broken piece of a clay pot and gratefully partook of his usual meal, sometimes plain bread and water in modest amounts and sometimes boiled legumes only. In season he satisfied himself with fruits from the trees and this alone. This courageous man often struggled to be satisfied with wild acorns from oak trees, myrtle berries and the fruits of the strawberry tree and other such foods. But because the master of the house, that is, his constitution, could not tolerate this diet, when he truly *became as a wineskin in the frost,* he turned again to the use of bread.

What more needs to be said? He practiced the regimens 2 that he had read about in each of the fathers of old. To be sure, he did not go forty days without food, since he was suspicious of the envy in men's praise and wanted *to crush the* most terrible *horn of conceit.* On three occasions, however, he went for twenty days tasting food only twice, and this he accomplished having learned it from the example of a pious woman in the *Practical History* of Theodoret. Having tried this in practice, he found that what had been written was true.

Neilos spent eleven months without consuming any 3

ὑγροῦ οἱουδήποτε ὅλως καὶ καθ᾽ ἑσπέραν ἐσθίων ἄρτον
ξηρὸν μετὰ δύσιν ἡλίου, δύο πραγματευόμενος ἐκ τούτου
μεγάλα, τό τε ὑπερμαχῆσαι δι᾽ αὐτοῦ τῇ μιᾷ τῶν τεσσάρων
ἀρετῶν, σωφροσύνη—καὶ γὰρ ἐφιλοτιμεῖτο καὶ αὐτῆς τῆς
φυσικῆς ἐκροῆς ἀπαλλάξαι τὸ σῶμα, ὅπερ ἠγωνίσαντο
τῶν ἁγίων οἱ πλεῖστοι, πολὺ δὲ συμβάλλεται ἡ τοῦ ὕδατος
ἔνδεια τοῖς τοιούτοις, ὡς ἔφη τις τῶν ἁγίων—καὶ τὸ ἀναστεῖλαι τὴν τοῦ λογισμοῦ φλυαρίαν, διστάζοντός τε καὶ
ἀπιστοῦντος ἐν τοῖς ὑπερφυῶς καὶ μεγαλοπρεπῶς τοῖς
ἁγίοις πατράσι πεπονημένοις. Πάντως γὰρ ἀκηκόαμεν
πάντες τὸν ἐν τῇ διακονίᾳ τοῦ φούρνου ποιήσαντα τρία
ἔτη καὶ μὴ πιόντα καὶ ἐν τούτῳ τελειωθέντα.

17

Ὅπερ ἐνθυμηθεὶς ὁ μακάριος οὗτος, μήπως ἡ παν-
τελὴς τοῦ πνεύμονος ψύξις κίνδυνον αὐτῷ ἐπαγάγῃ τὸν
οὐ τυχόντα, ἀνετράπη τῆς ἐργασίας. Οὔτε γὰρ δίψα αὐτῷ,
ὡς αὐτὸς ἐπληροφόρει, λοιπὸν παρηνόχλει, ἀλλὰ μέχρις
ὀγδόης ἡμέρας καὶ μόνον· ἐκ διαθέσεως ἐλάλει τε καὶ
ἐποίει τό· "Ἐκολλήθη τῷ ἐδάφει ἡ ψυχή μου, ζῆσόν με κατὰ
τὸν λόγον σου," μετέπειτα δὲ τό· "Ἐξήγειράς μου τὴν πνοήν,
καὶ παρακληθεὶς ἔζησα." Βεβαιοῖ δὲ τὸ εἰρημένον ὁ φήσας·
"Δίψα δίψαν ἰᾶται, πεῖνα δὲ πεῖναν οὐκ ἀναστέλλει." Τὴν δὲ
Ἁγίαν Τεσσαρακοστὴν διήρχετο πᾶσαν, μηδενὸς ἄλλου

liquid at all, eating dry bread every evening at sunset. He gained two great advantages from this. First, he was able thereby to conquer one of the four virtues, moderation—for he aspired to free his body even from the natural flow, something which most of the saints had also tried to accomplish, and, as one of the saints said, often *the avoidance of water is very profitable* to that end. Second, he refuted the nonsensical notion that both expresses doubt and does not believe in the extraordinary and magnificent struggles of the holy fathers. For we have all heard of the monk who spent three years tending the oven, without drinking anything, and thus ended his life.

Chapter 17

Reflecting on this example, this blessed one turned away from this practice, lest somehow the excessive dry chill of the lungs bring great danger upon him. Nor, as he asserted, did thirst afflict him until the eighth day, and only then. Prompted by this attitude he both spoke and carried out the verse, "*My soul has cleaved to the ground, quicken me according to Your word,*" and then "*You have revived my breath, and I am comforted and live.*" These sayings are confirmed by the one who says, "*Thirst* cures *thirst,* but *hunger* does not remove *hunger.*" He spent the entire forty days of Holy Lent

μετέχων εἰ μὴ τοῦ ἀντιδώρου καὶ μόνον, καὶ αὐτὸ δὲ διὰ τὸ καθ᾽ ἑκάστην ἡμέραν αἰτεῖσθαι τὸν ἐπιούσιον ἄρτον, ὅμως καὶ αὐτὰς ἀπότως ἤνυε πάσας πολλάκις. Πᾶσα μὲν οὖν ἡμέρα αὐτῷ ὑπῆρχεν ἐν ἀγῶνι κανόνος ἀπαραβάτου, νὺξ δὲ πάλιν ἐν τοῖς αὐτοῖς διήει ἀπαραβάτως ὁμοίως.

2 Ὥρᾳ μιᾷ ἐπληροῦτο τὸ χρέος τοῦ ὕπνου· οὐδὲ γὰρ εἶχεν ᾧ προσαναλώσῃ τὴν πέψιν· τὸ λεῖπον δὲ ἅπαν εἰς πλήρωσιν τοῦ Ψαλτηρίου καὶ πεντακοσίων γονυκλισιῶν μέτρον, τῶν τε μεσονυκτινῶν καὶ ὀρθρινῶν ἀνηλίσκετο ὕμνων. Πολλάκις γὰρ ἀπεμάχετο τῷ ἑαυτοῦ λογισμῷ καὶ ἐλάλει, ὅτι· "Οἱ ἐν τῷ κοινοβίῳ ὄντες ἡμέρας μὲν διακαρτεροῦσι τοῖς ἔργοις νηστεύοντες καθ᾽ ἑκάστην, νυκτὸς δὲ διαγρυπνοῦσι τοῖς ὕμνοις σχολάζοντες καὶ τῇ ἀναγνώσει, ψάλλοντες τόσα καὶ τόσα· ἐλεημοσύνας καὶ ξενοδοχίας ἐργάζονται πλείστας. Ἡμῶν δὲ ἐν ταύτῃ τῇ δοκούσῃ ἡσυχίᾳ καθεζομένων, ἐὰν μὴ περισσεύσῃ ἡ δικαιοσύνη καὶ ὁ ἔνθεος κόπος, ματαία ἡ ἐλπὶς ἡμῶν ἔσται καὶ ἀνοίκειος ὁ τρόπος."

3 Ἦν δὲ καὶ τὸ ἔνδυμα αὐτοῦ ἀπὸ τριχῶν αἰγῶν σάκκος, εἰς ἑνὶ ἐνιαυτῷ καὶ ἑτέρῳ ἄλλος. Ἡ δὲ ζώνη αὐτοῦ ἦν σχοινίον μὴ λυόμενον, εἰ μὴ μίαν τοῦ χρόνου. Διὸ καὶ ἐν πλήθει φθειρῶν ἐκαρτέρει, μὴ σιαινόμενος ἢ κνηθόμενος τῇ αὐτῶν ἐνοχλήσει. Θάμνος δὲ ὑπῆρχεν ἔμπροσθεν τοῦ σπηλαίου, ἔνθα μυρμήκων πλῆθος κατῴκει, ἐν ᾧ ῥιπτούμενος παρὰ τοῦ ἁγίου ὁ σάκκος ἐκαθαρίζετο ἀπὸ τῶν σκωλήκων ἐκείνων (οὕτω γὰρ αὐτοὺς καλεῖν δέον τραχυνθέντας τῷ χρόνῳ), δίκην εἰσπραττομένων παρὰ τῶν μυρμήκων, δι᾽ ὧν ἠνώχλησαν τῷ δικαίῳ. Κλίνη αὐτῷ οὐχ

partaking of nothing else except the blessed bread and this alone. This he did each day in order to ask for his *daily bread.* However, often he passed all these days of Lent without a drink. So he spent the entire day in a struggle to follow his inviolable rule, while passing the night in these same struggles.

Neilos satisfied his need for sleep with a single hour of rest, for he had nothing to digest, and the remainder of the night he used for the recitation of the Psalter, five hundred genuflections, and the singing of the midnight and matins hymns. Often he contended with his own wicked thoughts and said that "those who live in a cenobitic monastery pass the days with work and daily fasting, and spend the night in vigil, devoting themselves to hymns and reading and reciting many psalms; they also perform many works of charity and hospitality. But for those of us who are established in this supposed life of spiritual tranquility, unless we have abundant righteousness and a divinely inspired struggle, our hope will be in vain and our way of life unfitting."

Neilos's clothing was a garment made of goat hair; he used one for an entire year and another for the next. His belt was a rope that he did not unfasten more than once a year. As a result of this he endured a multitude of lice, neither loathing them, nor scratching himself from the irritation they caused. There was a shrub in front of his cave, home to a multitude of ants, upon which the saint used to toss his garment to clean it of those worms—for it was necessary to so call them, as they grew in size and strength over time—and the ants brought justice against the lice for having disturbed that just man. Neilos possessed no bed, no

ὑπῆρχεν, οὔτε θρονίον, οὐ κιβώτιον, ἢ γλωσσόκομον, ἢ
βαλάντιον, οὐδὲ πήρα, ἀλλ᾽ οὐδὲ μέλανος δοχεῖον σχολάζοντι ἐν τῷ γράφειν· κηρὸν δὲ πήξας ἐπὶ τῷ ξύλῳ, δι᾽ αὐτοῦ
τῶν τοσούτων βιβλίων τὸ πλῆθος ἐκαλλιγράφησε.

18

Ταῦτα δέ μοι φιλοπεπόνηται τὰ μικρὰ μὲν ἐκείνῳ,
ἑτέροις δὲ καὶ λίαν μεγάλα, οὐχ ἵνα προσθήκη τις ἐκ
τούτων γένηται αὐτῷ, ἀλλ᾽ ἵνα γνῶμεν μέχρι πόσου
κατώρθωσε ὧνπερ ἀρετῶν ἤρξατο τὴν ἐργασίαν, ἀκτημοσύνης, λέγω, καὶ ἐγκρατείας καὶ ἀγρυπνίας καὶ προσευχῆς, ἡσυχίας τε καὶ ἁγνείας καὶ ταπεινοφροσύνης καὶ
τῶν λοιπῶν, δι᾽ ὧν γίνεταί τις εἰκὼν καὶ ὁμοίωσις Θεοῦ. Τὰς
δ᾽ ἐκχύσεις τῶν θερμῶν δακρύων αὐτοῦ καὶ τοὺς πικροὺς
στεναγμοὺς καὶ στηθῶν τύψεις καὶ μετώπου ἐν τῇ γῇ
ἀραγμοὺς τίς ἂν ἐννοῆσαι ἢ κατ᾽ἀξίαν εἴποι; Τὰς δὲ
ἐπιπλήξεις καὶ ὀνειδισμοὺς καὶ ὕβρεις καὶ ἐξουδενώσεις,
ἃς αὐτῷ ἑαυτῷ ἐπήγαγεν ἐν ἅπασιν, ὡς ἐχθρὸν ἑαυτὸν
παραφυλάττων; Τὰς δὲ ἐπιβουλὰς καὶ πολέμους καὶ ἐπι-
φορὰς τῶν δαιμόνων, τὰς διὰ τῶν λογισμῶν καὶ φανερῶν
φαντασιῶν, καὶ μέντοι καὶ πόνων σωματικῶν ἐκ νόσων
χαλεπῶν, μόλις ἂν καὶ αὐτὸς ὁ παθὼν καθ᾽ ἑξῆς ἰσχύσας
φράσαιτο ἄν.

2   Πολλάκις ἐπολεμήθη δεινῶς ὑπ᾽ αὐτῶν τοῦ καταλεῖψαι

chair, neither chest nor moneybox, no purse, not even a pouch, and no inkwell, though he devoted himself to writing. But he fixed wax onto a wooden tablet and upon this he copied most of his books.

Chapter 18

I have thus far narrated those deeds which were insignificant to him, but to others they were extremely important, not so as to add to his reputation, but so that we may know to what extent he succeeded in practicing the virtues to which he aspired, I mean poverty and abstinence, vigilance and prayer, spiritual tranquility, purity, humility, and the rest, through which one becomes an *image and likeness* of God. Who could imagine or worthily recount Neilos's shedding of warm tears, his bitter groans, his pounding of his breast, his beating of his forehead on the ground in prostration? Who could relate the rebukes, the reproaches, the insults, the humiliation that he brought upon himself in all regards, as if he were his own enemy, on guard against himself? Neilos himself, who had suffered continuously the plots, the battles, and the assaults of the demons through wicked thoughts and visible phantoms, and even bodily suffering from grave illnesses, would scarcely be able to speak of them.

Often he was terribly assailed by demons to abandon his 2

τὴν ἡσυχίαν καὶ εἰς τὰ κοινόβια ἀπελθεῖν, ἵν᾽ ὡς φυγάδα καὶ δειλὸν αὐτὸν ἀπελέγξωσιν οἱ δεινοί. Ὅτε οὖν ἐστενοχωρεῖτο ἐν ἀνάγκῃ πολλῇ ὑπ᾽ αὐτῶν—ἐποίουν γὰρ αὐτὸν ἐμπεφυσημένον δοκεῖν ὑπὸ τῆς βίας τῶν λογισμῶν, ὥστε μὴ χωρεῖσθαι αὐτὸν ὑπὸ τοῦ σπηλαίου—ἐπαίρων οὖν τὸ τρίχινον ἔνδυμα αὐτοῦ, ὃ ἀπέκειτο ἐν ἑτέρῳ ἐνιαυτῷ, ἐτίθει εἰς ξύλον (οὐδὲ γὰρ ῥάβδον εἶχεν ἐπὶ τοῦ ὤμου), καὶ κατερχόμενος ἕως μεσασμοῦ τῆς ὁδοῦ, ἐν ᾧ ἵστατο δένδρον ὑψηλόν, ἐποίει αὐτῷ ὡς ὅτι ὁ ὅσιος Φαντῖνός ἐστιν, ἢ ἕτερος τῶν ἁγίων πατέρων. Εἶτα βαλὼν τῷ δένδρῳ μετάνοιαν, ἵστατο ὡς ἐρωτώμενος ὑπὸ τοῦ πατρὸς καὶ ἀποκρινόμενος τῆς ἐλεύσεως αὐτοῦ τὴν αἰτίαν καὶ πάλιν ὀνειδιζόμενος καὶ καταγελώμενος ὑπ᾽ αὐτοῦ καὶ τῶν ἀδελφῶν λεγόντων· "Ἴδε σοι καὶ ὁ ἡσυχαστής." Τούτοις τοῖς τρόποις καὶ τοῖς ἀντιρρητικοῖς συλλογισμοῖς τροπούμενος τοὺς πολεμίους ἐχθρούς, ὑπέστρεφεν ἐν τῷ σπηλαίῳ, ὡς εἴς τινα φυλακήν, διακαρτερῶν καὶ λέγων ἐν ἑαυτῷ· *"Καλόν μοι μᾶλλον ἀποθανεῖν, ἢ τὸ καύχημά μου ἵνα τις κενώσῃ."*

19

Πολλάκις προσευχομένῳ καὶ ψάλλοντι ἔλεγον οἱ λογισμοί· "Βλέψον εἰς τὸ θυσιαστήριον, ἴσως ἢ ἄγγελον, ἢ φλόγα πυρός, ἢ τὸ Ἅγιον Πνεῦμα θεάσῃ περὶ αὐτό, καθὼς

spiritual tranquility and return to the monastery, so the evil ones could deride him as a deserter and coward. Therefore, when they pressed him into a state of great misery—for they made him seem to be so swollen up by the violence of his thoughts that there was not room for him in the cave—he would take his goat hair garment, the one set aside for the following year, place it on a wooden stick over his shoulder—for he had no staff—and go halfway down the road; there stood a tall tree on which he would hang the garment, imagining it to be the blessed Phantinos or another of the holy fathers. Then, making obeisance to the tree, Neilos would stand before it as if being questioned by the father and then answer with the reason for his coming, all the while imagining that he was being reproached and derided by him and the other brothers who said, "Behold, here is your monk who claims spiritual tranquility!" In this manner and with counter arguments he would repel his enemy assailants and return to the cave, as if to a prison, persevering and saying to himself, "*I would rather die than have someone deprive me of my ground for boasting.*"

Chapter 19

His thoughts often spoke to him while he prayed and sang psalms, saying, "Look at the altar; perhaps you may see an angel, a fiery flame, or even the Holy Spirit around it, just

ἐθεάσαντο πολλοί." Αὐτὸς δὲ μύων τοὺς ὀφθαλμούς, τοσοῦτον κατεπόνει ἑαυτὸν ἐν πλήθει μετανοιῶν, ὡς κατέρχε-
σθαι τὸν ἱδρῶτα αὐτοῦ ὡς ὕδωρ ἐπὶ τὴν γῆν. Ὑπέβαλλε
δὲ αὐτῷ ὁ Πονηρὸς καὶ πύρωσιν δριμυτάτην ἐν τῇ σαρκί·
αὐτὸς δὲ τῇ προστρίψει τῶν ἀκανθῶν καὶ ἀγρίων κνιδῶν
ἐσβέννυε διὰ τῆς ὀδύνης τὴν ἡδονήν. Καθημένῳ ποτὲ ἀπὸ
τῆς ἀγρυπνίας καὶ μικρὸν ἑαυτὸν ἐκ τοῦ κόπου ὑπο-
χαυνώσαντι, ἐπέστησαν αὐτῷ δύο δαίμονες κατέχοντες
καὶ ἄλλον μέσον αὐτῶν· οὗ καὶ ἀνοίξαντες ὡσανεὶ τὰς
πλευρὰς καὶ ἐκβαλόντες ἅπαντα τὰ ἐντὸς αὐτοῦ, ἔρριψαν
ἐπὶ τὴν γῆν· ὁ δὲ σύντρομος ἀναστὰς καὶ ἀπὸ τῆς ναυσίας
ἐμέσας πικροτάτην χολήν, ἠσφαλίσατο ἑαυτὸν εἰς τὸ ἑξῆς.

2   Ποτὲ ἐν τῇ Ῥώμῃ ἀπελθὼν λόγῳ προσευχῆς καὶ ἀνερευνήσεως βιβλίων τινῶν, εἶδεν ἐν τῷ ναῷ τοῦ ἀποστόλου
Πέτρου ἐν παρόδῳ γυναῖκα Ἀλαμάναν, ὑψηλὴν τῷ σώματι
καὶ μεγάλην. Ταύτης τὴν θέαν τυπώσαντες οἱ πανοῦργοι,
ἐδείκνυον τῷ ἁγίῳ καὶ ψάλλοντι καὶ ἀναγινώσκοντι καὶ
γράφοντι καὶ πᾶν εἴ τι ἄλλο ποιοῦντι. Τούτου τοῦ πολέμου
κραταιουμένου, καὶ μηδὲν ὅλως ἔχοντος ἐννοῆσαι τί
ἀντιπράξασθαι πρὸς τοὺς πολεμίους, πρὸς τὸν Θεὸν κατα-
φεύγει, αὐτῷ τὴν οἰκείαν ἀσθένειαν ἀπαγγέλλων, καί,
ῥίψας ἑαυτὸν ἐνώπιον τοῦ ἱλαστηρίου ἐν συντετριμμένῃ
καὶ ταπεινῇ τῇ καρδίᾳ, ἔλεγε πρὸς τὸν Σωτῆρα· "Κύριε,
Σὺ ἐπίστασαι, ὅτι ἀσθενής εἰμι· ἐλέησόν με, καὶ κούφισόν
με ἐκ τοῦ πολέμου τῶν ἀκαθάρτων δαιμόνων, ὅτι λοιπὸν
τῆς ζωῆς μου ἀπεῖπον."

3   Ταῦτα εἰπὼν κείμενος ἐπὶ τῆς γῆς καὶ μικρὸν ἀφυπνώσας,
ὁρᾷ ἔμπροσθεν αὐτοῦ στήκοντα τὸν τίμιον σταυρὸν καὶ

as many have seen." He would close his eyes, and subdue himself with many penitential prostrations to such a degree that his sweat poured onto the ground like water. The Evil One would then subject his flesh to an extremely fierce burning desire, but Neilos, by rubbing himself against thorns and wild nettles, would quench his lust through the pain. Once after he had sat down following his night vigil, and was relaxing a bit from his laborious exercise, two demons appeared before him holding another demon between them; they ripped open his flanks, and, tearing out all of his innards, threw them on the ground. Neilos stood up trembling and, after vomiting the most bitter bile in his nausea, he fortified himself for the future.

Once when he went to Rome for the sake of prayer and 2 to search out some books, he saw in passing in the church of the apostle Peter a German woman conspicuous for her height and stature. The wicked spirits had fashioned a vision of her and would show it to the holy man while he was singing psalms, reading, writing, or engaging in any other activity. As this battle intensified and Neilos could not figure out any way to contend against his enemies, he sought refuge with God and proclaimed to Him his own weakness. Neilos threw himself in front of the altar with a contrite and humble heart, saying to the Savior, "Lord, You know that I am weak. Have mercy on me and release me from this struggle with the unclean demons because I despair of my life."

Having said this he lay upon the ground, and, falling 3 asleep for a while, he saw standing before him the venerable

ἐν αὐτῷ κρεμάμενον ζῶντα τὸν Κύριον ἡμῶν, μέσον δὲ αὐτῶν κρεμάμενον βῆλον καθαρὸν καὶ λίαν λεπτότατον. Καὶ βοήσας μετὰ φόβου πολλοῦ λέγει πρὸς αὐτόν· "Ἐλέησόν με, Δέσποτα, καὶ εὐλόγησόν με τὸν δοῦλόν σου." Τότε ὁ Σωτὴρ ἐξηλώσας τὴν δεξιὰν χεῖρα ἀπὸ τοῦ σταυροῦ, τρίτον ἐπεσφράγισεν αὐτὸν καὶ τέλος εἶχεν ἡ ἔνθεος ὀπτασία, σὺν αὐτῇ δὲ καὶ πόλεμος ἅπας καὶ ἡ τῆς φύσεως ῥεῦσις· καί, ὅπερ οὐκ ἴσχυσαν ἐκτελέσαι αἱ πολλαὶ πεῖναι καὶ δίψαι καὶ ἀγρυπνίαι, ἴσχυσεν ἡ ταπείνωσις καὶ ἡ ἐπίγνωσις τῆς οἰκείας ἀδυναμίας.

20

Διατρίβοντι τοίνυν τῷ ὁσίῳ ἐν ἀνέσει καὶ χαρᾷ καὶ εὐφροσύνῃ πνευματικῇ, ἔρχεταί τις πρὸς αὐτὸν ἀδελφὸς παρακαλῶν συμπαραμεῖναι αὐτῷ· ἴσως σωθήσεται δι' αὐτοῦ. Μόλις οὖν ἐπιτυχὼν τοῦ σκοποῦ, φησὶ πρὸς τὸν ὅσιον· "Πάτερ, ἔχω τρία νομίσματα, τί κελεύεις ποιῆσαί με αὐτά;" Ὁ δέ· "Ἄπελθε," φησί, "δὸς αὐτὰ τοῖς πτωχοῖς καὶ ἄρας τὸ Ψαλτήριόν σου ἔπου ταῖς ἐντολαῖς τοῦ Σωτῆρος·" εὐθέως δὲ ἐποίησεν οὕτως. Καὶ διακαρτερήσας μετὰ τοῦ ὁσίου πατρὸς οὐ μήκιστον χρόνον καὶ μαθὼν παρ' αὐτοῦ τὴν τῆς καλλιγραφίας δυσδιόρθωτον τέχνην, ἀχθεσθεὶς ἐπί τε τῇ σκληροτάτῃ διαίτῃ καὶ ἀπαραμυθήτῳ ἀσκήσει, ἤρξατο προφασίζεσθαι προφάσεις ἐν ἁμαρτίαις καὶ ζητεῖν πόρους λογομαχίας, δι' ὧν τὸν πατέρα πρὸς θυμὸν διεγείρει.

cross upon which our Lord was affixed while still alive, and between them was suspended a clean and exceptionally fine curtain. Neilos shouted aloud in great fear and said to Him, "Have mercy on me, Lord, and bless me Your servant." The Savior then unfastened His right hand from the cross, made the sign of the cross over Neilos three times, and the divine vision came to an end. At the same time his every struggle ended, and also the instability of his nature. What many fasts and thirst and vigils were not able to accomplish, humility and the knowledge of his own powerlessness could bring about.

Chapter 20

Afterward, as the blessed man was passing his time in repose, joy, and spiritual cheer, a brother approached asking to stay with him, so that he might be saved through Neilos's assistance. Hardly had he attained his goal when he said to the blessed man, "Father, I have three gold coins. What do you command me to do with them?" Neilos said, "Go and give them to the poor, and taking your Psalter follow the commandments of the Savior." Immediately the man did so. He remained with the blessed father for a short time and learned from him the complex art of calligraphy. Later as he became aggrieved by the very harsh regimen and comfortless ascetical practice, he began *to employ pretexts for sins* and to devise methods of argumentation through which he might rouse the father to anger.

2   Αὐτὸς δὲ ἀεὶ ἐν νῷ περιφέρων τὰς ἐντολὰς τοῦ
Δεσπότου, ὡς πρὸς μόνον αὐτὸν εἰρημένας, καὶ μνημο-
νεύων, ὅτι· "Ὁ λέγων τῷ ἀδελφῷ αὐτοῦ Ῥακά, ἔνοχος ἔσται
εἰς τὴν γέενναν τοῦ πυρός," οὐδέποτε εἶπε πρὸς αὐτὸν ῥῆμα
πονηρόν. Τότε δὲ λέγει πρὸς αὐτὸν πρᾴως καὶ ἐπιεικῶς·
"Ἀδελφὲ τιμιώτατε, ἐν εἰρήνῃ κέκληκεν ἡμᾶς ὁ Θεὸς ἐνταῦθα καὶ ἐν ἀγάπῃ, πνεύματί τε πραότητος, μὴ γὰρ ἐν
πικρίᾳ καὶ ὀργῇ καὶ θυμῷ. Εἰ δὲ τοσοῦτον βεβάρυσαι ἐμὲ
τὸν ταπεινὸν καὶ ἀφόρητος ἐγενόμην τοῖς σοῖς ὀφθαλμοῖς,
πορεύου ἐν εἰρήνῃ ὅπου ἂν βούλῃ, καὶ ἐμοὶ τῷ ἁμαρτωλῷ
μὴ ἐνόχλει· οἶδα γάρ σε ἐγὼ μὴ δυνάμενον, μᾶλλον δὲ καὶ
μὴ βουλόμενον, ἀποσείσασθαι τὸ παραβάλλον σοι πνεῦμα
τῆς φιλαρχίας καὶ φιλοϊερατείας. Ἄπελθε τοίνυν, ἐκπλη-
ρώσων τὸ σὸν βούλευμα, καὶ εὑρήσεις τὸ κατάλυμα πρόσφορον."

3   Ὁ δὲ ἀδελφὸς πλέον ὑπὸ τοῦ Πονηροῦ ἐξαφθεὶς ἐπὶ τῷ
ἐλέγχῳ τῶν κρυφίων αὐτοῦ λογισμῶν, φησὶν ὀργιζόμενος
πρὸς αὐτόν· "Δός μοι τὰ τρία μου νομίσματα καὶ πορεύομαι. Τί γὰρ ἀνάγκην εἶχον ἐγὼ δοῦναι αὐτὰ τοῖς πτωχοῖς,
εἰ μὴ ἐπειθόμην τῇ κελεύσει τῇ σῇ;" Ἀποκρίνεται εὐθέως
πρὸς αὐτὸν ὁ πατήρ· "Γράψον μοι," φησίν, "ἀδελφέ, εἰς
τμῆμα χαρτίου τοῦ ἀπολαβεῖν με τὸν μισθὸν αὐτῶν ἐν τῇ
βασιλείᾳ τῶν οὐρανῶν, καὶ θὲς αὐτὸ ἐπὶ τὸ θυσιαστήριον,
κἀγὼ ἄρτι παρέχω σοι τὰ τρία νομίσματα."

Neilos, however, always bore in mind the commandments 2
of the Lord, as if they had been spoken to him alone, and
remembering that he who *insults his brother shall be liable to
the hell of fire,* Neilos never said a harsh word to him. Then
he spoke to him mildly and appropriately, "Most honored
brother, *God has called us* here *to peace* and love with a spirit of
gentleness, not to bitterness, wrath, and anger. If you have
become so burdened by my humble self, and I have become
unbearable in your eyes, go in peace wherever you wish and
do not bother me, sinner that I am, any more. For I know
that you are not able, or rather that you are not willing, to
shake off your desire for authority and a priestly rank. Go
away, then, fulfill your desire, and you will find a suitable
abode."

The brother was inflamed even more by the Evil One as a 3
result of this rebuke of his hidden thoughts, and so he said
angrily to Neilos, "Give me my three coins and I shall go.
Why did I have to give them to the poor, if not in obedience
to your command?" The father immediately answered him,
"Write your request for me, brother, on a piece of paper
so that I may receive payment for them in the kingdom of
heaven, and put it on the altar, and then I shall give you the
three coins."

21

Ὁ δὲ θέλων ἀπιδεῖν πόθεν ἄρα ἐξῇ αὐτῷ πληρῶσαι τὸ ἐπαγγελλόμενον, μήτε κἂν ὀβολὸν ἔχοντι, ἰδίᾳ χειρὶ τὸ κελευσθὲν ἀπεπλήρωσε καὶ τῷ θυσιαστηρίῳ ἐπέθηκεν. Καὶ δὴ παραλαβὼν αὐτὸν ὁ πατὴρ κατέρχεται πρὸς τὸ τοῦ Καστελλίου κοινόβιον, κἀκεῖθεν δανεισάμενος τρία νομίσματα, δέδωκε μετὰ ἀγάπης τῷ ἀδελφῷ. Κἀκεῖνος δεξάμενος ἀνεχώρησε καὶ πεπλήρωκεν ἰδιοθελῶς ὅσα προεῖπεν αὐτῷ ὁ πατὴρ καὶ μετ᾽ ὀλίγον καιρὸν τετελεύτηκεν. Ὁ δὲ ὅσιος πατὴρ ἡμῶν Νεῖλος ὑποστρέψας ἐν τῷ σπηλαίῳ αὐτοῦ καὶ καθεσθεὶς ἐν ὑπομονῇ καὶ καρτερίᾳ πολλῇ, ἐντὸς ὀλίγων ἡμερῶν τρία Ψαλτήρια γεγραφώς (τότε γὰρ λέγεται πεπληρωκέναι ἐξ αὐτῶν διὰ τεσσάρων ἡμερῶν), ἐλύθη τοῦ χρέους τοῦ διὰ τὴν ἐντολὴν τοῦ Χριστοῦ.

2   Ἰδὼν οὖν ὁ τῶν δικαίων Ἐχθρός, ὅτι ἐν πάσῃ προσβολῇ ἡττᾶται καὶ καταβέβληται ὑπὸ τοῦ δικαίου ἀνδρός, μετατίθησι τὴν πάλην ἀπὸ τὸν ἐντὸς ἄνθρωπον ἐπὶ τὸν ἐκτὸς καὶ ἄρχεται πλήττειν αὐτὸν ἐν πόνοις δεινοῖς καὶ ἀρρωστίαις σωματικαῖς, ὥστε κἂν ἐμποδίσαι αὐτὸν ἀπὸ τῆς καθημερινῆς λειτουργίας αὐτοῦ καὶ τῆς οὐρανοδρόμου καὶ ἐχθρᾶς αὐτῷ προσευχῆς. Τί οὖν μηχανᾶται περὶ αὐτόν; Ὄγκῳ δεινοτάτῳ καὶ ἀφορήτῳ πόνῳ περιλαβὼν τὰ τὴν φωνὴν ἀποτελοῦντα ὄργανα αὐτοῦ, πεποίηκεν αὐτὸν ἄφωνον κατακεῖσθαι παντελῶς καὶ ἄβρωτον τῆς συνήθους τροφῆς. Ἀλλ᾽ ὅμως καὶ ἐν τούτῳ πολὺ πλέον ᾐσχύνετο καὶ ἡττᾶτο ὁ πολέμιος Ἐχθρός· ὅσον γὰρ ἐκεῖνος ἀπέκλειε τὴν

Chapter 21

Wishing to see how Neilos, who had not even an obol, would be able to fulfill his promise, he wrote down the request with his own hand and placed it upon the altar. The father took him and went down to the monastery of Kastellion, and there, borrowing three gold coins, he gave them with love to the brother. He took them, went away, and indulged his own desires just as the father had foretold to him. A short time later he died. Our blessed father Neilos then returned to his cave, and sitting down with patience and great perseverance within a few days he had copied three Psalters—he was said to have completed each one in four days—and so was released from the debt he incurred on account of Christ's commandment.

The Enemy of the just, seeing that in every encounter 2 he was defeated and cast down by the just man, changed his assault from the man's interior to his exterior, and began to afflict Neilos with terrible pains and bodily ailments, so that he might impede the father from his daily liturgy and heaven-traversing prayer that was so odious to him. What did he devise against Neilos? Covering the man's vocal cords with a terrible tumor and unbearable pain, he caused him to completely lose his voice, become unable to swallow his customary food, and be confined to his bed. Nevertheless, even in this the hostile Enemy was even more abashed and defeated. For the more he shut off the psalm-singing and

ψαλμολόγον καὶ ὑμνοφόρον φωνήν, τοσοῦτον αὐτὸς τὴν
διάνοιαν ὕψου πρὸς τὸν Θεὸν καὶ ἐνετρύφα ἀπερισπάστως
ταῖς θεαρέστοις καὶ μεγαλοπρεπέσιν ἐννοίαις. Ἵνα δὲ καὶ
τῇ λιμῷ μὴ ἐκλείψῃ καὶ ἀποκάμῃ, ὕδατι τὸν ξηρὸν ἄρτον
λειώσας, ταύτῃ ἐκέχρητο τῇ διαίτῃ.

22

Μετ᾽ οὐ πολὺ τοίνυν ἐλήλυθεν πρὸς ἐπίσκεψιν αὐτοῦ
Φαντῖνος ὁ ἁγιώτατος· παρέβαλλον γὰρ ἀλλήλοις πυκνότερον, ἀλλήλους, ὡς δύο φωστῆρες, πυκνότερον κατα-
φωτίζοντες· καὶ τὸν ἐβδομαρισιαῖον δὲ ἄρτον ὁ μέγας
Φαντῖνος σὺν πολλῇ παρακλήσει πείσας τὸν ὅσιον Νεῖλον
δέξασθαι, παρ᾽ αὐτοῦ ἐκ τῆς τῶν χειρῶν ἐργασίας τὴν
χάριν ἀντεσηκοῦτο. Ἰδὼν τοιγαροῦν αὐτὸν ἐν τῇ τοιαύτῃ
ἀνάγκῃ καὶ πολλὰ δυσωπήσας, ἀπήγαγεν εἰς τὸ μοναστήριον αὐτοῦ μετὰ πάσης σπουδῆς· ἀλλὰ καὶ τὸν Θεὸν
παρεκάλει περὶ τῆς ὑγείας αὐτοῦ ἐξ ὅλης ψυχῆς. Ὁ δὲ καρ-
τερικώτατος Νεῖλος μὴ δυνάμενος γεύσασθαί τινος, εἰ μὴ
μόνον ὕδατος καὶ αὐτοῦ μετὰ βίας καὶ πόνου, καὶ τοῦτο
ἐπὶ πολλὰς ἡμέρας, εἶπεν αὐτῷ ὁ λογισμός, ὅτι "Εἴπερ ἦν
ἀπὸ ἰχθύος μέρος μικρόν, ἐλάμβανον ἂν ἐξ αὐτοῦ, καὶ
διήνοιγέ μοι τὴν ὁδὸν τοῦ φαγεῖν."

2   Πυκτεύσας οὖν ἐπὶ ἡμέρας ὀκτώ, ἢ καὶ πρός, τοῦ μὴ
ἀναγγεῖλαι τὸ πρᾶγμά τινι, καὶ μάλιστα καθ᾽ ἑκάστην

hymn-bearing voice, the more Neilos raised up his mind to God and reveled continually in his thoughts that were magnificent and pleasing to God. And so that he might not faint nor become worn out by hunger, Neilos used to prepare a gruel of dry bread pounded fine with water and made this his diet.

Chapter 22

Not long thereafter the most holy Phantinos came to see him, for at that time they visited each other frequently, often illuminating one another like two stars. The great Phantinos had persuaded holy Neilos through much pleading to receive his weekly allotment of bread, and for this favor Neilos repaid him with the labor of his own hands. Phantinos, seeing the man in such great distress, after many entreaties led him to his monastery in all haste. Phantinos also called upon God with all his heart for his health. The most steadfast Neilos was unable to consume anything but water, and that only with much effort and struggle. This went on for many days until the thought occurred to him that "If I were to have a small portion of fish and to eat of it, then the passage of my throat might open up."

Neilos struggled for eight days and more not to reveal the matter to anyone, and all the while seeing each day one of   2

ὁρῶν διερχόμενόν τινα τῶν ἀδελφῶν ἔμπροσθεν αὐτοῦ
καὶ πρὸς τὸ ἁλιεῦσαι πορευόμενον, καὶ αὖθις μετ᾽ ἰχθύων
ὑποστρέφοντα, μετὰ πολλὴν ἄθλησιν καὶ πάλην τοῦ τοιούτου λογισμοῦ, ἰδοὺ ἔρχεταί τις πρὸς αὐτὸν κοσμικὸς
ἐπιφερόμενος κοφίνιον ἰχθύων μεστόν, τῶν μὲν τηγάνου,
τῶν δὲ ὀπτῶν τυγχανόντων, παρακαλῶν καὶ δεόμενος
αὐτοῦ ὅπως γεύσηται ἐξ αὐτῶν· "Ἐπειδή," φησίν, "ἑσπέρας,
ἀκούσας τὰ κατά σε, ἐξῆλθον τοῦ ἁλιεῦσαι ἐπὶ τῷ ὀνόματί
σου τῷ ἁγίῳ καί, τῶν εὐχῶν ἡμῶν συνεργησάντων,
ἠγρεύσαμεν ἀρκούντως καὶ δέον σε, πάτερ, μεταλαβεῖν ἐξ
αὐτῶν." Τότε ὁ μακάριος Νεῖλος τὸν μὲν ἄνθρωπον
ἀπέστειλεν εὐλογήσας καὶ μεγάλως εὐχαριστήσας ὑπὲρ
τοῦ αὐτοῦ κόπου, τῷ δὲ λογισμῷ αὐτοῦ διελέγετο οὕτως·
"Ταῦτα οὐχ ὁ Θεὸς ἡτοίμασεν, οὐδ᾽ ἄγγελος· οὐ γάρ εἰμι
τῶν φοβουμένων αὐτόν, ἵνα τὸ θέλημά μου ποιήσῃ. Ἀλλὰ
τοῦτο τὸ ἔργον τοῦ Διαβόλου τυγχάνει, ἐπειδή με ᾔσθετο
δουλωθέντα τῇ τοιαύτῃ ἐπιθυμίᾳ. Γέγραπται γάρ· ᾽Μὴ ἐπι-
θυμήσῃς,᾽ καί, *ζῇ Κύριος,* οὐκ εἰσέρχεται ἐξ αὐτῶν εἰς τὸ
στόμα μου."

3   Ὑπῆρχε δὲ τότε ἐκεῖ μοναχός τις παραγενάμενος ἐκ
τῶν ἄνω μερῶν, ὃς λίαν ἠγαπᾶτο παρ᾽ αὐτοῦ διὰ τὸ ᾀσμα-
τικὸν εἶναι αὐτὸν καὶ σφόδρα καλλίφωνον. Τοῦτον
καλέσας ὁ ὅσιος δέδωκεν αὐτῷ, καθὼς ἦν, τὸ κοφίνιον,
εἰπὼν πρὸς αὐτόν· "Λάβε τοῦτο τὸ ξένιον, ὅπερ σοι ὁ
Χριστὸς ἐξαπέστειλεν." Ὁ δὲ λαβὼν ἀνεχώρησεν.

4   Ἰδὼν οὖν ὁ Θεὸς τὴν μεγίστην αὐτοῦ ὑπομονὴν καὶ
καρτερίαν, ἀντελάβετο αὐτοῦ καὶ ἀπήλλαξεν αὐτὸν τῆς
ὀδύνης καὶ τῆς νόσου ἐκείνης τῆς πονηρᾶς, τοῦ πάθους

the brothers passing in front of his cell on the way out to go fishing, and thereafter returning with fish. After his great struggle and internal combat with this thought, behold, a layman came to him bearing a basket full of fish, some fried, and some baked, and entreated and begged Neilos to taste the fish. He said, "Since I heard about your condition last evening, I went out to fish in your holy name, and with the assistance of our prayers we made an abundant catch; and, father, you should eat some of them." Then the blessed Neilos sent the man away, blessing him and greatly thanking him for his efforts. He thought this, however, to himself: "God did not arrange this, nor did an angel, for I am not counted *among those who fear God* so that *He would fulfill my desire.* This must be the work of the Devil, since he perceives that I am enslaved by this longing. For it is written, '*You shall not covet.*' As *the Lord lives,* none of these fish will go into my mouth."

A monk who came from the upper region of the mountain, who was greatly loved by Neilos because he was a singer and had a most beautiful voice, was present at that time. After summoning him Neilos gave him the basket, just as it was, and said to him, "Take this gift which Christ has sent to you." The monk took it and departed.

Then God, seeing Neilos's very great perseverance and endurance, came to his aid and set him free from his pain and that wretched illness, as the tumor inside his throat

ἔνδον ἐν τῷ τραχήλῳ ῥαγέντος καὶ ἕλκους πολλοῦ διὰ τοῦ στόματος ἐξελθόντος. Μικρᾶς οὖν ἀνέσεως ἐπιτυχών, ἀνέρχεται πάλιν ἐν τῷ σπηλαίῳ, τῆς συνήθους ἐχόμενος πολιτείας καὶ τὴν ἡσυχίαν ἀσπαζόμενος ὡς οἰκείαν μητέρα. Ὁ δὲ Διάβολος οὐκ ἐπαύετο βρύχων κατ' αὐτοῦ τοὺς ὀδόντας καὶ ἀγωνιζόμενος, εἴγε ὑπὸ τῆς τοῦ Θεοῦ προνοίας παρεχωρεῖτο, ὥστε καὶ τοῦ ζῆν ἀπαλλάξαι τὸν δίκαιον ἄνδρα.

23

Καὶ δὴ κατὰ τὸ ἔθος σχολάζοντι ἐν μιᾷ νυκτὶ καὶ διαγρυπνοῦντι ἐν ψαλμοῖς καὶ γονυκλισίαις ἐν τῷ μικρῷ σπηλαρίῳ, τῷ ὑπ' αὐτοῦ λελατομημένῳ, καὶ τῆς τοῦ φέγγους αὐγῆς τὰ πάντα καταλαμπούσης—ἦν γὰρ τοῦ θέρους ἡ ὥρα—φαίνεται αὐτῷ ὁ Διάβολος ὀφθαλμοφανῶς ὡς Αἰθίοψ, ῥόπαλον εἰς τὰς χεῖρας κατέχων, μεθ' οὗ τύψας τὴν κεφαλὴν τοῦ ἁγίου, ἔρριψεν αὐτὸν ἐπὶ τὴν γῆν καὶ ἀφῆκεν, ἡμιθανῆ τυγχάνοντα.

2   Μετὰ οὖν μίαν ὥραν εἰς ἑαυτὸν ἐλθὼν ὁ ὅσιος, ἔγνω μὲν τοῦ Διαβόλου τὸν φθόνον καὶ τὴν ἄπειρον κατ' αὐτοῦ βασκανίαν, σφόδρα δὲ τὴν κεφαλὴν ἀλγυνόμενος καὶ τὸ ἥμισυ τοῦ προσώπου σὺν τῷ ἀριστερῷ ὀφθαλμῷ πεφυσημένον καὶ πελιδνότατον ἔχων, οὐ μὴν ἀλλὰ καὶ τὸν βραχίονα παραλελυμένον καὶ τεταριχευμένον, οὐκέτι μὲν

burst and a great ulcerated mass came out of his mouth. Having obtained a modicum of relief, he went up again to his cave, keeping to his usual daily routine and embracing spiritual tranquility as if it were his own mother. But the Devil did not stop gnashing his teeth against him and struggling to take away the just man's life, were it somehow permissible by God's providence.

Chapter 23

In fact, one night while Neilos was following his customary routine, keeping vigil, reciting psalms and making genuflections in the little cave that he had excavated with his own hands, as the light of dawn was illuminating everything — for the season was summer— the Devil appeared to him in the guise of an Ethiopian, grasping in his hand a club with which he struck the holy man on the head, knocking him to the ground, and leaving him half dead.

After an hour, the holy man came to his senses and then 2 recognized the Devil's envy and boundless animosity against him. His head ached terribly, while half his face and his left eye were swollen and bruised. Furthermore, his arm was paralyzed and withered. He had the strength neither to stand

ἴσχυσε στῆναι καὶ τὴν τῆς εὐχῆς λειτουργίαν ἀποπληρῶσαι. Κείμενος δὲ ἐπ᾽ ἐδάφους τὸν Κύριον ἐπεκαλεῖτο·
"Ὁ Θεός," λέγων, "εἰς τὴν βοήθειάν μου πρόσχες· Κύριε, εἰς
τὸ βοηθῆσαί μοι σπεῦσον. Αἰσχυνθήτωσαν καὶ ἐντραπήτω-
σαν οἱ ζητοῦντες τὴν ψυχήν μου," καὶ τὰ λοιπὰ τοῦ ψαλμοῦ.
Ἐν τούτοις διῆξεν τὸν ἅπαντα χρόνον ἐκεῖνον μυρίοις
πόνοις πυκτεύων καὶ συμφοραῖς ἀνηκέστοις. Πολλῶν
μέντοι συμβουλευόντων ἰατρικῆς ἐπιμελείας προσανασχέ-
σθαι, οὐδαμῶς κατεδέξατο τοῦτο, γινώσκων ἀθεράπευτον
εἶναι ὑπὸ χειρὸς ἀνθρωπίνης τὴν διαβολικὴν ἀλγηδόνα.

3   Τοῦ τοίνυν χρόνου παραδραμόντος καὶ τῆς μνήμης τῶν
ἁγίων ἀποστόλων ἐπιφθασάσης, συνῆλθον ἐν τῷ κοινοβίῳ
οἱ αὐτῶν μιμηταί, Φαντῖνος καὶ Νεῖλος, συνεορτάσαι καὶ
συμπαρακληθῆναι ἀλλήλοις, ὡς γνήσια τέκνα τῶν ἀποστόλων. Παννύχιον οὖν τὴν ὑμνῳδίαν ἐπιτελούντων καὶ τῶν
ἀδελφῶν ἀγαλλιωμένων ἐπὶ τῇ τῶν ἁγίων διδασκαλίᾳ καὶ
τῇ τῶν Γραφῶν ἀναπτύξει, παρακαλεῖ ὁ μέγας Φαντῖνος
τὸν ὅσιον Νεῖλον ἀναστῆναι καὶ ἀναγνῶναι ἐγκώμιον εἰς
τοὺς ἀποστόλους, συγγραφὲν παρὰ τοῦ ἐν ἁγίοις Δαμα-
σκηνοῦ Ἰωάννου, ἰαμβικοῖς καὶ ἐμμέτροις στίχοις καταπε-
ποικιλμένον.

4   Ὁ δὲ μακάριος Νεῖλος μηδέποτε παρακοῦσαι γινώσκων,
καίτοι σχεδὸν ὡς ἡμίξηρος τυγχάνων, ἀνέστη μετὰ πάσης
χαρᾶς καὶ προθυμίας· αὐτὸς τῆς ἀναγνώσεως ἀρχὴν ἐποι-
εῖτο, καὶ ἡ πονηρὰ νόσος ἐκείνη κατὰ μικρὸν τοῦ σώματος
ὑπεξήει. Ταύτης δὲ τῆς ἀντιλήψεως αἰσθηθεὶς παρὰ προσ-
δοκίαν ὁ μακάριος Νεῖλος, οὐδενὶ οὐδὲν εἶπε μέχρι τῆς
ἀπολύσεως τοῦ ὄρθρου. Καὶ τότε βαλὼν μετάνοιαν τῷ

nor to fulfill the liturgy of prayer. Lying on the ground he called out to the Lord, saying, *"Draw near, O God, to my help. Lord, make haste to help me. Let them be ashamed and confounded that seek my soul."* Then he added the remainder of the psalm. Thus he passed that whole year, struggling with numerous travails and terrible misfortunes. All the while many people encouraged him to seek medical care, though Neilos never agreed to this, knowing that demonic affliction could not be cured by human hands.

When the year had run its course and the feast day of 3 the holy apostles had arrived, their imitators Phantinos and Neilos met in the monastery to celebrate together and to support one another, as true children of the apostles. As they passed the night singing hymns and the brothers took pleasure in the holy men's teaching and their explanations of Scripture, the great Phantinos called upon holy Neilos to stand and read the encomium for the apostles composed by Saint John of Damascus, which is adorned with iambics and metrical verses.

The blessed Neilos, knowing never to disobey, even 4 though he was nearly half-paralyzed, stood up with all joy and eagerness. He began the reading, and little by little that wretched sickness disappeared from his body. Though this unexpected relief was apparent to him, the blessed Neilos said nothing to anyone until the dismissal from the matins service. Then prostrating himself before the righteous

δικαίῳ Φαντίνῳ εὐχαρίστει αὐτῷ, ὡς δι᾽ αὐτοῦ τῆς τοιαύτης ἀπαλλαγεὶς ἐπηρείας, αὐτὸς δὲ πάλιν τῇ ἐκείνου
ὑπακοῇ καὶ τῇ ἐπισκιάσει τῶν ἀποστόλων προσανατίθων
τὸ θαῦμα, διέμενον ἐν ταπεινοφροσύνῃ, τὸν τῶν θαυ-
μασίων Θεὸν δοξολογοῦντες.

24

ἩΗ δὲ πολύτροπος καὶ ἀπερινόητος τοῦ Θεοῦ περὶ
πάντας οἰκονομία (τί προνοουμένη περὶ τὸν ἑαυτῆς
οἰκέτην οὐκ οἶδα), εἴασεν αὐτὸν ἕως καὶ αὐτοῦ τοῦ γήρως
περιφέρειν τινὰ μικρὰ ἴχνη τῆς ἀρρωστίας ἐκείνης, ὑπο-
μιμνήσκοντα αὐτὸν τῆς αὐτοῦ περὶ αὐτὸν ἀντιλήψεως καὶ
κηδεμονίας. Ἐπὶ πᾶσι δὲ τούτοις ὑπερνικήσας διὰ τοῦ
ἀγαπήσαντος αὐτὸν Θεοῦ ὁ τῶν ἁγίων πάντων ζηλωτὴς
καὶ τῶν ἐντολῶν τοῦ Χριστοῦ πληρωτής, πρὸς ἑτέραν
ὡπλίζετο πάλην καὶ ἀγῶνα τοῦ Διαβόλου. Ἔδει γὰρ διὰ
πάντων ἀποκρουσθῆναι καὶ οὕτως ἀριδήλως τὸν νικητὴν
στεφανίτην ἀναδειχθῆναι.

2   Ἐν τῷ καιρῷ ἐκείνῳ ἔκστασις ἐπιπίπτει τῷ μακαρίτῃ
Φαντίνῳ, ἀληθῶς δὲ εἰπεῖν ἀλλοίωσις τῆς δεξιᾶς τοῦ
Ὑψίστου, καί, οἷον δὴ τὸν Ἰερεμίαν ἀκούομεν τὴν κεφαλὴν καὶ τὸν πώγονα ξυρίσαντα, τὴν Ἰερουσαλὴμ ἐν θρήνοις κατακομμῶντα περιϊέναι καὶ ὑπόληψιν ἐξεστηκότος
διδόναι τοῖς ἀνοήτοις, τὸν αὐτὸν τρόπον ἦν κατιδεῖν καὶ

Phantinos, Neilos thanked him, as it was through his aid
that Neilos was relieved from affliction, but Phantinos instead attributed the miracle to Neilos's obedience together
with the aid of the apostles. Persevering in humility, they
glorified God for His wondrous deeds.

Chapter 24

The manifold and unfathomable providence of God with
regard to all men—I know not what it has foreseen for His
servant—allowed Neilos to retain some small traces of that
malady to his old age, reminding him of God's assistance
and providential care. Neilos, who emulated all the saints
and fulfilled Christ's commandments, after overcoming all
trials through God's love for him, armed himself for another
combat and struggle with the Devil. For it was necessary for
the Devil to be defeated by all means and for the victorious
Neilos to receive the crown of victory in a conspicuous fashion.

At that time a state of ecstasy came over the blessed Phan- 2
tinos; to speak truly, *a change* came upon him *from the right
hand of the Most High.* And just as we hear that Jeremiah, having shaved his head and beard, went wandering about Jerusalem mourning with lamentations, giving to the foolish
ones the semblance of having gone out of his mind, the same

περὶ τὸν προφητικώτατον καὶ μακάριον ἄνθρωπον τοῦτον·
εἴτε γὰρ τὴν αἰσθητὴν ταύτης τῆς χώρας προφητεύων
κατάλυσιν καὶ τὴν τῶν Ἀγαρηνῶν οἰκιστάτην ἐπέλευσιν,
εἴτε τὴν τῆς ἀρετῆς παντελῆ ἔκλειψιν καὶ τῶν μοναστηρίων πρὸς κακίαν ἀπόκλισιν καὶ χυδαίωσιν, ὃ καὶ μᾶλλόν
ἐστι κυριώτερον, ὅμως καὶ αὐτὸς περιῄει θρήνοις κατα-
κομμῶν τάς τε ἐκκλησίας καὶ τὰ μοναστήρια καὶ τὰς
βίβλους, τὰς μὲν λέγων, ὅτι· "Ὄνων καὶ βορδονίων
ἐπλήσθησαν καὶ μεμόλυνται," τὰ δὲ "πυρίκαυστα," φησί,
"γεγόνασι, καὶ ἀπώλοντο," τὰς δὲ ὅτι "ἐβράχησαν καὶ
ἠχρείωνται καὶ λοιπὸν ποῦ ἀναγνῶναι οὐκ ἔχομεν." Ἡνίκα
δὲ ἀδελφὸν ἑώρα τῆς αὐτοῦ μονῆς, ὡς νεκρὸν ἐπένθει
αὐτόν, λέγων ὅτι· "Ἐγώ σε, ὦ τέκνον, ἀπέκτεινα." Ταῦτα
καὶ τὰ τοιαῦτα ἐλάλει τε καὶ ἐποίει, μήτε ὑπὸ στέγην
ἀνεχόμενος καταμεῖναι, μήτε τροφῆς ἀπογεύσασθαι, ἀλλὰ
τὰς ἐρήμους πλανώμενος διῃτᾶτο τοῖς ἀγριολαχάνοις.

3   Ταῦτα εἰς μεγίστην θλῖψιν καὶ λύπην ἤνεγκε Νεῖλον
τὸν ἀοίδιμον καὶ σχεδὸν νύκτωρ τε καὶ μεθ᾽ ἡμέραν
ἐπένθει καὶ αὐτὸς τὴν στέρησιν τοῦ καλοῦ συννόμου καὶ
συνεργάτου. Πολλάκις γὰρ ἀκολουθήσαντι αὐτῷ ἀναχω-
ροῦντι καὶ δυσωποῦντι τοῦ ὑποστρέψαι καὶ ἡσυχάσαι ἐν
τῷ μοναστηρίῳ, οὐχ ὑπήκουσε, λέγων ὅτι· "Οἱ ἐν τῇ μονῇ
οὔκ εἰσί μου ἀδελφοί, ἐπεὶ ἂν καὶ αὐτοὶ ἔκλαιον σὺν ἐμοί·
αὐτοὶ δὲ τοὐναντίον ποιοῦσιν, ἐξεστηκότα καὶ μαινόμενόν
με κρατοῦντες. Ἔσο τοίνυν γινώσκων, πολυπόθητε πάτερ,
ὅτι διαβήσομαι πρὸς τὴν ἄνω χώραν, κἀκεῖ τελειωθήσομαι
καὶ εἰς τὸ μοναστήριόν μου οὐκέτι ἐπιστραφήσομαι."
Αὐτὸς μὲν οὖν ὁ μακάριος, καθὰ καὶ προείρηκεν, οὕτω καὶ

thing also happened with regard to this most prophetic and blessed man Phantinos. Whether prophesying the actual destruction of this region, and the most deplorable attack of the Hagarenes, or predicting the complete disappearance of virtue, and the decline of the monasteries toward wicked decadence and vulgarity, which is even more important, Phantinos wandered about like Jeremiah, mourning with lamentations the churches, the monasteries, and the books, saying, "The churches have been filled with asses and mules and have been defiled, and the monasteries set on fire and destroyed, and the books have been drenched and rendered useless, and we have nothing to read from now on." And when he saw a brother from his own monastery, he mourned him as dead, saying, "O child, I have killed you." These and other such things he said and did. Neither did he allow himself to stay under a roof, nor to partake of any nourishment, but wandering in the wilderness he fed upon wild plants.

These practices caused great affliction and grief to the celebrated Neilos, and practically night and day he grieved at the absence of his good colleague and collaborator. Many times Neilos used to follow the wandering Phantinos, urging him to return to the monastery to live in spiritual tranquility, but he paid no heed, saying, "Those in the monastery are not my brothers, because if they were they would be crying out along with me. Instead they do the opposite, judging me to be out of my mind and raving mad. Know this, much-beloved father, that I shall go to the upper land and there end my life, and never shall I return to the monastery." Then, just as he had foretold, the blessed Phantinos died,

τετέλεκεν, καταλαβὼν τὸν τόπον, ἐν ᾧ προώρισεν αὐτῷ ὁ Θεὸς πρὸ πάντων τῶν αἰώνων τελειωθῆναι.

25

Ὁ δὲ ὅσιος πατὴρ ἡμῶν Νεῖλος ὑποστρέψας ἐν τῷ σπηλαίῳ, ἐν ὑπομονῇ διήρχετο τὴν στενὴν πύλην καὶ τεθλιμμένην ὁδόν, τὴν ὀλίγοις εὑρισκομένην. Ἔρχονται τοιγαροῦν πρὸς αὐτὸν οἱ τῆς μονῆς τοῦ ὁσίου Φαντίνου πατέρες, παρακαλοῦντες αὐτὸν σκυλῆναι καὶ ἡγούμενον αὐτοῖς καταστῆσαι, ὃν ἂν ἐκλέξηται ἡ αὐτοῦ ὁσιότης· περὶ γὰρ αὐτοῦ ἐκείνου ᾐδοῦντο καὶ ὀνομάσαι, γινώσκοντες τὸν ἄνδρα. Ὁ δὲ εἴξας τῇ αὐτῶν παρακλήσει καὶ εἰσελθὼν ἐν τῇ μονῇ μετ᾽ αὐτῶν, εἰσελθὼν δὲ ἐν τῇ ἐκκλησίᾳ τοῦ εὔξασθαι καὶ πάντων ἀκολουθησάντων αὐτῷ, μετὰ τὸ τελειωθῆναι τὴν εὐχήν, ὁ κατὰ σάρκα ἀδελφὸς τοῦ μακαριωτάτου Φαντίνου, Λουκᾶς τῷ ὀνόματι, προσδραμὼν καὶ τῶν ποδῶν τοῦ ὁσίου δραξάμενος, καὶ ὅρκοις αὐτὸν καὶ ἐπιτιμίοις φρικωδεστάτοις ἀπό τε τῆς Ἁγίας Τριάδος καὶ τῶν ἁγίων πατέρων ὑπέβαλλε τοῦ καταδέξασθαι εἶναι αὐτὸν αὐτοῖς ποιμένα καὶ καθηγούμενον. Τί οὖν εἶχε ποιῆσαι ὁ ἀγχίνους ἐκεῖνος ἀνὴρ καὶ περὶ τὸ διανοηθῆναι ὀξύς;

2   Ὑπερισχύσας τῶν χειρῶν τοῦ κρατοῦντος καὶ τῷ αὐτῷ σχήματι περιλαβὼν τοὺς πόδας αὐτοῦ, τοῖς αὐτοῖς

after reaching the very place where God before all the ages had preordained that he would die.

Chapter 25

As for our holy father Neilos, he returned to his cave; with endurance he went through *the narrow gate and along the hard way found by few.* Sometime thereafter, the fathers of the monastery of the holy Phantinos came to Neilos requesting that he come and appoint for them a superior, one whom his holiness Neilos might select; for they hesitated to nominate him themselves, since they were aware of Neilos's character. Neilos yielded to their entreaty and went to the monastery with them, entering the church to pray. All the brothers followed him and, after he finished his prayer, the blood brother of the most blessed Phantinos, Loukas by name, ran forward and grabbed hold of the holy man's feet. With oaths and threats of the worst punishments from the Holy Trinity and the holy fathers he proposed that Neilos should agree to become their shepherd and superior. What could that wise and keen-witted man do?

Overpowering the man's hands and grasping his feet in 2 the same way, Neilos bound him with the very same bonds

σχοινίοις, οἷσπερ ἐκέχρητο, αὐτὸν περιέδησεν, ὥστε λῦσαι
αὐτὸν τὰ ἴδια ἐπιτίμια καὶ γενέσθαι αὐτῷ ὅπερ τῷ πατρὶ
ἐπεβούλευσεν· ἦν γὰρ καὶ αὐτός, εἰ καὶ μὴ λίαν ἔμπειρος
τῶν θείων Γραφῶν, ἀλλ᾽ οὖν γε οἰκονομικὸς καὶ συνετὸς
καὶ τῷ βίῳ μηδὲν ἀποδέων τοῦ ἀδελφοῦ. Συστήσας οὖν τὰ
πάντα ὁ ὅσιος πατὴρ κατὰ τὸ τῷ Θεῷ δοκοῦν καὶ νουθεσίαις ἐνθέοις παρακαλέσας καὶ στηρίξας τόν τε ἡγούμενον καὶ τοὺς ἀδελφούς, ἀπηλλάγη καὶ τούτου τοῦ πει-
ρασμοῦ, εὐλογῶν τὸν Θεόν.

26

Καιρὸς δὲ λοιπὸν ἀνακάμψαι ἡμᾶς, εὐδοκοῦντος Θεοῦ,
καὶ ἐπὶ τὴν μνήμην τοῦ ὁμοζήλου καὶ συνάθλου καὶ συν-
αγωνιστοῦ τοῦ μεγάλου πατρός, Στεφάνου τοῦ μάκαρος,
ἵνα μὴ μόνον τὸ δένδρον ἀπὸ τῆς ἁγίας ῥίζης γνωρίζεται,
ἀλλὰ καὶ ἀπὸ τῶν ἁγίων καρπῶν καὶ κλάδων θαυμάζεται.
Πιστεύω δὲ τῷ Θεῷ, ὅτι οὐκ εἰς κενὸν ἡμῖν ἡ τοιαύτη
μνήμη γενήσεται. Ἀλλ᾽ εἰ μὴ καὶ ζηλωταὶ τῶν μεγάλων
αὐτῶν κατορθωμάτων γενέσθαι ἰσχύσωμεν τῶν γε, τὸ
μνημονεῦσαι μετὰ πίστεως αὐτῶν καὶ τῶν ἔργων αὐτῶν
ἀφέσεως ἡμῖν πλημμελημάτων πολλῶν πρόξενον γενήσεται, καθὼς διδασκόμεθα.

2   Οὗτος τοίνυν ὁ ἐν ἁγίοις Στέφανος, νέος ἔτι ὢν ὡς
ἐτῶν εἴκοσι, ἀγροῖκος δὲ καὶ ἐξ εὐτελῶν γονέων ὑπάρχων,

which Loukas had used, so that Loukas would release him from these punishments and subject himself to what he had wished upon father Neilos. For Loukas, though somewhat inexperienced in divine Scripture, was a capable manager, intelligent, and in no way inferior to his brother in his life-style. So the holy father arranged everything in accordance with God's will, and with divinely inspired admonitions he encouraged and supported the new superior Loukas and the brethren. So Neilos succeeded in freeing himself from this temptation as well, giving blessings to God.

Chapter 26

Now it is time for us, with God's approval, to turn the narrative to the commemoration of the blessed Stephen, an equal and a companion to the great father Neilos in zeal, in his spiritual struggle, and in combat, so that the tree may be recognized not only from its holy roots, but also be marveled at for its holy fruit and branches. I have faith in God that such a commemoration will not be in vain for us; for even if we cannot emulate their great achievements, at least the faithful remembrance of them and of their deeds will bring about the remission of our many sins, as we are taught.

When this Stephen, now among the saints, was still young, around twenty years of age, a peasant born from 2

ὀρφανὸν αὐτὸν καταλείψαντος τοῦ πατρὸς μετὰ τῆς μητρὸς καὶ μιᾶς ἀδελφῆς, τοσαύτη ἀκακίᾳ καὶ ἀπονηρίᾳ κεκόσμητο, ὡς εἴ τις αὐτὸν Ἰακὼβ εἴποι τὸν πατριάρχην, ἢ τὸν ἁπλούστατον Παῦλον τοῦ ἀββᾶ Ἀντωνίου, οὐκ <ἂν> ἀπεικότως στοχάσοιτο.

3   Οὗτος ἐρασθεὶς τοῦ μοναδικοῦ ἐπαγγέλματος καί, κατὰ τὸ Εὐαγγέλιον, τὸν Χριστὸν ὑπὲρ τὴν ἀδελφὴν καὶ μητέρα καὶ ὑπὲρ ἑαυτὸν ἀγαπήσας, ὡδηγήθη παρὰ τοῦ Θεοῦ ἀπελθεῖν ἔνθα ἦν ὁ μακάριος πατὴρ ἡμῶν Νεῖλος καὶ παρακαθίσας αὐτῷ μηδὲν εἰρηκώς, περὶ δυσμὰς ἡλίου λέγει αὐτῷ ὁ πατήρ· "Τί ζητεῖς, ἀδελφέ;" Ὁ δέ φησιν· "Καλόγηρος θέλω γενέσθαι." Λέγει αὐτῷ ὁ μέγας· "Καὶ εἰ καλόγηρος θέλεις γενέσθαι, ἐγώ σοι δεικνύω τὰ μοναστήρια, καὶ ἄπελθε ἐκεῖ· ὧδε γὰρ κατοικῆσαι οὐ δύνῃ, μὴ ἔχων τί φαγεῖν, καὶ ἀποθνήσκεις ἀπὸ λιμοῦ." Ὁ δὲ ἀπεκρίθη, ὅτι· "Τὰ μοναστήρια," φησί, "γινώσκω καὶ οἶδα, ἀλλ᾽ οὐκ ἀρέσκουσί μοι· ὧδε δὲ ἀρέσκει μοι." Πάλιν ἐρωτηθείς, εἰ ἔχει τινά, καὶ ἀποκριθείς, ὅπερ ἦν, ἐβιάζετο ἀπελθεῖν καὶ θρέψαι τήν τε μητέρα καὶ τὴν ἀδελφήν· καί φησιν, ὅτι· "Οὐκ ἀπέρχομαι οὐδαμοῦ· ἐκείνας γὰρ οὐκ ἐγώ, ἀλλ᾽ ὁ Θεός, καὶ ἔθρεψε καὶ τρέφει."

parents of no means, he was left an orphan together with his mother and sister when his father passed away. He was adorned with such goodness and lack of malice that if someone were to say that he resembled the patriarch Jacob or Paul the Simple, the disciple of father Anthony, he would not be far from the truth.

This man loved the monastic profession and, in accordance with the Gospel, loved Christ more than his sister and mother and even more than himself. He was shown by God the path that led to our blessed father Neilos, and sat down next to him without saying a word. At sunset the father said to him, "What do you seek, brother?" And Stephen said, "I wish to become a monk." The great man said to him, "If you wish to become a monk, I shall show you the monasteries. Go there, for you cannot live here. Since you have nothing to eat, you will die from hunger." He responded, "I know the monasteries and am familiar with them, but they do not suit me; I like it here." He was again asked if he had any family, and when he responded that he did, Neilos urged him to leave and take care of his mother and sister. Stephen said, "I am not going anywhere; for it is not I but God who has fed them and feeds them now."

27

Λοιπὸν μὴ ἰσχύσας ἀποδιῶξαι αὐτὸν ὁ πατήρ, δέδωκεν αὐτῷ ὅπερ εἶχεν ἥμισυ ἄρτου φαγεῖν, αὐτὸς δὲ διέμεινεν ἄγευστος μέχρι τῆς αὔριον· Παρασκευῆς γὰρ οὔσης, τέλος εἶχε καὶ ἡ μεμετρημένη δίαιτα. Τοῦτο δὲ ἦν ἐν τῷ δευτέρῳ ἔτει τῆς τοῦ πατρὸς παροικησίας ἐκεῖσε. Ὁρῶν οὖν αὐτὸν ὁ πατὴρ φύσει ὄντα ἁπλοῦν καὶ ἀργόν, ὅπερ ἦν ἐναντίον τῇ ἐκείνου ἀστειότητι, ἤχθετο μὲν ἐπὶ τῇ ἀργότητι αὐτοῦ καὶ ἐθλίβετο, οὐ μὴν ἐλάλει αὐτῷ τι σκληρόν, ἔχων τὸν νοῦν αὐτοῦ ἐν ταῖς εὐαγγελικαῖς ἐντολαῖς· νουθετῶν δὲ αὐτὸν μετ᾽ ἐπιεικείας καὶ πρᾳότητος, ἔσπευδεν ἀστεῖον καὶ γοργὸν ἀποδεῖξαι αὐτόν, ὡς καὶ αὐτὸς ἦν. Ἀκμὴν γὰρ οὐκ ᾔδει σαφῶς, ὅτι τὸ ἐκ φύσεως οὐ μεθίσταται.

2   Ὡς οὖν ἀπετύγχανε τοῦ σκοποῦ καὶ διῆλθον ἡμέραι τριῶν ἐτῶν, λέγει ἐν ἑαυτῷ ὁ πατήρ· "Ἆρά γε, εἰ ἦν μοι ἀδελφός, ἢ υἱός, ἢ ἀνεψιός, οὐκ ἂν καὶ ὕβρεσι καὶ ὀνειδισμοῖς ἐχρησάμην πρὸς παίδευσιν αὐτοῦ; Δοκιμάσωμεν πάλιν τὸ τοιοῦτον εἶδος ἐπ᾽ αὐτῷ, μή ποτε μείνῃ ἀπαίδευτος ὁ ἀδελφός." Τότε ἤρξατο αὐστηρῶς λέγειν πρὸς αὐτὸν καὶ ὕβρεσιν στύφειν αὐτόν· πολλάκις δὲ καὶ ἀπὸ χειρὸς ἐδίδει αὐτῷ. Βουλόμενος γὰρ διδάξαι αὐτὸν τὰς συνήθεις εὐχὰς καὶ τὸ Ψαλτήριον, ἀνάγκην εἶχε καὶ κολαφιστικῶς ἅπτεσθαι αὐτοῦ. Αὐτὸς δὲ πάντα ὑπέφερεν ἀβαρῶς καὶ μετὰ χαρᾶς, μήτε τὴν σκληροτάτην ἄσκησιν καὶ τὴν ἄληκτον ἀγρυπνίαν δειλιάσας, ἐν πᾶσιν ἐξισούμενος τῷ

Chapter 27

In short the father was unable to send Stephen away and so gave him to eat the half loaf of bread that he had, while Neilos himself remained with no food until the following day, because, since it was Friday, he had consumed his allotted portion. This happened during the second year of the father's residence there. Then Neilos, seeing that Stephen was by nature simple and slow, which was the opposite of his own cleverness, was irritated by the man's slow-wittedness and was distressed. But he did not say anything harsh to him, keeping in mind the commandments of the Gospels. He admonished him with equity and kindness, commending him to become quick-witted and spirited as Neilos himself was; for he still clearly did not know that innate characteristics never change.

As he did not attain his goal despite the passage of three 2 years, the father Neilos said to himself, "If he were my brother or son or nephew, wouldn't I use insults and reproaches to train him? Let us try this approach instead, so that the brother does not remain forever incorrigible." Then Neilos began to speak sternly to him and to treat him harshly with abusive language, often even raising his hand against him. For when Neilos decided to teach him the customary prayers and the Psalter, he even found it necessary to slap him. Stephen bore all this without taking offense, even joyfully, fearing neither the most severe asceticism nor unceasing vigil. He made himself an equal in all regards to

μεγάλῳ, μήτε τὰ ὀνείδη καὶ τὰς παρὰ τοῦ πατρὸς ἐπηρείας ἀποδράσας.

3   Διὸ καὶ πρὸς τοῦ Θεοῦ ἐφυλάχθη, μείνας ἀπείραστος τῆς δαιμονικῆς πανουργίας. Πολλάκις γὰρ ἐρωτηθεὶς παρὰ τοῦ ὁσίου ποίοις ἄρα λογισμοῖς ἐνοχλεῖται, ἀπεκρίθη, ὅτι· "Οὐκ ἔχω λογισμὸν τίποτε, μόνον δὲ νυστάζω πολλὰ καὶ διὰ τοῦτο θλίβομαι." Τότε ποιεῖ αὐτῷ ὁ πατὴρ σκαμνίον ἔχον πόδιον ἕν, καὶ λέγει αὐτῷ, ὅτι· "Σὺ μὲν ἔχεις πόδια δύο καὶ τὸ σκαμνίον ἕν, ἰδοὺ τρία πόδια· καὶ οὕτω καθήμενος, τῆς μελέτης μὴ ἀμελήσῃς." Ὁ δὲ τὴν παραγγελίαν δεξάμενος, οὐδαμοῦ ἐκάθητο ἔκτοτε εἰ μὴ ἐν τῷ σκαμνίῳ ἐκείνῳ καὶ ἐν τῇ μελέτῃ καὶ ἐν τῇ ἐκκλησίᾳ καὶ ἐν τῷ γεύσασθαι. Νικώμενος δὲ πολλάκις ὑπὸ τοῦ νυσταγμοῦ καὶ πίπτων ἐπὶ τὴν γῆν, ποτὲ μὲν τὸν βραχίονα, ποτὲ δὲ τὸ πρόσωπον συνετρίβετο.

28

Πάλιν ἐρχόμενος ἐπὶ τὸ ἐψῆσαι τὸ ὄσπρεον καὶ τίθων πλέον ἢ τὸ σκεῦος χωρῆσαι ἠδύνατο, ὑπὸ τῆς βίας ἀθρόον ἐρρήγνυτο. Ἐν μιᾷ οὖν τῶν ἡμερῶν συναγαγὼν ἅπαντα τὰ κλάσματα, ὑπεδείκνυε τῷ πατρί, τὸ σφάλμα ἐξομολογούμενος. Ὁ δὲ λέγει πρὸς αὐτόν· "Καὶ τί τὸ ὄφελος, ὅτι ἐξομολογεῖ μόνῳ ἐμοί; Ὕπαγε εἰς τὰ μοναστήρια, δεῖξον αὐτά, ἵνα γνωρίσωσιν ὁποῖοι ἀσκηταὶ ἡμεῖς ἐσμεν χυτροκλάσται."

the great man Neilos, and did not seek to escape the father's reproaches and insults.

Therefore he was also protected by God, remaining un- ₃ tested by demonic cunning. For many times, when the holy man asked him which thoughts were troubling him, he would respond, "I don't have any such thoughts; only I doze off a lot, and this bothers me." Then the father made for him a one-legged stool and said to him, "You have two legs, and this stool has one—all together that is three legs. Sitting thus, you will not be neglectful of your meditation." He accepted the command and from that time on sat only on that stool, whether he was meditating, or in church, or partaking of food. But many times he was overcome by drowsiness and tumbled to the ground, injuring his arm on one occasion and another time his face.

Chapter 28

Another time when Stephen went to boil legumes, he filled the pot with more than it could hold and suddenly it burst from the pressure of the boiling. Then on one of the subsequent days, he gathered all the broken pieces and showed them to the father, confessing his fault. Neilos said to him, "What is the benefit that you confess it to me alone? Go to the monasteries, and show the fragments there so that they know what sort of monks we are—potbreakers."

2   Τότε, λαβὼν τὰ κλάσματα, ἀπέρχεται πρὸς Φαντῖνον, τὸν ὁσιώτατον, καὶ τὸ πρᾶγμα αὐτῷ ἐξηγήσατο. Αὐτὸς δὲ τῷ σκοπῷ ἑπόμενος τοῦ θεόφρονος καὶ ὁμόφρονος, συναγαγὼν πάντα τὰ κλάσματα καὶ σχοινίῳ συνδήσας καὶ τῷ τραχήλῳ αὐτοῦ κρεμάσας, πεποίηκεν αὐτὸν οὕτω παρασταθῆναι ἐν τῷ ἀριστηρίῳ τῶν ἀδελφῶν γευομένων. Τούτου δὲ γενομένου ἀπέστειλεν αὐτὸν πάλιν πρὸς τὸν ὅσιον ἐν τῷ σπηλαίῳ τοῦ λοιποῦ διορθωθέντα.

3   Περιερχόμενος δέ ποτε ὁ μακάριος Στέφανος, εὗρε τὰ λεγόμενα σπαράγγια· καὶ συναγαγὼν αὐτὰ καὶ ἑψήσας, παρέθηκεν ἐν τῇ ὥρᾳ τοῦ γεύσασθαι. Μεταλαβὼν δὲ ἐξ αὐτῶν ὁ πατὴρ καὶ ὡς παρὰ συνήθειαν μικρᾶς ἡδονῆς αἰσθόμενος, ἐπύθετο τοῦ ἑταίρου, εἴγε καὶ αὐτὸς τῆς αὐτῆς γλυκύτητος ᾔσθετο. Τοῦ δὲ συμφωνήσαντος, ῥῖψαι αὐτὰ ἔξω παρὰ τοῦ πατρὸς ἐκελεύετο· "Ταῦτα γάρ," φησί, "πικρὰ φύσει τυγχάνοντα ὁ Διάβολος ἤρτυσε, καὶ γλυκεῖα πεποίηκεν." Ἕως τοσούτου ἐγκρατεύοντο οἱ μακάριοι καὶ βίᾳ τὴν φύσιν διηνεκεῖ κατεδάμαζον.

4   Μετὰ δὲ ταῦτα ἔκρινεν ὁ ὅσιος Νεῖλος φροντίσαι καὶ περὶ τὸ ἀδύνατον μέρος τοῦ μακαρίου Στεφάνου· καὶ ἀποστέλλει αὐτὸν μετὰ γραμμάτων πρὸς τὴν ὄντως Θεοδώραν τὴν μακαριωτάτην παρθένον, ἀσκουμένην τῷ τότε καιρῷ ἐν τῷ λεγομένῳ Ἀριναρίῳ καὶ καθηγουμένην ὀλίγων παρθένων, γραῦν ἁγίαν καὶ λίαν συνετωτάτην καὶ σοφωτάτην ἐκ νεαρᾶς ἡλικίας τὴν μοναδικὴν ἀσκουμένην σκληραγωγίαν· οὐκ οἶδα, εἰ τοιαύτην ἄλλην τὸ Ῥυσιάνον ἐξήνεγκεν· ἥτις, ὡς υἱὸν γνήσιον ἀγαπῶσα τὸν ἅγιον πατέρα ἐκ νεαρᾶς αὐτοῦ τῆς ἡλικίας, πείθεται δέξασθαι

Then taking the broken pieces, Stephen went to the most 2
holy Phantinos and explained the matter to him. Understanding the aim of Neilos, who was of godly mind and likeminded to him, Phantinos gathered together all the pieces,
tied them together with a cord, and hung them around Stephen's neck. He then made him stand in the refectory while
the brothers ate. When this was done Phantinos sent him,
henceforth edified, back to the holy Neilos in his cave.

Once, while walking around, the blessed Stephen found 3
some plants called asparagus, and, after picking them, he
cooked and served them at suppertime. After eating some
of them Neilos experienced a modicum of pleasure contrary
to his norm and then asked his companion if he as well had
enjoyed the sweet taste. When Stephen agreed, the father
ordered him to throw the rest away, saying, "For asparagus is
by nature bitter, but the Devil has seasoned them and made
them sweet." To such an extent did the blessed men discipline themselves, and by force continually subdued their na-
tures.

Afterward the blessed Neilos decided to concern himself 4
also with the defenseless female relatives of the blessed Stephen and sent him with letters to Theodora, the truly most
blessed virgin, who was leading an ascetic life at that time
in the place called Arinarion and serving as mother superior to a few virgins. An old woman, she was most clever and
holy and wise, and from her youth had practiced the harsh
training of monastic life—I do not know if Rossano produced any other woman like her. As someone who had loved
holy Neilos as her own son from the time of his youth, she

τήν τε μητέρα καὶ τὴν ἀδελφὴν τοῦ ὁσίου ἐν τῷ μοναστηρίῳ, ἐν ᾧ καί, γνησίως δουλεύσασαι τῷ Κυρίῳ καὶ
μεγάλως εὐαρεστήσασαι, ἐτελειώθησαν ἐν εἰρήνη. Τὰ μέν
τοι τῆς ζωῆς αὐτῶν ἔτη ἅπαντα κατὰ καιρόν, τῇ ὥρᾳ τοῦ
θέρους, ἀπήρχετο ὁ μακάριος Στέφανος ἐν τῷ μοναστηρίῳ
ἐκείνῳ, καί, τελέσας τὸν ἐκεῖσε ἀμητόν, πάλιν ὑπέστρεφεν
εἰς τὰ μοναστήρια καὶ συνεκοπία ἐν παντὶ ἔργῳ τοῖς ἀδελφοῖς, διπλοῦν ἀγῶνα ἀγωνιζόμενος, τόν τε τῆς ἐγκρατείας
καὶ τὸν πανημέριον κόπον.

29

Τῶν τοίνυν ἀθέων Ἀγαρηνῶν παραδραμόντων πᾶσαν
τὴν Καλαβρίτιδα χώραν ἕνα χρόνον καὶ πάντα ληϊσα-
μένων, μελλόντων δὲ ἐπιβαίνειν καὶ τοῖς Μερκουριακοῖς
μέρεσιν, μήτε μοναστήριον καταλιπεῖν ἀχείρωτον λογισά-
μενοι, μήτε μοναχὸν ἐλέους καὶ φειδοῦς ἀξιῶσαι, προέλα-
βεν ἡ φήμη αὐτῶν καὶ πάντες κατέφευγον ἐπὶ τὰ τυχόντα
καστέλλια. Τότε δὴ καὶ ὁ μακάριος Στέφανος, εὑρεθεὶς ἐν
τῷ κοινοβίῳ τοῦ μεγάλου Φαντίνου, ἀνῆλθεν σὺν τοῖς
ἀδελφοῖς ἐν τῷ γειτνιάζοντι καστελλίῳ, μὴ δυνηθεὶς
ὑποστρέψαι ἐν τῷ σπηλαίῳ διὰ τὸ κατεπεῖγον τῆς φήμης.
2   Ὁ δὲ πατὴρ ἄνωθεν ἀπὸ τοῦ σπηλαίου θεασάμενος τὸν
κονιορτὸν καὶ τὸ πλῆθος ἐπερχόμενον τῶν Σαρακηνῶν,
ἐλογίσατο ἀποκρυβῆναι ἀπὸ τῆς δολιότητος αὐτῶν, μή

was persuaded to receive the holy Stephen's mother and sister into her convent, where they truly served the Lord and, greatly pleasing Him, ended their days peacefully. For the rest of their lives the blessed Stephen used to go to her convent during the summer, and having finished the harvest there, he would return again to the monasteries and labor with his brethren in all endeavors, thus striving in two contests, one of self-discipline and one of daily labor.

Chapter 29

Then for one year the godless Hagarenes overran the entire land of Calabria and sacked everything, and were about to attack the region of Merkourion as well, intending to leave no monastery untouched nor deem any monk worthy of mercy or being spared. The report of their incursion preceded them, and everyone fled to the nearest fortresses. At that time the blessed Stephen, who was in the monastery of the great Phantinos, went up with the brethren to the neighboring fortress, since he could not return to the cave on account of the urgent report.

Father Neilos observed from above his cave the dust 2 cloud and the size of the advancing Saracen host, and decided to conceal himself from their malice, so that he would

ποτε καὶ ὡς πειράζων τὴν δύναμιν τοῦ Θεοῦ εὑρεθῇ. Λαβὼν οὖν μεθ᾽ ἑαυτοῦ τὸ κεράμιον τοῦ ὕδατος, ἐπορεύθη ἐν ἀποκρύφῳ τόπῳ, ἔνθα ἀφόβως διῆγε. Τῇ δὲ νυκτὶ ἐκείνῃ ἀναπατῶν περὶ τὸ ὄρος ἐκεῖνο καὶ τὸν Δαβὶδ κατὰ τὴν συνήθειαν μεθ᾽ ἑαυτοῦ περιφέρων, μᾶλλον δὲ τὸν τοῦ Δαβὶδ βασιλέα, ἤκουσε κτύπον ὡσεὶ ποδῶν ἵππου περιερχόμενον καὶ κυκλεύοντα αὐτὸν καὶ μὴ δυνάμενον προσεγγίσαι αὐτῷ. Καὶ τὰ μὲν πρῶτα νομίσας ἄνθρωπόν τινα εἶναι αὐτόν, οὐδὲν ἐλάλησε, πληρῶσαι βουλόμενος τὸν ψαλμόν. Ὡς δὲ εἶδεν αὐτὸν μήτε ὑπάγοντα, μήτε προσεγγίζοντα, λέγει πρὸς αὐτόν· "Τίς εἶ σύ;" Καὶ ἅμα τῷ λόγῳ ἀκούει ὅτι συνέτριψε τὸ κεράμιον τοῦ ὕδατος καὶ ἄφαντος γέγονεν.

3   Τότε γνοὺς ὁ μακάριος τὸν ἐργάτην ἐκ τῶν οἰκείων ἔργων, ἤρξατο πάλιν τοῦ ψάλλειν καὶ λέγειν· "Κυκλώσαντες ἐκύκλωσάν με οἱ ἐχθροί μου, καὶ τῷ ὀνόματι Κυρίου ἠμυνάμην αὐτούς." Ἐμέμφετο δὲ πάλιν ἑαυτὸν καὶ ἔλεγε τῷ λογισμῷ· "Ἄρτι τοῦ ἐλθεῖν τοῦτον ἐνταῦθα ὁ ἡμέτερος ῥεμβασμὸς γέγονεν αἴτιος αὐτῷ, διότι τῷ μὲν στόματι θεολογοῦμεν, τῷ δὲ νοῒ ἀλογοῦμεν." Καὶ ἔλεγεν ἀεί, ὅτι· "Οὐδὲν ἄλλο διεγείρει τοὺς δαίμονας κατὰ τοῦ μοναχοῦ, ὡς ὁ ῥεμβασμὸς ἐν τῇ προσευχῇ καὶ τὸ μὴ προσέχειν τοῖς ἐξερχομένοις λόγοις ἐκ τοῦ στόματος αὐτοῦ."

not seem to be testing God's power. So taking with him a jug of water, he went to a hiding place and stayed there without fear. But that evening while walking around the mountain, bearing the words of David on his lips, or rather the words of David's king, as was his custom, he heard a clatter like that of a horse's hooves surrounding and encircling him, though unable to get near him. Even though at first he thought it was a human being, he did not speak, wishing to complete the psalm. When Neilos saw that the person was neither going away nor coming near, he said, "Who are you?" Just as he spoke he heard him break the water jug and disappear.

The blessed one recognized the culprit from his deeds, 3 and so began again the psalm, "My enemies *completely compassed me about, but in the name of the Lord I repulsed them.*" He again reproached himself, and thought, "My distraction was responsible for the person coming here just now, for while I may speak of God with my mouth, I do not speak with my mind." As Neilos always said, "Nothing rouses demons against the monk as much as distraction during prayer and lack of attention to the words coming from his mouth."

30

Τότε τοίνυν ὁ ὅσιος πατὴρ ἡμῶν Νεῖλος, ἡμέρας καταλαβούσης, ἀπελθὼν ἐν τῷ σπηλαίῳ, εὗρεν ὅτι ἀνῆλθον
ἕως ἐκεῖ οἱ Σαρακηνοὶ καὶ ἀφείλαντο τὸ τρίχινον τῆς
ἀλλαγῆς αὐτοῦ, γεμίσαντες αὐτὸ ἀπιδίων ἀγρίων κειμένων
ἐκεῖσε. Κατελθὼν δὲ καὶ εἰς τὸ μοναστήριον καὶ ἰδὼν
ἅπαντα κατεστραμμένα καὶ κατηρημωμένα, ἐλογίσατο
ὑπὸ τῶν Σαρακηνῶν κρατηθῆναι τὸν ὅσιον Στέφανον,
εἴτε ἐν τῷ σπηλαίῳ, εἴτε ἐν τῷ μοναστηρίῳ. Ἤρξατο οὖν
σφόδρα λυπεῖσθαι καὶ λέγειν ἐν ἑαυτῷ· "Ὄντως, ταπεινὲ
Νεῖλε, ὁ ἀδελφὸς Στέφανος δοῦλος ὑπάγει· πάντως γὰρ
περιμένων ἡμᾶς, εἴτε ὧδε, εἴτε ἐν τῷ σπηλαίῳ, ἐκρατήθη.
Ὄντως δίκαιόν ἐστιν, ἵν᾽ ὑπάγωμεν καὶ δουλεύσωμεν μετ᾽
αὐτοῦ." Καὶ ταῦτα λέγων ἐδάκρυε, φοβούμενος μὲν τὸ
ἀναιδὲς καὶ ἀκάθαρτον τῶν παγανῶν, ἀναγκαζόμενος δὲ
πάλιν θεῖναι τὴν ψυχὴν ὑπὲρ τοῦ φίλου αὐτοῦ διὰ τὴν ἐντολὴν τοῦ Χριστοῦ.

2   Ταῦτα τοίνυν ἐνθυμηθείς, ἀπέρχεται καὶ καθέζεται
ἀναμέσον τῆς δημοσίας ὁδοῦ, ἐκδεχόμενος τὴν διάβασιν
τῶν Σαρακηνῶν. Οὐ πολὺ τὸ ἐν μέσῳ, καὶ ἰδοὺ ἤρχοντο
ὡσεὶ δέκα καβαλλάριοι, ἐνδύματα καὶ ὅπλα καὶ φακιόλια
καὶ ὅλον τὸ σχῆμα ἔχοντες τῶν Σαρακηνῶν· οὓς ἰδών, ὁ
μακάριος πατὴρ εὐθέως ἀνέστη καί, κατασφραγισάμενος
ἑαυτὸν τῷ σημείῳ τοῦ τιμίου σταυροῦ, ἔστη περιμένων
αὐτούς. Αὐτοὶ δὲ μακρόθεν ἐπιγνόντες αὐτόν, ἀπέβησαν
τῶν ἵππων καὶ πεζοὶ ἦλθον καὶ προσεκύνησαν τοὺς πόδας

Chapter 30

Then right at daybreak our blessed father Neilos went back in the cave and discovered that the Saracens had come that far up the mountain, and had carried off his spare goat-hair garment, filling it with wild pears found in the area. After going down to Phantinos's monastery and seeing it entirely overrun and destroyed, he thought that the blessed Stephen had been captured by the Saracens either in the cave or in the monastery. So he began to grieve exceedingly, and to say to himself, "Truly, wretched Neilos, brother Stephen has become a slave. Assuredly while waiting for me, either here or in the cave, he was taken captive. Truly it is right for me to go and become a slave along with him." So speaking he wept, fearing on the one hand the ruthless and unclean pagans, though constrained by Christ's *commandment to lay down his life for his friend.*

With this weighing on his mind, Neilos went forth and 2 sat in the middle of the public road, expecting the Saracens to pass by. Shortly thereafter, behold, ten horsemen arrived there with the garb and weapons and turbans and all the other trappings of a Saracen. Upon seeing them, the blessed father immediately arose, and making the sign of the venerable cross he stood awaiting them. From afar they recognized him, dismounted from their horses, and, approaching him on foot, prostrated themselves at his feet. Removing

αὐτοῦ. Περιελόμενοι δὲ τὰ φακιόλια ἀπὸ τῶν προσώπων αὐτῶν, τότε ἐγνωρίσθησαν ὑπὸ τοῦ πατρὸς ἐκ τοῦ καστελλίου εἶναι αὐτοὺς καὶ χάριν τοῦ ἀποσκεπάσαι τὸν τόπον ποιῆσαι ταῦτα αὐτούς.

31

Καὶ μαθὼν παρ' αὐτῶν ὅτι σεσωσμένοι εἰσὶ πάντες οἱ ἀδελφοὶ καὶ ὁ ἀββᾶς Στέφανος μετ' αὐτῶν, ὑπέστρεψεν ἐν τῷ σπηλαίῳ εὐχαριστῶν τῷ Θεῷ. Ἀναχωρησάντων δὲ τῶν Σαρακηνῶν, ἦλθε καὶ ὁ μακάριος Στέφανος καὶ πάλιν εἴχοντο τῆς προτέρας ὁδοῦ. Ὄντος δὲ αὐτοῦ ἐν τῷ μοναστηρίῳ τὸ πρὶν διὰ τὸν θερισμόν, ἤν τις γέρων ἐκεῖ ποιῶν τὰ σπυρίδια· καὶ μαθὼν παρ' αὐτοῦ πλέκειν τὴν σειράν, ἐποίησεν ἓν μαλάκιον καὶ ἤνεγκεν εἰς τὸ σπήλαιον, ὡς νομίζων ὅτι χαριεῖται ἐπ' αὐτῷ ὁ πατήρ. Ὁ δὲ ἰδών, λέγει πρὸς αὐτόν· "Δεῦρο, ἀδελφὲ Στέφανε, πληρώσωμεν καὶ ἡμεῖς μίαν ἐντολήν· ἐπειδὴ ἄνευ παραθέσεως καὶ βουλῆς ἐποίησας αὐτό, βάλωμεν καὶ καύσωμεν αὐτό, οὕτως γὰρ λέγει ὁ μέγας Βασίλειος." Καὶ σὺν τῷ λόγῳ ἀναστάς, ἀνῆψε πυρὰν καὶ ἔβαλε τὸ μαλάκιον. Ἰδὼν δὲ αὐτόν, ὅτι βαρέως ἤνεγκε τὸ πρᾶγμα καὶ οὐ μετ' εὐχαριστίας, ἀλλὰ μετὰ γογγυσμοῦ, εἴασε τὸ μαλάκιον καῆναι παντελῶς καὶ ἀπήλλαξεν αὐτὸν τῆς προσπαθείας αὐτοῦ.

2   Ἐν μιᾷ οὖν ἔρχεται ὁ γέρων ὁ διδάξας αὐτὸν τὰ

their turbans and uncovering their faces, they were recognized by the father as men from the fortress who had disguised themselves in order to reconnoiter the place.

Chapter 31

Learning from them that all the brethren were safe and father Stephen with them, he returned to the cave, giving thanks to God. When the Saracens withdrew, the blessed Stephen came back and they again directed themselves upon their former path. There was an elder in the monastery making baskets when Stephen was there earlier for the harvest. He learned from the elder how to weave fiber and made a single basket and brought it to the cave, thinking that the father would be pleased. But when Neilos saw it, he said, "Come here, brother Stephen, and let us fulfill a commandment; since you made this without permission and consent, let us throw it into the fire and burn it, as the great Basil says." With these words Neilos stood up, kindled a fire, and threw the basket into it. Seeing that Stephen took the matter hard and not with gratitude but with grumbling, Neilos allowed the basket to burn up completely, and liberated him from his attachment.

One day the elder who had taught Stephen basket 2

σπυρίδια, ζητῶν αὐτὸν παρὰ τοῦ πατρός, ἵνα πορευθῇ μετ᾿ αὐτοῦ πρὸς τὴν τοῦ χόρτου συλλογήν. Ὁ δὲ κελευσθεὶς ἀπῆλθεν. Ἔχων οὖν ὁ γέρων μεθ᾿ ἑαυτοῦ τὸ Ψαλτήριον αὐτοῦ, ὅπου δήποτε τέθηκεν αὐτὸ καὶ ληθαργηθὲν ἀπώλετο. Ἐλθὼν οὖν ὁ γέρων πρὸς τὸν ὅσιον, ἤρξατο θλίβεσθαι περὶ τοῦ Ψαλτηρίου αὐτοῦ. Ὁ δὲ πατὴρ ἰδὼν αὐτὸν σφόδρα λυπούμενον, εὐσπλαγχνίσθη ἐπ᾿ αὐτῷ καὶ ἤρξατο ἐπιτιμᾶν τῷ μακαρίῳ Στεφάνῳ, καὶ λέγειν· "Ὄντως σύ, ἀναίσθητε καὶ ἀνόητε, διατί οὐκ ἀνεζήτησας τὸ Ψαλτήριον; Σὸν τὸ πταῖσμά ἐστιν. Δίκαιον οὖν ἐστιν ἵν᾿ ἐπάρῃ ὁ γέρων τὸ σὸν Ψαλτήριον," καὶ ἐπάρας δέδωκε τῷ γέροντι, καὶ ἀπῆλθεν ἀγαλλιώμενος.

32

Ἄλλοτε πάλιν ἀπέστειλεν αὐτὸν ὁ πατὴρ εἰς τὸ Ῥυσιάνον ἀγοράσαι μεμβράνας· καὶ δὴ πορευθεὶς ὑπέστρεψε μετὰ καὶ ἄλλου τινὸς γέροντος τῶν μεγάλων τοῦ κάστρου καὶ εὐγενῶν ἀνθρώπων, Γεωργίου ὀνόματι. Ὅστις ἐρωτηθεὶς ὑπὸ τοῦ ἁγίου πατρὸς τό, τί ἂν ἐθέλῃ, ἀπεκρίθη, ὅτι, φησίν· "Καθημένῳ μοι μιᾷ τῶν ἡμερῶν ἐν τῷ οἴκῳ μου καὶ διαλογιζομένῳ τὴν τοῦ βίου ματαιότητα καὶ τὰς ἁμαρτίας μου, ἐπῆλθέ μοι καὶ ὁ φόβος τοῦ θανάτου καὶ ἡ ἀπολογία τῆς Κρίσεως. Ταῦτα οὖν διαλογιζόμενος, μικρὸν ἀπενύσταξα· καὶ ὁρῶ ἐμαυτὸν εἰσερχόμενον διὰ τῆς μεγάλης πύλης τῆς πόλεως, ἐν ᾗ τῶν ἁγίων ἀποστόλων καθίδρυται

weaving came and asked the father that Stephen might accompany him to gather wild grasses. Stephen was commanded to go with him. Now the elder had his Psalter with him, but he had put it down some place, forgotten where it was, and lost it. So the elder came to the blessed Neilos distressed over the Psalter. The father, seeing him grieving, was struck with pity and began to upbraid the blessed Stephen, saying, "Truly you are insensible and absent-minded. Why didn't you search for the Psalter? It is your fault. It is right that the elder take your Psalter." So Neilos took it and gave it to the elder who went away rejoicing.

Chapter 32

Another time the father sent Stephen to Rossano to buy parchment, and after making the journey, he returned with an old man named George who was from one of the city's great and noble families. This man was asked by the holy father what he wanted, and he responded, "One day while sitting at home and contemplating the vanity of life and my sins, the fear of death and the reckoning of Judgment Day came upon me. Then after contemplating this, I fell asleep for a little while, and I saw myself entering through the great gate of the city near which stands the house of the holy

οἰκητήριον. Ἔνθα ἀκούσας ἐνθέου μελῳδίας ἀπήχημα, οἵας οὐδέποτε ἤκουσα, ὥρμησα ἐκεῖ τοῦ ἰδεῖν τίνες οἱ ψάλλοντες. Καὶ λοιπὸν θεωρῶ ἅπαν τὸ βῆμα μεστὸν εὐειδῶν εὐνούχων καὶ λευχειμόνων, οἷα ἀγγέλων, καὶ σὺν αὐτοῖς ἱστάμενον σέ, τὸν νῦν μοι ὁρώμενον, ἐν δὲ τῷ τοῦ ἐπισκόπου θρόνῳ καθήμενον πάνυ εὔμορφον νεώτερον καὶ ὑπέρλαμπρον, οὗ τὸ κάλλος ἀμήχανον διηγήσασθαι.

2   "Ἐν τῷ οὖν εἰσελθεῖν με ἐν τῷ ναῷ καὶ θεωρεῖν τὰ πανθαύμαστα κάλλη ἐκεῖνα καὶ ἀκούειν τὴν εὔηχον μελῳδίαν, ὁρῶ δύο τῶν λευκοφόρων ἐλθόντας πρός με, νεύσαντος τοῦ ἐπὶ θρόνου, καὶ λέγοντάς μοι· Δεῦρο, καλεῖ σε ὁ Δεσπότης.' Ἐγὼ δὲ σὺν φόβῳ πολλῷ πορευθεὶς καὶ σταθεὶς ἔμπροσθεν αὐτοῦ, ἤκουσα αὐτὸν λέγοντά σοι· Ἀπελθὼν κούρευσον αὐτόν.' Σὺ δὲ προσελθὼν ἐκούρευσας καὶ ἐποίησάς με μοναχόν. Εὐθέως οὖν ἐξυπνισθείς, ἠρξάμην διστάζειν τῷ λογισμῷ καὶ λέγειν, ὅτι· Ὄντως φάντασμά ἐστι τὸ φανέν μοι, καὶ οὐ θεόπεμπτον·' ἐγὼ γὰρ οὐδέποτε ἐνεθυμήθην τοῦ γενέσθαι μοναχός.

3   "Ὅμως ἐστοίχησα ἐν ἐμαυτῷ τοῦτο, ἵνα, εἰ κατὰ τὴν ἡμέραν ἐκείνην ἔλθοι ἀδελφὸς τῶν μοναστηρίων ἐν τῷ οἴκῳ μου, ἀληθῶς βούλημα Θεοῦ εἶναι τὸ μονάσαι με, εἰ δὲ μὴ τοῦτο γένηται, ὡς οὐ θεϊκῷ ὄντι τῷ φανέντι ὀνείρῳ ἀπροσεξῆσαί με. Ἀπὸ πολλῆς οὖν ἀδολεσχίας ἐξελθὼν ἐπὶ τὰ προαύλια, θεωρῶ ἱστάμενον τὸν ἀδελφὸν Στέφανον· καὶ μαθὼν παρ' αὐτοῦ τὴν αἰτίαν τῆς ἐλεύσεως, σπουδαίως ἅπαντα διευθέτησα καὶ πρὸς τὴν σὴν ἁγιωσύνην ἐλήλυθα. Νῦν οὖν, ὡς δοκεῖ τῷ Θεῷ καὶ σοὶ τῷ ἁγίῳ πατρί, ἐπ' ἐμοὶ ποίησον."

apostles. There hearing the faint echo of a divine melody, such as I had never heard, I rushed to see who was chanting. And upon entering I saw the entire sanctuary filled with handsome eunuchs, dressed in white like angels, and you—whom I see at present—were standing with them. Sitting on the bishop's throne was a very comely young man, utterly resplendent, whose beauty was indescribable.

"As I was entering the church to see those beautiful marvels and to hear the melodious song, I saw two of the white-robed eunuchs coming toward me, at a nod from the man on the throne, and saying, 'Come, the Master is calling you.' With great fear I went and stood before him, and I heard him say to you, 'Go and tonsure him.' Then you came forward, tonsured me, and so made me a monk. Thereupon I immediately awoke from sleep and began to consider its meaning and to say, 'It clearly was a figment of my imagination that appeared to me, and not something sent by God,' for I had never even considered becoming a monk. 2

"I made the following decision, however, that if that very day a brother from the monasteries were to come to my house, truly it would be God's will that I become a monk. If this were not to happen, I would disregard the dream I had seen, since it was not sent by God. So after much consideration I went into the forecourt and saw brother Stephen standing there; after learning from him the reason for his visit, I quickly set all my affairs in order, and now I have come to your holiness. Now do with me as is pleasing to God and to you, holy father." 3

33

Τούτων τοίνυν τῶν λόγων ἀκούσας ὁ θεοφόρος πατήρ, λέγει πρὸς αὐτόν· "Ἡμεῖς, ὦ τιμιώτατε ἀδελφέ, οὐ διὰ τὸν Θεόν, ἢ ἕνεκεν ἀρετῆς καθήμεθα ἐν τῇ ἐρημίᾳ ταύτῃ, ἀλλὰ διὰ τὸ μὴ δύνασθαι ὑπενεγκεῖν τοῦ κοινοβιακοῦ κανόνος τὸ ἄχθος κεχωρίκαμεν ἑαυτοὺς ἀπὸ τῶν ἀνθρώπων, ὥσπερ τινὲς λεπροὶ καὶ ἀκάθαρτοι. Σὺ οὖν καλῶς ποιεῖς φροντίζων τῆς σωτηρίας τῆς σῆς ψυχῆς. Πορεύου τοίνυν εἰς τὰ κοινόβια, ἔνθα ἀναπαήσῃ ψυχῇ καὶ σώματι."

2   Ὁ δέ, ὥσπερ ἀδάμας ἀπείραστος μένει τῇ τοῦ σιδήρου προσβολῇ, οὕτω διέκειτο πρὸς τοὺς ἐν πειρασίᾳ λόγους τοῦ πατρός. Τῆς δὲ Κυριακῆς ἡμέρας καταλαβούσης, ἐν ᾗ τὰ κοινόβια μικρᾶς τινος παρακλήσεως σωματικῆς μεταλαγχάνουσι, λαμβάνει αὐτὸν ὁ πατὴρ εἰς τὸ τοῦ Καστελλάνου λεγόμενον μοναστήριον, ἔνθα τροφῆς δαψιλοῦς ἐμφορηθέντες καὶ μεταλήψεως οἴνου μετρίως τυχόντες, μετὰ τὸ ἀναστῆναι τῆς τραπέζης λέγει ὁ πατὴρ πρὸς τὸν γέροντα· "Κύρι Γεώργιε, μεῖνον ὧδε μικρόν, ἕως οὗ, ἀπελθὼν εἰς ἐπίσκεψιν ἑτέρων ἀδελφῶν, ὑποστρέψω." Τοῦτο δὲ εἶπεν, θέλων αὐτὸν ἐκεῖ τοῦ λοιποῦ καταλεῖψαι. Ὅπερ νοήσας ὁ γέρων, εὐθέως ἀπεκρίθη· "Οὐκ ἔστι δίκαιον, τίμιε πάτερ, ἀλλ᾽ ὅπου ὁ δεσπότης ἀπέλθοι, ἐκεῖ καὶ ὁ κύων ἀκολουθήσει." Ἀγασθεὶς οὖν ὁ πατὴρ ἐπὶ τῷ παραδείγματι αὐτοῦ, παρέλαβεν αὐτὸν μεθ᾽ ἑαυτοῦ καὶ ὑπέστρεψαν ὁμοθυμαδόν.

Chapter 33

When the divinely inspired father heard his words, he said to George, "O most honorable brother, we are not living here in the wilderness because of God or for the sake of virtue, but because we cannot bear the burden of the monastery's cenobitic rule. So, just like lepers and unclean people, we have removed ourselves from humankind. You do well to consider the salvation of your soul, so go to the monastery and there repose your soul and body."

Just like a diamond that remains unscathed when scratched by iron, George resisted Neilos's attempts to persuade him. On Sunday, the day on which cenobitic monasteries allow some small bodily comforts, the father took George to the monastery of Kastellanos and there they filled themselves with plentiful food and drank a moderate amount of wine. After they got up from the table, the father said to the old man, "Sir George, remain here awhile, since I am going to visit some other brothers and shall return." He said this, wishing to leave him behind there. The old man, realizing this, immediately replied, "This is not right, venerable father. Rather, wherever the master goes, there also follows the dog." The father was pleased by his comparison, and taking him along, they returned to the cave with one accord.

34

Λέγει οὖν αὐτῷ ὁ Γεώργιος κατὰ τὴν ὁδόν· "Οἴῃ με, τίμιε πάτερ, ἀπορεῖν ἐν τῷ οἴκῳ μου τρυφῆς καὶ παντοίας χλιδῆς καὶ δελεασθῆναί με νομίζεις ὡς βρέφος ὑπὸ δαψιλείας τροφῆς; Πέπεισο ὅτι οὐ θροήσεις με οὔτε ὑπὸ ἐγκρατείας, οὔτε ὑπὸ ἄλλης οἱασδήποτε κακουχίας. Ἐγὼ γάρ, πολλὰ πλεύσας καὶ πολλὰς χώρας γυρεύσας, πολλῶν καλῶν καὶ κακῶν ἐπειράσθην. Καὶ δύναται ὁ Θεὸς διὰ τῶν ἁγίων εὐχῶν σου ἐνδυναμῶσαί με τοῦ ὑποστῆναι, ὥσπερ ἐκεῖνα διὰ τὴν δόξαν τοῦ κόσμου, οὕτω καὶ ταῦτα διὰ τὴν αὐτοῦ ἀγάπην. Μὴ οὖν ἄλλο τί ποτε ὑπολάβῃς· ὁ γὰρ Θεὸς πρὸς σέ με ἀπέστειλεν, καὶ ἀδύνατόν ἐστι σοῦ χωρισθῆναί με."

2   Ταῦτα ἀκούσας ὁ μέγας, ἐκύρωσεν εἰς αὐτὸν ἀγάπην καὶ τοῦ λοιποῦ ἔσχεν αὐτὸν ὡς πατέρα· αὐτὸς δὲ πάλιν κατοχυρώσας ἑαυτὸν τῇ πρὸς τὸν ὅσιον πίστει καὶ ἐλπίσας δι' αὐτοῦ τυχεῖν οὐρανῶν βασιλείαν, ἠγάπησεν αὐτὸν ὡς αὐτὸν τὸν Θεόν· τοὺς δὲ λόγους, οὓς ἤκουεν ἐκ τοῦ στόματος αὐτοῦ νουθετοῦντος ἀφ' ἑαυτοῦ, ἢ καὶ ἑρμηνεύοντος τὰς Γραφάς, οὕτως ὑπεδέχετο καὶ ἡδύνετο ἐπ' αὐτοῖς, ὡς ἐν διαθέσει γίνεσθαι τοῦ εἰπόντος· "Ὡς γλυκέα τῷ λάρυγγί μου τὰ λόγιά Σου, ὑπὲρ μέλι τῷ στόματί μου." Διὸ καὶ ὑπέφερε τὴν ἄφατον ἄσκησιν ἐκείνην, μεταβληθεὶς ἀθρόον ἀπὸ τῆς ἔξω συνηθείας εἰς ταύτην, εἰς ἣν πολλοὶ δοκιμάσαντες εἰσελθεῖν καὶ καρτερῆσαι, ταχέως ἀπεπήδησαν καὶ ἀπέδρασαν.

Chapter 34

During their journey back George said to him, "Do you think, venerable father, that in my house I lack food and every sort of luxury, and you think to entice me like a babe with abundant food? Be assured that you will never scare me away either through abstinence or any other such mortification. For I have sailed a great deal, traveled the breadth of many lands, and experienced much good and evil. And through your holy prayers God can empower me to endure those privations for the sake of His love, just as I also endured those worldly travails for the glory of the material world. So you need not assume anything else; for God sent me to you and it is impossible for me to separate myself from you."

Upon hearing this, the great Neilos confirmed his love for George, and ever after considered him as a father. On the other hand, this George fortified himself with his faith in the holy man, and hoping through him to achieve the kingdom of heaven, he loved Neilos as he loved God Himself. George welcomed the words that he heard from the holy man's mouth, whether in the form of Neilos's own admonitions or in the form of his interpretation of Scripture, and found such great delight in them that his reaction was that of the psalmist who said, *"How sweet are Your words in my throat, more so than honey in my mouth."* For this reason, George also endured that unspeakably severe ascetic life, suddenly changing his routine from a layman's way of life to this ascetic one which many endeavor to undertake and master, but quickly turn away from and abandon.

3   Τὸ δὲ θαυμαστὸν ὅτι, μηδέποτε γράμματα μαθών, οὕτως ἔψαλλεν εἰς τὴν ὑμνῳδίαν ἔν τε ψαλμοῖς καὶ κανόσιν, ὥστε θαυμάζειν καὶ ἐκπλήττεσθαι πάντας τοὺς ἀκούοντας αὐτοῦ καὶ αὐτὸν τὸν ὅσιον πατέρα ἀναπαύεσθαι ἐπὶ τῇ εὐρύθμῳ καὶ εὐκατανύκτῳ ψαλμῳδίᾳ αὐτοῦ. Παρὰ τὰς ἀρχὰς μὲν οὖν, ὡς ἀπὸ συνηθείας, ἡνίκα μικρὸν ηὐκαίρει, ἐξηγεῖτο πρὸς τὸν τυχόντα, ἃ εἶδεν καὶ ἤκουσεν ἐν τῷ κόσμῳ. Εἶτα, ὡς παρὰ τοῦ πατρὸς ἐνεκόπτετο, λέγοντος πρὸς αὐτόν· "Οὐᾶ, κύρι, ποῖος συγγραφεύς, ὁ Λουκᾶς, ἐγένου, ἢ ὁ Ματθαῖος;", εὐθέως κρούων εἰς τὸ στόμα αὐτοῦ ἀνίστατο, καὶ ἀπερχόμενος κατὰ μόνας, τοσοῦτον ἑαυτοῦ τὰς παρειὰς ἐμάστιζεν, ὑβρίζων καὶ ἐπιτιμῶν ἑαυτῷ, ἕως οὗ ἀρκούντως ἐδάκρυε.

35

Γέγονε δὲ καὶ τοιοῦτόν τι ἐν τῷ κάστρῳ τῷ καλουμένῳ Βισινιάνῳ. Νεώτερός τις τῶν σφόδρα ἀκαταστάτων ὑπηντήθη Ἑβραίῳ ὑποστρέφοντι ἀπὸ πραγματείας καί, δελεασθεὶς ἐπὶ τοῖς ὑπ᾽ αὐτοῦ ἀποφερομένοις, μαχαίρᾳ τοῦτον συγκατακόψας, ἀπέκτεινε καί, ἄρας τὴν ὄνον αὐτοῦ σὺν τῷ γόμῳ, φυγῇ ἐχρήσατο. Κρατηθεὶς ὁ τούτου κηδεστὴς ὑπὸ τῶν τότε πραττόντων παραδίδοται τοῖς Ἰουδαίοις τοῦ σταυρωθῆναι ἀντὶ τοῦ σφαγέντος Ἑβραίου.

2   Καὶ τοῦτο μαθὼν ὁ σοφώτατος Νεῖλος παρὰ τῶν ἰδίων

It was a marvel that George, who never learned how to read, chanted both psalms and canons in such a way that all those who heard him marveled and were astonished, and even the holy father himself used to be spiritually refreshed from hearing his well-intoned chanting full of compunction. At the beginning of his ascetic life, when he had a little free time, George would talk to all and sundry about what he had seen and heard in the world, as he had previously been accustomed to do, but the father would then interrupt him, saying, "What is this, sir? What sort of author are you? Luke or Matthew?" George would immediately strike his mouth, stand up, and go off by himself, scourging his cheeks, abusing and reproaching himself until he wept profusely.

Chapter 35

The following incident took place at the fortified city called Bisignano. A particularly rowdy youth encountered a Jew who was returning from his business. Enticed by the merchandise he was carrying, the youth struck him with a knife and killed him. Then he took the Jew's donkey together with its load and fled. The authorities of that time apprehended the youth's father-in-law and *delivered him* to the Jews *to be crucified* in exchange for the slain Jew.

Upon learning this from the relatives of the condemned

τοῦ κατακεκριμένου, γράφει πρὸς τοὺς ἀδίκους κριτὰς ταῦτα· "Ἔδει μὲν ὑμᾶς, τὸν νόμον ἐπισταμένους, κατὰ τὸν νόμον ἀποφαίνεσθαι καὶ τὰς κρίσεις, τὸν κελεύοντα ἀπόλλυσθαι ἕνα Χριστιανὸν ἀντὶ ἑπτὰ Ἰουδαίων. Ἢ τοίνυν δότωσαν ἐξ αὐτῶν οἱ Ἑβραῖοι ἑτέρους ἓξ τοῦ ἀποκτανθῆναι ὑπὲρ τοῦ μέλλοντος σταυρωθῆναι, ἤ, εἴγε ὅλως ἔδοξεν ὑμῖν παρακρίνειν τὰ καλῶς νομοθετημένα, ὅνπερ αὐτόθι μετὰ τῶν γραμμάτων ἐξαποστέλλω (εὐγενής ἐστι τῶν πρώτων τοῦ Ῥυσιάνου), δοθήτω τοῖς Ἰουδαίοις τοῦ σταυρωθῆναι καὶ ὁ πτωχὸς ἐλευθερωθήτω, ἵνα σὺν αὐτῷ καὶ γυνὴ καὶ τέκνα ἐλεηθῶσιν." Καλέσας οὖν τὸν ἀββᾶν Γεώργιον ὁ ὅσιος καὶ μηδὲν αὐτῷ εἰρηκὼς ὥνπερ ἔγραψεν, δίδωσιν αὐτῷ τὴν ἐπιστολὴν καὶ ἀποστέλλει εἰς τὸ Βισινιάνον.

3   Δεξάμενοι δὲ οἱ κριταὶ καὶ ἀναγνόντες τὰ γεγραμμένα, λέγουσι πρὸς τὸν γέροντα· "Ὧδε, καλόγηρε, ὁ πατὴρ ἔγραψεν ἵνα σε δῶμεν τοῖς Ἰουδαίοις τοῦ σταυρωθῆναι· ἀρέσκει σοι;" Λέγει αὐτοῖς ἐκεῖνος· "Ἕτοιμός εἰμι εἰς πᾶν ὃ ἔγραψεν ὁ κύριός μου πληρῶσαι. Εἰ δὲ καὶ τὸν σταυρὸν οὐκ ἔστι τίς ὁ κατασκευάζων, ἐγὼ καλῶς οἶδα αὐτὸν πελεκῆσαι." Οἱ δέ, αἰδεσθέντες τὴν τοῦ γέροντος προθυμίαν καὶ τὴν τοῦ ἀποστείλαντος μεγαλοφυΐαν, καὶ τὸν πτωχὸν ἠλευθέρωσαν καὶ τὸν γέροντα μετὰ τιμῆς μεγίστης ἀπέλυσαν.

man, the most wise Neilos wrote as follows to the unjust judges: "Since you know the law that prescribes that one Christian must be executed for the killing of seven Jews, you ought to apply it in your verdict. Therefore, let the Jews surrender another six men from among them to be killed in exchange for the one Christian who is going to be crucified. Or, if you have decided to issue a verdict in defiance of what is well established in law, surrender to the Jews for crucifixion the man I am sending there with my letters, a nobleman from among the first citizens of Rossano. In return, let the poor man be freed, so that mercy may be shown to his wife and children as well as to him." Then the holy Neilos summoned brother George, gave him the letter without telling him what was written in it, and sent him to Bisignano.

When the judges received Neilos's letter and read it, they 3 said to the elder, "Look here, monk. The father wrote that we should hand you over to the Jews to be crucified. What do you say to this?" George said to them, "I am prepared to fulfill all that my lord Neilos has written. And if there is no one to prepare the cross, I know well how to fashion one." Abashed by the elder's eagerness and the cleverness of the one who sent him, they let the poor man go free, and released the elder with great honor.

36

Ἔτι δὲ καὶ ἔτι κατὰ καιρὸν ἐπερχομένων τῶν ἀθέων Σαρακηνῶν τοῖς τόποις ἐκείνοις, καὶ μὴ δυναμένων καθίσαι ἐν τῷ σπηλαίῳ τῶν ὁσίων πατέρων (ἐκεῖθεν γὰρ ἦν ἡ δίοδος τοῦ φουσσάτου), ἔδοξε τῷ μεγάλῳ καταλιπεῖν τὰ ἐκεῖσε· καὶ καταλαβὼν τὰ περίχωρα τῆς πατρίδος, ἔμεινεν ἐν τόπῳ οἰκείῳ, ἐν ᾧ τοῦ Ἁγίου Ἀδριανοῦ μικρὸν εὐκτήριον ἵδρυτο, νομίσας μηδέποτε ἐκεῖ εἰσελεύσεσθαι ἔθνος διὰ τὸ δύσβατον καὶ παρόδιον εἶναι τὸν τόπον.

2   Τούτου δὲ γενομένου, ἤρξαντό τινες τῶν πτωχῶν τῷ πνεύματι, οὓς καὶ εἰς τὸ οἰκεῖον δεῖπνον ἐκάλει ὁ Κύριος, προσέρχεσθαι τῷ πατρὶ καὶ τὴν συνοίκησιν δέεσθαι. Ὁ δὲ σπλαγχνιζόμενος ἐπ᾽ αὐτοῖς, ἐδέχετο τούτους καὶ ψυχῶν καὶ σωμάτων αὐτῶν τὴν σωτηρίαν ἐπραγματεύετο. Κατὰ μικρὸν δὲ προϊόντος τοῦ χρόνου συνήχθησαν μέχρι τῶν δώδεκα ἀδελφῶν, ἢ καὶ πλέον, καὶ μοναστήριον, Θεοῦ συνεργοῦντος, ὁ τόπος ἐγένετο, πλείστων μὲν ἀποδιδρασκόντων τὸ δραστικὸν τοῦ κανόνος καὶ τὸ σκληρὸν τῆς διαίτης, ὅσοι *τὴν πλατεῖαν ὁδὸν τῆς στενῆς* προετίμων, τῶν δέ γε φιλοθέων ἐγκαρτερούντων καὶ πάντα ὑποφερόντων *διὰ τὴν τῶν οὐρανῶν βασιλείαν.*

Chapter 36

From time to time there were still raids by the godless Saracens against those places, and the holy fathers could not remain in the cave—for the route of the armies was nearby—so Neilos decided to leave. After reaching the outskirts of the land of his birth, he took up residence in a place of his own in which was built a small chapel in honor of Saint Adrianos, being confident that the Saracens would not enter there, as the place was remote and difficult to access.

When this happened, some of those who were poor in spirit, whom the Lord had invited to His supper, began to approach the father and begged to be allowed to stay. Neilos, feeling pity for them, welcomed them and provided for the salvation of both their souls and their bodies. Gradually, as time passed, around twelve or more brethren assembled there, and, with God's assistance, the place became a monastery. Although most of the brethren, those who preferred *the wide way to the narrow one,* fled the austerity of the monastic rule and the harsh regimen, those who loved God persevered and endured all *for the sake of the kingdom of heaven.*

37

Ἦσαν οὖν δύο ἀδελφοὶ ὁμαίμονες πλησίον ἐκεῖ καθήμενοι, οἵτινες ὑπὸ τοῦ Πονηροῦ πειραζόμενοι καὶ τῷ φθόνῳ βαλλόμενοι, ἤρξαντο καταλαλεῖν τοῦ δικαίου καὶ ἐν παντὶ αὐτὸν διασύρειν, πλάνον λέγοντες εἶναι καὶ μάγον, ὑποκριτήν τε καὶ ψεύστην καὶ εἴ τι ἄλλο ἔτικτεν ἡ κακία.

2   Ταῦτα δὲ ὁ μακάριος ἀκούσας, ἠγωνίζετο παντοίῳ τρόπῳ τὸν φθόνον αὐτῶν κατασβέσαι καὶ ἀποθεραπεῦσαι αὐτῶν τὰς καρδίας, ὃ καὶ πεποίηκε μετ᾿ ὀλίγον. Ἐκείνων γὰρ διαβαλλόντων καὶ σφόδρα κακολογούντων, οὗτος τὸ ἐναντίον οὐκ ἐπαύετο εὐφημῶν καὶ ἐπαίνους πολλοὺς δι᾿ αὐτῶν ἀναγγέλλων εἰς πάντας ὡς ἐπὶ ἁγίων. Ἡνίκα δὲ πάλιν ἐκεῖνοι μικρᾶς τινος ἀφορμῆς ἐπελαμβάνοντο, ἢ κτήνους διαβάντος τὸ κλεῖσμα, ἢ φρυγάνου παραρρυέντος ὑπὸ ἀνέμου, ἐξερχόμενοι ἄντικρυς τοῦ δικαίου μυρίας λοιδορίας ἐλάλουν, ἀναισχύντως λοιπὸν μαχόμενοι καὶ ὑβρίζοντες. Ὁ δὲ πατὴρ παραγγείλας τοῖς ἀδελφοῖς μηδένα μηδὲν αὐτοῖς ἀνταποκριθῆναι, αἴρων ἐν τῷ στόματι αὐτοῦ τὸν Δαβὶδ ὑπεχώρει .

3   Κἀκεῖνοι αὐτὸν θεωροῦντες, κραυγάζοντες ἔλεγον· "Βλέπεις τὸν ὑποκριτήν; Ἑαυτὸν ποιεῖ ἅγιον καὶ ἡμᾶς δαίμονας. Οὐ καλῶς ἐλέγομεν, ὅτι ὁ Διάβολός σε ἐνταῦθα ἤγαγεν, ἵνα καθ᾿ ἡμέραν μαχόμεθα;" Ὁ δὲ ἀκούων οὐκ ἀπεκρίνετο· ἀλλὰ τῆς ἑσπέρας καταλαβούσης, εἴτε τῇ ἐπαύριον ἡμέρᾳ, ἡνίκα ἐθεώρει ὅτι εἰσῆλθον τοῦ γεύσασθαι,

Chapter 37

Dwelling nearby were two brothers by blood who, tempted by the Evil One and driven by envy, began to slander the righteous Neilos and disparage him in every way, calling him a deceiver, a wizard, a hypocrite, and a liar, and whatever else their wickedness prompted them to say.

Upon hearing this, the blessed Neilos strove in every way 2 possible to appease their envy and heal their hearts, and was soon successful. For although they kept slandering and violently abusing him, he never stopped speaking well of them or greatly praising them to all, as if they were saints. Whenever they found some small pretext, however, either that the monks' cattle had crossed into their land, or that dry sticks were blown into their property by the wind, they would come out openly against the righteous one, hurling countless insults, and then shamelessly challenging and abusing him. The father, however, warning his brethren to make no response, would withdraw, keeping the words of David on his lips.

When the two brothers saw him, they would cry out, "Do 3 you see the hypocrite? He makes himself holy and demonizes us. Weren't we right to say that the Devil brought you here so that we would quarrel every day?" Neilos, however, would listen without responding to them, but that evening or the following day, when he saw that they had gone in to

ἀπερχόμενος πρὸς αὐτοὺς ἐποίει αὐτοῖς μετάνοιαν, αἰτούμενος τὴν συγχώρησιν. Εἶτα συνεστιώμενος αὐτοῖς καὶ συναγαλλόμενος, τῇ καλῇ συνέσει αὐτοῦ ἐθεράπευε τὰς καρδίας αὐτῶν καὶ ὑπέστρεφε μετὰ χαρᾶς εἰς τὸ κελλίον αὐτοῦ. Μετὰ δὲ χρόνον ἱκανόν, τελευτῶν ὁ μειζότερος ἀδελφός, ἐν ταῖς χερσὶ τοῦ ἁγίου πατρὸς κατέλιπεν εἴ τι ἂν ἐκέκτητο καὶ τὸν ἀδελφὸν αὐτοῦ· καὶ αὐτὸς αὐτὰ οἰκονόμησε κατὰ τὸ τοῦ Θεοῦ βούλημα.

38

Μιᾷ δὲ τῶν ἡμερῶν ἐλήλυθεν ὁ υἱὸς τοῦ ἀββᾶ Γεωργίου ἐν τῷ μοναστηρίῳ, φέρων μεθ᾽ ἑαυτοῦ βοΐδια τρία πάνυ εὐειδῆ καὶ μεγάλα. Καλέσας οὖν ὁ μέγας τὸν γέροντα, λέγει αὐτῷ· "Τί ἤνεγκας ὧδε τὰ βοΐδια ταῦτα;" Ὁ δὲ δήσας τὰς χεῖρας ὡς ἐπὶ ἀρχόντων, ἀπεκρίνατο μετὰ φόβου· "Τιμιώτατε πάτερ, ἐπειδὴ κοπιῶσιν οἱ ἀδελφοὶ ἵν᾽ ἐργάσονται τὸν ἐπιούσιον ἄρτον, καλόν ἐστιν, εἰ κελεύεις, ἵν᾽ ἔχωσι ταῦτα βραχύ τι παραμύθιον."

2 Λέγει οὖν πρὸς αὐτὸν ὁ πατήρ· "Οὐ χρείαν ἔχουσι τούτων οἱ ἀδελφοί, μᾶλλον δὲ συμφέρει αὐτοῖς, ἵνα κοπιῶσιν. Ἀλλ᾽ ἀπελθὼν σφάξον καὶ διάδος αὐτὰ τοῖς πτωχοῖς." Εὐθέως δὲ ὁ γέρων ἀκούσας καὶ μηδὲ πρὸς ὥραν μελλήσας, ἀνεκομβώσατο τὰς χεῖρας καί, τῆς μαχαίρης δραξάμενος, ὥρμησε τοῦ τελέσαι τὸ κελευόμενον. Καὶ

eat, he would approach them, make obeisance, and request their forgiveness. Then he would share their meal and celebrate with them, and so with his subtle understanding Neilos would heal their hearts and joyfully return to his cell. A long time afterward, as the elder brother was dying, he left all his possessions in the hands of the holy father as well as the care of his younger brother, and the holy man took care of them in accordance with God's will.

Chapter 38

One day father George's son came to the monastery, driving three fine-looking and large oxen. The great Neilos called the elder and said to him, "Why did you bring us these oxen?" George, clasping his hands, as if he were in the presence of the authorities, fearfully answered him, "O most honored father, since the brethren are struggling to procure their daily bread, it would be nice if you permitted them to have these oxen as some small assistance."

But the father said to him, "The brethren have no need of 2 these oxen. Rather it is better for them to exert themselves. So go now to slaughter them, and *distribute* them *to the poor.*" As soon as the elder heard this, without any delay he girded himself for action, and taking a knife set off to fulfill the command. He would have done so, had the holy one not

ἐπλήρωσεν ἂν αὐτό, εἰ μὴ ταχέως φωνήσας ὁ ὅσιος τὴν χεῖρα ἐκώλυσεν. Τότε γνοὺς ὁ πατὴρ τὸ Ἀβραμιαῖον τῆς αὐτοῦ ψυχῆς, "Μὴ φονεύσῃς αὐτά," ἔφη, "ἐπειδὴ ὀλίγον ὄφελος γίνεται, ἀλλὰ τὰ μὲν δύο δώσωμεν ἐπὶ τὰ ἐνδεῆ μοναστήρια καὶ πληθυντικώτερα, τὸ δὲ ἕτερον μίξαντες μετὰ τῶν γειτόνων ἡμῶν, τὴν χρείαν ἡμῶν ἐργασώμεθα· ὅτι πᾶν τὸ ὑπὲρ τὴν χρείαν πλεονεξία λογίζεται." Ποιήσαντες οὖν ὡς ὁ πατὴρ διετάξατο, ἐποίησαν τῷ ἐνιαυτῷ ἐκείνῳ σῖτον πολὺν καὶ πάντες ἐδόξαζον τὸν Θεόν.

3   Ποτὲ δὲ τριῶν ἀδελφῶν ἐν τῷ μύλωνι ἀπελθόντων μετὰ καὶ τριῶν ζῴων πεφορτωμένων, μετὰ τὸ ἀλέσαι τῇ ἐπαύ-ριον ὑποστρεφόντων καὶ ἤδη τῇ μονῇ ἐγγιζόντων, ὁρῶσιν ἐν τῇ ὁδῷ πυρὰν καιομένην καὶ λέγουσιν· "Ἄρτι ἐν τῷ μοναστηρίῳ νηστεύουσιν· ποιήσωμεν ὧδε ἄρτον καὶ φά-γωμεν, μήποτε νήστεις ἀπελθόντες καὶ ἡμεῖς μετ' αὐτῶν νηστεύσωμεν." Καὶ ἐποίησαν καθὼς ἐβουλεύσαντο. Γνοὺς δὲ ὁ πατὴρ τῷ πνεύματι τὰ περὶ αὐτούς, ἐκέλευσεν ἑτοι-μάσαι τῷ κελλαρίτῃ, "ἵνα," φησί, "τῶν ἀδελφῶν φθασάντων ἀπὸ τοῦ μύλου γευσόμεθα ἄρτου."

4   Εὐθέως τοίνυν ἐκείνων ἐλθόντων καὶ πάλιν μετὰ τοῦ πατρὸς καὶ τῶν ἀδελφῶν γευσαμένων, μετὰ τὸ τῆς τρα-πέζης ἐξαναστῆναι καλεῖ αὐτοὺς ὁ πατὴρ κατὰ μόνας, καὶ λέγει αὐτοῖς· "Διατί ὑπηκούσατε τῷ Διαβόλῳ συμβου-λεύσαντι ὑμῖν ποιῆσαι κατὰ τὴν ὁδὸν ἄρτον καὶ φαγεῖν; Μὴ μακρὰν τῆς μονῆς ἐτυγχάνετε, ἢ δοῦλοί μου ὑπάρχετε, ἵνα διὰ τὸν ἐμὸν φόβον λάθρα ἐσθίετε; Ὑμεῖς ἀδελφοί μού ἐστε καὶ ὁ ἄρτος ὑμέτερος κόπος ἐστὶν καὶ οὐδείς ἐστιν ὁ βιάζων ὑμᾶς παρὰ τὴν προαίρεσιν ὑμῶν. Τοῦτο τοίνυν

quickly spoken and stayed his hand. Then the father realized that George had a soul like that of Abraham and said, "Don't kill them, since that would be of little use. Rather let us give two to the monasteries that are in need and have more monks, and we will meet our needs by yoking the third with those of our neighbors. For anything that exceeds our needs is avarice." The monks did everything as the father ordered, and that year grew abundant grain, and they all gave glory to God.

One day three of the brethren went to the mill with three 3 pack animals loaded with grain. As they returned the next day after grinding the grain, just as they were drawing near to the monastery, they saw a fire burning in the road and said, "Right now they are fasting in the monastery, so let's make bread here and eat it, so that we don't leave here without a bite and have to fast with them." So they did just as they had planned. The father, knowing in his spirit what they were doing, ordered the cellarer to make preparations, "so that," he said, "as soon as the brethren arrive from the mill we may eat bread."

As soon as they arrived, they ate for a second time with 4 the father and the brethren. When they got up from the table, the father summoned them privately and said to them, "Why did you listen to the Devil who advised you to make bread on the road and to eat it? Were you that far from the monastery? Or are you my slaves that you eat in secret in fear of me? You are my brothers and the bread is the fruit of your toil, and no one is forcing you against your will. Now

γινώσκοντες, μηδέποτέ τι παρὰ κανόνα ποιήσητε." Οἱ δὲ ἀκούσαντες ἔβαλον μετάνοιαν, καὶ ἐπηγγείλαντο τοῦ λοιποῦ διορθώσασθαι.

39

Ἄλλοτε πάλιν, τοῦ μεγάλου πατρὸς ἐν τῇ μονῇ μὴ ὑπάρχοντος, ἐλήλυθέ τις παρθένος συντυχεῖν αὐτῷ βουλομένη, μὴ εἰδυῖα ὅτι προαιρεῖται μᾶλλον ἀσπίδι ἢ γυναικὶ ὁμιλῆσαι. Τῶν δὲ ἀδελφῶν εἰς τὰ κελλία ἡσυχαζόντων, ἰδοῦσα αὕτη τὴν ἐκκλησίαν μεμονωμένην, εἰσῆλθε καὶ ηὔξατο. Ἰδόντες δὲ αὐτὴν οἱ ἀδελφοὶ ἐξελθοῦσαν, ἐγόγγυσαν κατ᾽ αὐτῆς ὡς παρὰ συνήθειαν ποιησάσης. Ἡ δὲ μαθοῦσα ὅτι ὁ πατὴρ οὐκ ἔστιν ἐκεῖσε, εὐθέως ἀπῆλθε. Καταλαβὼν οὖν ὁ μέγας μετὰ τετάρτην ἡμέραν, καὶ τῶν ἀδελφῶν εἰς προσκύνησιν αὐτοῦ συνελθόντων, ἤρξατο αὐτοὺς ἐπιμέμφεσθαι καὶ λέγειν· "Τοιοῦτοι μοναχοί ἐστε ὑμεῖς, ὅτι μία γυνὴ ἐλθοῦσα κατεπάτησεν ὑμᾶς, καὶ συνώζεσε τὴν ἐκκλησίαν ὑμῶν; Ὄντως μεγάλου ἐπιτιμίου ἐστὲ ἄξιοι." Οἱ δὲ καταπλαγέντες ἐπὶ τῷ θαύματι, ἔβαλον μετάνοιαν καὶ συγχώρησιν ἐξαιτήσαντο.

2 Ὁ τοίνυν μακάριος ἀληθῶς Γεώργιος μεγάλως κατὰ Θεὸν πολιτευσάμενος καὶ εὐαρεστήσας αὐτῷ ἔν τε ἐγκρατείᾳ καὶ κακουχίᾳ καὶ ὑπακοῇ ἀδιακρίτῳ καὶ ταπεινώσει μεγίστῃ καὶ τῇ κοπῇ τοῦ οἰκείου θελήματος,

that you know this, do not do anything contrary to the rule."
Upon hearing this they prostrated themselves and promised
to mend their ways thereafter.

Chapter 39

Another time, when the great father Neilos was not at
the monastery, a virgin woman came there wishing to meet
with him, not knowing that he would have preferred to con-
verse with a viper rather than with a woman. As the brethren were engaged in spiritual contemplation in their cells,
she saw that the church was empty, went inside, and prayed.
When the brethren saw her coming out of the church, they
grumbled against her, as she had acted contrary to their custom. When she learned that the father was not there, she
immediately left. When the great Neilos returned four days
later and the brothers assembled to greet him, he began to
rebuke them, saying, "What sort of monks are you that a
woman came here, trampled upon you, and defiled your
church? Truly you deserve a severe penance." They were
amazed at his miraculous discernment, prostrated themselves, and begged his forgiveness.

At this time the truly blessed George, who had conducted   2
himself entirely in accordance with God and pleased the
Lord through his abstinence and mortification, complete
obedience, great humility, and in the restraint of his own

ὅπερ μαρτύριόν ἐστι καὶ λέγεται, πρὸς Κύριον ἀπεδήμησεν, ἀποληψόμενος τὰ δι' ἃ πάντα ὑπέμεινεν. Ἐπὶ τοῦτο μεγάλως τὸν Θεὸν εὐχαρίστησε, πληροφορηθεὶς ὅτι ἀληθῶς δόκιμον γεώργημα καὶ εὐπρόσδεκτον ἀναφαίρεμα τὸν πρῶτον καρπὸν αὐτοῦ τῷ Χριστῷ προσηγάγετο.

40

Αὐτὸς δέ, ἀνεξάλειπτα ἔχων ἐν τῇ ψυχῇ τὰ τοῦ ἁγίου Εὐαγγελίου ἐντάλματα καὶ τό, "Ὑμεῖς δὲ μὴ κληθῆτε ῥαββί, μηδὲ κληθῆτε καθηγηταί," οὐδέποτε κατεδέξατο ἀκοῦσαι οἱονδήποτε ὄνομα δόξης ὑπόληψιν ἔχον, ἀλλ' ἀεὶ τὸ φρόνημα πάντων κατώτερον ἔχων, ὡς ἕνα τῶν ἐσχάτων ἀδελφῶν ἑαυτὸν ἐλογίζετο. Διὸ καὶ τῶν τέκνων τῆς ἐρήμου πληθυνομένων καὶ καθ' ἡμέραν ὑπ' αὐτοῦ πνευματικῶς γεννωμένων καὶ εὐαγγελικῶς ποιμαινομένων, ἑτέρῳ τὸ τῆς ἡγουμενίας ὄνομα πάσας τὰς ἡμέρας τῆς ζωῆς αὐτοῦ ἐνεχείριζεν· ὧν εἷς ὑπῆρξε καὶ πρῶτος ὁ παμμακάριστος καὶ τρισόσιος Πρόκλος, ἀνὴρ τῆς ἐγκυκλίου παιδεύσεως σφόδρα πεπειραμένος, βιβλίων τε τῶν ἔξωθεν καὶ τῶν ἡμετέρων ἐνδιαθέτων τε καὶ τῶν ὕστερον ἐκτεθέντων κιβώτιον τὴν οἰκείαν καρδίαν ἀποτελέσας.

2   Ὅστις ἐλέγετο, πρὶν τοῦ μονάσαι νέος ἔτι ὢν ἐν τῷ κάστρῳ τυγχάνων, τοιαύτην ἐσχηκέναι τὴν ἐργασίαν· καθ' ἑκάστην νηστεύων ἕως ἑσπέρας καὶ τῇ ἀναγνώσει

will (which is and is said to be the mark of a martyr), departed to the Lord, to receive the reward for which he had endured everything. Neilos greatly thanked God for this, because he was assured that the first fruit he had offered to Christ was a truly worthy harvest and an acceptable offering.

Chapter 40

Neilos, keeping indelibly in his soul the precepts of the holy Gospel and the verse, "*You are not to be called rabbi, neither be called masters,*" never consented to be called by any name signifying glory, but always maintained a self-conception humbler than all the others, so that he considered himself as one of the least among his brethren. Therefore, although the children of the wilderness were increasing in number, and every day were given spiritual rebirth by him and shepherded in the manner of the Gospels, throughout his life Neilos entrusted to others the title of superior. One of them, in fact the first, was the most blessed and thrice-holy Proklos, a man with great experience of general education who had perfected his heart into a treasure chest of secular and religious books, both those previously composed and those composed more recently.

It is said of Proklos that while still young, before he took [2] monastic vows, he already maintained the following way of life in the city, fasting each day until evening, devoting

σχολάζων, ἀπεχόμενός τε τῶν ἐκκαιόντων καὶ ἡδυνόντων
βρωμάτων τε καὶ πομάτων, περιήρχετο ἀφ᾽ ἑσπέρας ἕως
ὄρθρου πάσας τὰς ἐκκλησίας τοῦ κάστρου, πληρῶν τὸ
Ψαλτήριον καὶ καθ᾽ ἑκάστην θύραν αὐτῶν ποιῶν μετα-
νοίας, ὅσας ἑαυτῷ τυπώσας ἐκεῖνος ἐγίνωσκεν. Οὐδεὶς
γὰρ τὴν ἐν κρυπτῷ αὐτοῦ ἐργασίαν ἠπίστατο.

3   Οὗτος, εἰσελθὼν εἰς τὸ μοναχικὸν στάδιον καὶ ὑπὸ τοῦ
ὁσίου πατρὸς ἡμῶν Νείλου τῆς ἐναρέτου πολιτείας τὴν
σφραγῖδα ἐνσημανθείς, τοσαύτῃ ἐγκρατείᾳ καὶ ἀσκήσει
ἑαυτὸν καθυπέβαλεν, ὥστε *νεκρῶσαι αὐτοῦ τὰ μέλη τὰ ἐπὶ
τῆς γῆς* καὶ ἀσθενείαις πικραῖς προσπαλαῖσαι μέχρι τῆς
ἐσχάτης ἀναπνοῆς. Ἀλλὰ τὰ μὲν ἐκείνου, ἱκανὰ ὄντα ἰδίαν
συγγραφὴν ὠφελείας μεστὴν ἐκτελέσαι, τῷ τὰ πάντα
ἐπισταμένῳ καὶ πᾶσιν ἀποδιδοῦντι *κατὰ τὸν ἴδιον κόπον*
Θεῷ ἀναθήσωμεν, ἡμεῖς δὲ ἐπὶ τὴν τοῦ μεγάλου πατρὸς
διήγησιν ἀνακάμψωμεν.

41

Ἐν τῷ καιρῷ ἐκείνῳ, σεισμοῦ μεγάλου καταλαβόντος
τὸ Ῥυσιάνον μετὰ πολλῶν νυχθημέρων ὀμβροκλυσίαν καὶ
τοῦ ἀνωτέρου μέρους ἐπαναστάντος σὺν οἴκοις καὶ
εὐκτηρίοις καὶ ἐπελθόντος τοῖς κατωτέροις, καλύψαντός
τε οἴκους καὶ ἐκκλησίας καὶ μὴ αἰδεσθέντος εἰ μὴ μόνον
τὴν καθολικὴν ἐκκλησίαν καὶ τὸ ὄνομα τῆς Ἁγίας Εἰρήνης,

himself to reading, and abstaining from hot or sweetened food or drink. From evening to dawn he would make the rounds of all the churches of the city, reciting the entire Psalter, and at each church door making as many prostrations as he prescribed for himself. For no one knew about his secret labors.

Once he had entered the monastic arena and was stamped 3 by our holy father Neilos with the seals of the virtuous life, he subjected himself to such abstinence and asceticism that *he mortified his earthly limbs* and struggled with bitter illnesses until his final breath. Although this man's deeds are sufficient for a separate and beneficial composition, let us dedicate them to God who knows all things and gives to all *in accordance with their toil,* and now return to the account of our great father.

Chapter 41

Around that time, after a torrential rain lasting many days and nights, a great earthquake struck Rossano. In the resulting landslide the upper part of the city along with the houses and chapels collapsed and fell on the lower part, covering houses and churches with rubble. Nothing was spared except for the cathedral and the church of Saint Irene. This

θαυμαστὸν ἦν καὶ φοβερὸν τὸ γεγονὸς τοῖς ὁρῶσιν, ἄλλα ἐξ ἄλλων φαινόμενα τὰ πάντα καὶ ἕτερα ἀνθ᾽ ἑτέρων. Τὸ δὲ παράδοξον, ὅτι ἐν τοιούτῳ κατακλυσμῷ φοβερῷ οὐδὲ μία ψυχὴ ἀνθρωπίνη ἢ κτήνους ἀπώλετο.

2   Ταῦτα τοίνυν πολλῶν ἐξηγουμένων τῷ μακαρίτῃ καὶ ἐπὶ τούτοις ἐκπληττομένου, ἔδοξεν αὐτῷ μετὰ ταῦτα εἰσελθεῖν καὶ ἱστορῆσαι τὰ γεγονότα. Ὁ δὲ τρόπος τῆς ἐλεύσεως αὐτοῦ ἦν τοιόσδε· εὑρὼν γὰρ κατὰ τὴν ὁδὸν δέρμα ἀλώπεκος ἐρριμμένον καὶ τοῦτο τῇ κεφαλῇ αὐτοῦ περιδήσας, τὸ δὲ περιβόλαιον ἐν τῇ ῥάβδῳ παρὰ τὸν ὦμον κρεμάσας, οὕτω διῆλθεν ἅπαν τὸ κάστρον ὑπ᾽ οὐδενὸς γνωριζόμενος. Οἱ δὲ παῖδες ἰδόντες αὐτὸν ἐν τοιούτῳ σχήματι διερχόμενον, ἠκολούθουν αὐτὸν λιθάζοντες καὶ λέγοντες, "Ἀΐ, σύ, Βούλγαρι καλόγηρε," καὶ ἕτεροι Φράγγον αὐτὸν ἀπεκάλουν καὶ ἄλλοι Ἀρμένιον. Αὐτὸς δὲ σιωπῶν περιβλεψάμενος πάντα, ὀψίας ἤδη οὔσης, ἀπέρχεται ἐν τῇ μεγάλῃ ἐκκλησίᾳ καί, ῥίψας ἀπὸ τῆς κεφαλῆς τὸ δέρμα, θείς τε τὸ εὐτελὲς περιβόλαιον ἐπὶ τῶν ὤμων, εἰσέρχεται μετὰ πόθου καὶ κατανυκτικῶν δακρύων προσκυνῆσαι τὴν ὑπέραγνον Θεοτόκον, τὴν αὐτοῦ παιδαγωγὸν καὶ προστάτιν. Ἰδὼν δὲ αὐτὸν ὁ προσμονάριος, ὃς ἐλέγετο Κανισκᾶς, διδάσκαλος αὐτοῦ χρηματίσας ποτέ, καὶ ἄλλοι τῶν ἱερέων τινές, καὶ ἐπιγνόντες ὅτι ὁ μέγας πατήρ ἐστιν, ἦλθον καὶ προσέπεσον τοῖς ποσὶν αὐτοῦ, ξενιζόμενοι ἐπὶ τῇ παραδόξῳ παρουσίᾳ αὐτοῦ.

event caused amazement and awe to those who witnessed it, as everything was displaced and changed in appearance. But the most miraculous thing was that in such a terrifying catastrophe not a single human or animal life was lost.

When many people described the event to the blessed 2 man, Neilos was amazed at the news, and decided to enter the city and observe what had happened. The manner of his arrival was as follows: on the road he found an abandoned fox's pelt and wrapped it around his head. He hung his cloak as well on a stick across his shoulder. Thus he traversed the whole city without anyone recognizing him. The children who saw him walking around in such a guise began to follow him, pelting him with stones and saying, "Hey Bulgar monk!" Others called him a Frank and yet others an Armenian. Neilos, keeping silent, observed everything, and since it was already evening he went into the cathedral. Removing the fox skin from his head and placing his worn cloak on his shoulders, he entered the church full of longing and with tears of contrition to venerate the immaculate Mother of God, his guide and protector. The custodian, who was called Kaniskas, saw him. The man had once been Neilos's teacher and along with some other priests recognized that he was the great father. They came to him and threw themselves at his feet, astonished by his extraordinary visit.

42

Αὐτὸς δέ, πᾶσι τὰ συμφέροντα προσειπὼν καὶ μεγάλως ὠφελήσας καὶ ἀπολύσας, παρέμεινεν ἐν τῇ ἐκκλησίᾳ μετὰ τοῦ αὐτοῦ διδασκάλου, συμβουλεύων αὐτῷ ἐκβῆναι ἀπὸ τοῦ κόσμου καὶ διασῶσαι τὴν ψυχὴν αὐτοῦ· ἦν γὰρ μηδέποτε γυναικὶ συνδεθείς, μηδὲ γαστριμαργίᾳ, ἢ λαιμαργίᾳ, ἢ βλακείᾳ καταδεδουλωμένος, τῇ δὲ φιλαργυρίᾳ τοσοῦτον ὑπῆρχεν ἐμπεπλεγμένος, ὅσον καὶ μυῖα τῇ ἀράχνῃ περιπαρεῖσα. Διὸ καὶ ὁ πατὴρ τὴν παραβολὴν ταύτην πρὸς αὐτὸν εἴρηκεν, ὅτι· "Οἱ μὲν τῇ τῆς γαστρὸς ἀναγκαζόμενοι χρείᾳ, εὐλόγως τοῖς ὑπηρεσίοις προσκαρτεροῦσι· σὺ δὲ ταύτης ἐκτὸς τυγχάνων, τί καὶ μάτην παρακάθησαι τοῖς ἐκκοπρουμένοις, καὶ τῆς ἐκείνων δυσωδίας μεταλαμβάνεις;"

2   Ἐπὶ τούτοις ἀπεκρίθη ἐκεῖνος· "Ὄντως, τίμιε πάτερ, πολλοί ἐσμεν οἱ μακαρίζοντές σου τὴν πολιτείαν καὶ πολλάκις ἐβουλευσάμεθα τοῦ ἐξελθεῖν πρὸς τὴν σὴν ἁγιωσύνην, ἀλλὰ διὰ τὸ μὴ δύνασθαι ἡμᾶς ἄνευ οἴνου βιῶσαι ἱλιγγιάσαμεν τοῦτο πρᾶξαι." Λέγει αὐτῷ ὁ μέγας· "Δεῦτε καὶ ποιήσατε ὑμῖν αὐτοῖς καινοὺς λάκκους συγκεκλεισμένους καὶ γεμίσαντες αὐτοὺς οἶνον, ἀντλήσατε ἀεννάως καὶ πίετε." Τοῦ δὲ πάλιν προφασιζομένου προφάσεις ἐν ἁμαρτίαις καὶ τῆς παραινέσεως μὴ ἀνεχομένου, ἔννυχον λίαν ἀναστὰς ὁ μέγας ἐξῆλθε καὶ ὑπεχώρησε τῶν ἐκεῖσε, εἰπὼν πρὸς τὸν φιλάργυρον ἐκεῖνον ἓν ῥῆμα, ὅτι· "Οἴμοι, διδάσκαλε, τότε μετανοήσεις, ὅταν οὐκ ὠφελήσεις."

Chapter 42

Neilos addressed them all with beneficial words, edified them, and then dismissed them. He then remained in the church with his teacher, advising him to abandon the material world and save his soul. For Kaniskas had never married a woman, nor was he enslaved by gluttony, greediness for food, or indolence, but he was ensnared by avarice like a fly entangled in a spider web. Therefore, the father spoke this parable to him: "Those who are constrained by the needs of their bowels with good reason spend their time in latrines. But why do you, who have no such need, sit without reason next to those who are defecating, and suffer their stench?"

Kaniskas responded to this, "Truly, honorable father, 2 there are many of us who bless your way of life, and we have often thought about joining your holiness, but because we cannot live without wine, we grew dizzy at the prospect of doing so." The great man said to him, "Come and make yourselves new basins that are tightly covered and, after filling them with wine, draw from them continually and drink." Kaniskas again *employed pretexts for sins* and did not heed his advice, so at night the great Neilos stood up, departed, and went away from there, with a single comment for that miser, "Alas, my teacher, you will repent when it will be of no avail to you."

3   Ὀλίγου τοίνυν καιροῦ διελθόντος καί, τοῦ ὁσίου πατρὸς
ἐν τῷ μοναστηρίῳ ποτὲ τοὺς ὀρθρινοὺς ὕμνους ἐπιτε-
λοῦντος, πόνος κατέσχεν αὐτὸν ἐξαίφνης ἀφόρητος, ὥστε
μὴ δυνηθέντα αὐτὸν τὴν λειτουργίαν ἀποτελέσαι, ἐξελθεῖν καὶ ῥίψαι ἑαυτὸν ἐν τῷ σκιμποδίῳ, καὶ οὕτως ὑπο-
φέρειν τὰς ἀλγηδόνας. Ἐπὶ τούτοις, ἰδοὺ ὁ ἀνεψιὸς ἐκείνου
τοῦ Κανισκᾶ δρομαίως εἰσῆλθεν, φέρων ἐπιστολὴν ἐξ αὐτοῦ πρὸς τὸν πατέρα τοιαύτην· "Δεῦρο, πάτερ ἅγιε,
παράλαβε τὸν πολὺν πλοῦτον, ὃν ἀκαίρως συνῆξα πρὸς
ἀπώλειαν τῆς ψυχῆς μου, μήπως ὁ Διάβολος αὐτὸν καθαρ-
πάξας ἄμοιρόν με ποιήσῃ τοῦ ἐξ αὐτοῦ κέρδους. Ἰδοὺ γὰρ
λοιπὸν ἀποθνήσκω, καί με τὸ ἐκεῖθεν εἰσδέχεται δικα-
στήριον."

43

Ταῦτα ἀναγνοὺς ὁ πατήρ, ἠβούλετο μὲν ἀπελθεῖν πρὸς
αὐτὸν τοῖς οἰκείοις σπλάγχνοις νικώμενος, τοῖς δὲ πόνοις
δεινῶς συνεχόμενος τοῦ βουλεύματος ἐνεκόπτετο. Λέγει
δὲ τῷ ἀποκομιστῇ τῶν γραμμάτων· "Οὐ χρείαν ἔχει ὁ
Χριστὸς τῶν τοῦ σοῦ θείου χρημάτων· αὐτὸς γὰρ εἴρηκεν·
'Ἀπόδοτε τὰ Καίσαρος Καίσαρι, καὶ τὰ τοῦ Θεοῦ τῷ Θεῷ.'
Σὺ δὲ ἄγε, πορεύου, ἴσως γὰρ ζῶντα αὐτὸν οὐκέτι θεάσῃ."
Ὁ δὲ ὑποστρέψας δρομαίως, εὗρεν αὐτὸν τεθνηκότα καὶ
πάντα τὰ αὐτοῦ ὑπὸ τοῦ δημοσίου διαρπασθέντα. Ὁ δὲ

And in fact not long after, while the holy father was in the $_3$ monastery performing the matins hymns, a sudden unbearable pain overwhelmed him, so that being unable to finish the liturgy he went out and threw himself on a couch so he could bear the pain. While this was happening, behold, the nephew of that Kaniskas came running up, carrying a letter from his uncle for the father, with the following message, "Come, holy father, take this great wealth which I inopportunely accumulated to the destruction of my soul, so that the Devil may not take it from me and thus leave me without profit from it. For, behold, I am dying and the tribunal in the other world awaits me."

Chapter 43

When the father read this, he was overcome by compassion, and wished to visit the man, but the terrible pain he was suffering prevented him from carrying out his wish. He said to the bearer of the letter, "Christ has no need of your uncle's riches, for He has said, '*Render to Caesar the things that are Caesar's, and to God the things that are God's.*' So be on your way; for perhaps you will not see him still among the living." The nephew returned home at a run and found his uncle dead, and all his possessions confiscated by the imperial

ὅσιος, εὐθέως τῇ τοῦ ἀποκρισιαρίου ἀναχωρήσει ὑπο-
χωρήσαντος καὶ τοῦ κατέχοντος πόνου, ἐν ἐκπλήξει καὶ
θαύματι κατέστη, ἐξιστάμενος ἐπὶ τῇ τοῦ Θεοῦ ἀφάτῳ
προνοίᾳ, ὅτι βουληθέντα αὐτὸν πρᾶξαί τι παρὰ τὸ αὐτοῦ
θέλημα, καὶ ἄκοντα διεκώλυσε.

2   Τῶν δὲ ἀδελφῶν ἐν τῷ ὄρει ἐργαζομένων καὶ κυλιόντων
τὰ κεκαυμένα δένδρα πρὸς τὸ ἀνοῖξαι καὶ ποιῆσαι χώραν
σιτοφόρον ἀντὶ ξυλοφόρου, εἶπεν τὸ Ἅγιον Πνεῦμα τῷ
οἰκείῳ θεράποντι· "Ἔξελθε ἐν τῷ ὄρει πρὸς τοὺς κο-
πιῶντας, ἐπειδὴ ὁ Ἐχθρὸς ἡμῶν Διάβολος περιέρχεται,
ζητῶν τίνα καταπίει." Παραχρῆμα δὲ ἀναστὰς ἐπορεύθη
καὶ πᾶσαν τὴν ἡμέραν ἐκείνην οὐκ ἐπαύσατο περιερχόμενος, τοὺς ἀδελφοὺς πάντας ἐπιφωνούμενός τε καὶ παρ-
αγγέλλων ἀεὶ προσεύχεσθαι καὶ τῷ ὀνόματι Ἰησοῦ Χριστοῦ ἀποδιώκειν τὸν Ἀντικείμενον.

3   Ἰδὼν οὖν ὁ Διάβολος τὴν τοῦ ἀρχηγοῦ ἀσφάλειαν καὶ
τὴν τῶν ὑπηκόων περίφραξιν, περὶ ὥραν δεκάτην ῥίψας
μέγιστον δένδρον καὶ ἕνα κύνα φονεύσας, ἀπῆλθε κατ-
ῃσχυμμένος. Τινῶν δὲ ἀδελφῶν περὶ τοῦ κυνὸς θλιβομέ-
νων, ἔφη ὁ μέγας· "Καλῶς, ὦ ἀδελφοί, προσέταξεν ἡ θεία
φωνὴ ἀεὶ προσεύχεσθαι ἡμᾶς μὴ εἰσελθεῖν εἰς πειρασμόν·
βουληθεὶς γὰρ ὁ Διάβολος ἀδελφῷ ἐπαγαγεῖν τὸν θυμὸν
αὐτοῦ, ὃν εἰς τὸν κύνα ἐπέδειξεν, ἐκωλύθη ὑπὸ ἀγγέλου
Θεοῦ, καθὼς λέγει ὁ ψαλμός· Παρεμβαλεῖ ἄγγελος Κυρίου
κύκλῳ τῶν φοβουμένων αὐτὸν καὶ ῥύσεται αὐτούς.'"

treasury. Immediately after the messenger's departure the holy man was relieved of his pain, and was filled with amazement and astonishment, marveling at the ineffable providence of God, who prevented Neilos, even against his will, from doing something contrary to His will.

Meanwhile as the brethren were laboring on the mountain, rolling down the burned trees in order to clear a plot of land and make it grow grain instead of wood, the Holy Spirit said to His servant Neilos, "Go to those working on the mountain, since our Enemy *the Devil* is afoot, *seeking someone to devour.*" Forthwith he stood up and set out, and for that entire day he did not cease to make the rounds of all the brethren, calling out to them, encouraging them to pray always, and to chase away the Adversary in the name of Jesus Christ. 2

The Devil then, seeing their leader's steadfast vigilance and his protection of his subordinate monks, around the tenth hour felled a huge tree, killing a dog, and went away abashed. While some of the brethren were grieving for the dog, the great man said, "O brothers, rightly did the divine voice ordain that we should always *pray not to enter into temptation.* For whereas the Devil wished to direct against a brother the wrath he displayed against the dog, he was prevented from doing so by an angel of God, and as the psalm says, '*The angel of the Lord will encamp round about them that fear Him and will deliver them.*'" 3

44

Τούτοις τοῖς λόγοις καὶ τρόποις ἐδίδασκεν αὐτοὺς ἐν παντὶ καὶ ἀεὶ προσεύχεσθαι καὶ οὕτω τὰς ἐπιβουλὰς τῶν δαιμόνων ἐκτρέπεσθαι. Ἵνα δὲ καὶ τῆς τῶν γηΐνων προσπαθείας ἑαυτοὺς ἀπαλλάξῃ καὶ παιδεύσῃ αὐτοὺς προτιμᾶν τὴν ὑπακοὴν καὶ αὐτῆς τῆς ζωῆς, ἄλλο πεποίηκε καὶ αὐτὸ μνήμης ἄξιον. Ἔθος ἦν τῷ μακαρίῳ ἐξ ἀρετῆς κτηθέν, οὐκ ἐκ φύσεως, τὸ ἐν παντὶ πράγματι ἑαυτὸν ἐπιμέμφεσθαι.

2   Ὅθεν πολλάκις ἐν ἑαυτῷ λογιζόμενος τὴν τῆς ἡσυχίας γλυκύτητα καὶ τὸ τῆς ἀκτημοσύνης ἀμέριμνον, καὶ ὅτι ὁ καθήμενος μετὰ ἀδελφῶν ἀγωνιστὴς εἰς ἀρετὴν οὐ προκόπτει, βία δὲ μὴ καὶ ὑστερήσει, ταῦτα πάντα ἐνθυμούμενος, ἐδυσχέραινε σφόδρα τῇ τῶν πολλῶν συνοικήσει καὶ ἤχθετο μέχρι καὶ τῆς αὐτῶν συντυχίας, ὡς ἐμποδιζούσης αὐτὸν τῆς κατὰ νοῦν θεωρίας καὶ τῆς ἔνδοθεν κρυπτῆς ἐργασίας, ἧς μόνοι πεπείρανται οἱ περὶ Ἀντώνιον καὶ Ἀρσένιον καὶ Ἰωάννην τὸν Κολοβόν, τοὺς θεοφόρους πατέρας. Τούτοις τοῖς λογισμοῖς ἀντεισῆκτο τὸ τοῦ ἀποστόλου· "Μηδεὶς τὸ ἑαυτοῦ ζητείτω, ἀλλὰ τὸ τῶν πολλῶν, ἵνα σωθῶσιν."

3   Ἔδοξε τοίνυν αὐτῷ πειρᾶσαι αὐτοὺς ἔν τινι παραλόγου ἐπιταγῆς πράγματι, καὶ εἰ μὲν ἀδιακρίτως καὶ ἀπολυπραγμόνως συγκαταθήσονται, αἱρήσασθαι τὴν συνοίκησιν, ὡς καὶ αὐτῶν οὕτω δυναμένων σωθῆναι κἀκεῖνον τὴν ἰδίαν τάξιν φυλάξαι, εἰ δέ τι γένηται τοὐναντίον, τὴν ἀναχώρησιν προτιμῆσαι. Διὰ ταύτην οὖν τὴν αἰτίαν τῆς

Chapter 44

With these words and in such a manner, Neilos used to teach them to pray always, wherever they were, and so deflect the attacks of demons. In order to relieve their attachment to earthly things and instruct them to prefer obedience to life itself, he did something else worthy of mention. The blessed man had a habit, acquired from virtue, not from nature, to blame himself in every matter.

For this reason, he often reflected on the sweetness of 2
spiritual tranquility and the freedom from care that results from poverty, and how the spiritual athlete who lives among brethren does not advance in virtue, but despite himself falls short in his quest. Neilos took all this into account and was much disturbed by his cohabitation with many people. He was annoyed even to meet them, as this distracted him from mental contemplation and the hidden, interior labor, which only the monastic companions of Anthony, Arsenios, and John Kolobos, the divinely inspired fathers, had experienced. To these base thoughts he opposed the words of the apostle, "*Let no one seek his own good, but that of many, that they may be saved.*"

He then decided to test the brethren with an irrational 3
command. If they were to agree without protest and objections, Neilos would choose to continue to live with them, as they would thus be proved capable of salvation, and he would be able to maintain his own regimen. If it turned out otherwise, he would give preference to solitude. For this

ἑωθινῆς ὑμνῳδίας ἐν μιᾷ τελεσθείσης, καὶ πάντων συνη-
θροισμένων, λέγει αὐτοῖς ὁ μέγας· "Πολλοὺς ἀμπελῶνας
πεφυτεύκαμεν, ὦ πατέρες, καὶ τοῦτο λογίζεται ἡμῖν ὡς
πλεονεξία, διότι πλέον τῆς χρείας ἡμῶν ὑπεκτησάμεθα.
Δεῦτε κόψωμεν ἐξ αὐτῶν καὶ μὴ ἐάσωμεν, εἰ μὴ μόνον τὸ
αὔταρκες."

45

Ταῦτα εἰπὼν καὶ ἰδὼν ὅτι συγκατέθεντο, ἄρας τὸν
πέλεκυν ἐπὶ τὸν ὦμον αὐτοῦ, ὥρμησεν ἐπὶ τὸ κάλλιον καὶ
εὐφορώτερον μέρος τοῦ ἀμπελῶνος· ὁμοίως δὲ καὶ αὐτοὶ
ἅπαντες ἠκολούθησαν ὀπίσω αὐτοῦ, ἓν ῥῆμα καὶ μόνον μὴ
ῥήξαντες. Καὶ οὐκ εἶπον ὅτι· "Ὁ ἄνθρωπος ἐμάνη, οὐκ
οἶδε τί ποιεῖ· τοῦτό ποτε οὔτε ἐφάνη, οὔτε ἠκούσθη," ἀλλά
εὐχῆς γενομένης, ἤρξαντο κόπτειν ἀπὸ πρωῒ ἕως τῆς
τρίτης ὥρας. Τότε γνοὺς ὁ πατὴρ τὴν τῶν τέκνων ὑπακοὴν ἁμιλληθεῖσαν τοῖς πάλαι ἱστορουμένοις, δέδωκε τῷ
Θεῷ δεξιὰς μηδὲν αὐτῶν προτιμῆσαι ἕως ἐσχάτης ἀναπνοῆς.

2   Τούτου οὖν τοῦ ἔργου περιφήμου γεγονότος καὶ ἕως
αὐτοῦ τοῦ Ἁγίου Ὄρους καὶ ἕως τῆς Σικελίας, οὐδεὶς
ἠδυνήθη καταλαβέσθαι τοῦ πράγματος τὴν αἰτίαν, ἀλλ᾽ οἱ
μὲν ἔλεγον ὅτι οἱ μοναχοὶ ἐμεθύσθησαν, οἱ δὲ ὅτι ὁ πατὴρ
ἐθυμώθη καὶ διὰ τοῦτο καὶ ἄλλοι ὅτι, πολλὰ ὄντα, καμεῖν

reason, one day when the matins hymnody was completed and all were assembled, the great father said to them, "We have planted many vines, O fathers, and this seems to be greed on our part, since we possess more than we need. Let us cut down some of them, and leave only what is essential."

Chapter 45

When Neilos had said this and saw that they consented, he hoisted an ax upon his shoulder and set off to the best and most fruitful part of the vineyard. All the brothers followed likewise behind him, without saying a single word. No one said, "The man is mad; he does not know what he is doing. This has never been seen or heard." Instead they prayed and began to cut the vines from morning until the third hour. Then, when the father realized that his children's obedience emulated that of those recounted in the stories of old, he promised God to prefer nothing to them until his final breath.

This deed became famous and reached as far as the Holy 2 Mountain of Athos and Sicily, though no one could understand the reason for it. Some said the reason was that the monks were drunk, others that the father became enraged on this account, yet others said that there were so many

αὐτὰ οὐκ ἴσχυον. Καὶ τοῦτο οὐ θαυμαστόν, ὅπου γε οὐδὲ αὐτοὶ οἱ συγκόψαντες εἶδον δι' οὗ ἔκοψαν, εἰ μὴ αὐτὸς ὁ μέγας, οἷς ἠβουλήθη, τὸ μυστήριον ἀπεκάλυψεν.

3 Ποτὲ τῆς Ἁγίας Πέμπτης τοῦ Πάσχα καταλαβούσης, ἤνεγκέ τις ἰχθύας ἐν τῇ μονῇ καλοὺς καὶ μεγάλους, ἕνα κόφινον πλήρη, ἵνα μικρὰν παράκλησιν οἱ ἀδελφοὶ ποιήσωσιν ἐκ τῆς μακρᾶς καὶ πολλῆς νηστείας καὶ ἐγκρατείας· καὶ ἰδὼν αὐτοὺς ὁ πατὴρ ὅτι μικρὸν ἠγαθύνθησαν ἰδόντες, εἴασε μὲν αὐτοὺς ξύσαι καὶ πλῦναι καὶ ἑτοιμάσαι πρὸς τὸ ἑψῆσαι· τινὸς δὲ προσαίτου καταλαβόντος, δέδωκεν αὐτῷ αὐτοὺς ἅπαντας, μὴ ἐάσας ἐξ αὐτῶν οὐδένα. Οὕτως ἐπαίδευσεν αὐτοὺς ἐκ διαθέσεως ψάλλειν τό· "Κύριε, ἐναντίον Σου πᾶσα ἡ ἐπιθυμία μου," καὶ τό· "Μερίς μου εἶ, Κύριε, καὶ κλῆρος ἐπιπόθητος."

46

Εὐκτήριόν ἐστιν ἐν τῷ ἄκρῳ τοῦ Ῥυσιάνου τερπνότα- τον ἐπ' ὀνόματι τῆς Ἁγίας Ἀναστασίας, κτισθὲν μὲν ὑπὸ Εὐπραξίου, τοῦ βασιλικοῦ κριτοῦ γεγονότος Ἰταλίας καὶ Καλαβρίας, φροντιστήριον δὲ χρηματίσαν παρθένων. Τούτου τὴν προστασίαν ἐπιστεύθη παρὰ τοῦ αὐτοῦ Εὐπραξίου, ὄντος ἐν Κωνσταντινουπόλει, μοναχός τις Ἀντώνιος τῷ ὀνόματι· ὅς, χρημάτων ὑπάρξει περιεχόμενος καὶ ὑπὸ τοῦ θανάτου κατεπειγόμενος, ὑφορώμενος τὸ τῶν

vines that the monks could not cultivate them. This is not a cause for wonder, since even those who cut down the vines would not have known why they cut them, unless the great Neilos had revealed the mystery to those whom he chose.

Once on the Holy Thursday before Easter, someone 3 brought to the monastery a basket filled with fine large fish, so the brethren could have some small relief from their long and intensive fast and abstinence. Seeing them, the father realized that the brothers were quite pleased to see the fish, so he allowed the brothers to scale and clean the fish and prepare them for cooking. But when a beggar arrived, Neilos gave him all the fish, without keeping a single one. Thus he taught them to chant from deep within their heart the psalm verses, "Lord, *all my desire is before You,*" and "*You are my portion, Lord, and my desired inheritance.*"

Chapter 46

There is a very charming chapel at the top of Rossano, named after Saint Anastasia, built by Eupraxios, who was imperial judge of Italy and Calabria; it became a monastery for virgins. While Eupraxios was in Constantinople, he entrusted a monk named Anthony with the custody of this place. This Anthony possessed a lot of money, but was oppressed by the proximity of death. Since he was suspicious

ἀρχόντων εὐάρπακτον καὶ εὐρούφιστον, ἐπὶ τὸν ἄσυλον πύργον προσφεύγει, πατέρα τὸν ὅσιον, καὶ τοῦτον πάντων τῶν αὐτοῦ καταστήσας ἐπίτροπον, οὕτω λοιπὸν ἄφροντις τετελεύτηκεν.

2   Ὅπερ ἀκούσας ὁ τοῦ Θεοῦ οἰκονόμος καὶ σπλαγχνισθείς, οὐ τοσοῦτον ἐπὶ τῷ ἀπελθόντι, ὅσον ἐπὶ τῇ τῆς μονῆς καταστάσει—ἦν γὰρ λοιπὸν ἐξ ἐκείνου ἀφανισθεῖσα καὶ διασκορπισθεῖσα—εἰσέρχεται ἐν τῷ ἄστει, καὶ τὰ μὲν ἐγκαταλείμματα τοῦ ἀποιχομένου διεμέρισε πτωχοῖς καὶ ἐκκλησίαις καὶ τῷ μοναστηρίῳ, πᾶσαν δὲ σπουδὴν κατεβάλετο τοῦ τὴν μονὴν καταστήσασθαι καὶ παρθένους ἐν αὐτῇ ἐμφυτεῦσαι ἀξίας τοῦ ἐπαγγέλματος.

3   Ὅπερ καὶ Θεοῦ συνεργοῦντος τετέλεκεν, πάσας τὰς διεσκορπισμένας συνάξας, καὶ ἡγουμένην αὐταῖς ἐπιστήσας, οἵαν ἀπαιτεῖ ὁ λόγος, παρακαλέσας τοὺς οἰκήτορας πάντας τοῦ κάστρου φροντίζειν αὐτῶν, ὡς ἀσθενεστέρου μέρους καὶ ὡς μέγα ὄφελος δι᾽ αὐτῶν καρπουμένους, λέγων αὐτοῖς καὶ τοῦτο, ὅτι· "Ἐάν τις ἐξ ὑμῶν τελευτήσῃ καὶ βουληθῇ ἡ γυνὴ αὐτοῦ τοῦ λοιποῦ ἐν ἁγνείᾳ βιῶσαι, μὴ ἔχουσα δὲ ποῦ καταφυγεῖν, ἑτέρῳ γάμῳ προσομιλήσῃ, ὑμέτερόν ἐστι πταῖσμα, τῶν μὴ σπουδασάντων, ἵνα τοιαύτη πόλις ἓν μοναστήριον ἔχῃ."

of the rapacity and greed of the officials, he sought refuge with the unassailable tower, the holy father. After designating Neilos as custodian of all his possessions, Anthony thus died freed of all worries.

When Neilos, the steward of God, heard this, he took 2 pity, not so much for the departed, as for the condition of the monastery; from the time of Anthony's death it was left in a disastrous and precarious state. He went to the city and distributed the dead man's possessions to the poor, to churches, and to the monastery. He then exerted much zeal to restore the monastery, and settled in it virgins worthy of their vocation.

With God's assistance he accomplished this, reassem- 3 bling all the scattered nuns, and appointing for them an appropriate mother superior. He urged all the inhabitants of the city to look after them, as they were of the weaker sex, and because the inhabitants themselves would obtain a great benefit from them. He also added this, "If any of you should die, and his widow wished to spend the rest of her life in chastity, but having no other refuge, she entered into a second marriage, it would be your fault, since you did not ensure that this city should have a nunnery."

47

Ἔτι δὲ αὐτοῦ ἐν τῷ κάστρῳ προσκαρτεροῦντος καὶ μικρὸν ὑπὸ νόσου καταληφθέντος, εἰσῆλθε καὶ ὁ μητρο-πολίτης Καλαβρίας Θεοφύλακτος, σὺν αὐτῷ δὲ καὶ ὁ δομέστικος Λέων, ἄνδρες γραμματικώτατοι καὶ σοφώτα-τοι. Ὁ δὲ ὅσιος πατὴρ ἡμῶν Νεῖλος, φεύγων τὴν τοῦ λαοῦ ὄχλησιν καὶ τὴν φίλην ἡσυχίαν ἀεὶ ἀσπαζόμενος, ἐξῆλθεν μικρὸν ἀπὸ τοῦ ἄστεως ἐν τῷ ναῷ τοῦ φιλερήμου καὶ Βαπτιστοῦ Ἰωάννου, οὗ καὶ τὸν βίον ἐζήλου, κἀκεῖ προσ-ωμίλει τῷ Θεῷ καὶ τῇ μελέτῃ προσεῖχεν.

2   Ἐξῆλθεν οὖν πρὸς αὐτὸν ὁ μητροπολίτης καὶ ὁ δομέστι-κος καὶ οἱ ἄρχοντες καὶ τῶν ἱερέων πολλοὶ καὶ λαοῦ μέρος οὐ βραχύτατον. Ἐβουλεύσαντο δὲ κατὰ τὴν ὁδόν, τίς τί αὐτὸν ἐρωτήσει τῶν τῆς Γραφῆς ἀπορρήτων, οὐ τοσοῦτον μαθεῖν, ὅσον πειρᾶσαι βουλόμενοι. Καθήμενος δὲ ἐξ ἐναντίας ὁ ὅσιος καὶ θεασάμενος αὐτοὺς πρὸς αὐτὸν ἐρχομένους, λέγει ἐν ἑαυτῷ· "Ἰδοὺ νῦν οὗτοι ἐλθόντες, εἰς ἀργολογίας ἡμᾶς ἐμβαλοῦσιν. Ἀλλά, Κύριε Ἰησοῦ Χριστέ, λύτρωσαι ἡμᾶς ἐκ τῶν παγίδων τοῦ Ἀλλοτρίου καὶ δώρη-σαι ἡμῖν νοεῖν καὶ λαλεῖν ἃ δεῖ, καὶ πράττειν τὰ Σοὶ εὐ-άρεστα."

3   Καὶ ταῦτα εὐξάμενος, ἀνοίγει τὴν ἐν τῇ χειρὶ αὐτοῦ βίβλον, καὶ κατὰ συγκυρίαν εὑρίσκει τὴν γενομένην ἀποκάλυψιν πρὸς τὸν ἐν ἁγίοις Συμεῶνα, τὸν εἰς τὸ Θαυ-μαστὸν Ὄρος. Ἐκείνων οὖν ἐγγισάντων καὶ μετὰ τὴν προσκύνησιν καθισάντων, ἐπιδίδει ὁ μέγας τὴν βίβλον τῷ

Chapter 47

While Neilos was still staying in the city and was mildly indisposed, the metropolitan of Calabria, Theophylaktos, came along with the *domestikos* Leo, men most erudite and wise. The holy father Neilos, trying to escape the tumult of the crowd and embrace his beloved spiritual tranquility, withdrew from the city to the church of the desert-loving John the Baptist, whose way of life he emulated. There he conversed with God and devoted himself to study.

So the metropolitan and the *domestikos* came out of the 2 city to him, along with the officials, many priests, and a large part of the townspeople. Along the road they deliberated over who would ask him what about various obscure passages of Scripture, wishing not so much to learn as to test him. As the holy man sat facing them and watching them as they approached, he said to himself, "Behold now those who are coming to ensnare us in idle chatter. Lord Jesus Christ, deliver us from the snares of the Alien One, and grant that I may think of and say what is appropriate, and act in a manner pleasing to You."

With this prayer he opened the book in his hands and by 3 chance found the revelation disclosed to Saint Symeon of the Wondrous Mountain. When they had all drawn near, they made obeisance and sat down. The great Neilos gave

δομεστίκῳ τοῦ ἀναγνῶναι, ἔνθα τὸ σημεῖον ὑπῆρχεν. Ὁ δὲ ἀνοίξας τὸ στόμα, ἤρξατο πάνυ εὐφυῶς καὶ νουνεχῶς ἀναγνῶναι. Ἐλθόντος δὲ εἰς τὸν τόπον ὅπου λέγει, "ἀπὸ μυρίων μόλις εὑρίσκεσθαι μίαν ψυχὴν ἐν τοῖς ἐνεστῶσι χρόνοις τὴν ἐν ταῖς χερσὶ τῶν ἁγίων ἀγγέλων προερχομένην," ἤρξαντο πάντες, ὡς ἐξ ἑνὸς στόματος, λέγειν· "Μὴ γένοιτο! Οὐκ ἔστιν ἀληθές· αἱρετικός ἐστιν ὁ λαλήσας. Λοιπὸν ἡμεῖς δωρεὰν ἐβαπτίσθημεν καὶ τὸν σταυρὸν προσκυνοῦμεν καὶ κοινωνοῦμεν καὶ Χριστιανοὶ λεγόμεθα;"

4   Ταῦτα καὶ τὰ ὅμοια τούτοις πάντων ἀντιλεγόντων, ἰδὼν ὁ μακάριος ὅτι ὁ μητροπολίτης καὶ ὁ δομέστικος οὐδὲν αὐτοῖς λέγουσιν, ἀπεκρίθη πρᾴως καὶ εἶπεν· "Ἐὰν δὲ ὑμῖν ἀποδείξω καὶ τὸν μέγαν Βασίλειον καὶ τὸν Χρυσόστομον καὶ Ἐφραὶμ τὸν πανόσιον καὶ Θεόδωρον τὸν Στουδίτην καὶ αὐτὸν τὸν ἀπόστολον καὶ τὸ ἅγιον Εὐαγγέλιον τὸν αὐτὸν σκοπὸν καὶ φρονοῦντας καὶ λέγοντας, τί πείσεσθε ὑμεῖς, οἱ ἀσκόπως τὰ στόματα διανοίγοντες καὶ τῷ Ἁγίῳ Πνεύματι ἀντιπίπτοντες καὶ τοὺς τῶν ἁγίων πατέρων φρικώδεις λόγους αἱρετικοῖς ὑποβάλλοντες διὰ τὴν ὑμῶν τοῦ βίου φαυλότητα; Λέγω δὲ ὑμῖν, ἀδελφοί, ὅτι ἐκ πάντων, ὧν ἐψηφίσασθε, οὐδεμία ὑμῖν χάρις παρὰ τῷ Θεῷ. Ποῖα εἴδωλα, ἢ ποίαν αἵρεσιν καταλείψαντες, τῷ Χριστῷ προσεδράμετε; Τολμᾷ τις ὑμῶν εἰπεῖν ὅτι· 'αἱρετικός εἰμι,' καὶ εἰσελθεῖν εἰς τὴν πόλιν αὐτοῦ; Οὐχὶ λιθοβοληθεὶς ὑπὸ πάντων ἀποκτανθήσεται; Πληροφορήθητε ὅτι, ἐὰν μὴ ἐνάρετοι γένησθε καὶ σφόδρα ἐνάρετοι,

the book to the *domestikos* to read from the point where the revelation began. Opening his mouth, the *domestikos* began to read very gracefully and with thorough understanding. When he came to the passage that says, "*From the thousands living in these times scarcely is found one soul who is received in the hands of the holy angels,*" everyone began to say with one voice, "God forbid! It is not true, the one who said this is a heretic. In this case, we would be baptized for naught and so in vain we would venerate the cross, take communion, and be called Christians."

After everyone voiced these and similar objections, the 4 blessed Neilos, seeing that the metropolitan and the *domestikos* were saying nothing to them, responded calmly and said, "If I demonstrate to you that even the great Basil, Chrysostom, the most holy Ephraim, Theodore the Stoudite, the apostle Paul himself, and even the holy Gospel, all think and speak along these same lines, what should happen to those of you who open your mouths aimlessly and *resist the Holy Spirit,* and assign the awe-inspiring words of the holy fathers to heretics, because of the wickedness of your own lives? I say to you, brothers, of all the deeds that you have reckoned for yourselves, not one gives you grace in the presence of God. What idols or which heresy did you abandon in order to have recourse to Christ? Does any one of you dare say, 'I am a heretic,' and enter into his own city? Will not such a person be stoned by all and killed? Know well that unless you are virtuous—in fact very virtuous—no one

οὐδεὶς ὑμᾶς ἐξαιρήσεται τῆς κολάσεως." Τούτων ἀκούσαντες ἅπαντες καὶ σφόδρα καταπλαγέντες, ἤρξαντο
στενάζειν καὶ λέγειν· "Οὐαὶ ἡμῖν τοῖς ἁμαρτωλοῖς καὶ
ἀθλίοις."

48

Λέγει αὐτῷ Νικόλαος ὁ πρωτοσπαθάριος· "Διατί,
πάτερ, λέγει τὸ Εὐαγγέλιον· *Ὅς ἐὰν ποτίσῃ ἕνα τῶν μικρῶν
ποτήριον ψυχροῦ ὕδατος, οὐ μὴ ἀπολέσῃ τὸν μισθὸν αὐτοῦ*';"
Ἀπεκρίθη αὐτῷ ὁ πατήρ· "Τοῦτο πρὸς τοὺς μηθὲν ἔχοντας
εἴρηται, ἵνα μηδεὶς προφασίσηται, ὅτι· 'ξύλα οὐκ ἔχω, ἵνα
ποιήσω θερμόν.' Τί δὲ ποιήσετε ὑμεῖς, οἱ καὶ αὐτὸ τὸ ψυ-
χρὸν ποτήριον τοῦ πτωχοῦ ἀφαιρούμενοι;"

2   Τούτου δὲ σιωπήσαντος, ἀνίσταται ἕτερος καί φησιν·
"Ἤθελον γνῶναι, ἅγιε πάτερ, εἴγε σέσωσται ὁ πανθαύμα-
στος Σολομών, ἢ ἀπώλετο." Γνοὺς δὲ τῷ πνεύματι αὐτὸν
ὁ πατὴρ τῷ τῆς πορνείας πάθει κατεχόμενον, ἔφη πρὸς
αὐτόν· "Ἤθελον γνῶναι κἀγὼ περὶ σοῦ, εἴγε σώζῃ, ἢ
ἀπόλλυσαι. Τί γὰρ ὄφελος ἐμοὶ καὶ σοὶ ἀπὸ τοῦ σωθῆναι
τὸν Σολομῶντα ἢ κατακριθῆναι; Οὐ γὰρ ἐκείνῳ, ἀλλ᾽ ἡμῖν
ἐντέταλται τό· *Πᾶς ὁ ἐμβλέψας γυναικὶ πρὸς τὸ ἐπιθυμῆσαι,
ἤδη ἐμοίχευσεν αὐτήν*,' καὶ τό· *Εἴ τις τὸν ναὸν τοῦ Θεοῦ
φθείρει, φθερεῖ τοῦτον ὁ Θεός*.' Περὶ δὲ τοῦ Σολομῶντος
μηδαμοῦ εὑρισκομένου ἐν τῇ Γραφῇ μετανοήσαντος μετὰ
τὴν ἁμαρτίαν, καθὼς εὑρίσκεται ὁ Μανασσῆς, τίς δύναται
εἰπεῖν ὅτι ἐσώθη;"

will save you from hell." They all were quite dumbfounded upon hearing this, and began to groan and say, "Woe to us sinners and wretches!"

Chapter 48

Nicholas the *protospatharios* said to him, "Father, why does the Gospel say, '*Whoever gives to one of these little ones even a cup of cold water, he shall not lose his reward*'?" The father responded to him, "This was said to those who have nothing, so that no one may make an excuse, saying, 'I have no wood to heat it.' What will you do, you who have snatched the very same cup of cold water from the poor man?"

When Nicholas was silent, someone else stood up and said, "I wanted to know, holy father, whether the all-admirable Solomon was saved or doomed?" Since Neilos knew in his spirit that the man was possessed by the passion of fornication, he said to him, "I wanted to know the same about you, if you are to be saved or doomed. For what benefit is it to me and to you whether Solomon was saved or condemned? For it was not to him, but to us that it was commanded, '*Everyone who looks at a woman lustfully has already committed adultery with her*,' and also, '*If anyone destroys God's temple, God will destroy him*.' With regard to Solomon, since nowhere is it found in Scripture that he repented after his sin, as is found for Manasses, who can say that he was saved?"

3   Μετὰ τοῦτον ἀνίσταταί τις τῶν ἱερέων καὶ λέγει·
"Πάτερ ἅγιε, τί ἦν τὸ ξύλον, ὃ ἔφαγεν ὁ Ἀδὰμ ἐν τῷ
παραδείσῳ καὶ κατεκρίθη;" Ὁ δὲ ἀπεκρίθη· "Ἄγριον μῆ-
λον." Μειδιασάντων δὲ πάντων, λέγει αὐτοῖς ὁ μέγας· "Μὴ
γελάσητε ἐπὶ τούτῳ· πρὸς γὰρ τὴν ἐρώτησιν ἡ ἀπόκρισις.
Τὸ ξύλον ἐκεῖνο Μωϋσῆς οὐκ ὠνόμασεν· οἱ διδάσκαλοι
πάντες τὴν μὲν ἐνέργειαν εἶπον, τὸ δὲ εἶδος οὐκ εἶδον. Ὁ
δὲ ἡ Γραφὴ ἀπέκρυψεν, πῶς ἡμεῖς ἀποκαλύψωμεν; Σὺ δέ,
ἐάσας τὸ ἐρωτῆσαι πῶς ἐπλάσθης καὶ ἐτέθης ἐν τῷ παραδείσῳ καὶ σύ, καθὼς ὁ Ἀδάμ, καὶ τίς ἡ ἐντολή, μᾶλλον δὲ
<αἱ> ἐντολαί, ἃς παρέλαβες καὶ οὐκ ἐφύλαξας, διὸ καὶ
ἀπέρριψαι τοῦ παραδείσου, μᾶλλον δὲ τῆς βασιλείας, καὶ
πῶς ἄρα ἰσχύσῃς ἐπανακάμψαι ἐπὶ τὴν ἀρχαίαν σου δόξαν
καὶ τιμήν, ἠρώτησας ὄνομα ξύλου μαθεῖν, ἑνὸς τῶν ἄλλων
ἁπάντων, ὃ καὶ μετὰ τὸ μαθεῖν, ἀπορήσεις, τί τὰ φύλλα καὶ
τίς ἡ ῥίζα, ἢ τίς ὁ φλοιὸς καὶ εἰ μέγα ἢ μικρόν· καὶ τίς
δύναται ἑρμηνεῦσαι, ὅπερ τοῖς ὀφθαλμοῖς οὐδέποτε εἶδεν;"

49

Ἀπεκρίθη ὁ δομέστικος καὶ εἶπεν· "Ἐρωτήσω κἀγώ,
πάτερ· Τί ἐστιν, ὃ λέγει ὁ Θεόλογος Γρηγόριος· '*Πῶς γὰρ
σώσει ῥᾳδίως ἡ ἀλλοτρία, ὃν ἀπώλεσεν ἡ ἰδία;*'" Ὁ δὲ πατὴρ
πρὸς αὐτόν· "Τοῦτό σοι εἴρηκεν ὁ διδάσκαλος, ἵνα μὴ
θαρρήσῃς ὡς διὰ γυναικὸς ἰσχύων σωθῆναι, ὅπερ καὶ ὁ

After him one of the priests stood up and said, "Holy fa- 3
ther, what was the tree, of whose fruit Adam ate in paradise and was condemned?" Neilos answered, "A wild apple."
When they all began to smile, the great man said to them,
"Don't laugh at this, as the answer is appropriate for the
question. Moses did not name that tree, and all the teachers
spoke of its effect, but they did not know its species. How
shall we reveal that which Scripture has concealed? You,
however, instead of asking how you were created and how
you were also placed in paradise, just like Adam, and which
was the commandment, or rather the commandments, that
you received and did not keep, because of which you were
cast out of paradise, or rather out of the kingdom of heaven,
and how you can regain your first glory and honor, instead of
asking these questions, you ask to be informed about the
name of that tree, one out of many. Even if you were to learn
that, will you next ask what the leaves were like and the
root, or the bark, and whether it was big or small? But who
can describe what his eyes have never seen?"

Chapter 49

The *domestikos* responded, saying, "I too have a question,
father; what does Gregory the Theologian mean when he
says, *'How will an unfamiliar woman more easily save a man
whom his own wife has destroyed?'"* The father said to him,
"The teacher has said this to you, so that you may not be
confident that you can be saved by a woman. And this is also

ἀπόστολος κεκολασμένον εἴρηκεν, εἰπών, 'Τί γὰρ οἶδας, γύναι, εἰ τὸν ἄνδρα σώσεις;', πάντως ὡς συνήθειαν ἐχούσης τοῦ αὐτὸν ἀπολλύειν. Εἰ γοῦν ἐκείνη ἡ ἐκ τῶν σαρκῶν τοῦ Ἀδὰμ ἐξελθοῦσα, καὶ ἰδία αὐτῷ οὖσα, ὡς εἰπεῖν, ἀδελφὴ ἢ θυγάτηρ, μᾶλλον δὲ ὑπὲρ ταῦτα, παραβάσει τὸν ἄνδρα ὑπέβαλε καὶ ἀπώλεσε, πῶς εἰς ἀρετὴν ἐλάσειε καὶ σώσει ἡ σοῦ ἀλλοτρία καὶ γνώμη καὶ θέσει καὶ ἕξει καὶ διαπλάσει; Πρόσεχε τοίνυν καὶ σὺ ἑαυτῷ καὶ ἀπὸ τῆς συγκοίτου σου φυλάσσου." Ταῦτα εἰπὼν αὐτῷ καὶ ἕτερα πολλά, διὰ παρα-βολῶν ἐνῆγεν αὐτὸν εἰς τὴν μοναδικὴν πολιτείαν· πάνυ γὰρ ἠγάπα αὐτὸν διὰ τὴν συνετὴν κατάστασιν αὐτοῦ.

2   Ὁ δὲ ἀποκρίνεται καί φησιν· "Ὄντως, πάτερ ἅγιε, πάντα ὠφέλιμα καὶ συμβουλεύεις καὶ νουθετεῖς. Ἀλλὰ λέγει τὸ ἅγιον Εὐαγγέλιον, ὅτι· 'Ὁ ὁ Θεὸς συνέζευξεν, ἄνθρωπος μὴ χωριζέτω.'" Λέγει αὐτῷ ὁ μέγας· "Εἰ μὲν ἄνθρωπος χωρίζει, καλῶς εἶπας, 'μὴ χωριζέτω,' εἰ δὲ ὁ λόγος τοῦ εἰπόντος ἐστὶν ὁ χωρίζων· 'Ὃς οὐκ ἀφῆκεν οἰκίας, ἢ ἀδελφούς, ἢ γυναῖκα, ἢ τέκνα, καὶ τὰ λοιπά, οὐκ ἔστιν μου ἄξιος,' τίς ἐστιν ὁ τὸ θεάρεστον τοῦτο κωλύσων; Τίς δὲ καὶ οἶδεν, εἰ ὁ Θεός ἐστιν ὁ συζεύξας καὶ οὐχὶ ἔρως σωματικὸς καὶ ἡδονὴ σαρκός, καθὼς ὁ ἀπόστολος λέγει, ὅτι· 'διὰ τὰς πορνείας ἕκαστος τὴν ἑαυτοῦ γυναῖκα ἐχέτω.'" Ταῦτα καὶ τὰ πλείονα τούτων ἀκούσαντες καὶ μεγάλως ὠφεληθέντες, ἀνεχώρησαν θαυμάζοντες τὴν ἀρετὴν καὶ σοφίαν τοῦ μακαρίου, ὡς καὶ αὐτὸν τὸν μητροπολίτην εἰπεῖν ὅτι· "Ὁ Θεὸς οἶδε, μέγας ἐστὶν ὁ καλόγηρος οὗτος."

what the apostle stated in a more restrained way by saying, *'Wife, how do you know whether you will save your husband?'* For in general it is the norm for women to destroy men. If that woman who came from the flesh of Adam, and was his, so to speak, sister or daughter, or something greater than this, subjected her husband to transgression and destroyed him, how can a woman who differs from you in her views, in her opinions, in her habits, and in her physical form lead you to virtue and save you? Therefore take care of yourself and be on guard against your spouse." With these and many other words, Neilos was leading him through parables toward the monastic way of life; for he loved the man because of his wisdom.

The *domestikos* responded, saying, "Holy father, truly all 2 of your counsel and advice is very beneficial, but as the holy Gospel says, *'What God has joined together, let not man put asunder.'"* The great man said to him, "If man is the agent of separation, you spoke well by saying, 'May he not separate.' If, however, separation is effected by the words of the One who said, 'He who does not leave his home, his brothers, his wife, his children, and all else, *is not worthy of me,'* who would impede something so pleasing to God? Moreover, who knows if it is God who joined together rather than physical passion and even pleasure of the flesh? Just as the apostle says, *'Because of the temptation to immorality, each man should have his own wife.'"* Upon hearing this and much more, all found great benefit in Neilos's words and went away, marveling at the blessed man's virtue and wisdom; even the metropolitan himself said, "God bears witness that this monk is great."

50

Τῇ ἐπαύριον κατελθόντος τοῦ ὁσίου ἐκεῖθεν καὶ ἐν τῷ κάστρῳ εἰσεληλυθότος, ἔρχεται πρὸς αὐτὸν Ἰουδαῖός τις ὀνόματι Δόμνουλος, ὃς ἦν αὐτῷ γνωστὸς ἐκ νεότητος αὐτοῦ, διὰ τὸ εἶναι αὐτὸν σφόδρα νομομαθῆ καὶ ἱκανὸν περὶ τὴν ἰατρικὴν ἐπιστήμην. Ἤρξατο οὖν λέγειν πρὸς τὸν μακάριον οὕτως· "Ἤκουσα περὶ τῆς ἀσκήσεώς σου καὶ πολλῆς ἐγκρατείας καί, γινώσκων τὴν κρᾶσιν τοῦ σώματός σου, ἐθαύμαζον πῶς οὐ περιπέπτωκας ἐπιλήψει· ἀλλὰ κἂν ἀπὸ τοῦ νῦν, εἰ κελεύεις, ἐγώ σοι φάρμακον δώσω πρὸς τὴν σὴν κρᾶσιν, ἵνα ἔχων αὐτὸ πάσας τὰς ἡμέρας τῆς ζωῆς σου, μηδεμίαν ἀσθένειαν φοβηθήσῃ."

2 Ἔφη αὐτῷ ὁ μέγας· "Εἴπε πρὸς ἡμᾶς ἐξ ὑμῶν εἷς Ἑβραῖος· Ἀγαθὸν πεποιθέναι ἐπὶ Κύριον, ἢ πεποιθέναι ἐπ᾽ ἄνθρωπον.' Πεποιθότες οὖν ἡμεῖς ἐπὶ τὸν ἰατρὸν ἡμῶν Θεὸν καὶ Κύριον ἡμῶν Ἰησοῦν Χριστόν, οὐ χρείαν ἔχομεν τῶν ὑπὸ σοῦ γινομένων φαρμάκων. Σὺ δὲ οὐκ ἄλλως δυνήσῃ ἐμπαῖξαι τοὺς τῶν Χριστιανῶν ἀκεραίους, εἰ μὴ ἐν τῷ καυχᾶσθαί σε τῶν σῶν φαρμάκων μεταδοῦναι τῷ Νείλῳ." Τούτων ὁ ἰατρὸς ἐπακούσας, οὐδὲν ἔτι πρὸς τὸν ἅγιον ἀπεκρίνατο.

Chapter 50

On the next day as the holy man departed from there and entered the city, a Jew by the name of Domnoulos came up to him. Neilos had known him since his youth as someone very learned in the law and adept at medical science. He began to speak to the blessed man as follows: "I have heard about your asceticism and intensive abstinence, and knowing the temperament of your body, I am amazed that you have not fallen victim to epilepsy. But from now on, if you agree, I can administer a medicine appropriate to your bodily temperament, so that with its help you will not feel threatened by any disease for the rest of your life."

The great one said to him, "One of your Jews said to us, '*It* 2 *is better to trust in the Lord, than to trust in man.*' So, having placed trust in our physician, that is, our God and Lord Jesus Christ, we have no need of the medicines prepared by you. You will not be able to mock the pure Christians in any other way than by boasting that you administered your medicines to Neilos." The physician heard this, but made no response to the holy man.

51

Ἦν δὲ ἐλθὼν μετ᾽ αὐτοῦ ἄλλος, καὶ λέγει· "Εἶπον ἡμῖν περὶ Θεοῦ τί ποτε· ἐπιθυμοῦμεν γάρ σου ἀκοῦσαι τῶν λόγων." Ὁ δὲ πατὴρ πρὸς αὐτόν· "Ἔοικεν ὁ λόγος σου, ὦ Ἰουδαῖε, ἀνθρώπῳ προστάσσοντι βρέφει τῇ χειρὶ κρατῆσαι τοῦ ὑψηλοῦ δένδρου καὶ πρὸς τὴν γῆν αὐτὸ ὑποκλῖναι. Ὅμως εἰ βούλει μικρόν τι περὶ Θεοῦ ἀκοῦσαι, λάβε σου τοὺς προφήτας μετὰ τοῦ νόμου, καὶ δεῦρο εἰς τὴν ἔρημον, ὅπου κἀγὼ ἡσυχάζω· ἔνθα σχολάσας τῇ ἀναγνώσει ὅσας ἡμέρας ὁ Μωϋσῆς ἐν τῷ ὄρει, ἐρώτησον μετὰ ταῦτα, κἀγώ σοι ἀποκρινοῦμαι· ʽΣχολάσατε γάρ,ʼ φησί, ʽκαὶ γνῶτε, ὅτι ἐγώ εἰμι ὁ Θεός.ʼ Ὡς ἐὰν νῦν σοι περὶ Θεοῦ τι λαλήσω, καθ᾽ ὕδατος γράφω καὶ ἐπὶ θάλασσαν σπερῶ."

2   Ἀπεκρίθησαν ἅμα καὶ εἶπον· "Οὐ δυνάμεθα τοῦτο ποιῆσαι, ἐπεὶ ἀποσυνάγωγοι γενόμεθα, καὶ ὑπὸ τῶν ἰδίων λιθοβολούμεθα." "Οὕτω," φησὶν ὁ πατήρ, "καὶ οἱ πατέρες ὑμῶν ἐναπέθανον τῇ ἀπιστίᾳ ἑαυτῶν, ὥς φησιν ὁ εὐαγγελιστής, ὅτι· ʽπολλοὶ ἐκ τῶν ἀρχόντων ἐπίστευσαν εἰς τὸν Ἰησοῦν, ἀλλὰ διὰ τοὺς Ἰουδαίους οὐχ ὡμολόγουν, ἵνα μὴ ἀποσυνάγωγοι γένωνται· ἠγάπησαν γὰρ τὴν δόξαν τῶν ἀνθρώπων μᾶλλον ἤπερ τὴν δόξαν τοῦ Θεοῦ.ʼ" Ταῦτα εἰπὼν καὶ ἀπαλλαγεὶς αὐτῶν, ἐξῆλθε πρὸς τὸ μοναστήριον εἰς τὸ κελλίον αὐτοῦ, σχολάζειν τῇ θεωρίᾳ καὶ τῇ μελέτῃ τῶν θείων Γραφῶν.

Chapter 51

Another man had come with Domnoulos, and he said to Neilos, "Tell us something about God, for we desire to hear your words." The father said to him, "Your words, O Jew, are like a man ordering an infant to grab a tall tree with his hand and bend it to the ground. If you wish to hear something brief about God, take your prophets along with the law, and go to the wilderness where also I live in spiritual tranquility, and there devote yourself to reading for as many days as Moses spent on the mountain. After that you may ask me questions, and I shall respond, *'Be still and know that I am God.'* For if I should speak to you now about God, I would be writing on water and sowing seeds in the sea."

The two men responded, "We cannot do so, since we will 2 be cast out of the synagogue and stoned by our own people." The father said, "Thus did your fathers die in their lack of belief. As the evangelist said, *'Many of the authorities believed in* Jesus, *but for fear of the* Jews *they did not confess it, lest they should be put out of the synagogue, for they loved the praise of men more than the praise of God.'*" With these words, Neilos left them and returned to his cell in the monastery, to devote himself to contemplation and the study of divine Scripture.

52

Καὶ μετ᾽ ὀλίγον χρόνον ἐξέρχονται πρὸς αὐτὸν ἐκεῖσε Νικόλαος ὁ πρωτοσπαθάριος καὶ ὁ δομέστικος Λέων, ἱμειρόμενοι ἀκούειν τῆς ὀνησίμου διδασκαλίας καὶ νουθεσίας αὐτοῦ. Καὶ δὴ γενομένης ἱκανῆς συντυχίας καὶ παραινέσεως, ὁ μὲν ἅγιος εἰσῆλθεν ἐν τῷ κελλίῳ αὐτοῦ, τῷ Θεῷ πάλιν προσανέχειν σπουδάζων, ἐκεῖνοι δὲ ἔξω που ἀνακλιθέντες ἐπὶ τοῦ χόρτου καὶ μικρὸν κουκούλιόν τινος ἀδελφοῦ εὑρόντες, ἐτίθουν ἐπὶ τὰς κεφαλὰς ἀλλήλων ὅ τε δομέστικος καὶ ὁ πρωτοσπαθάριος, γελοιάζοντες ἅμα καὶ παίζοντες. Ὅπερ θεασάμενος διὰ τῆς θυρίδος ὁ ὅσιος καὶ σφόδρα καταγνοὺς τῆς εὐτραπελίας αὐτῶν, ἐπέπληξεν αὐτοῖς αὐστηρῶς, καί φησιν, ὅτι· "Τοῦτο, ὅπερ ὑμεῖς γελοιάζετε νῦν, ἰδοὺ ἐλεύσεται ὥρα, ἐν ᾗ ζητήσετε ἐπιθυμητικῶς τοῦ περιβαλέσθαι αὐτό, καὶ αὐτοῦ οὐ καταξιωθήσεσθε."

2   Καὶ ἅμα τῷ προορατικῷ τούτῳ λόγῳ φρίκη τε καὶ κεφαλαλγία τὸν δομέστικον περιέσχεν· ὅστις καὶ παραχρῆμα ἐπιστρέψας εἰς τὸν ἴδιον οἶκον καὶ ῥίψας ἐν τῇ κλίνῃ, ἐκέλευσε κληθῆναι αὐτῷ τινα τῶν εὐλαβῶν ἱερέων. Ὃς ἐλθὼν καὶ τῇ κλίνῃ ἐγγίσας πρὸς τὸ μαθεῖν τῆς κλήσεως τὴν αἰτίαν, εὗρεν αὐτὸν ἤδη ἀποθανόντα. Τούτου δὲ γενομένου, φόβος ἐπέπεσε τοῖς αὐτῷ συνοδεύσασιν ἀπὸ τοῦ μοναστηρίου καὶ πάντες ἐθαύμαζον τὴν πρόρρησιν τοῦ ἁγίου.

Chapter 52

A little later, the *protospatharios* Nicholas and the *domestikos* Leo went out to visit Neilos, desiring to hear his beneficial teaching and admonition. After a lengthy meeting and exhortation, the holy man went into his cell, eager to devote himself to God once more; meanwhile the *domestikos* and *protospatharios* were outside the monastery reclining upon the grass, and after finding a small monk's hood, they were putting it on each other's heads, fooling around playfully. When the holy man saw this from his window, he greatly condemned their jocularity, reprimanded them severely, and said, "Behold, the time will come when you will ardently seek to be invested with this hood which you now mock, but you will not be deemed worthy of it."

Just as these prophetic words were spoken, the *domestikos* 2 was seized with shivering and a headache, and immediately returned to his house. Throwing himself on his bed, he asked that one of the pious priests be summoned. The priest arrived, but as soon as he drew near the bed to find out the reason for the summons, he found Leo already dead. After this happened, fear struck those who had accompanied him from the monastery, and they all marveled at the holy man's prophecy.

53

Τινὲς οὖν κακεντρεχεῖς καὶ κόλακες ἄνθρωποι, ἀνελθόντες ἐν Κωνσταντινουπόλει, ἐλοιδόρησαν τὸν μακάριον εἰς τὰ ὦτα τοῦ βασιλικοῦ Εὐπραξίου, ὡς λεηλατήσαντα τὸ αὐτοῦ μοναστήριον καὶ τὰ τοῦ Ἀντωνίου πράγματα νοσφισάμενον. Ὃς ταῖς τοιαύταις συκοφαντίαις ἀγριωθείς, γράφει τινὶ τῶν ἐπιτρόπων αὐτοῦ, ἀπειλῶν τῷ ἁγίῳ καὶ λέγων ὅτι· "Ἀξιώσει με ὁ Θεὸς ὑγιαίνοντα κατελθεῖν καὶ γνωρίσαι τίς ἐστιν ὁ καλόγηρος Νεῖλος καὶ τίς ἐστιν ὁ βασιλικὸς Εὐπράξιος."

2 Κατελθόντος δὲ αὐτοῦ μετὰ πολλῆς ἐπάρσεως καὶ φαντασίας διὰ τὸ κατασταθῆναι αὐτὸν ὑπὸ τῶν βασιλέων κριτὴν Ἰταλίας τε καὶ Καλαβρίας, ἅπαντες μὲν οἱ ἡγούμενοι τῆς χώρας προσήρχοντο αὐτῷ μετὰ δώρων καὶ κολακείας, τὴν αὐτοῦ ἀντίληψιν καὶ βοήθειαν ἔχειν παρακαλοῦντες, ὁ δὲ θεσπέσιος ἡμῶν πατὴρ Νεῖλος, ἵνα μὴ δόξῃ ἢ ἀπειλὰς ἀνθρωπίνας θροεῖσθαι, ἢ πεποιθέναι ἐπ᾽ ἄρχοντας, τοὺς ὀνειδιστικῶς υἱοὺς ἀνθρώπων παρὰ τοῦ προφήτου κληθέντας, οἷς οὐκ ἔστιν σωτηρία, οὔτε προσῆλθε θωπευτικῶς καὶ κολακευτικῶς, οὐδὲ δώροις ἐκμειλίξατο τὴν ἀπειλὴν τῆς αὐτοῦ αὐθαδείας τε καὶ θρασύτητος, ἡσυχάζων δὲ μόνον ἐν τῷ ἰδίῳ μοναστηρίῳ, τὸν Θεὸν ἐδυσώπει ὑπέρ τε τῆς τοῦ κόσμου παντὸς καὶ τῆς τοῦ ἄρχοντος ψυχικῆς σωτηρίας.

3 Ὅπερ εἰς πλείονα θυμὸν καὶ μανίαν ἀνῆψε τὴν καρδίαν τοῦ ὑψηλοφρονοῦντος, ὡς παρὰ πάντων τιμωμένου καὶ

Chapter 53

Some wicked and parasitic men went to Constantinople and slandered the blessed Neilos to the ears of the imperial judge Eupraxios, saying that Neilos had plundered his monastery and appropriated the property of Anthony. Eupraxios was enraged by these false charges, and wrote to one of his procurators, threatening the holy man with these words, "May God deem me worthy to visit Rossano in good health, and make known who this monk Neilos is and who the imperial judge Eupraxios is."

Eupraxios arrived with much pomp and spectacle, be- 2 cause he had been appointed judge of both Italy and Calabria by the emperors, and all the superiors of the region approached him with gifts and flattery, calling on his protection and his assistance. However, not wishing to give the impression that he was afraid of human threats, or trusted *in princes,* whom the prophet reproachfully calls *the children of men in whom there is no safety,* our godly father Neilos did not approach the judge in a fawning or flattering manner, nor did he try to appease with gifts his insolent and arrogant threats, but remained in spiritual tranquility in his monastery, entreating God for the spiritual salvation of the whole world and the official.

This inflamed the heart of the haughty judge to greater 3 anger and rage since he was honored and revered by all, but

θεραπευομένου, ὑπὸ δὲ τοῦ ὁσίου σαφῶς περιφρονου-
μένου· διὸ καὶ <οὐκ> ἐξέλειπεν ἐξερευνῶν κατὰ τοῦ δικαίου πρόφασιν ἀνομίας. Οὐ γὰρ δυνατὸν γνωσθῆναι
ἴχνος ὄφεως ἐπὶ πέτρας, ὥσπερ οὖν οὐδὲ πονηρίαν ἄρχοντος ἐν ἀνθρώπῳ κατεστεμμένῳ.

54

Ἐν τούτῳ γνωσιμαχοῦντος καὶ πονηρευομένου, ἐπέστη
ὄλεθρος αἰφνίδιος καὶ ἡ εὐχὴ τοῦ τιμίου πατρὸς αὐτὸν
προκατελάβετο· πάθος γάρ τι, τὸ λεγόμενον γάγγραινα,
περὶ τὸν βάλανον τοῦ παιδογόνου μορίου αὐτοῦ ἐκφυέν,
τῶν μὲν ἰατρῶν ἄπρακτον διήλεγχε τὴν περιοδείαν, δίκας
δὲ εἰσεπράττετο τὸ τῆς ἀσωτίας ὄργανον, δι᾿ ὧν ἀκρατῶς
τὸν τῆς φύσεως νόμον ἐξύβρισεν.

2   Ἐλθὼν τοίνυν εἰς συναίσθησιν ἑαυτοῦ καὶ μεμψάμενος
τὴν κατὰ τοῦ ἁγίου θρασύτητα ἑαυτοῦ—ἦν γὰρ ἐχέφρων
ἱκανῶς ὁ ἀνήρ, εἰ καὶ τετύφωτο τῇ τῆς ἐξουσίας ὑπερ-
οχῇ—ἱκέτης καθίσταται ὁ πρώην ἐμβριμώμενος ταῖς
ἀπειλαῖς, εἴ πως τῆς θέας ἐπιτύχει καὶ μόνον, εὐλογίας τε
καὶ συγχωρήσεως τῆς παρ᾿ ἐκείνου ἀξιωθείη. Ὁ δὲ πατὴρ
πρὸς μὲν τὸ παρὸν ἀνεβάλλετο τὴν κατὰ πρόσωπον
ὁμιλίαν, μήτε ἐκεῖνον καταδεχόμενος ἐρχόμενον ἐν τῷ μοναστηρίῳ, μήτε αὐτὸς βουλόμενος ἀπελθεῖν καὶ τὴν δέη-
σιν αὐτοῦ ἐκτελέσαι, τῷ τοιούτῳ τρόπῳ τὴν σωτηρίαν

was clearly held in contempt by the holy man. Therefore the judge did not cease searching for a pretext for iniquity against the righteous one. Just as one cannot trace the *track of a serpent on a rock,* so one cannot detect the wickedness of an official against an honored person.

Chapter 54

While the judge was preoccupied with these conflicting and wicked thoughts, a sudden disaster befell him, and the prayer of the venerable father anticipated it. For an affliction called gangrene grew around the tip of his penis, rendering ineffective the routine treatment by doctors, and exacting punishment on his organ of sexual desire for the unrestrained violations it had made against the law of nature.

Coming, therefore, to his senses and blaming himself for 2 his own insolence against the holy man—for the man was very sensible, even though he was swollen up with arrogance on account of the eminence of his authority—he who previously had shouted threats became a suppliant, hoping to obtain an audience with the holy man, and be deemed worthy of his blessing and forgiveness. The father postponed for the moment any personal interaction with him, neither receiving Eupraxios when he came to the monastery, nor being willing to go out himself to the city and fulfill his request,

αὐτῷ πραγματευόμενος. Ἤιδει γὰρ ἐν εὐθέτῳ καιρῷ καὶ τῷ τύφῳ δεόντως κατὰ τῶν ἀναισθήτων χρήσασθαι.

3   Ὡς γοῦν ἐπὶ τριετῆ χρόνον ἡ θεόπεμπτος νόσος ἐκείνη κατὰ μικρὸν ἀναλώσασα τὰ κρυπτόμενα μόρια, προσήγγισε λοιπὸν τῷ καιριωτάτῳ τῶν μελῶν καὶ θάνατον ἠπείλει τῇ τούτου διαφθορᾷ, τότε πορεύεται πρὸς αὐτὸν ὁ ψυχικὸς ἰατρός, δυσωπηθεὶς ταῖς οἰκτροτάταις αὐτοῦ ἐπιστολαῖς. Ἰδὼν τοίνυν τὸν ὅσιον ὁ βασιλικὸς καὶ περιλαβὼν τοὺς τιμίους πόδας αὐτοῦ, τοσοῦτον πλῆθος δακρύων ἐξέχεε καταφιλῶν αὐτούς, ὥστε καὶ αὐτὸν τὸν ἅγιον πατέρα καὶ πάντας τοὺς παραστήκοντας συνθρηνεῖν αὐτῷ καὶ κλαίειν σφοδρῶς. Οὐδὲν γὰρ ἄλλο εἰκάσαι ἦν καὶ ἰδεῖν παρ' αὐτοῖς, ἢ τὴν πόρνην ἐν κατανύξει κατέχουσαν τοὺς πόδας τοῦ Σωτῆρος καὶ ἄφεσιν αἰτοῦσαν τῶν πεπλημμελημένων.

55

Ἰδὼν οὖν αὐτὸν ὁ πατὴρ χορτασθέντα τοῦ κλαυθμοῦ, καθάπερ βρέφος τοῦ οἰκείου μασθοῦ, ἐκτείνας τὴν χεῖρα ἐπελάβετο καὶ ἀνέστησεν αὐτόν. Ὁ δέ, πᾶσι κελεύσας ἐξελθεῖν ἀπ' αὐτοῦ, ἤρξατο ἀπογυμνοῦν σὺν τοῖς ψυχικοῖς πάθεσι καὶ τὰ σωματικὰ καὶ δακρύων ἔλεγεν· "Ἰδού, τιμιώτατε πάτερ, τριετίαν, ἡμέραν καὶ νύκτα, βεβασάνισμαι ὑπὸ τούτου τοῦ δεινοτάτου πάθους, πόνοις δριμυτάτοις καὶ ἀφάτῳ δυσωδίᾳ πυκτεύων, ἥν, οὔτε πλῆθος προστριβόμενος μύρων, οὔτε τῇ πυκνότητι τῶν ἱματίων

effecting in this way the man's salvation. For Neilos knew how, at the proper time, to use even arrogance in a fitting manner against senseless people.

So for three years that divinely-sent disease gradually 3 consumed his private parts, and was advancing to the most vital of his members, and threatening death through its destruction. Then Neilos, the physician of souls, moved by his most piteous letters, went to Eupraxios. Upon seeing the holy man, the imperial judge clasped his venerable feet and kissed them, shedding such abundant tears that the holy father and all those in attendance lamented together with the man and wept profusely. For it seemed to them that they saw nothing else than the prostitute clasping the Savior's feet in contrition and asking forgiveness for her transgressions.

Chapter 55

Therefore, seeing that he was sated with weeping, just as an infant by a familiar breast, the father reached out his hand and taking hold of him, made him stand. Eupraxios ordered everyone to leave the room and began to disclose the sufferings of his soul and also those of his body, and tearfully said, "Behold, most reverend father, for three years I have been tormented day and night by this most terrible affliction, contending with acute pain and an unspeakable stench, which I have never been able to get rid of, neither by rubbing on a great quantity of perfumed ointments, nor through

παλαίων, ἑπτάκις γὰρ τῆς ἡμέρας ἀλλάσσων, ἐκφυγεῖν ἠδυνήθην."

2   Ἦν δὲ τὸ πάθος, ὡς ὁ μακάριος ἔλεγεν, ὑπὸ τὸ ἦτρον αὐτοῦ ὥσπερ ἀπὸ διαβήτου τηχθὲν καὶ ἔχων ἐκ τῶν κεχωρισμένων μορίων οὐδέν. Πάλιν οὖν, τὰς χεῖρας τοῦ δικαίου κρατῶν ὁ βασιλικὸς καὶ πλύνων αὐτὰς τοῖς δάκρυσιν, ἔλεγεν· "Ἐλέησόν με διὰ τὸν Κύριον, μιμητὰ τοῦ Δεσπότου Χριστοῦ, καὶ καταξίωσον ταῖς τιμίαις σου ταύταις χερσὶν ἀποκεῖραί με τὸν πανάσωτον, ἐπειδὴ ὡμολόγησα τῷ Θεῷ τοῦ γενέσθαι με μοναχόν."

3   Λέγει δὲ πρὸς αὐτὸν ὁ πατήρ· "Οὐκ ἔξεστί σοι, ἀνθρώπῳ συνετῷ ὄντι καὶ σφόδρα πεπαιδευμένῳ, τὰ τῶν κοινῶν ἀνθρώπων λόγια φρονεῖν τε καὶ λέγειν· ἅπαντες γὰρ οἱ τοῦ θείου βαπτίσματος καταξιωθέντες καὶ ἀμόλυντον ἀπὸ πάσης ἁμαρτίας μὴ φυλάξαντες τοῦτο, χωρὶς πάσης ὁμολογίας χρεωστοῦσιν ἀναδέξασθαι πάλιν τὸ μακάριον βάπτισμα τοῦτο, ὅπερ διὰ πολλὴν εὐσπλαγχνίαν καὶ ἀγαθότητα ὁ Θεὸς τοῖς ἀνθρώποις ἐδωρήσατο, πλουσίοις καὶ πένησι, βασιλεῦσι καὶ ἄρχουσι, ἱερεῦσί τε καὶ ἀρχιερεῦσιν καὶ πάσῃ ψυχῇ τῇ βουλομένῃ ἐν μιᾷ καιροῦ ῥοπῇ ἀναγεννηθῆναι, ὡς ἀετοῦ ἡ νεότης, καὶ πάντων ἀπαλλαγῆναι τῶν προημαρτημένων.

4   "Καθὼς δὲ ἔφης περὶ τοῦ με ἀποκουρεῦσαί σε, εὐτελὲς καλογηρίτζιν εἰμὶ ἐγώ, μηδένα κεκτημένος βαθμὸν ἱερατικόν. Ὧδε μητροπολίτης ἐστίν," (ἦν γὰρ τότε ἐκεῖ ὁ τῆς Ἁγίας Σεβηρίνης μητροπολίτης), "ὧδε ἐπίσκοποι καὶ ἀρχιμανδρῖται εἰσίν· αὐτοὶ τὴν ἐπιθυμίαν σου πληρωσάτωσαν. Καὶ ἐγὼ τίς εἰμι, ἵνα μεσάζομαι;" Ὁ δὲ πάλιν τὰς χεῖρας

frequent change of garments, changing them seven times a day."

Furthermore, as the blessed Neilos said, the affliction 2 had resulted in a wasting away of the genitals as if they were cut by a stonemason's rule and Eupraxios had no testicles at all. Again the imperial official grasped the hands of the righteous Neilos, and washing them with his tears said, "Have mercy on me for the sake of the Lord, O imitator of Christ the Master, and deem me, the most profligate one, worthy of being tonsured by your venerable hands, since I have promised God to become a monk."

The father then said to him, "It is not fitting for you, as a 3 wise and extremely educated man, to believe and speak the thoughts of common men; for all who were deemed worthy of holy baptism and did not preserve it immaculate from every sin ought to receive again this blessed baptism without a second thought. This God gave as a gift to humanity, on account of His abundant compassion and goodness, to rich and poor, to kings and rulers, to priests and high priests, and to every soul wishing to be born again in the twinkling of an eye, *like the youth of the eagle,* and to be delivered from all one's prior sins.

"As for your suggestion about my tonsuring you, you 4 should know that I am a humble monk, who holds no ecclesiastical office. There is a metropolitan here"—at that time the metropolitan of Saint Severina was there—"there are bishops and archimandrites here, let them fulfill your desire. Who am I to intervene?" But Eupraxios kissed again

καταφιλῶν τοῦ θείου πατρὸς παρεκάλει ὁμοῦ καθορκίζων
τοῦ μὴ ἄλλῳ τινὶ τὸ τοιοῦτον ἔργον παραχωρῆσαι, ἀλλὰ
δι' αὐτοῦ τὸ ἅγιον καὶ ἀποστολικὸν σχῆμα ἀμφιασθῆναι
καὶ πρὸς τὸν Θεὸν αὐτὸν μεσίτην καὶ προστάτην γενέσθαι.

56

Καμφθεὶς οὖν ὁ πατὴρ τοῖς δάκρυσιν καὶ ταῖς ἱκεσίαις
αὐτοῦ, ταῖς οἰκείαις χερσὶν αὐτὸν ἀπεκείρατο καὶ τὰ τῇ
σεμνῇ ταπεινώσει δεδοξασμένα ῥάκη περιεβάλετο τὸν
ἁπαλῇ καὶ περιρρεούσῃ ἐσθῆτι πρώην μαλακιζόμενον,
παρόντος τοῦ μητροπολίτου Στεφάνου σὺν τῷ ἐπισκόπῳ
τοῦ κάστρου, ἡγουμένοις τε οὐκ ὀλίγοις καὶ ἄλλοις ἱε-
ρεῦσιν. Παρειστήκει δὲ καὶ ὁ Ἰουδαῖος Δόμνουλος ὡς
ἰατρός, οὗ καὶ πρώην ἐμνήσθην, θεωρῶν ἅπαντα τὰ τε-
λούμενα· ὃς ἐξελθὼν ἔξω καὶ τὰ γεγενημένα θαυμάσας,
ἔφη πρὸς τοὺς παρόντας· "Σήμερον ἐθεασάμην θαυμάσια,
ἅπερ πάλαι γενέσθαι ἀκήκοα. Νῦν εἶδον τὸν προφήτην
Δανιὴλ ἡμεροῦντα τοὺς λέοντας. Τίς γὰρ ἠδυνήθη ποτὲ
χεῖρα ἐπιβαλέσθαι τούτῳ τῷ λέοντι; Ὁ δὲ νέος οὗτος Δανιὴλ καὶ τὴν κόμην ἀπέτεμε καὶ κουκούλιον ἐπιτέθεικεν."
Καὶ ταῦτα μὲν ὁ Ἑβραῖος.

2   Ὁ δὲ βασιλικός, μετὰ τὸ πᾶσαν τὴν ἀγγελικὴν ἀκο-
λουθίαν τελεσθῆναι ἐπ' αὐτῷ, προτρεψάμενος ἅπαντας
ἐπὶ τὸ γεύσασθαι καὶ συντάξας δι' ἑαυτοῦ, αὐτὸς παρίστατο

the holy father's hands, beseeching him and binding him with oaths not to entrust this deed to anyone else, but that he should be garbed in the holy and apostolic habit by Neilos, who should be for him a mediator with God and his protector.

Chapter 56

Then the father was moved to pity by the man's tears and supplications, and so tonsured him with his own hands. Neilos garbed in the habit that is glorified by sacred humility this man who had previously indulged in soft and luxurious clothing, in the presence of the metropolitan Stephen along with the bishop of the city of Rossano and many superiors as well as other priests. Also in attendance as a physician was the Jew Domnoulos, whom I mentioned earlier, who carefully observed the entire ceremony; upon leaving he marveled at what had happened and told those present, "Today I saw amazing deeds, such as I have heard happened long ago. Now I have seen the prophet Daniel taming the lions. For who could ever place his hand upon this lion? This new Daniel both cut off its hair and placed the monastic hood upon it." And this is what the Jew said.

After the completion of the rite of angelic investiture, 2 the imperial official invited everyone to dine and arranged everything himself. Furthermore, he, who for so many days

καθάπερ οἰκέτης προθυμούμενος ὑπουργῆσαι, ὁ πρὸ
πολλῶν ἡμερῶν τῆς κλίνης μὴ δυνάμενος ἀναστῆναι, ῥω-
σθεὶς τῇ δυνάμει τοῦ Πνεύματος καὶ τῆς τοῦ ὁσίου χειρὸς
χάριτι. Παρακελευσθεὶς καθεσθῆναι ἔγγιστα αὐτοῦ,
ᾐτήσατο πάλιν τοῦ διατάξασθαι ἐπὶ τῆς τραπέζης λύσιν
λαβεῖν. Καὶ τούτου γενομένου, πάντες ἐξίσταντο ἐπὶ τῇ
ἀναρρώσει καὶ προθυμίᾳ τοῦ ἀνδρὸς καὶ ἐδόξαζον τὸν
Θεόν.

3   Μετὰ δὲ ταῦτα, πάντα τὰ ὑπάρχοντα αὐτῷ τῇ ἰδίᾳ χειρὶ
δοὺς πένησι καὶ ἐκκλησίαις καὶ πᾶσι τοῖς δεομένοις, ληγα-
τεύσας τε ἅπασαν τὴν οἰκετείαν αὐτοῦ καὶ ἐλευθερίας
καταξιώσας, τῇ τρίτῃ ἡμέρᾳ πρὸς Κύριον ἀπεδήμησε μετὰ
πάσης κατανύξεως καὶ εὐχαριστίας, πίστεώς τε καὶ ἐλπίδος
βεβαίας, ἀπελθὼν πρὸς τὸν εἰρηκότα διὰ τοῦ προφήτου·
"Οὐ θέλω τὸν θάνατον τοῦ ἁμαρτωλοῦ, ὡς τὸ ἐπιστρέψαι καὶ
ζῆσαι αὐτὸν ζωὴν τὴν αἰώνιον."

57

Μετὰ δὲ τὸ κατατεθῆναι τὸ σῶμα αὐτοῦ ἐν τῷ μοναστηρίῳ τῆς ἁγίας παρθένου Ἀναστασίας, προσέρχεται τῷ
θεσπεσίῳ πατρὶ ὁ ῥηθεὶς μητροπολίτης, ὑποδεικνύων
αὐτῷ τὴν τοῦ βασιλικοῦ διαθήκην, ἐν ᾗ πάσῃ τῇ τε κινητῇ
καὶ ἀκινήτῳ αὐτοῦ ὑποστάσει ἐπίτροπον καὶ δεσπότην τὸν
ὅσιον διεγράψατο. Ἥνπερ θεασάμενος ὁ μακάριος καὶ τὴν

previously was unable to rise from his bed, stood at the table as a servant eager to attend them, fortified by the power of the Spirit and the grace of the holy man's hand. Though bidden to sit next to Neilos, he asked again for permission to serve at table. When this happened, they all were amazed at the man's recovery and zeal, and praised God.

After this, with his own hands he gave all his belongings 3 to the poor, to the churches, and to all those in need, and he gave legacies to all his household servants and granted them their freedom. On the third day he departed to the Lord with great compunction and gratitude, departing with faith and sure hope to the One who said through the prophet, "*I do not desire the death of the sinner, but that he turn from his way and live forever.*"

Chapter 57

After Eupraxios's body was laid to rest in the monastery of the holy virgin Anastasia, the aforementioned metropolitan went to the divine father and showed him the testament of the imperial official, in which Eupraxios had appointed the holy Neilos as the custodian and owner of all his movable and immovable properties. When he saw this

ἐν ἐκείνοις τοῖς πράγμασιν ἀσχολίαν παγίδα εἶναι καὶ χλεύην τοῦ Διαβόλου κατανοήσας, πάντα ἐπιτρέψας τῷ αὐτῷ μητροπολίτη δικαίως οἰκονομῆσαι, ὡς τῷ τὰ πάντα ἐφορῶντι Θεῷ ἀποδώσοντα τὴν περὶ τούτων ἀπολογίαν, αὐτὸς τὸ οἰκεῖον κατέλαβεν μοναστήριον, ἑαυτῷ προσέχων καὶ τῷ Θεῷ προσανέχων καὶ πειθόμενος τοῖς ἁγίοις ἀγγέλοις αὐτῷ συναινοῦσι καὶ λέγουσι· "Μεταναστεύου ἐπὶ τὰ ὄρη ὡς στρουθίον, ὅτι ἰδοὺ οἱ ἐξ ἡμῶν ἁμαρτωλοὶ ἐνέτειναν τόξον, τὴν τῶν ἀνθρωπίνων πραγμάτων ἐπιμέλειαν καὶ φροντίδα, καὶ ἡτοίμασαν βέλη εἰς φαρέτραν, τὰ τῇ διανοίᾳ ἐξ αὐτῶν ἐναποτιθέμενα πονηρὰ βουλεύματα καὶ διανοήματα, ὑφ' ὧν κατατοξεῦσαι ἐν σκοτομήνῃ βουλεύονται οἱ ἀλάστορες τοὺς εὐθεῖς τῇ καρδίᾳ."

58

Τοῦ τοίνυν θαυμασίου πατρὸς τῇ προσευχῇ καὶ τῇ διακονίᾳ τοῦ λόγου μετὰ τῶν ἀδελφῶν φιλοθέως προσκαρτεροῦντος, ἔρχεταί τις πρὸς αὐτὸν στρατηλάτης, Πολύευκτος τοὔνομα, ἀπὸ τῆς παροικίας Μεσουβιάνου τῆς Καλαβρίας, φέρων μεθ' ἑαυτοῦ τὸν υἱὸν αὐτοῦ κατεχόμενον ὑπὸ σφοδροτάτου δαίμονος. Προσπεσὼν οὖν παρὰ τοὺς πόδας τοῦ μακαρίου πατρός, παρεκάλει αὐτὸν σπλαγχνισθῆναι ἐπ' αὐτῷ καὶ ἐλεῆσαι τὸν υἱὸν αὐτοῦ, ἀπαλλάξας αὐτὸν τοῦ δεινοῦ πνεύματος.

testament, the blessed man realized that involvement in these affairs was a snare and deception of the Devil, so he entrusted everything to the same metropolitan for his just administration, as he would have to make an accounting for these things to God who oversees all. Neilos himself withdrew to his monastery, focusing on himself, devoting himself to God, and obeying the holy angels who advised him, saying, *"Flee to the mountains as a sparrow, for, behold, those* of us who are *sinners have bent the bow"* — that is, concern and solicitude for human affairs — *"and have prepared the arrows for the quiver"* — that is, the wicked counsels and inclinations in their mind — "with which the wicked devise *to shoot in the darkness at the upright in heart."*

Chapter 58

While the marvelous father and his brethren *devoted themselves to prayer and to the ministry of the word* with love for God, a military officer named Polyeuktos, from the region of Mesoubianon in Calabria, came to him, bringing along his son who was possessed by a most violent demon. Throwing himself at the feet of the blessed father, the officer beseeched Neilos to have compassion for him and to take pity on his son and deliver him from the terrible spirit.

2   Ὁ δὲ ὄντως υἱὸς τῆς χριστομιμήτου ταπεινοφροσύνης
ἀπεκρίνατο πρὸς αὐτόν· "Πίστευσον, ἄνθρωπε, ὅτι οὐδέποτε παρεκάλεσα τὸν Θεὸν τοῦ δωρήσασθαι τῇ ταπεινώσει μου χάριν ἰαμάτων, ἢ πονηρῶν πνευμάτων ἐκδίωξιν.
Εἴθε τῶν πολλῶν μου ἁμαρτημάτων δυναίμην συγγνώμην
αἰτήσασθαι τὸν Θεὸν καὶ ἀπαλλαγὴν τῶν ἀεὶ παρεν-
οχλούντων μοι πονηρῶν λογισμῶν! Δεῦρο τοίνυν αὐτὸς
παρακάλεσον τὸν Θεὸν μᾶλλον ὑπὲρ ἐμοῦ, ἀδελφέ, εἴ πως
ἂν ῥυσθείην τῶν περικυκλούντων με δαιμονίων πολλῶν.
Ὁ γὰρ σὸς υἱὸς ἓν δαιμόνιον ἔχει, καὶ αὐτὸ ἀκουσίως, ἴσως
δὲ καὶ πρὸς σωτηρίαν τῆς ἰδίας ψυχῆς, εἴτε πρὸς παρ-
ῳχηκότων ἁμαρτημάτων ἐκλύτρωσιν, εἴτε καὶ πρὸς μελλόντων ἀνακοπήν. Ἐγὼ δὲ τῇ ἐμῇ ῥαθυμίᾳ καὶ ἀμελείᾳ
καθ᾽ ἑκάστην δουλοῦμαι χιλιάσι καὶ μυριάσι δαιμόνων
πρὸς ἀπώλειαν τῆς ψυχῆς μου."

3   Ταῦτα εἰπὼν καὶ ὑπαναχωρήσας μικρόν, ἀπέκρυψεν
ἑαυτὸν ἡμέρας τινάς, δεδοικὼς μήπως, ἰαθέντος τοῦ δαι-
μονιζομένου, ἐξέλθοι ἡ φήμη καθ᾽ ὅλης τῆς χώρας καὶ οὐκ
ἐάσωσιν αὐτὸν ἠρεμῆσαι ἐν τῷ τόπῳ ἐκείνῳ. Ὁ δὲ Πολύευκτος, κατοχυρώσας ἑαυτοῦ τὴν καρδίαν τῇ πίστει καὶ τῇ
ἐλπίδι, διεκαρτέρει ἐν τῷ μοναστηρίῳ νηστεύων καὶ κακο-
χούμενος καὶ μετὰ δακρύων λέγων· "Οὐκ ἀναχωρήσω τῶν
ὧδε, ἕως οὗ ὁ υἱός μου ἰάσεως ἐπιτύχει."

4   Ἰδὼν οὖν ὁ μακάριος τὴν ἔνθεον αὐτοῦ πίστιν καὶ ὑπομονὴν αὐτοῦ, ἐσπλαγχνίσθη ἐπ᾽ αὐτῷ καὶ ἐπὶ τῷ υἱῷ αὐτοῦ
καί, ἐν τῷ μοναστηρίῳ ἐλθών, ἐδυσφόρει ἐν ἑαυτῷ λέγων·
"Τί ποιήσω τῷ ἀνθρώπῳ τούτῳ οὐκ οἶδα· καὶ γὰρ ἀμφοτέρωθεν πειρασμὸς ἡμῖν πρόσκειται, εἴτε ἰαθεὶς ὁ υἱὸς

Neilos, a true son of Christ-imitating humility, responded 2
to him, "My good man, be assured that I never called upon
God to grant to my humble self the grace of healing nor the
expulsion of wicked spirits. If only I were able to ask God
for forgiveness for my many sins and deliverance from the
wicked thoughts that constantly torment me! Come then,
brother; it is rather you who should entreat God on my behalf, that I may be liberated from the many demons that
surround me. For your son has only one demon and that one
he has against his will. Perhaps this is also for the salvation
of his soul, either as redemption for past sins or as a check
against future ones. Yet I, through my idleness and negli-
gence, am enslaved every day by thousands and tens of thousands of demons for the perdition of my soul."

With these words he withdrew a short distance, and went 3
into hiding for several days, fearing that, if the youth were
somehow cured from demonic possession, the rumor would
spread throughout the whole region and the people would
not let him continue his quiet life in that place. Polyeuktos
fortified his own heart with faith and hope, and waited patiently in the monastery, fasting and mortifying himself,
while he kept saying tearfully, "I shall not go away from here
until my son attains healing."

The blessed man, upon seeing his divinely inspired faith 4
and his perseverance, was moved to compassion for him and
his son, and returned to the monastery, but he was distressed and said to himself, "I do not know what to do for
this man; for on either side lies a temptation for me, whether

αὐτοῦ, εἴτε μή." Ὅμως οὖν, μηδ᾽ ὅλως καταδεξάμενος κἂν θεάσασθαι τὸν πνευματιζόμενον, καλέσας τὸν τῆς ἱερατείας τὴν τάξιν ἐνδεδυμένον, κελεύει αὐτῷ ἀπελθεῖν ἐν τῷ εὐκτηρίῳ καί, ἐπευξάμενον τῷ νοσοῦντι, ἀλεῖψαι αὐτὸν ἐλαίῳ τῆς κανδήλας καὶ ἀπολῦσαι.

59

Τούτου δὲ γενομένου, παραχρῆμα ὁ νέος ἰάσεως ἠξιώθη, τοῦ δαίμονος ἀπὸ τῶν αἰσθητηρίων αὐτοῦ ὡσεὶ καπνοῦ ἐξελθόντος. Ὅπερ ἰδὼν ὁ πατὴρ αὐτοῦ καὶ χαρᾷ σὺν θαύματι συσχεθείς, παραλαμβάνει αὐτὸν καὶ προσπίπτει μετ᾽ αὐτοῦ τοῖς γόνασι τοῦ πατρός, εὐχαριστῶν τῷ Θεῷ καὶ αὐτῷ τῷ διὰ μόνης προστάξεως τὸ πονηρὸν πνεῦμα τοῦ υἱοῦ ἀπελάσαντι. Ἐμβριμησάμενος δὲ αὐτῷ ὁ μακάριος, παρήγγειλε μηδενὶ τοῦτο εἰπεῖν. "Ὁ Θεὸς γάρ," φησίν, "ἰάσατο τὸν σὸν υἱόν, οὐκ ἐγώ," καὶ εὐλογήσας αὐτούς, ἀπέλυσεν ἐν εἰρήνῃ εἰς τὸν οἶκον αὐτῶν δοξάζοντας τὸν Θεόν.

2 Τούτῳ δὲ τῷ τρόπῳ πολλοὺς ἀπὸ δαιμόνων ὁ θαυμάσιος ἐθεράπευσεν, μοναχούς τε καὶ λαϊκούς, τοὺς μὲν ἐλαίῳ διὰ τῶν ἱερέων ἀλείφων, αὐτὸς μηδέποτε καταδεξάμενος μέχρι καὶ τῆς διὰ χειρὸς σφραγῖδος ἐπ᾽ αὐτοῖς, τοὺς δὲ ἀποστέλλων πρὸς τὰς τῶν μακαρίων ἀποστόλων τε καὶ μαρτύρων θήκας τὰς ἐν τῇ Ῥώμῃ, οἵτινες κατὰ τὴν ὁδὸν ἐκαθαρίζοντο, τοῦ μακαρίου πατρὸς ὀφθαλμοφανῶς

his son is healed or not." Nevertheless, although he would not consent to even look upon the young man possessed by a spirit, Neilos summoned a brother who was invested with the priestly rank and bade him go to the chapel and pray for the afflicted youth, anoint him with oil from the lamp, and send him on his way.

Chapter 59

As soon as this was done, the young man was immediately healed, as the demon departed from his sensory organs in the form of smoke. At this sight, his father, Polyeuktos, was seized by joy and amazement. He took the youth and with him prostrated himself at the knees of the father, expressing gratitude to God and to him, who by virtue of his command alone expelled his son's wicked spirit. But the blessed man rebuked him and told him to reveal this to no one. "For it was God," he said, "who healed your son, not I," and, after giving his blessing, he dismissed them in peace to return home, glorifying God.

The wondrous man cured many people of demons — monks and laypeople alike — in this manner, that is, either by having the priests anoint them with oil (as he himself never consented even to make the sign of the cross upon them with his own hand), or by sending them to the tombs of the blessed apostles and martyrs in Rome. In this case these people were cleansed along the way, as the blessed

αὐτοῖς ὀπτανομένου καὶ τοὺς δαίμονας ἐξ αὐτῶν ἀπελαύ-
νοντος. Τοῦτο δὲ ἐγίνετο, ἵνα μὴ κενὴ ἡ πρὸς τὸν ὅσιον
πίστις αὐτῶν δειχθῇ καὶ ὁ κόπος ἀνόνητος τῆς καταφυγῆς.
Εἰ γὰρ καὶ λόγῳ ταπεινοφροσύνης φανερῶς οὐκ ἐπεύχετο
αὐτοῖς ἀποφεύγων τὸν ἀνθρώπινον ἔπαινον, ἀλλά γε, τῇ
φιλανθρωπίᾳ νικώμενος, ἀπὸ τοῦ κρυπτοῦ τῆς κέλλης
αὐτοῦ ταῖς πυρίναις ἐντεύξεσι κατέφλεγε τὰ δαιμόνια καὶ
τὰς νόσους ἀπήλαυνεν. Ἅπερ ἅπαντα εἰ κατὰ μέρος βου-
ληθείην γραφῇ παραδοῦναι, οὐκ ἐπαρκέσει μοι ὁ χρόνος
τῇ δρομῇ παρατρέχων· ἀρκεῖ δὲ τοῖς εὐλαβέσι καὶ ἐκ
μέρους τὸ ὅλον καταλαβέσθαι, ὡς ἐξ ὀνύχων τὸν λέοντα.

60

Δέδωκε δὲ αὐτῷ χάριν ὁ τῶν ὅλων Θεός, οὐ μόνον τοὺς
καθ᾽ ἕκαστον προσερχομένους αὐτῷ θλιβομένους καὶ
παντοίαις ἀνάγκαις συνεχομένους ἐλεεῖν καὶ ἰᾶσθαι, ἀλλὰ
καὶ πόλεων ὁλοκλήρων ἐν κινδύνοις ἀντιλαμβάνεσθαι καὶ
λυτροῦσθαι τῶν περιστάσεων. Δηλώσει δὲ τὸ νῦν ῥη-
θησόμενον. Ἐκράτει ποτὲ ἀμφοτέρων τῶν χωρῶν, Ἰταλίας
τε καὶ τῆς καθ᾽ ἡμᾶς Καλαβρίας, Νικηφόρος ὁ μάγιστρος,
πρῶτος καὶ μόνος τῷ μεγίστῳ ἀξιώματι τούτῳ παρὰ τῶν
εὐσεβῶν βασιλέων ταῖς ῥηθείσαις χώραις ἀποσταλείς. Ὅς
τε ὁ μάγιστρος, τῇ μεγαλοφυΐᾳ νυττόμενος καὶ τῇ ἀξίᾳ
φιλοτιμούμενος, βουλὴν ἐβουλεύσατο ταῖς μὲν ἀνθρωπί-
ναις ἐννοίαις ἀπόδεκτον καὶ δοκοῦσαν ὠφέλιμον, τῷ θεϊκῷ

father appeared visibly before their very eyes and drove out their demons. This was done so that their faith in the holy man should not prove to be in vain, nor their labor of seeking refuge in him be unrewarded. Although on account of his humility he did not openly pray for them, avoiding men's praise, nonetheless Neilos, overcome by his love for humanity, burned up demons and drove out afflictions with his fiery prayers from the seclusion of his cell. And if I wished to write down in detail all these deeds, the swift passage of time would not suffice for me. It is enough for pious readers to conceive the whole from a part, as *the lion* is recognized *by his claws.*

Chapter 60

The God of all things granted him the grace not only to have mercy on and heal those coming to him individually—those suffering and oppressed by every sort of need—but even to rescue entire cities in danger and to deliver them from their misfortunes. I shall now demonstrate this with a story. Some time ago the *magistros* Nikephoros, the first and only one sent to these regions invested with such high dignity by the pious emperors, was the governor of both Italy and our Calabria. The *magistros,* overcome by the importance of his mission and the loftiness of his rank, conceived a plan that was worthy of approval by human minds and

δὲ βουλήματι ἀνθισταμένην καὶ μηδ' ὅλως εὐπρόσιτον, ὡς τὸ τέλος ἀπέδειξεν.

2   Ἐλογίσατο γὰρ ἐφ' ἑκάστῃ τῶν τῆς Καλαβρίας πόλεων κατασκευάσαι τὰ λεγόμενα χελάνδια, καὶ δι' αὐτῶν, οὐ μόνον ἑαυταῖς φυλάττειν τὸ ἀσφαλὲς καὶ ἀνεπιβούλευτον, ἀλλὰ καὶ τὴν γείτονα καὶ ἐχθρὰν Σικελίαν ἀφανισμῷ παραδοῦναι. Τοῦτο δὲ μὴ ἐνεγκόντες οἱ πάροικοι Ῥυσι-άνου, ὡς ἀσυνήθεις ὄντες τοῦ χελανδίοις δουλεύειν, μετὰ τὸ ἤδη ταῦτα κατασκευάσαι καὶ μέλλειν τοῖς τῆς θαλάσσης νώτοις ἐπιβιβάζειν, ζήλου θερμότητι ἀναφθέντες—ᾧπερ ἀεὶ νικῶνται ὑπὲρ πάντας Καλαβριώτας—παμπληθεὶ ὁρ-μήσαντες μετὰ πυρὸς καὶ μεγίστου θορύβου τά τε πλοῖα κατέκαυσαν καὶ τοὺς πρωτοκαράβους ἐκεφαλαίωσαν.

3   Τοῦτο δὲ εἰς μεγίστην ὀργὴν καὶ ἀγανάκτησιν κατὰ τῶν Ῥυσιανιτῶν τὸν μάγιστρον ἤγαγεν, ὡς δι' αὐτῶν καὶ τὰ λοιπὰ κάστρα τὸ βούλευμα ἀνατρέψαντα. Ὅπερ νοή-σαντες οἱ τοῦ Ῥυσιάνου πάροικοι καὶ καταγνόντες τῆς ἑαυτῶν ἀβουλίας καὶ ἀταξίας, τῶν δύο τὸ ἓν ἐβουλεύ-σαντο, ἢ παντελῆ ἀποστασίαν καὶ φανερὰν ἀνυποταξίαν ἐργάσασθαι καὶ κακῷ τὸ κακὸν ἰάσασθαι, ἢ τῇ τῶν χρημά-των ἐκδόσει καὶ τῷ πλήθει τῶν δώρων τὰ πάντα ἐξευμα-ρίσασθαι. Ἀμφοτέρωθεν δὲ αὐτοῖς δεινὸν καὶ ἐπαχθὲς τυγχάνον τὸ ἐπιχείρημα, βουλὴν βουλεύονται ἀγαθὴν καὶ σφόδρα ὠφέλιμον· ἐπὶ τὸν ἄσειστον πύργον, πατέρα τὸν ὅσιον, καταφεύγουσι, μεσίτην γενέσθαι αὐτὸν τοῦ πράγματος ἱλεούμενοι καὶ τῇ δυσωπήσει τῆς αὐτοῦ ἀρετῆς τὸν θυμὸν κατασβέσαι τοῦ ἄρχοντος.

seemingly beneficial, but was against the divine will and not at all acceptable to it, as the conclusion of this plan demonstrated.

He proclaimed that each city of Calabria should construct war ships, the so-called *chelandia,* and with these they would not only preserve their security and freedom from attack, but also bring destruction to their hostile neighbor Sicily. But the inhabitants of Rossano did not tolerate this, as they were unaccustomed to corvée labor on the *chelandia,* and after the ships were already built and ready to launch on the sea, driven by the heat of their furor—in which they always surpass all Calabrians—the citizens rushed *en masse* with torches and great uproar, and burned the ships and beheaded the captains.

This drove the *magistros* to very great anger and indignation against the inhabitants of Rossano, since because of them the other Calabrian cities had also overturned his plans. When the inhabitants of Rossano understood this, they blamed themselves for their own poor planning and disorder, and debated which of two alternatives to follow: either to carry out complete secession and open insubordination, attempting to heal evil with evil, or to make amends for everything by paying money and giving a great many gifts. However, since both options were grievous and onerous for them, they made a good and very beneficial decision; they went to the unshakable tower, the holy father, beseeching him to be a mediator in the affair and, with the authority of his virtue, to quench the magistrate's anger.

61

Τότε δὴ ὁ θεσπέσιος μηδὲν εἰς αὖθις ἀναβαλόμενος, ἀλλὰ τὸ τοῦ Χριστοῦ ὄνομα προβαλλόμενος, τὸ ἄστυ κατέλαβε καὶ τοῖς οἰκήτορσι τὰ πρέποντα συνεβούλευεν. Οὗπερ τῇ πεποιθήσει τὰς πύλας ἀνοίξαντες, θαρροῦντες τὸν μάγιστρον ὑπεδέξαντο, τῇ ὀργῇ πεπρισμένον καὶ τῷ θυμῷ κατοιδαίνοντα. Πάντων τοίνυν ἀπὸ προσώπου αὐτοῦ πτοηθέντων, ἀρχόντων τε καὶ ἱερέων καὶ τῶν λοιπῶν, μόνος ὁ τοῦ Θεοῦ δοῦλος προΐστατο καὶ ὑπὲρ πάντων ἀπολελόγητο. Οὗτινος τὴν ἀρετὴν ὁ ἄρχων αἰδούμενος καὶ τὴν ἔνθεον παρρησίαν σὺν τῇ ἐπιλαμπούσῃ τῷ προσώπῳ αὐτοῦ χάριτι τοῦ Ἁγίου Πνεύματος ἐκπληττόμενος, αὐτῷ τὴν κρίσιν τῆς τοιαύτης ἀταξίας τε καὶ ζημίας ἐπέτρεπεν.

2   Πρὸς ὃν ὁ ὅσιος πρᾴως τε καὶ μάλα σαφῶς ἀπεκρίνατο· "Ὁμολογητέον, ὅτι σφόδρα κακὸν καὶ ἄτακτον πρᾶγμα γεγένηται· ἀλλ' εἰ μὲν ὑπὸ εὐαριθμήτων ἀνθρώπων καὶ αὐτῶν τῶν ὑπερεχόντων ἀνθρώπων τὸ ἔργον προκεχώρηκε, κατάγνωστοι ἂν ὑπῆρχον καὶ ὑπόδικοι τῇ σοφωτάτῃ σου κρίσει· ἐπειδὴ δὲ τοῦ πλήθους παντός ἐστι τὸ ἐγχείρημα καὶ πᾶσι κοινὸν τὸ τῆς κακοπραγίας ἀβούλημα, ἔξεστί σοι μαχαίρᾳ παραδοῦναι πλῆθος τοσοῦτον καὶ ἔρημον καταστῆσαι τὸ τοιοῦτον φρούριον Θεοῦ καὶ τοῦ βασιλέως;"

3   Καὶ ὁ μάγιστρος ἔφη· "Οὐ μαχαίρῃ παραδώσομεν, πάτερ, οὐδ' ἀποκτενοῦμέν τινα, ἀλλὰ τὰ αὐτῶν ἀποθησαυρίσομεν τοῖς βασιλικοῖς βαλαντίοις, ἵν', ἐν τούτῳ

Chapter 61

Then the godly Neilos did not delay, but, setting before himself the name of Christ, he went down to the city and offered suitable advice to the inhabitants. With trust in him they opened the city gates and boldly received the *magistros,* who was gnashing his teeth in anger and swollen with rage. Whereas they were all terrified by him—the officials, priests, and all the others—the servant of God alone approached him and spoke on behalf of all the citizens in their defense. The *magistros* admired his virtue and was struck by his godly and bold speech, and by the grace of the Holy Spirit shining in his face, and so he entrusted to Neilos the judgment about the great disorder and damage.

To him the holy man gently and very clearly responded, 2 "It must be acknowledged that an exceedingly wicked and lawless offense has been committed; if the deed were done by only a few people, or by the leading citizens, then they could be condemned and submitted to your most wise judgment. However, since this was an undertaking of the whole multitude and the impulsive crime was committed by all, can you put such a great number of people to the sword and render desolate this citadel of God and the emperor?"

The *magistros* said, "We shall not put to the sword or kill 3 anyone, father, but store up their possessions in the imperial coffers, so that after being chastened in this way they will

σωφρονισθέντες, μηκέτι τολμήσωσι μείζοσιν ἐγχειρῆσαι."
"Καὶ τί ὄφελος τῇ σῇ ἐνδοξότητι," ἔφη ὁ ἅγιος, "εἰ, τὰ
βασιλικὰ βαλάντια καταφορτίζων, τὴν σὴν ψυχὴν ἀπολέσῃς; Πῶς δὲ καὶ ἀφεθήσεταί σοι, οὐ μόνον τὰ τῷ ἐπου-
ρανίῳ βασιλεῖ ὀφειλήματα, ἀλλὰ καὶ τῷ ἐπιγείῳ, μὴ ἀφιέντι
τοῖς ἀφελῶς καὶ ἀσυνέτως τῷ κράτει σου πταίουσι, σήμερον ὄντι, καὶ αὔριον οὐχ ὑπάρχοντι; Εἰ δὲ καί, ὡς εὔλογόν
τινα πρόφασιν, τὴν τοῦ βασιλέως ἀπόφασιν ἡμῖν προβαλλόμενος, οὐ βούλῃ παραχωρῆσαι τὸ ἔγκλημα, ἔασον
τὴν ἐμὴν οὐθενότητα χαράξαι τι πρὸς τὴν ἐκείνου
θειότητα· καί, εἴ τι δ᾽ ἂν κελεύσῃ τὸ εὐσεβὲς αὐτοῦ κράτος,
μετὰ πάσης προθυμίας τελέσωμεν."

4   Ταῦτα ἀκούσας ὁ μάγιστρος ἀπεκρίνατο· "Ἡμεῖς μέν,
ὁσιώτατε, τὴν πρός σε τοῦ ἁγίου βασιλέως εὔνοιαν ἐπι-
στάμενοι, δωρούμεθά σοι τὴν τοσαύτην τῶν νομισμάτων
ἔκτισιν, πλέον ἢ δύο χιλιάδων ἀριθμὸν περιέχουσαν. Τὸ δὲ
τῶν ἀρχόντων κεφαλοκλάσιον καὶ τὸ ἄτιμον σύντριμμα
παριδεῖν οὐκ εὔλογον, οὐδὲ δίκαιον." Τότε ὁ παμμακάριστος παραινετικοῖς καὶ συμβουλευτικοῖς λόγοις πέπεικε
καὶ αὐτοὺς μεγαλοψύχως χαρίσασθαι αὐτῷ τὴν αὐτῶν δι-
εκδίκησιν, μὴ μέχρι τῶν πεντακοσίων νομισμάτων ἐκπλη-
ρουμένην.

never dare to undertake a major offense." The holy man replied, "What benefit is it to you, your excellency, if you load up the imperial coffers, but destroy your own soul? How will your debts be forgiven—not only those due to the heavenly king but the earthly one as well—if you do not forgive those who foolishly and unwisely offend your might? For today you are alive, though tomorrow you may not be. But if you do not wish to forgive the crime, presenting to me the emperor's decision as a legitimate reason, permit my humble self to scribble a note to his holiness, that whatever his pious authority should command we will carry out eagerly."

Upon hearing these words, the *magistros* responded, "Most 4 holy one, as we know well the holy emperor's goodwill toward you, we shall rescind for your sake the payment of the financial penalty, which amounts to more than two thousand gold coins. However, it is neither reasonable nor just to disregard the beheading of the officers and the dishonorable destruction of the ships." Then the most blessed Neilos, using words of exhortation and counsel, persuaded them to entrust him magnanimously with the collection of the penalty, which amounted to less than five hundred gold coins.

62

Τούτων τοίνυν τῇ τοῦ ὁσίου πατρὸς ἀντιλήψει καλῶς ἀποπεραιωθέντων, μετετράπη ἡ ἀγανάκτησις ἐπὶ τὸν κατὰ τὰς ἡμέρας ἐκείνας πράττοντα, Γρηγόριος δ᾽ οὗτος ἦν ὁ καλούμενος Μαλεΐνος, ὅνπερ σὺν πολλῷ ἀγῶνι καὶ σφοδρᾷ παρακλήσει ἐξίσχυσεν ὁ μακάριος καταξιῶσαι τῆς τοῦ μαγίστρου ἐπόψεως κεκρυμμένον τυγχάνοντα.

2   Ὅν ὁ μάγιστρος θεασάμενος καὶ μὴ ἔχων πῶς ἀπο-κενώσῃ τὸ ἔκβρασμα τῆς καρδίας αὐτοῦ, τὸν ὅσιον εὐλα-βούμενος, ἀναστὰς μετ᾽ ὀργῆς κατηράσατο αὐτὸν καὶ πάντας τοὺς ἐν τῷ οἴκῳ αὐτοῦ καὶ πάντα τὰ ὑπάρχοντα αὐτῷ, ἀπὸ ἵππου καὶ βοὸς μέχρι καὶ ὄρνιθος καὶ κυνὸς καὶ πάντων τῶν λοιπῶν. Αὐτοῦ δὲ τῷ φόβῳ συνεχομένου καὶ μηδὲν ὅλως ἀποκριναμένου, ἐπετράπη καθίσαι διὰ τὸ πρω-τοσπαθάριον αὐτὸν εἶναι. Καὶ λέγει πρὸς αὐτὸν ὁ μάγι-στρος· "Ὕπαγε, ταπεινέ, σὺν τοῖς ὁμοίοις σου κακόφροσι, ποιήσατε εἰκόνα Νεῖλον τὸν ὅσιον καὶ μὴ παύσησθε προσ-κυνοῦντες καὶ εὐχαριστίας αὐτῷ ἀναφέροντες, ἐπεί, μὰ τὴν κεφαλὴν τοῦ ἁγίου βασιλέως, πλέον ὑμεῖς δόξαν οὐκ ἐδίδοτε."

3   Ἅπαντα δὲ λοιπὸν ἡμερώσας καὶ συνετῶς εὐμαρίσας, ὁ τῶν εἰρηνοποιῶν τοῦ μακαρισμοῦ ὄντως ἄξιος ἀνεχώρη-σεν εἰς τὸ μοναστήριον, τῷ Θεῷ τὰς εὐχὰς αὐτοῦ ἀποδίδων καὶ τῇ χάριτι αὐτοῦ τὸ πᾶν λογιζόμενος· σφόδρα μὲν δυσ-χεραίνων καὶ ἀχθόμενος ἐν τῷ συνδυάζειν μετὰ τῶν ἐργαζομένων τὴν ἀνομίαν καὶ βλέπειν τὴν τοῦ κόσμου

Chapter 62

Then after these affairs were brought to a good conclusion through the intervention of the holy father, the indignation of the *magistros* turned against the man serving as *praktor* at that time; this was Gregory, surnamed Maleinos. Although Maleinos was in hiding, the blessed one managed with much effort and fervent entreaty to secure for him an audience with the *magistros*.

When the *magistros* saw him, and was unable to remove 2 the boiling rage in his heart, even though he revered the holy man, he stood up and angrily cursed Gregory, and everyone in his house and all his possessions, from his horse and ox to his chicken and dog, and everything else. Gregory was overcome by fear and in no way able to respond; but since he was a *protospatharios* he was permitted to sit down. Then the *magistros* said to him, "Off with you, wretched one, together with your likeminded evildoers; make the holy Neilos into an icon and do not stop venerating him and offering thanks to him, since I swear, by the head of the holy emperor, there is no way you would honor him more."

Afterward when Neilos had prudently calmed and 3 smoothed over this matter, the one truly worthy of the blessedness of the peacemakers went back to the monastery, *giving his prayers* to God, and assigning all things to His grace. Although Neilos, who contemplated the heavens and was a true son of spiritual tranquility, was greatly distressed and upset *to associate with workers of lawlessness,* and to see

ματαιότητα καὶ τὸν κενὸν θόρυβον, ὁ τῶν οὐρανίων
ἐπόπτης καὶ τῆς ἡσυχίας υἱὸς γνήσιος, συγκαταβαίνων δὲ
καὶ ὄχλοις καὶ ἄρχουσι συναγελαζόμενος, δεινά τε πολλὰ
πάσχων καὶ κινδυνεύων διὰ τὴν τῶν ἀδικουμένων, ἢ καὶ
δικαίως πολλάκις πασχόντων, ἀντίληψιν καὶ θερμὴν προστασίαν.

63

Ποσάκις γὰρ ὑπὲρ ἐκδικήσεως καταπονουμένης ψυχῆς
ὑπὸ τῶν μὴ φοβουμένων τὸν Κύριον πεζοπορίαν ἐστεί-
λατο καὶ κακοπάθειαν ἀνεδέξατο, χειμῶνος μὲν κατὰ κεφαλῆς τὸν ὄμβρον δεχόμενος καὶ τῇ πικρότητι τῶν ἀέρων
χεῖράς τε καὶ πόδας ἀποναρκούμενος καὶ ἅπαν τὸ σῶμα τῷ
ψύχει καταπονούμενος διὰ τὸ ἑνὶ καὶ σμικρῷ χιτῶνι περι-
στέλλεσθαι, θέρους δὲ θάλπει καυσούμενος καὶ κόπῳ καὶ
πείνῃ καὶ δίψει συνεχόμενος; Ἅπερ ἅπαντα γενναίως
ὑπέφερε διὰ τὴν ἐντολὴν τὴν λέγουσαν· "Ῥῦσαι ἀπαγο-
μένους εἰς θάνατον, καὶ ἐκπρίω κτεινομένους, μὴ φείσῃ."

2   Ποτὲ γὰρ πορευόμενος ὁ τρισόσιος εἰς ἐκδίκησίν τινος
ἀδελφοῦ παρὰ τῶν ἀδίκων ἀδικουμένου, ἠναγκάσθη ὑπὸ
τῶν πατέρων περιθεῖναι τοῖς ποσὶν αὐτοῦ εὐτελῆ δέρματα,
διὰ τὸ πάγος καὶ ψῦχος εἶναι σφοδρότατον. Κατὰ δὲ τὴν
ὁδὸν κειμένου ξύλου μεγίστου, δι' οὗπερ τὴν ὁδὸν ἔμελλε
ποιεῖσθαι ὁ ὅσιος, ἐν τῷ τὸν πόδα ἐπάνω αὐτοῦ τεθηκέναι,

the vanity of the world and its empty commotion, he still condescended to mingle with crowds and officials, suffering many ills and putting himself at risk in order to provide aid and ardent protection for those suffering injustice, or often even those who suffered justly.

Chapter 63

How many times did Neilos set off on foot and endure suffering, for the vindication of a soul oppressed by those who do not fear the Lord? In wintertime the rain would beat down upon his head, and because of the bitter weather his hands and his feet would be numbed, and his entire body suffered from the chill since he wore nothing more than a light cloak. And as he burned with the heat of summer, he would be afflicted by fatigue, hunger, and thirst. He endured all this nobly for the sake of the commandment which says, *"Deliver them that are led away to death and redeem them that are appointed to be slain; spare not Your help."*

Once, when the thrice-holy man set off to defend a 2 brother wronged by some wicked men, the fathers of the monastery compelled him to wrap some old animal hides around his feet, because the frost and chill were extreme. On the road lay a large piece of wood, over which the holy man had to make his way, and when he placed his foot upon

τῇ τοῦ Ἐχθροῦ συνεργείᾳ ὄλισθος μὲν τῇ τῶν δερμάτων γλισχρότητι περιγίνεται, ἐπελθὸν δὲ τῷ σκέλει τὸ ξύλον πληγὴν ἀφόρητον κατεργάζεται, ὥστε, λιποθυμήσαντα τὸν μακάριον ὑπό τε τοῦ πόνου καὶ τοῦ κρύους καὶ τῆς τοῦ αἵματος καταρρεύσεως, ἀπολέγεσθαι τὴν ψυχὴν καὶ τὸ τέλος ἐκδέχεσθαι. Ἐκβαλὼν δὲ ἀπὸ τοῦ κόλπου αὐτοῦ, ὅπερ ἀεὶ ἐβάσταζεν φυλακτήριον—τοῦτο δὲ ἦν πυκτίον, τῆς Νέας Διαθήκης τυγχάνον θησαύρισμα—καὶ τοῦτο τοῖς ὀφθαλμοῖς καὶ τοῖς χείλεσιν καὶ τῷ στήθει περιβαλὼν καὶ εἰπών· "Κύριε, *εἰς χεῖράς Σου παρατίθημι τὸ πνεῦμά μου,*" μικρὸν ἀπενύσταξεν, ἢ μᾶλλον εἰπεῖν, ὠλιγοψύχησεν.

3   Ὤφθη δὲ αὐτῷ ἄγγελος Κυρίου ἐνισχύων αὐτὸν καὶ τίθων *ἐν τῷ στόματι αὐτοῦ τί ποτε ὡς μέλι γλυκάζον·* πάραυτα τοίνυν ἀναστὰς καὶ γενόμενος ἐν εὐθυμίᾳ, εὐτονώτερον τὴν ὁδὸν ἢ πρότερον ἐπορεύετο τῇ τοῦ ὀφθέντος ἀντιλήψει, καὶ τοῦ αἵματος σταθέντος καὶ τοῦ πόνου λωφήσαντος. Ἔλεγε δὲ ὁ θεσπέσιος, ὅτι· "Πολλάκις μὲν ᾐσθόμην ἐν πολλοῖς πράγμασιν Θεοῦ ἀντιλήψεως, ὡς δὲ τότε, οὐδέποτε οὕτω ταχείας καὶ μεγίστης καὶ πλήρους οὔσης πολλῆς παρακλήσεως." Ἐνταῦθα γὰρ δεῖ προσθεῖναι τό· *Ὅταν πέσῃ, οὐ καταρραχθήσεται, ταχέως ἀνορθωθήσεται παρὰ Κυρίου τὰ διαβήματα ἀνθρώπου κατευθύνοντος καὶ τὴν ὁδὸν αὐτοῦ θέλοντος.*

it, by the work of the Enemy he slipped because of the slick hides covering his feet; the wood struck his leg, causing such an agonizing injury that the blessed man fainted from the pain and the icy cold and the loss of blood, and he despaired of his life and expected to die. Taking from his bosom a phylactery which he always carried—this was a small book, an anthology of the New Testament—and placing this on his eyes, his lips, and his breast, he said, "Lord, *into Your hands I commit my spirit,*" and fell asleep for a bit, or, to put it better, fainted.

An angel of the Lord appeared to Neilos, giving him 3 strength and placing *in his mouth* a substance that was *sweet as honey.* Immediately he stood up, and continued his journey down the road in good spirits and more vigorously than before with the assistance of the angelic vision; the flow of blood stopped as well, and his pain subsided. The holy man used to say, "Up to that time often and in many circumstances I had experienced God's assistance, but never so swift, so great, and full of such consolation." At this point one should add these scriptural verses: "*When he falls, he shall not be ruined,* for he will quickly be restored by *the Lord who rightly orders man's steps and takes pleasure in his way.*"

64

Ταύτην οὖν τὴν παρὰ τοῦ μακαρίου βοήθειαν τοῖς ἀνθρώποις χορηγουμένην ψυχικῶς τε καὶ σωματικῶς ὁρῶν ὁ τῶν δικαίων Ἐχθρὸς καὶ πᾶσι βασκαίνων τοῖς ἀγαθοῖς, ἔσπευδεν εἰ δυνατὸν ἦν αὐτῷ πᾶσαν τὴν δόξαν καὶ τὸν πλοῦτον τοῦ κόσμου συναγαγεῖν πρὸ τῶν ὀφθαλμῶν αὐτοῦ καὶ ἀμβλυωπῆσαι αὐτὸν μὲν ἀπὸ τῆς τῶν ἀρετῶν θεωρίας, στερῆσαι δὲ τὸν κόσμον τῆς αὐτοῦ ὠφελείας. Πολλοὶ γοῦν τῶν κατερχομένων ἀρχόντων πλήθη χρημάτων προσφέροντες αὐτῷ, τὴν οἰκονομίαν τῶν μετ᾽ αὐτοῦ ἀδελφῶν καὶ τὴν προστασίαν τῶν πτωχῶν προεβάλλοντο· ὁ δὲ ὥσπερ σκύβαλα ἀποστρεφόμενος ταῦτα, ἔλεγε τοῖς παρέχουσιν, ὅτι· "Οἱ μὲν ἀδελφοὶ παρὰ τοῦ Δαβὶδ μακαρίζονται, εἴπερ τοὺς πόνους τῶν χειρῶν αὐτῶν φάγονται καὶ ἀλλοτρίαις ἁμαρτίαις μὴ κοινωνήσουσιν. Οἱ δὲ πτωχοὶ καθ᾽ ὑμῶν μὲν κεκράξονται, ὡς τὰ τούτων κατέχουσιν, ἐμὲ δὲ θαυμάσονται, ὡς μηδὲν ἔχοντα καὶ πάντα κατέχοντα."

2   Εὐνοῦχος ὁ κοιτωνίτης εἰσελθών ποτε ἐν τῷ Ῥυσιάνῳ καὶ εἰδὼς τὸν μακάριον μηδαμῶς αὐτῷ προσδραμόντα— ἠπίστατο γὰρ αὐτὸν ἐκ μόνης τῆς φήμης—ἔλεγε θαυμάζων πρὸς τοὺς παρόντας· "Ποῦ κάθηται ὧδε Νεῖλος ὁ καλόγηρος; Καὶ πῶς οὐ προσῆλθέ μοι μετὰ πάντων τῶν ἡγουμένων, ἀκούσας τὴν ἐμὴν ἄφιξιν; Τοῦτο γὰρ οὐδ᾽ αὐτὸς ὁ πατριάρχης ἐτόλμησεν ἂν ἐν ἐμοὶ καυχήσασθαι καὶ καταφρονῆσαι τῆς ἐμῆς ἐλεύσεως."

3   Οἱ δὲ παρεστῶτες αὐτῷ ἀπεκρίναντο· "Οὗτος, ὃν ἔφη

Chapter 64

The Enemy of the just, who is envious of all good men, seeing the aid the blessed Neilos provided to people for their spiritual as well as their bodily needs, strove, to the extent possible, to amass before Neilos's eyes all the glory and wealth of the world, and to blind him to the contemplation of virtue, and to deprive the world of Neilos's aid. In fact many officials came to him, offering him a great deal of money for the financial support, they claimed, of his brother monks and for the care of the poor; but Neilos refused it all as if it were rubbish and said to those who made these offerings, "My brethren are blessed by David, if *they shall eat the labors* of their hands, and *do not participate in another man's sins.* But the poor will cry out against you, since you seize what belongs to them, and they will admire me *since I have nothing and yet possess everything.*"

The *koitonites,* who was a eunuch, once came to Rossano, 2 and seeing that the blessed one in no way at all hastened to meet him—for he knew of Neilos by reputation only—he was astounded by this and said to those present, "Where does the monk Neilos reside? And why did he not come to me with all the other superiors, upon hearing of my arrival? For not even the patriarch would dare to be so arrogant toward me and disregard my arrival."

Those standing around him responded, "This monk, of 3

ἡ σὴ ἐνδοξότης, καλόγηρος, οὔτε πατριάρχης ἐστίν, οὔτε πατριάρχην φοβεῖται, ἀλλ᾽ οὐδ᾽ αὐτὸν τὸν πᾶσι φοβερὸν βασιλέα. Κάθηται δὲ ἅμα ὀλίγοις μοναχοῖς ἐν τῷ ὄρει, μὴ δεόμενός τινος ἀντιλήψεως· οὔτε γὰρ πλάτει ὁρίων συνέχεται, οὔτε πλήθει βοσκημάτων συνδέδεται. Διὸ οὐδ᾽ ἀμφιβολίαν κέκτηται πρός τινα. Μονόκερώς ἐστιν οὗτος, ζῷον αὐτόνομον· καὶ εἰ θελήσῃς αὐτὸν μετ᾽ ἐξουσίας ἀγάγαι, οὐδέποτε δυνήσῃ τὸ πρόσωπον αὐτοῦ κατιδέσθαι." Ταῦτα ἀκούσας ὁ κοιτωνίτης καὶ ἐπὶ πλεῖον τὸν ἄνδρα θαυμάσας, γράφει αὐτῷ ἐπιστολὴν δυσωπητικήν, συμπλέξας αὐτῇ καὶ ὅρκους φρικτούς, ἵνα εἴτε πρὸς αὐτὸν ἐξερχομένῳ μὴ ἀποκρύψῃ ἑαυτὸν ἀπ᾽ αὐτοῦ, εἴτε καταξιώσῃ ἐν τῷ κάστρῳ εἰσελθεῖν καὶ εὐλογῆσαι αὐτὸν καὶ πάντας τοὺς σὺν αὐτῷ.

65

Ὁ δὲ ὅσιος πατὴρ ἡμῶν Νεῖλος, τὸ μὲν διὰ τοὺς γεγραμμένους ὅρκους, τὸ δὲ ἵνα πάλιν ὁ ἄρχων αὐτῷ ὑπακούσῃ ἐν τῇ περὶ τῶν πτωχῶν παρακλήσει, καταλαμβάνει τὸ κάστρον, καὶ πρὸς τὸν κοιτωνίτην εἰσῆλθεν. Ὁ δέ, θεασάμενος σχῆμα καὶ πρόσωπον προφητικόν, μᾶλλον δὲ ἀγγελικόν, προσεκύνησεν ἐπὶ τοὺς πόδας αὐτοῦ καί, κρατήσας αὐτὸν τῆς χειρός, εἰσῆλθον ἄμφω ἐν τῷ κοιτῶνι αὐτοῦ. Κελεύσας δὲ ἑνὶ τῶν πιστοτάτων αὐτοῦ τὸ

whom your excellency speaks, is neither a patriarch, nor does he fear the patriarch or even the emperor who is feared by all. He resides with a few monks on the mountain, not requiring any assistance, for he is neither constricted by any boundaries, nor is he tied to a flock of herd animals. Accordingly, he has not come into conflict with anyone. This man is an independent being, like the unicorn, and if you try to bring him here by force, you will not even be able to see his face." Hearing this, the *koitonites* was all the more amazed at Neilos, and wrote a letter of entreaty, interweaving terrible oaths, that Neilos should either not hide himself when he, the *koitonites,* came to visit, or that Neilos should deign to come to the city to bless him and all those in his entourage.

Chapter 65

Our holy father Neilos, because of the oaths contained in the letter and expecting that the official would listen to him when he made pleas for the poor, went to the city and visited the *koitonites.* When the latter saw his habit and prophetic or, rather, angelic face, he prostrated himself at Neilos's feet, took him by the hand, and went together with Neilos into his chamber. He bade one of his most faithful

Εὐαγγέλιον ἐνεγκεῖν, λέγει τῷ μακαρίτῃ· "Ἐπειδή, ἅγιε πάτερ, τῇ τοῦ ψεύδους ὑπολήψει τὸ ἄπιστον προσγίνεται τοῖς ἀνθρώποις, θέλω σοι ὀμόσαι πρὸς πληροφορίαν τῶν παρ' ἐμοῦ ἐπαγγελλομένων σοι."

2   Ὁ δὲ πατὴρ πρὸς αὐτόν· "Τοῦ ἁγίου Εὐαγγελίου ἀποφαντικῶς ἐντελλομένου καὶ λέγοντος, 'Ἐγὼ δὲ λέγω ὑμῖν μὴ ὀμόσαι ὅλως· ἤτω δὲ ὁ λόγος ὑμῶν· ναί, ναί, καὶ τὸ οὔ, οὔ· τὸ δὲ περισσὸν τούτων ἐκ τοῦ Πονηροῦ ἐστιν,' διατί ἀπιστίας ὑπόθεσιν σπεύδεις περιθεῖναι τῇ σῇ ἐνδοξότητι καὶ ἀπὸ παρανομίας τὴν συντυχίαν ἀπάρξασθαι; Πᾶς γὰρ ὁ ἕτοιμος εἰς εὐορκίαν, ταχὺς εἰς ψευδολογίαν, ὥσπερ καὶ τὸ ἀνάπαλιν."

3   Καὶ ὁ κοιτωνίτης ἀπεκρίνατο· "Δίκαιόν ἐστιν, ὁσιώτατε, μήτε ὑμῖν τοῖς τοῦ Θεοῦ δούλοις τινὰ ψεύδεσθαι, μήτε ὑμᾶς ἀπιστεῖν τοῖς μετὰ πίστεως τὰ δόξαντα λέγουσιν. Λοιπὸν οὖν ἀκούων, παρακαλῶ, τοὺς λόγους μου, πίστευε. Οὐκ ἔστι μοί τις προσγενὴς ἐν τῷ βίῳ τούτῳ ἐξ αἵματος, εἰ μὴ μόνη μήτηρ ἀδύνατος, τὸ εἰς ἐμὲ φίλτρον στέργουσα· ὑπάρχει δέ μοι πλοῦτος πολὺς καὶ κτῆσις ἄπειρος, ἀνδραπόδων πλῆθος, καὶ βοσκημάτων ἑσμὸς ἀναρίθμητος. Ἐλογισάμην οὖν ταῦτα πάντα τῷ Θεῷ προσκυρῶσαι, μοναχῶν φροντιστήριον συστησάμενος, εἴπερ κατένυξεν ὁ Θεὸς τὴν ἁγιωσύνην σου καὶ ἐν τῇ Κωνσταντινουπόλει συνήρχου μοι, ὅπως διὰ τῶν ἁγίων σου χειρῶν ἐγώ τε καὶ ἡ τεκοῦσα τὸ ἀγγελικὸν σχῆμα ἐνεδυσάμεθα, ἐποίουν δέ σε, ὡς νῦν μετ' ἐμοῦ, οὕτω τοῖς ἁγίοις βασιλεῦσι συγκαθεσθῆναι."

servants to bring in the Gospel and then said to the blessed man, "Holy father, since mistrust among people results from the suspicion of a falsehood, I wish to confirm with an oath what I am going to promise you."

The father responded to him, "The holy Gospel explic- 2 itly commands and says, '*I say to you, Do not swear at all,* let this be *your word: yes for yes, and no for no, anything more than this comes from the Evil One.*' Why then are you eager to lay upon your estimable self a suspicion of mistrust and to begin our meeting with an unlawful act? For everyone who is ready to swear an oath is just as quick to lie; the reverse is true as well."

The *koitonites* responded, "It is right, most holy one, that 3 no one should lie to you, the servant of God, nor should you mistrust those who speak their mind in good faith. Now then, listen, I beseech you, and trust my words. In this life I have no blood relatives, except for my old, feeble mother who feels great affection for me, but I do have great wealth and boundless possessions, a great many slaves, and countless flocks of animals. Therefore, I have resolved to donate all this to God, to build a monastery for monks, if only God would prompt your holiness to come to Constantinople with me, so that through your holy hands my mother and I could be garbed in the angelic habit. I would arrange it so that you would sit together with the holy emperors, just as you do now with me."

66

Ταῦτα τὰ μέλιτος καὶ πίσσης ἀνάπλεα ῥήματα ὁ τῆς διακρίσεως λύχνος ἐκεῖνος ἀκούσας, οὐ συνηρπάγη τοῖς ὑψηλοῖς ἐπαγγέλμασι τούτοις, ἀλλ᾽ ἡσυχῇ τὴν χεῖρα βαλὼν ἐν τῷ στήθει—ὅπερ αὐτῷ ἀεὶ ἔθος ὑπῆρχε—καὶ τὸ σημεῖον τοῦ σταυροῦ ποιησάμενος, τῷ κοιτωνίτῃ ἀπεκρίνατο· "Ὁ μὲν σκοπὸς τῆς ὑμετέρας θεοφιλείας τε καὶ συνέσεως εὐκλεὴς καὶ Θεῷ εὐαπόδεκτος. Πρὸς τοῦτον γὰρ ἐνάγων ἡμᾶς ὁ Σωτήρ, παραβολικῶς ἔφησεν, ὅτι· Ὁμοία ἐστὶν ἡ βασιλεία τῶν οὐρανῶν θησαυρῷ κεκρυμμένῳ ἐν τῷ ἀγρῷ, ὃν εὑρὼν ἄνθρωπος ἔκρυψε, καὶ ἀπὸ τῆς χαρᾶς ὑπάγει καὶ πωλεῖ πάντα ὅσα ἔχει καὶ ἀγοράζει τὸν ἀγρὸν ἐκεῖνον.᾽ Ἐμοὶ δὲ ἀσύμφορόν ἐστι καταλείψαντα τὴν ἐρημίαν καὶ τοὺς συγκακοπαθοῦντάς μοι πτωχούς, ἀνὰ τὰς πόλεις ἀλᾶσθαι καὶ ἀναδέχεσθαι φροντίδας πραγμάτων. Μὴ γὰρ ἐξέλιπεν ἀπὸ Κωνσταντινουπόλεως μοναχὸς καὶ ἡγούμενος, ἵνα δι᾽ ἐμοῦ κουρευθῶσιν οἱ ἐκεῖσε ἀποτασσόμενοι;

2 "Εἰ δὲ καὶ ὅλως προτιμᾷς τὴν ἐμὴν οὐθενότητα, κατάλαβε τὴν ἐσχατιὰν ἐν ᾗ καθεζόμεθα, καὶ μεθ᾽ ἡμῶν τὴν τεθλιμμένην ὁδὸν διάνυε. Οὐδέποτε γὰρ δυνήσῃ πτωχὸς γενέσθαι τῷ πνεύματι, πρὶν παντελῶς πτωχεῦσαι τῷ σώματι· ὅπερ γινώσκων κατώρθωσεν ὁ ἐν ἀγγέλοις Ἀρσένιος. Τὰ δὲ σὰ πάντα κατάλειπε τῇ ἐξουσίᾳ τοῦ φήσαντος· Ἐμόν ἐστι τὸ χρυσίον καὶ τὸ ἀργύριον,᾽ καί, "Ὅστις οὐκ ἀποτάσσεται πᾶσι τοῖς ἑαυτοῦ, οὐ δύναταί μου εἶναι

Chapter 66

When that beacon of superior discernment heard these words full of honey and pitch, he was not seduced by these lofty promises, but calmly placed his hand on his chest, as was always his custom, and made the sign of the cross. He then responded to the *koitonites,* "The goal of your love for God and your prudence is noble and well pleasing to God. For the Savior, leading us toward this goal, said in a parable, '*The kingdom of heaven is like treasure hidden in a field, which a man found and covered up; then in his joy he goes and sells all that he has and buys that field.*' But it is unsuitable for me to abandon my solitude and the poor people who suffer together with me, and to wander through cities and concern myself with these affairs. Is there such a lack of monks and superiors in Constantinople that I need to tonsure there those who renounce the world?

"But if you really prefer my humble self, come to the remote place where we reside and walk the *hard way* along with us. For you will never be able to be *poor in spirit* until you have become utterly poor in body. This is what Arsenios (who is now among the angels) knew and was able to accomplish. Leave all your possessions at the disposal of the One who says, '*Mine is the gold and the silver,*' and '*Whoever does not renounce all that he has cannot be my disciple.*'" But since the

μαθητής.'" Πρὸς ταῦτα τοῦ κοιτωνίτου ἐνισταμένου καὶ τὸ ἴδιον θέλημα γενέσθαι φιλονεικοῦντος, καταλιπὼν αὐτὸν ὁ μακάριος ἐξῆλθεν.

67

Καὶ δὴ πορευομένῳ σὺν Δαβὶδ τῷ προφήτῃ καὶ πρὸς τὸ οἰκεῖον ὑποστρέφοντι μοναστήριον, ἐν τῷ λέγειν αὐτόν, "*Ἐν ὁδῷ ταύτῃ ᾗ ἐπορευόμην, ἔκρυψαν παγίδα μοι,*" ὑπαντᾷ αὐτῷ κατὰ μέσην τὴν ὁδὸν μία κόρη μοναχή, ἥτις, προδραμοῦσα ἔμπροσθεν αὐτοῦ, ἔρριψεν ἑαυτὴν ἐν στενῇ διαβάσει, ἐν ᾗ οὐκ ἦν ἄλλοθεν διέρχεσθαι τὸν μακάριον. Τότε ὁ θεῖος ἀνὴρ πνευματικὴν ἀνδρείαν ἀναλαβὼν καὶ τὸν δόλον τοῦ Σατανᾶ ἐπιγνούς, τύπτει μὲν αὐτὴν τῇ βακτηρίᾳ τῆς χειρὸς αὐτοῦ ἐμβριμησάμενος, ἀπεπήδησε δὲ ταχέως μὴ ἐγχρονίσας, κατὰ τὴν παροιμίαν, καὶ ᾤχετο. Ἔκτοτε τοίνυν συνοῖδεν, μήτε ἑαυτῷ, μήτε οἱῳδήποτε τῶν ἀδελφῶν κατὰ μόνας ἐπιτρέπειν πορεύεσθαι. "*Ἀγαθοὶ γάρ,*" φησίν, "*δύο ὑπὲρ τὸν ἕνα,*" καί, "*Οὐαὶ τῷ ἑνὶ ὅτι ἐὰν πέσῃ, οὐκ ἔστιν ὁ ἐγείρων αὐτόν.*"

2 Ἐν τούτοις πᾶσιν ὑπερνικήσας ὁ ὅσιος πατὴρ ἡμῶν Νεῖλος τὸν Ἀντικείμενον διὰ τοῦ ἀγαπήσαντος αὐτὸν Θεοῦ καὶ δόκιμος παλαιστὴς ἀναδειχθεὶς ἔν τε τῇ τῆς πείνης ὑπομονῇ καὶ τῇ τῶν ἐκ λίθων ἀρτοποιήσεων προσβολῇ, πρὸς τούτοις τῇ τοῦ παντὸς κόσμου δόξῃ καὶ τῇ τῶν

koitonites objected to all this and insisted that his own wishes prevail, the blessed Neilos left him and went away.

Chapter 67

While returning to his monastery and reciting the psalms of the prophet David as he went along, just as Neilos recited the verse, "*In the very way wherein I was walking they hid a snare for me,*" in the middle of the road he met a young nun; she ran toward him and then threw herself down in a narrow passage where there was no other way for the blessed one to pass. The godly man, taking on spiritual courage, and knowing this to be a trick of Satan, became angry, beat her with the staff he had in his hand, and quickly moved away without delay in accordance with the proverb. From then on he decided that neither he nor any of his brethren should be permitted to travel alone. "For *two are better than one,*" he said, and, "*Woe to him who is alone when he falls, and there is no one to lift him up.*"

In all these conflicts, our holy father Neilos was victorious over the Adversary through God who loved him, and he proved to be a skillful athlete in enduring hunger, and against the temptation of making bread out of stones, and moreover in the rejection of all worldly glory and money

χρημάτων ἀποστροφῇ, δι᾽ ὧν τις πίπτων τῷ Πειραστῇ προσκυνεῖ, καὶ ταῦτα οὐχ ἅπαξ, ἀλλὰ πολλάκις καὶ ἐν ἑτέροις πλείστοις πειρασθεὶς καὶ νικήσας πολυμερῶς τε καὶ πολυτρόπως, ἔδει δὲ αὐτὸν καὶ ἐν τῷ πτερυγίῳ τοῦ ἱεροῦ ἀκολούθως δοκιμασθῆναι, εἴγε καταδέξοιτο διὰ τούτου καταβληθῆναι, ὅρα πῶς μιμητὴς ἀνεδείχθη κἂν τούτῳ τοῦ Δεσπότου καὶ Διδασκάλου.

68

Ἐν ἐκείναις γὰρ ταῖς ἡμέραις τελευτήσαντος τοῦ ἀρχιερατεύοντος ἐν τῷ Ῥυσιάνῳ, ἑτέρου δὲ ζητουμένου τοῦ δυναμένου τὸν τόπον ἀναπληρῶσαι, μιᾶς γνώμης γεγόνασι πάντες, μικροί τε καὶ μεγάλοι, τοῦ ἀπροσδοκήτως περικρατεῖς γενέσθαι τοῦ θεσπεσίου πατρὸς καὶ βίᾳ τοῦτον τῷ θρόνῳ τῆς ἐκκλησίας ἐγκαθιδρῦσαι, ὡς ἄτε βίον ἔχοντα ὑπὲρ λόγον καὶ τὸν λόγον ἐφάμιλλον κεκτημένον τῷ βίῳ. Τοῦτο τοίνυν βουλευσαμένων καὶ ὁρμησάντων ἀρχόντων τε καὶ τῶν ἐξόχων τοῦ κλήρου πρὸς τὸ πληρῶσαι τὸ δόξαν, προλαμβάνει τις καὶ τῷ πατρὶ ἀναγγέλλει τὸ πρᾶγμα, προσδοκῶν ἐν τούτῳ αὐτῷ προσαρέσκειν καὶ τὰ μέγιστα χαριεῖσθαι, ὡς τοιούτου αὐτῷ πράγματος ἀγγέλου γεγενημένου.

2   Καὶ μέντοι γε τοῦ σκοποῦ οὐ διήμαρτεν· ἀπευχαριστήσας γὰρ αὐτῷ ὁ μέγας καὶ τότε καὶ ὕστερον, ἀπέλυσεν ἐν

CHAPTER 68

through which man *falls down and worships* the Tempter. This happened not only once, but many times. Neilos was tempted on many other occasions and emerged victorious in various circumstances and in many ways. Consequently, it was necessary that he be tested even on *the pinnacle of the temple,* to see if he would choose to cast himself down from it. See how in this temptation as well he made himself an imitator of the Lord and Teacher.

Chapter 68

For at that time when the bishop of Rossano died and a replacement was being sought, everyone, small and great alike, decided unanimously to suddenly seize the godly father and install him by force upon the throne of the church, since he led a life beyond description and possessed an eloquence comparable to his way of life. Both the officials and the preeminent members of the clergy hastened to act upon this decision. Then someone took the initiative and announced the decision to the father, expecting to find favor and great acceptance from him, as a herald of such a great matter.

In fact, he did not fail in his goal in this regard, for 2 the great man gave many thanks to him both then and

εἰρήνῃ, κελεύσας αὐτῷ δοθῆναι καί τινα εὐλογίαν. Αὐτὸς δὲ μελετήσας τὸ ἐμφερόμενον ἐν τῷ ἁγίῳ Εὐαγγελίῳ, τό· "Γνοὺς δὲ ὁ Ἰησοῦς, ὅτι μέλλουσιν ἔρχεσθαι καὶ ἁρπάζειν αὐτόν, ἵνα ποιήσωσι βασιλέα, ἀνεχώρησε μόνος εἰς τὸ ὄρος," ἀναχωρεῖ καὶ οὗτος ἐπὶ τὸ ἐνδότερον ὄρος μετὰ ἑνὸς ἀδελφοῦ καὶ μόνον, ἀποκρυβόμενος μικρὸν ὅσον ὅσον, ἕως ἂν παρέλθῃ ἡ βουλὴ ἐκείνη. Καταλαβόντες δὲ τὸ μοναστήριον οἱ ἱερεῖς σὺν τοῖς ἄρχουσι καὶ πολλὰ γυρεύσαντες καὶ ζητήσαντες, τὰ μέγιστα ἔστενον ἀστοχήσαντες τοῦ βουλεύματος. Ὡς δὲ ἐπὶ πλεῖον καρτερήσαντες οὐδὲν ἤνυον— εὐκοπώτερον γὰρ ἦν μονοκέρωτος ἢ ἐκείνου περιγενέσθαι—ὑπέστρεψαν εἰς τὰ ἴδια, ἑτέρῳ τὴν προστασίαν ἐγχειρισάμενοι.

3   Ὁ δὲ ὅσιος, ἀγαλλιώμενος ἐπὶ τῷ Κυρίῳ, σὺν τῷ προφήτῃ ἀνέμελπεν, "Ἐκράτησας," λέγων, "Κύριε, τῆς χειρὸς τῆς δεξιᾶς μου, καὶ ἐν τῇ βουλῇ Σου ὡδήγησάς με καὶ μετὰ δόξης προσελάβου μου. Τί γάρ μοι ὑπάρχει ἐν τῷ οὐρανῷ, καὶ πλήν Σου τί ἠθέλησα ἐπὶ τῆς γῆς; Ἐναντίον Σου γάρ ἐστι πᾶσα ἡ ἐπιθυμία μου, Κύριε· καὶ Σὺ ἐπίστασαι, ὅτι ἡμέραν ἀνθρώπου οὐκ ἐπεθύμησα." Τῷ τοιούτῳ φρονήματι ὁ μακάριος παρεῖδε τὸ μικρὸν τοῦ βίου τούτου δοξάριον καὶ τὴν ἀνθρωπίνην τιμὴν ἐβδελύξατο· νυνὶ δὲ κατέστησεν αὐτὸν ὁ Θεὸς ἐπάνω δέκα πόλεων, ὡς ἀψευδῶς ἐπηγγείλατο. Οὐδὲ γάρ, διότι τὴν ἱερωσύνην οὐ κατεδέξατο, τὸ τάλαντον οὐκ ἐπολυπλασίασε· πλείους γάρ εἰσιν οἱ σωθέντες διὰ τῆς διδασκαλίας τοῦ στόματος αὐτοῦ ἔν τε τῷ κοινοβίῳ καὶ ἐν τῷ μοναδικῷ, ἢ οὔσπερ ἐκεῖνο τὸ ἄστυ συγκλείει οἰκήτορας.

afterward, and dismissed him in peace, bidding that he be given some gift. Then Neilos, pondering the passage in the holy Gospel, "*Perceiving that they were about to come and take Him by force to make Him king, Jesus withdrew to the mountain by Himself,*" departed for a remote part of the mountain with only one of the brethren, to stay in hiding for a little while until that plan to make him bishop should be forgotten. The priests and the officials came to the monastery, and after a thorough search and inquiry were greatly distressed because their plans were frustrated. And since after more delay, they accomplished nothing—for it was easier to catch a unicorn than Neilos—they returned home and entrusted the bishopric to another.

The holy man, rejoicing in the Lord, sang with the prophet, saying, "Lord, *You took hold of my right hand. You guided me by Your counsel, and You have taken me to Yourself with glory. For what have I in heaven but You, and what have I desired upon the earth* beside *You? All my desire is before You, Lord,* and *You know* that *I have not desired the day of man.*" With such thoughts the blessed one disregarded the vainglory of this life and despised the honor of men; but now God put him in charge *over ten cities,* as he truly promised. While he did not accept the bishopric, he did not fail to multiply his *talent,* for through the teaching of his lips, both while he was in the monastery and while he was a solitary, more were saved than the inhabitants of the city of Rossano.

69

Βλάττων ποτέ, ὁ μητροπολίτης, ἐρχόμενος ἀπὸ Ἀφρικῆς μετὰ πολλῶν αἰχμαλώτων διὰ τὸ προσκεῖσθαι αὐτῷ ἕως καιροῦ τὸν τῶν Σαρακηνῶν βασιλέα, ἐν προφάσει τοῦ ἀδελφὴν αὐτῷ εἶναι τὴν γαμετὴν ἐκείνου—ὅπερ οὐκ ἦν— παρέβαλε τῷ αἰγιαλῷ Ῥυσιάνου καὶ δυσωπητικῶς τὸν μακάριον μετεπέμψατο, ἱμειρόμενος ἀκοῦσαι παρ' αὐτοῦ τὰ δέοντα καὶ τὰς εὐχὰς αὐτοῦ καρπώσασθαι.

2   Μετὰ δὲ τὸ θαρρῆσαι αὐτῷ τὸν ἀρχιεπίσκοπον ἅπαντα τὰ αὐτοῦ ἐγκάρδια καὶ διαβούλια, λέγει αὐτῷ ὁ μακάριος· "Ἄκουσόν μου, δέσποτα, τῆς συμβουλίας καὶ μηκέτι ὑποστρέψῃς πρὸς τὰ τῶν ἐχιδνῶν γεννήματα. Μετὰ γὰρ τὸ λίαν κολακεῦσαί σε καὶ τιμῆσαί σε τὸ αἷμά σου πίονται, μαχαίρᾳ σε θανατώσαντες. Καὶ περὶ τῆς εἰρήνης τῆς Καλαβρίας μὴ κοπιῶ, μηδὲ ἀξίου· οὐ γὰρ εὐδοκεῖ ὁ τῶν ὅλων Δεσπότης ἐν τούτῳ." Λέγει δὲ πρὸς αὐτὸν ὁ ἀνεψιὸς τοῦ μητροπολίτου· "Ὁρᾷς, πάτερ ἅγιε, πόσας ὁ δεσπότης ψυχὰς ἠλευθέρωσεν;" Ἀπεκρίθη αὐτῷ ὁ ὅσιος· "Οὐ ψυχὰς ἠλευθέρωσεν, ἀλλὰ σώματα. Λυσιτελεῖ δὲ τοῖς πολλοῖς καὶ ἡ τῶν σωμάτων κάκωσις, ὅσοις τὸ ἐλευθεριάζειν πολλῶν κακῶν αἴτιον γίνεται, ὥσπερ αἱ παρὰ τῶν ἰατρῶν τοῖς μαινομένοις συγκλείσεις καὶ λιμαγχονίαι. Εἰ δὲ μὴ ταῦτα, δοκοῦντα λυπηρά, τῇ τῶν πολλῶν σωτηρίᾳ συνέβαλλε, οὐκ ἂν πρὸς τοῦ Θεοῦ συνεχωρήθησαν γίνεσθαι. Δεῖ δὲ ὅμως τοὺς δυναμένους βοηθεῖν τοῖς τοιούτοις, ὅσον ἐνδέχεται." Ταῦτα ὁ μητροπολίτης ἀκούσας καὶ τῇ τοῦ πατρὸς

Chapter 69

Once the metropolitan Blatton, returning from Africa with many released war captives, came to the shore of Rossano—for at that time the king of the Saracens had friendly relations with him, under the pretext that Blatton's sister was the king's wife, which was not true. And Blatton sent for the blessed Neilos with an entreaty, desiring to hear from him the proper course of action and to receive his blessing.

After the archbishop confided everything in his heart and his plans, the blessed man said to him, "Listen to my advice, lord. Do not return to that *brood of vipers;* for after they excessively flatter and honor you, they will kill you with a sword and drink your blood. Also, you should not toil for the peace of Calabria, nor insist on it, for the Lord of all things is not in favor of this." The metropolitan's nephew said to him, "Do you see, holy father, how many souls our lord, the archbishop, has freed?" The holy one responded to him, "He has not freed souls, but bodies. For the many for whom absence of moral restraint is the cause of many evils, affliction of the body is beneficial, just as the confinement and starvation prescribed by doctors is beneficial for the insane. For if these seemingly painful experiences did not contribute to the salvation of many, they would not have been allowed by God. It is necessary, however, for those who can help such people to do so as much as possible." The metropolitan, 2

συμβουλίᾳ μὴ ὑπακούσας, τὸ προφητευθὲν αὐτῷ ἐπ᾽ αὐτὸν ἐτελέσθη.

70

Ὁ δὲ ὅσιος πατὴρ ἡμῶν Νεῖλος, τὸ μὲν ἐκ τοῦ πολλοῦ τῆς ἀσκήσεως πόνου, τὸ δὲ ἐκ τῆς τῶν χρόνων ἱκανῆς περιόδου—περὶ γὰρ τὰ ἑξήκοντα ἔτη ὑπῆρχεν—ἀδυνατήσας λοιπὸν καὶ μηκέτι ἰσχύων τὰς μακρὰς ὁδοὺς ἀκινδύνως πεζοπορεῖν, ἐκέχρητο ἵππῳ πρὸς θεραπείαν τῆς πολλῆς ἀτονίας· ἐν γὰρ τῷ πλείονι τῆς ὁδοῦ μέρει, λόγῳ τῆς περιεκτικῆς ἐγκρατείας, ἐπισύρων αὐτὸν ἐπορεύετο.

2 Τοῦτον τὸν ἵππον, ἐν τῷ τὸν ὅσιον συντυγχάνειν μετὰ τοῦ ἀρχιεπισκόπου, ὑποβληθείς τις ὑπὸ τοῦ Διαβόλου, κλέψας ἀνεχώρησεν. Κατὰ δὲ τὴν ὁδὸν χειμῶνος αὐτῷ ἐπελθόντος, ἀποβὰς τοῦ ἵππου ἵστατο ὑφ᾽ ἑνὶ τῶν δένδρων, ἐκδεχόμενος παρελθεῖν τὴν σφοδρότητα τοῦ ἀέρος. Βροντὴ δὲ οὐρανόθεν ἐλθοῦσα, ἐπάταξε τὸν ταλαίπωρον καὶ τῷ Ἅιδῃ παρέπεμψε, μὴ πεισθέντα τῷ λέγοντι· "Ζημιοῦν ἄνδρα δίκαιον οὐ καλόν," καί "Ὁ κλέπτων μηκέτι κλεπτέτω, ἀλλὰ κοπιάτω ἐργαζόμενος ταῖς ἰδίαις χερσίν, ἵνα ἔχῃ μεταδοῦναι τῷ χρείαν ἔχοντι." Καὶ ὁ μὲν ἄθλιος ἐκεῖνος ἥμαρτεν, ἀνομήσας διακενῆς, τινὲς δὲ τῇ ἐπαύριον τὴν ὁδὸν διερχόμενοι καὶ τὸν ἵππον γνωρίσαντες ἐπὶ τοῦ τόπου νεμόμενον, πρὸς τὸ μοναστήριον διεσώσαντο καὶ ἀπέδοντο τῷ δικαίῳ τὸ ἴδιον.

hearing this, did not heed the father's advice, and so Neilos's prediction came to pass for him.

Chapter 70

Our holy father Neilos, because of his great ascetic toils and his advancing age—for he was about sixty—became feeble and could no longer take long journeys on foot without difficulty. He began to ride a horse to support his increasingly frail body. Nonetheless due to his all-embracing self-restraint, he used to walk the greater part of the journey, pulling the horse behind him.

While the holy man was conversing with the archbishop, 2 someone stole this horse, at the prompting of the Devil, and fled. As the thief was on his way, a storm broke, so he got off the horse and stood under a tree, waiting for the vehemence of the wind to pass. Then a lightning bolt came from the sky and struck the wretched man, and sent him to Hades, since he did not obey the one who said, "*It is not right to punish a righteous man,*" and, "*Let the thief no longer steal, but rather let him labor, doing honest work with his hands, so that he may be able to give to those in need.*" That wretched man had sinned, breaking the law in vain. The next day some people traveling along the road recognized the horse grazing on the spot, and they safely led it to the monastery, returning the horse to the righteous Neilos.

3   Ἄλλοτε πάλιν τῶν στρατιωτῶν τις ὁρμήσας πρὸς τὸ τὸν
ἵππον ἀπὸ τοῦ μοναστηρίου συλῆσαι καὶ περὶ δυσμὰς
ἡλίου ἐλθὼν τῆς μονῆς ἐξ ἐναντίας, ὥστε καὶ ὀφθαλμοῖς
αὐτὴν βλέπειν, περιέμενε τὴν νύκτα, ἵν᾽ ἐν σκότει ποιήσῃ
τὸ ἔργον τοῦ σκότους. Περιπατήσας δὲ πᾶσαν τὴν νύκταν
ἐκείνην, οὐδ᾽ ὅλως ἴσχυσε τῇ μονῇ προσεγγίσαι, ἀλλὰ φα-
ράγγοις καὶ κρημνοῖς ἐντυχὼν ἀβάτοις, ἀρκούντως ἐταρι-
χεύθη. Ἡμέρας δὲ γεναμένης, ἔμπροσθεν αὐτοῦ τὸ μοναστήριον εἶδεν, καὶ τῷ θαύματι σφόδρα καταπλαγείς,
εἰσήει μετανοῶν καὶ τὴν οἰκείαν ἐξομολογούμενος κακο-
βουλίαν.

71

Ἐν τῷ καιρῷ ἐκείνῳ, ἐπιδραμόντων τῶν ἀθέων Ἀγαρηνῶν τῷ θέματι τῆς Καλαβρίας καὶ πάντα ληϊζομένων, ὁ
μὲν ὅσιος πατὴρ τὸ φρούριον καταλαβὼν σὺν τοῖς ἀδελφοῖς διεσώζετο· τρεῖς δὲ ἐξ αὐτῶν ἰδιορρύθμως προσκαρ-
τερήσαντες τῷ μοναστηρίῳ, ὑπὸ τῶν Σαρακηνῶν
ἐκρατήθησαν καὶ ἐν Σικελίᾳ ἀπήχθησαν. Ἔκρινε γοῦν ὁ
μακάριος μὴ παρεωραθῆναι τούτους, ἀλλ᾽ ὡς οἰκεῖα μέλη
ἀναζητηθῆναι καὶ εἰς τὸν ἴδιον τόπον ἀποκατασταθῆναι.
Ἐπισυνάξας τοίνυν ἀπό τε σίτου καὶ οἴνου καὶ καρποῦ
ἑτέρου μέχρι τῶν ἑκατὸν χρυσίνων καὶ βορδόνιον, ὃ ἦν
αὐτῷ δεδωκὼς Βασίλειος ὁ στρατηγὸς Καλαβρίας, καὶ

Another time, one of the soldiers made an attempt to 3 steal the horse from the monastery. Just around sunset he approached from the opposite side of the monastery, and came close enough to see it with his eyes; he waited for nightfall so that he might carry out in darkness *the work of darkness*. Although he walked around that whole night, he was unable to reach the monastery, but encountering gullies and impassable precipices he became completely worn out. At daybreak, he saw the monastery in front of him, and astonished by the miracle, he went inside repenting and confessed his wicked plan.

Chapter 71

At that time, when the godless Hagarenes invaded the theme of Calabria and were looting everything, the holy father along with the brethren fled for safety to the fortress of Rossano, but three of the monks who remained in the monastery, following their own individual regimen, were captured by the Saracens and abducted to Sicily. The blessed man decided that they should not be overlooked, but sought after like members of his own body, and brought back to their place. Then Neilos collected from the sale of grain, wine, and other crops up to one hundred gold coins, and together with the mule which Basil, the *strategos* of Calabria,

δοὺς αὐτά τινι τῶν ἀδελφῶν λίαν δοκιμωτάτῳ, ἀπέστειλεν αὐτὸν ἐν Πανόρμῳ, γράψας ἐπιστολὴν πρὸς τὸν νοτάριον τοῦ τῶν ἐκεῖσε φυλάρχου χριστιανικώτατον καὶ φιλευσεβῆ τυγχάνοντα.

2 Ὅστις νοτάριος ὑποδείξας τῷ λεγομένῳ ἀμμηρᾷ τὰ παρὰ τοῦ ὁσίου σταλέντα, ἑρμηνεύσας δὲ αὐτῷ καὶ τὴν θαυμασίαν ἐκείνην ἐπιστολήν, κατεπλάγη ἐπὶ τῇ σοφίᾳ καὶ συνέσει τοῦ μακαριωτάτου, ἐπιγνοὺς αὐτὸν φίλον τοῦ Θεοῦ ὄντα καὶ ἀνάπλεων πάσης ἀγαθοσύνης. Ἐπειδὴ τοίνυν οἶδεν ἀρετὴ αἰδεῖσθαι καὶ παρὰ πολεμίοις, ἀγαγὼν τοὺς μοναχοὺς καὶ φιλοφρονήσας πρεπόντως, κατασχών τε δι᾽ ὑπόμνησιν καὶ καύχημα τὸ βορδόνιον, ἀπέλυσεν αὐτοὺς σὺν τοῖς ταρίοις, προσθεὶς καὶ ἱκανὰ δέρματα ἐλάφων καὶ μηνύσας τῷ πατρὶ τοιάδε· "Σὸν τὸ πταῖσμά ἐστιν ὑπὲρ τοῦ κολασθῆναι τοὺς σοὺς μοναχούς, ἐπειδὴ οὐκ ἐγνώρισάς μοι ἐν πρώτοις σαυτόν· εἰ γὰρ τοῦτο ἐγίνετο, ἀπέστελλον ἄν σοι τὸ ἐμὸν σημεῖον, ὅπερ εἰ ἐκρέμνας ἔξω ἐν τῇ πλατείᾳ, οὐκ εἶχες ἀνάγκην οὐδεμίαν τοῦ σαλευθῆναι ἀπὸ τῆς μονῆς σου, ἢ κἂν ποσῶς ταραχθῆναι· εἰ δὲ καὶ ἠξίους πρός με παραγενέσθαι, εἶχες ἂν ἐξουσίαν ἐν πάσῃ μου τῇ περιχώρῳ κατασκηνῶσαι καὶ πολλῆς ἀπήλαυες τῆς παρ᾽ ἡμῖν τιμῆς τε καὶ εὐλαβείας."

3 Ταῦτα ἀκούσας ὁ θεσπέσιος Νεῖλος καὶ θαυμάσας τὴν ἐπ᾽ αὐτῷ τοῦ Θεοῦ οἰκονομίαν, τὸ τοῦ Σαμψὼν ἐφθέγξατο πρόβλημα, ὅτι· "Ὄντως νῦν ἀπὸ ἐσθίοντος ἐξῆλθε βρῶσις, καὶ ἀπὸ μισανθρώπου φιλανθρωπία," προσθεὶς καὶ τοῦτο πρὸς τὰς τοῦ ἀμμηρᾶ ἐπαγγελίας, ὅτι· "Ταῦτα πάντα σοι δώσω, ἐὰν πεσὼν προσκυνήσῃς μοι."

had given him, gave all this to one of the brethren, who was very trustworthy, and sent him to Palermo. He also wrote a letter to the local ruler's notary, who happened to be a very pious Christian.

This notary displayed the gifts sent by the holy man to 2 the emir, as their ruler was called, and translated that wonderful letter for the emir, who was struck by the wisdom and prudence of the most blessed Neilos, and recognized that he was a friend of God and filled with great goodness. Since virtue is admired even by enemies, the emir asked that the monks be brought to him, treated them in a kindly manner, and kept, as a memento and a trophy, only the mule. He freed them, returning the coins paid in ransom, and adding several deerskins. He also wrote this to the father, "The suffering of your monks is your fault, because you did not make yourself known to me before. For if this had been the case, I would have sent you my banner, and if you had hung it outside the monastery you would not have needed either to flee from your monastery or be disturbed at all. If you should ever deign to come visit me, you would have permission to reside in the entirety of my territory and you would receive from us much honor and reverence."

Upon hearing this, the godly Neilos was amazed at God's 3 dispensation toward him, and recited the riddle of Samson, "'Truly now *meat came forth* from the eater,' and kindness from the misanthrope." He added also this to the emir's promises, that "*All these things I will give to you, if you will fall down and worship me.*"

72

Ὁ δὲ συνετώτατος καὶ ἐστυμμένος τῷ νοῒ Βασίλειος ὁ στρατηγός, τοσαύτην πίστιν καὶ ἀγάπην ἔχων πρὸς τὸν πατέρα, ὅσην ὁ ἑκατόνταρχος πρὸς τὸν Σωτῆρα, προσήνεγκεν αὐτῷ μέχρι τῶν πεντακοσίων χρυσίνων, ὀμνύων καὶ λέγων ὅτι· "Οὔκ εἰσί μου ταῦτα ἀπὸ ἀδικίας, ἀλλ᾽ ἀπὸ τοῦ ἐμοῦ σπαθίου. Ἡνίκα γὰρ ἐκρατήσαμεν τῆς Κρήτης μετὰ τοῦ μακαριωτάτου Νικηφόρου, ἀκμὴν οὐκ ὄντος βασιλέως, εὑρήκαμεν παρά τινι πρεσβυτέρῳ ἐπ᾽ ἀληθείας τὸ ἔνδυμα τοῦ Προδρόμου, ἐκ τριχῶν καμήλου τυγχάνον καὶ περὶ τὸν τράχηλον ἡμαγμένον· ὅπερ λαβὼν ὁ μακάριος ἐκεῖνος, ἅπαν τὸ χρυσίον ἐμοὶ παρεχώρησεν. Ἐξ αὐτῶν οὖν τυγχάνοντα ταῦτα δέξαι διὰ τὸν Κύριον καὶ εὖξαί μοι."

2 Ὁ δὲ ὄντως ὑπερόπτης τῶν ἐπιγείων πατὴρ ἡμῶν Νεῖλος, μὴ καταδεχόμενος κἂν πρὸς αὐτὰ ἐπιβλέψαι, λέγει πρὸς αὐτόν, ὡς ἐν προφάσει δῆθεν τοῦ φοβεῖσθαι τὸν θάνατον· "Θέλεις, ἵνα διὰ τὰ σκύβαλα ταῦτα ἐνεδρεύσας τις ἀποκτείνῃ με καὶ ἀπολέσῃς τὸν φίλον σου;" Ὁ δὲ πάλιν εἶπεν· "Καὶ ἄφες με ἀμφιάσαι τὸ θυσιαστήριον ἐνδύμασι πολυτίμοις." Λέγει αὐτῷ ὁ μέγας· "Ἀπελθὼν βάλε αὐτὰ ἐν τῇ καθολικῇ τοῦ κάστρου, ὅπου φυλάττονται, ἐπεὶ ἔνθεν κλέπτονται." "Καὶ ἔασόν με," φησίν, "οἰκοδομῆσαί με τὸ εὐκτήριον μέγιστον καὶ τερπνότατον· οὐ γὰρ ἀνέχομαι πήλινον θεωρεῖν αὐτό." Καὶ ὁ πατήρ· "Ὥρα σοι," φησί, "μηδὲ ἐμὲ ἀνέχεσθαι θεωρεῖν, ὅτι ἐκ πηλοῦ τὴν

Chapter 72

Basil, the *strategos,* was a rather prudent and austere man who had as much faith and love for the father as the centurion had for the Savior. One day he brought him five hundred gold coins, swearing an oath and saying, "I did not acquire these through injustice, but through my sword. For when we conquered Crete with the most blessed Nikephoros who was not yet emperor, we found in the possession of a priest the true garment of Saint John the Baptist the Forerunner, which was made of *camel's hair* and bloodied around the neck. That blessed man Nikephoros took this for himself and gave me all the gold. This then is the origin of these coins. Take them for the sake of the Lord and pray for me."

But our father Neilos, who truly disdained worldly goods, did not deign even to look at the coins, but said to him, using as a pretext his supposed fear of death, "Are you willing to let someone lie in ambush and kill me on account of this rubbish, and to lose your friend?" In response Basil said, "Then let me cover the altar with costly fabrics." The great Neilos said to him, "Go and put them in the city's cathedral where they will be protected, since here they would be stolen." The other man said, "Then allow me at least to enlarge and beautify the chapel, for I cannot bear looking at it, since it is built of clay." And in reply the father said, "Then neither can you bear to look upon me, since my substance is also of

ὑπόστασιν κέκτημαι. Περὶ τοῦ εὐκτηρίου μηδὲν κοπιάσῃς· ὑπὸ γὰρ τῶν ἀθέων Ἀγαρηνῶν ἀφανισθήσεται καὶ πᾶσα δὲ ἡ Καλαβρία ταῖς χερσὶν αὐτῶν παραδοθήσεται."

3   Τοῦτο δὴ γνοὺς ὁ ὅσιος πατὴρ ἡμῶν Νεῖλος τῷ προορατικῷ αὐτοῦ ὄμματι καὶ βουληθεὶς τόπον δοῦναι τῇ θεϊκῇ ὀργῇ, οὐκ εὐδόκησεν ἀπελθεῖν πρὸς τὰ ἑῷα μέρη, τὴν ὑπόληψιν ὑφορώμενος τὴν περὶ αὐτοῦ τῶν ἐκεῖσε— καὶ μέχρι γὰρ αὐτῶν τῶν φιλοχρίστων ἡμῶν βασιλέων ἡ ἐνάρετος αὐτοῦ φήμη διῆλθεν—, καὶ τὴν τιμὴν τὴν παρ' αὐτῶν ἀποφεύγων. Ἐξελέξατο δὲ τὴν μετὰ τῶν Λατίνων ἀναστροφήν, ὡς ἄγνωστος ὢν παρ' αὐτοῖς καὶ μηδαμῶς παρ' αὐτῶν τιμώμενος· ὅσον δὲ αὐτὸς τὴν τῶν ἀνθρώπων δόξαν ἀποδιδράσκειν ἐσπούδαζεν, τοσοῦτον ἡ οὐράνιος εὔκλεια αὐτὸν περιέστελλεν καὶ πάντες ὡς ἕνα τῶν ἀποστόλων αὐτὸν ὑπεδέχοντο καὶ τὸ σέβας ὁμοίως ἀπένεμον.

73

Ἐλθὼν γὰρ ἐν Καπούῃ, ἵνα τὰ ὄπισθεν ἐάσω διὰ τὸ πλῆθος, καὶ τιμῆς μεγίστης τυχὼν παρά τε τοῦ πρίγκιπος Πανδούλφου καὶ τῶν ἀρχόντων, ὥστε βουλεύσασθαι αὐτοὺς ἐπίσκοπον αὐτὸν ἑαυτοῖς καταστῆσαι· καὶ προεχώρησεν ἄν, εἰ μὴ ὁ θάνατος τὸν πρίγκιπα περιέκοψε. Τότε δὲ καλέσαντες τὸν τοῦ Ἁγίου Βενεδίκτου ἡγούμενον τοῦ Ὄρους Κασίνου—Ἀλιγέρνος οὗτος ἦν ὁ ὁσιώτατος—,

clay. Nor should you waste your toil on the chapel, for it will be destroyed by the godless Hagarenes and all of Calabria will fall into their hands."

Our holy father Neilos, knowing this with his prophetic 3 eye and wishing to yield to the wrath of God, refused to leave for the east, fearing the admiration toward him of the men of that region—for his virtuous reputation had even reached our Christ-loving emperors—and avoiding the honor paid by these men. He chose rather to go among the Latins, in the hopes that he would be unknown to them and so receive no honor. But the more he strove to avoid human glory, the more heavenly glory surrounded him; and all received him as one of the apostles, and venerated him in like fashion.

Chapter 73

When he came to Capua—for I am omitting the intervening events because of their multitude—Neilos received so much honor from the prince Pandulf and the officials that they decided to enthrone him as their bishop, and this would have happened had death not cut short the prince's life. Then they summoned the abbot of the monastery of Saint Benedict of Monte Cassino—this was the most blessed

παρήγγειλαν αὐτῷ τοῦ δοῦναι τῷ μακαρίτῃ μοναστήριον, οἷον ἂν θέλῃ ἐκ τῶν τοῦ ὁσίου πατρὸς ἡμῶν Βενεδίκτου μετοχίων.

2   Πορευθεὶς δὲ ὁ ὅσιος πρὸς τὸ θεάσασθαι τὸ λεχθὲν περίδοξον μοναστήριον, ὑπήντησεν αὐτῷ ἅπαν τὸ πλῆθος τῶν μοναχῶν ἕως τῶν θεμελίων τοῦ ὄρους, οἵ τε ἱερεῖς αὐτῶν καὶ διάκονοι τὰς ἱερὰς στολὰς ὡς ἐν ἑορτῇ περιβεβλημένοι, κηρούς τε καὶ θυμιατήρια μετὰ χεῖρας φέροντες, οὕτω τὸν μακάριον εἰς τὸ μοναστήριον ἀνήγαγον, οὐδὲν ἄλλο δοκοῦντες ἀκούειν καὶ βλέπειν, ἢ ὅτι ὁ μέγας Ἀντώνιος ἀπὸ Ἀλεξανδρείας πρὸς αὐτοὺς παρεγένετο, ἢ ἐκ νεκρῶν ἠγέρθη ὁ μέγας Βενέδικτος, ὁ θεῖος νομοθέτης αὐτῶν καὶ διδάσκαλος.

3   Καί γε ὀρθῶς ἐλογίζοντο καὶ τοῦ σκοποῦ οὐ διήμαρτον. Ἅπαντες γὰρ αὐτῶν, οἵ τε σωματικοῖς, οἵ τε ψυχικοῖς συνεχόμενοι πάθεσιν ἐθεραπεύθησαν καὶ πάντα τὰ πρόσφορα παρ᾿ αὐτοῦ ἐκομίζοντο· οἱ ἐν λόγῳ τὴν διδασκαλίαν, οἱ ἐν ἔργῳ τὴν ποδηγίαν, οἱ ἐν ἁμαρτίαις τὴν διόρθωσιν, οἱ ἐν ἀρεταῖς τὴν παράκλησιν, οἱ ἐν ὑγιείᾳ τὴν ἐγκράτειαν, οἱ ἐν ἀρρωστίᾳ τὴν ἴασιν καί, συντόμως εἰπεῖν, ὥσπερ ποτὲ τοῖς Ἰσραηλίταις τὸ μάννα ἑκάστῳ πρὸς τὴν κρᾶσιν καὶ τὴν ὄρεξιν μετεβάλλετο, διὸ καὶ οὐκ ἦν ταῖς φυλαῖς αὐτῶν ὁ ἀσθενῶν, οὕτω κἂν τούτοις ὁ θαυμαστὸς διεγίνετο.

4   Ἀποθεραπεύσας τοίνυν αὐτοὺς τῇ θεοπεμπεῖ αὐτοῦ παρουσίᾳ καὶ πληρώσας εὐφρασίας πνευματικῆς, πάνυ δὲ καὶ αὐτὸς ἀγασθεὶς ἐπὶ τῇ εὐταξίᾳ καὶ πεπαιδευμένῃ καταστάσει αὐτῶν καὶ θαυμάσας τὰ αὐτῶν ὑπὲρ τὰ ἡμῶν, προεπέμπετο πάλιν ὑπό τε τοῦ ἀββᾶ καὶ τῶν ἐν ἐξοχῇ ἀδελφῶν

Aligernus—and they demanded that he give the blessed Neilos a monastery, whichever he preferred from among the dependencies of our holy father Benedict.

The holy man then journeyed to see the aforementioned 2 illustrious monastery, and the whole community of monks came to meet him at the foot of the mountain. The priests and deacons were dressed in their holy vestments as they would be on a feast day, carrying in their hands candles and censers; and thus they escorted the holy man to the monastery, thinking that what they saw and heard was nothing less than the advent of the great Anthony from Alexandria or the rising from the dead of the great Benedict, their divine lawgiver and teacher.

Indeed they reasoned rightly and did not fail to achieve 3 their purpose, for all who suffered from ailments, whether in soul or in body, were healed, and all they received from him was suited to their need: those devoted to study received instruction, the workers received guidance, the sinners correction, the virtuous exhortation, the healthy temperance, the sick a cure. To speak succinctly, just as once among the Israelites manna was transformed to suit each one's temperament and appetite—for which reason *there was not a feeble one among their tribes*—in the same manner the marvelous Neilos spent his time among them.

After healing them with his God-sent presence and filling 4 them with spiritual joy, Neilos also greatly admired their orderly and disciplined conduct, even praising their ways over our own. Neilos was then escorted by the abbot and the foremost of the brothers to the monastery where he was

εἰς τὸ μοναστήριον, ὅπου ἔδει σὺν τοῖς τέκνοις αὐτοῦ καθ-
εσθῆναι· ὁ Ἀρχιστράτηγος δὲ τοῦτο ἦν, τὸ καλούμενον
Βαλλελούκιον. Παρεκάλεσαν δὲ αὐτὸν ὅ τε ἡγούμενος καὶ
οἱ ἀδελφοὶ τοῦ σὺν πάσῃ τῇ ὑπ᾽ αὐτὸν ἀδελφότητι ἀνελ-
θεῖν ἐν τῷ μεγίστῳ μοναστηρίῳ καὶ τῇ Ἑλλάδι φωνῇ ἐν
τῇ αὐτῶν ἐκκλησίᾳ τὸν κανόνα πληρῶσαι, ἵνα γένηται,
φησίν, "ὁ Θεὸς τὰ πάντα ἐν πᾶσιν"· ὅπερ καὶ ὁ προφήτης
προαναφωνῶν ἔλεγεν, ὅτι· "Λέων καὶ βοῦς ἅμα βοσκηθή-
σονται, καὶ ἅμα τὰ παιδία αὐτῶν ἔσονται."

74

Ὁ δὲ θεσπέσιος Νεῖλος τὰ μὲν πρῶτα οὐκ ἐπένευσεν
ἀπὸ ταπεινοφροσύνης, λέγων· "Πῶς ᾄσωμεν τὴν ᾠδὴν
Κυρίου ἐπὶ γῆς ἀλλοτρίας, οἱ σήμερον ταπεινοὶ ἐν πάσῃ τῇ
γῇ διὰ τὰς ἁμαρτίας ἡμῶν ὑπάρχοντες;" Ὅμως διὰ τὸ συμπαρακληθῆναι ἐν τῇ ἀλλήλων πίστει καὶ τὸ μέγα ὄνομα
τοῦ Χριστοῦ δοξασθῆναι κατεδέξατο αὐτὸ τοῦτο ποιῆσαι.
Καὶ τυπώσας ἀπὸ καρπῶν χειλέων αὐτοῦ ὑμνῳδίαν πρὸς
τὸν ὅσιον πατέρα ἡμῶν Βενεδίκτον, περιέχουσαν πάντα τὰ
ἐν τῷ Βίῳ αὐτοῦ τεράστια γεγραμμένα, παραλαβών τε
πάντας τοὺς ἀδελφούς, ὑπὲρ τοὺς ἑξήκοντα ὄντας, ἀνῆλθεν ἐν τῷ μοναστηρίῳ Κασίνῳ, καὶ τὴν ἀγρυπνίαν ἐτέλεσε
παναρμονίως. Εἶχε γὰρ ἀδελφοὺς μεθ᾽ ἑαυτοῦ συνετοὺς
καὶ ἱκανοὺς ἔν τε ἀναγνώσει καὶ ψαλμῳδίᾳ, οὓς αὐτὸς κατ᾽
ἀμφότερα ἐξεπαίδευσεν.

meant to take up residence with his spiritual children. This was the monastery of the Archangel Michael, the so-called Valleloukion. The abbot and his brethren requested that Neilos return to the great monastery with the entire monastic brotherhood and celebrate the office in their church in the Greek language, *so that,* as the abbot said, "*God* would be *everything to everyone*"; the prophet also proclaimed this previously, saying, "*the lion and the ox shall feed together, and their young shall be together.*"

Chapter 74

At first the godly Neilos did not consent, saying in humility, "*How should we sing the Lord's song in a strange land,* we who are humble men today on all the earth because of our sins?" Nevertheless, so that they might find solace in their common faith and the great name of Christ be glorified, Neilos agreed to do this. He composed *from the fruits of his lips* a hymn of praise for our blessed father Benedict, including all the marvelous events written in his *Life.* Then taking with him all the brothers, more than sixty in number, he ascended to the monastery of Cassino and performed the night office in perfect harmony, since he had with him brethren who were skilled and capable in both reading aloud and singing the psalms, in both of which he had instructed them himself.

2   Μετὰ δὲ τὴν συμπλήρωσιν τοῦ κανόνος συνῆλθον πρὸς αὐτὸν ἅπαντες οἱ μοναχοὶ μετὰ παραθέσεως τοῦ ἀββᾶ αὐτῶν—καὶ μέχρι γὰρ τούτου τὴν εὐταξίαν φυλάττουσι— καὶ θαυμάζοντες ἐπὶ τῇ αἴγλῃ τοῦ Πνεύματος τῇ ἐκπεμπομένῃ ἀπὸ τῆς εἰδέας αὐτοῦ, ἐγλίχοντο καὶ ἀπὸ τῶν ῥημάτων ἐνωτίζεσθαι τοῦ στόματος αὐτοῦ. Διὸ καὶ προβλήματα συνεχῆ προσῆγον αὐτῷ, λέγοντες· "Εἰπὲ ἡμῖν, ἅγιε πάτερ, τί ἐστι τὸ ἔργον τοῦ μοναχοῦ, καὶ πῶς εὕρωμεν ἔλεος;" Ὁ δὲ μακάριος, ἀνοίξας τὸ στόμα αὐτοῦ, τῇ Ῥωμαϊκῇ γλώσσῃ ἔφη· "Μοναχός ἐστιν ἄγγελος· τὸ δὲ ἔργον αὐτοῦ ἐστιν ἔλεος, εἰρήνη, θυσία αἰνέσεως. Ὥσπερ γὰρ οἱ ἅγιοι ἄγγελοι τῷ μὲν Θεῷ ἀδιαλείπτως θυσίαν αἰνέσεως προσφέρουσιν, ἐν ἀλλήλοις δὲ εἰρήνην ἀγαπητικῶς κέκτηνται, ἐλεῶσι δὲ καὶ ἀντιλαμβάνονται τῶν ἀνθρώπων ὡς μικροτέρων ἀδελφῶν, οὕτω δεῖ καὶ τὸν ἀληθῆ μοναχόν, ἔλεος μὲν ἐπιδείκνυσθαι πρὸς τοὺς ἐλαχιστοτέρους καὶ ξένους τῶν ἀδελφῶν, ἀγαπᾶν δὲ ἐν εἰρήνῃ τοὺς ἰσοτίμους, τοῖς προκόπτουσι μὴ φθονοῦντα, πίστιν δὲ ἄδολον καὶ ἐλπίδα ἔχειν πρός τε τὸν Θεὸν καὶ τὸν ἐν πνεύματι πατέρα. Ὁ κεκτημένος τὰ τρία ταῦτα ἀγγελικὸν βίον ἐπὶ τῆς γῆς διάγει, ὁ δὲ τὰ ἐναντία, τουτέστιν ἀπιστίαν καὶ μῖσος καὶ ἀσπλαγχνίαν, παντὸς κακοῦ καταγώγιον γίνεται καὶ δαίμων προφανῶς ἀναδείκνυται. Ἀφ' οὗ γάρ τις μονάσῃ, οὐκέτι διαμένει τοῦ εἶναι ἄνθρωπος, ἀλλ' ἐκ τῶν δύο ἕν, ἢ ἄγγελος ἢ δαίμων, φανήσεται. Πέπεισμαι δὲ περὶ ὑμῶν, ἀδελφοί, τὰ κρείττονα καὶ ἐχόμενα σωτηρίας."

After the completion of the office, all the monks came 2
to him with the permission of their abbot,—as even in this
they followed orderly conduct—, and they were amazed at
the splendor of the Spirit sent forth from his countenance
and longed to hearken to the words from his mouth. Wherefore they kept asking him questions, saying, "Tell us, holy
father, what is the work of a monk? And how may we find
mercy?" The blessed man, opening his mouth, said in the
Roman tongue, "A monk is an angel, his work is mercy, peace,
a sacrifice of praise. For just as the holy angels ceaselessly offer a sacrifice of praise to God, maintain peace among themselves in loving kindness, and take pity on and assist mankind like younger brothers, thus the true monk should
demonstrate mercy toward the least of his brethren and the
foreign among them, love in peace his equals and not bear a
grudge against those who advance, and have a sincere faith
and hope in God and in his spiritual father. The man who
possesses these three qualities leads an angelic life on earth,
but the man who possesses the opposite qualities, that is
to say, lack of faith, hatred, and mercilessness, becomes an
abode of all evil and distinctly reveals himself as a demon.
For, from the moment that one becomes a monk no longer
does he continue to be a man, but he will appear as one of
the two, either an angel or a demon. *Yet in your case,* brothers,
I feel sure of better things that belong to salvation."

75

Τ αῦτα καὶ ἕτερα ὑπὲρ συγγραφὴν διαγορεύσαντος τοῦ ἁγίου, κατενύγησαν ταῖς καρδίαις αὐτῶν· καὶ ἀποκριθείς τις ἐξ αὐτῶν, εἶπεν· "Διατί λέγει ὁ Δαβίδ, 'Μετὰ ὁσίου ὅσιος ἔσῃ, καὶ μετὰ ἐκλεκτοῦ ἐκλεκτός, καὶ μετὰ στρεβλοῦ διαστρέψεις';" Λέγει αὐτῷ ὁ μέγας· "Τοῦτο πρὸς τὸν Θεὸν ἐλάλησεν ὁ προφήτης, οὐ πρὸς ἄνθρωπον· καὶ γὰρ Θεῷ πρέπει τὸ ἀκόλουθον, οὐκ ἀνθρώπῳ, τό· 'Ὅτι Σὺ λαὸν ταπεινὸν σώσεις, καὶ ὀφθαλμοὺς ὑπερηφάνων ταπεινώσεις.' Ἤκουσε γὰρ ὁ Δαβὶδ τοῦ Θεοῦ λέγοντος ὅτι· 'Ζῶ ἐγὼ Κύριος· ἐὰν ὀρθῶς πορεύσῃ μετ' ἐμοῦ, ὀρθῶς πορεύσομαι κἀγὼ μετὰ σοῦ.' Καὶ πάλιν γέγραπται πρὸς τοὺς σκολιούς—ταὐτὸν δέ ἐστι καὶ ὁ στρεβλός—, 'Σκολιὰς ὁδοὺς ἀποστελεῖ Κύριος, καὶ οὐχὶ ἄνθρωπος.' Ἀνθρώποις δὲ νενομοθέτηται τὸ ἀγαπᾶν τοὺς ἐχθρούς, τὸ καλῶς ποιεῖν τοῖς μισοῦσι, καὶ κακὸν ἀντὶ κακοῦ τινι μὴ ἀποδοῦναι."

2 Πάλιν ἠρώτησεν ἕτερος· "Τί ἐστιν ὃ λέγει Ἀμβακοὺμ ὁ προφήτης, 'Ἀναπαύσομαι ἐν ἡμέρᾳ θλίψεώς μου, τοῦ ἀναβῆναί με εἰς λαὸν παροικίας μου';" Ὁ δὲ ὅσιος ἀπεκρίθη· "Τοῦ ἀποστόλου λέγοντος, ὅτι· 'Ταῦτα πάντα τυπικῶς συνέβαινεν ἐκείνοις, ἐγράφη δὲ πρὸς τὴν ἡμῶν νουθεσίαν,' ἐγὼ πᾶσαν τὴν Γραφὴν εἰς ἐμαυτὸν ἑρμηνεύω. Τὸν γὰρ Ἀδὰμ ἀκούων καὶ τὸν Κάϊν καὶ τὸν Λάμεχ καὶ πάντας τοὺς τῷ Θεῷ ἐπταικότας, ἐνθυμοῦμαι ὅτι ἐγώ εἰμι ὁ τοιοῦτος καὶ οὐχὶ ἄλλος. Τοῦτο τοίνυν τὸ ῥητὸν τοῦ προφήτου ἀνθρώπῳ πρέπει συνετῷ, καθημένῳ κάτω εἰς τὴν ὕλην τοῦ

Chapter 75

When the holy Neilos imparted this and other teachings that cannot be included in our account, they felt compunction in their hearts. Then one of them responded, "Why did David say, '*With the holy* You will be holy, *and with the excellent man You will be excellent, and with the crooked You will pervert*'?" The great man said to him, "The prophet said this to God, not to man, for the following verse is appropriate for God, not man, '*You will save the lowly people and will humble the eyes of the proud.*' For David heard God saying, 'I your Lord live; if you rightly journey with me, I shall rightly journey with you.' And again it is written regarding the twisted, that is to say the crooked man, that the Lord and not man '*sends crooked ways.*' But to men it has been commanded *to love your enemy and to do well to those who hate,* and *not to repay evil for evil.*"

Someone else asked Neilos, "What does the prophet Habakkuk mean when he says, '*I will rest in the day of* my *affliction from going up to the people of my sojourning*'?" The holy man responded, "When the apostle says that '*all these things happened to them as a warning, but they were written down for our instruction,*' I interpret the entire Holy Scripture as if it referred to me. For when I hear about Adam, Cain, Lamech, and all those who have sinned against God, I am reminded that I am such a person and not someone else. Indeed, the saying of the prophet Habakkuk is appropriate for a person of understanding, who lives here below amid worldly

κόσμου, λογιζομένῳ τε καθ᾽ ἑαυτὸν καὶ λέγοντι, "Ἕως
πότε προσεύχομαι, καὶ ἃ λέγω οὐ νοῶ;᾽ Τότε ἐπάγει λέγων·
'Ἐφυλαξάμην,᾽ τουτέστιν, ἐσκόπησα, καὶ ἐσκεψάμην τὴν
προσευχὴν τῶν χειλέων μου᾽, εὔχομαι δέ, ὅτι· Εἰ ἀνταπέδωκα
τοῖς ἀνταποδιδοῦσί μοι κακά, πείσομαι τόδε καὶ τόδε,᾽ καί,
'Κρῖνόν με, Κύριε, κατὰ τὴν δικαιοσύνην μου καὶ κατὰ τὴν
ἀκακίαν μου, ὁ Θεός,᾽ καὶ ὅτι, "Ο Θεὸς ἐμφανῶς ἥξει καὶ οὐ
παρασιωπήσεται, πῦρ ἐνώπιον αὐτοῦ καυθήσεται,᾽ 'καὶ φλο-
γιεῖ κύκλῳ τοὺς ἐχθροὺς αὐτοῦ.᾽

3   "Ταῦτα καὶ τὰ ὅμοια τούτοις ἐννοήσας ἐξερχόμενά μου
τῶν χειλέων, κατανοήσας δὲ ἐμαυτὸν τὰ ἐναντία πράττοντα τούτων, ἐφοβήθη μου ἡ καρδία, καὶ ἐτρόμασαν τὰ
ὀστᾶ μου, ἡ δὲ ἰσχὺς τῶν γονάτων μου ὑποκάτω μου
ἐταράχθη, ὥστε στῆναι μὴ δύνασθαι. Ἐν ταύτῃ τοίνυν τῇ
τῆς θλίψεώς μου ἡμέρᾳ οὐκ ἄλλως ἔγνων ἀναπαῆναι καὶ
ἀπαλλαγῆναι τοῦ τρόμου τε καὶ τοῦ φόβου, εἰ μὴ ἐν τῷ
ἀναβῆναί με ἔνθα ὁ λαὸς τῆς ξενιτείας μου, ὅπου εἰσὶ
πάντες ξένοι καὶ παρεπίδημοι καὶ τὸ πολίτευμα ἐν οὐρανοῖς
ἔχοντες, οἱ μηδὲν ἔχοντες ἴδιον καὶ πάντα κατέχοντες· διότι
ἡ συκῆ μου καὶ ἡ ἐλαία μου καὶ ἡ ἄμπελος καὶ τὰ κτήνη μου
οὐδέν με ὠφελήσουσιν ἐν ἡμέρᾳ θλίψεως, οὐδὲ μετὰ
θάνατόν μοι καρποφορήσουσιν. Εἰ δὲ ποιήσω ὃ ἐβουλευ-
σάμην, ἀγαλλιάσομαι τότε ἐν τῷ Κυρίῳ, χαρήσομαι ἐπὶ τῷ
Θεῷ τῷ Σωτῆρί μου."

tribulations, and thinking to himself says, 'How long shall I pray and not understand what I say?' Then he added the words, '*I watched,*' that is, 'I paid attention and considered *the prayer from my lips,*' and I prayed, '*If I have requited with evil those who requited me with good,* I should suffer this and that.' I prayed also, '*Judge me, Lord, according to my righteousness, and according to my innocence,* O God,' and that, '*God shall come manifestly and shall not keep silence; a fire shall be kindled* before *Him,*' '*and burn up His enemies round about.*'

"Such prayers as these I noted issuing forth from my lips, 3 but saw myself doing the opposite. My heart was afraid, my bones trembled, and the strength of my knees was shaken such that I was unable to stand. *On* this *day of* my *affliction* I did not know how to find peace and be freed of the trembling and fear except by going there to the place where there are people who live in solitude, where all are *strangers and exiles,* and those whose *commonwealth is in heaven. They have nothing* of their own, *and yet possess everything. Wherefore* my *fig tree,* my *olive tree,* my *grape vine,* and my beasts of burden are of no benefit to me *on the day of affliction,* nor *shall they bear fruit* for me after death. If instead I do what I have decided, then *I will exult in the Lord, I shall rejoice in God, my Savior.*"

76

Τούτου δὲ οὕτως ἑρμηνευθέντος κατὰ τὴν τοῦ ἠθικοῦ τροπολογίαν, λέγει πρὸς τὸν ὅσιον ἄλλος· "Ἰδού, τίμιε πάτερ, ἀποστέλλομαι παρὰ τοῦ ἀββᾶ εἰς διακονίαν, ἐξ ἧς οὐ μικρὰν βλάβην ὑπομένω, ὁ δὲ κανὼν παραγγέλλει ὑπακοὴν ἀδιάκριτον ἔχειν. Τί οὖν προτιμῆσαι τῶν ἀμφοτέρων οὐκ οἶδα." Ὁ δὲ πατὴρ ἔφη· "*Πείθεσθε τοῖς ἡγουμένοις ὑμῶν καὶ ὑπείκετε· αὐτοὶ γὰρ ἀγρυπνοῦσιν ὑπὲρ τῶν ψυχῶν ὑμῶν, ὡς λόγον ἀποδώσοντες,*' ὁ ἀπόστολος λέγει. Τοίνυν ἡμεῖς πάντα τὰ τῆς καρδίας ἡμῶν τῷ ἀββᾶ ἐξομολογησάμενοι, τῷ κρίματι αὐτοῦ τὸ πᾶν καταλείψωμεν."

2 Πάλιν οὖν ἕτερος εἶπεν· "Ἐὰν ἅπαξ τοῦ ἔτους συγκαταβῶ τῷ σώματί μου καὶ κρεοφαγήσω, μὴ τί ποτέ ἐστιν;" Ὁ ὅσιος ἀπεκρίθη· "Καὶ εἰ πάντα τὸν χρόνον ὑγιαίνων, ἐν μιᾷ ὥρᾳ κρημνισθεὶς κατεάξεις τὸ σκέλος, τί κακόν ἐστι;"

77

Ταῦτα καὶ πλείονα τούτων ἀπὸ Γραφῶν προβαλόντες, ἠρώτησαν καὶ περὶ τῆς τοῦ Σαββάτου νηστείας. Ὁ δὲ σύντομον ἀπόκρισιν δεδωκὼς αὐτοῖς, ἀπηλλάγη εἰπών· "*Ὁ ἐσθίων τὸν μὴ ἐσθίοντα μὴ ἐξουθενήτω καὶ ὁ μὴ ἐσθίων τὸν ἐσθίοντα μὴ κρινέτω· ὁ Θεὸς γὰρ ἀμφοτέρους προσελάβετο. Σὺ δὲ διατί κρίνεις τὸν ἀδελφόν σου;*' Εἴτε οὖν

Chapter 76

When Neilos had interpreted the passage in this morally allegorical sense, another monk said to the holy man, "Behold, reverend father, if I am sent by my superior on an errand which will cause me great harm, but the monastic rule commands me to have unconditional obedience, I do not know which of the two imperatives to honor." The father said, "'*Obey your superiors and submit to them, for they are keeping watch over your souls, as men who will have to give an account.*' So says the apostle. Therefore, when we have confessed all the thoughts in our heart to the superior, let us leave everything to his judgment."

Then another monk said, "If I were to indulge my body 2 once a year and eat meat, would this be of any consequence?" The holy man responded, "If you were healthy all year long and on one occasion you fell and broke your leg, what harm is that?"

Chapter 77

After proposing these questions and more from Scripture, they also asked him about the Sabbath fast. He gave them a concise response, and concluded by saying, "'*Let not him who eats despise him who abstains, and let not him who abstains pass judgment on him who eats, for God has welcomed* both. *Why do you pass judgment on your brother?*' Let us do

ἐσθίομεν ἡμεῖς, εἴτε ὑμεῖς νηστεύετε, πάντα εἰς δόξαν Θεοῦ ποιῶμεν.

2 "Εἰ δέ τι ἐπιλαμβάνεσθε ἡμῶν, διότι τὸ Σάββατον οὐ νηστεύομεν, βλέπετε μήπως εὑρεθῆτε ἐναντιούμενοι τοῖς ἁγίοις πατράσιν καὶ στύλοις τῆς Ἐκκλησίας, Ἀθανασίῳ καὶ Βασιλείῳ καὶ Γρηγορίῳ καὶ Ἰωάννῃ τῷ Χρυσοστόμῳ καὶ ἄλλοις μυρίοις καὶ ταῖς ἁγίαις συνόδοις, οἵτινες ὃ οὐκ ἐποίησαν, οὐδὲ ἐνομοθέτησαν· οὐ μὴν δὲ ἀλλὰ καὶ Ἀμβροσίῳ τῷ ὑμῶν διδασκάλῳ, περὶ οὗ γέγραπται ἐν τῷ αὐτοῦ Βίῳ ὅτι πᾶσαν τὴν ἑβδομάδα ἐνήστευεν ἐκτὸς Σαββάτου καὶ Κυριακῆς. Ἐγὼ δὲ οὐδ' αὐτὸν τὸν ἅγιον Σίλβεστρον οἶμαι ἐναντιούμενον τοῖς ἁγίοις πατράσι ταύτην τὴν νηστείαν νομοθετῆσαι· οὐδὲ γὰρ δύνασθε ἀποδεῖξαι λόγον ἢ κανόνα περὶ τούτου, εἰ μὴ μόνον τὸν συγγραψάμενον τὸν ἐκείνου Βίον, ᾧ οὐδεὶς εὐχερῶς πιστεύει διὰ τὸ ἀναπόδεικτον. Ὅμως ἡμεῖς ἐάσαντες τὰς λογολεσχίας—οὐδὲν γὰρ κακὸν ἡ νηστεία—εἴπωμεν τὸ τοῦ ἀποστόλου· ὅτι 'βρῶμα ἡμᾶς οὐ παρίστησι τῷ Θεῷ,' καὶ τὰ ἑξῆς. Εἴθε δὲ καὶ οἱ ταπεινοὶ Ἰουδαῖοι προσεκύνουν τὸν ἐσταυρωμένον Δεσπότην καί, εἰ ἐνήστευον καὶ αὐτὰς τὰς Κυριακάς, οὐδέν μοι ἔμελεν περὶ τούτου."

3 Λέγουσιν αὐτῷ ἐκεῖνοι· "Καὶ οὐκ ἔστιν ἁμαρτία τὸ τὴν ἁγίαν Κυριακὴν νηστεῦσαι;" Ἀπεκρίθη· "Καὶ εἰ ἁμαρτία ἐστί, πῶς ὁ Ἅγιος Βενέδικτος καὶ τὰς Κυριακὰς καὶ τὰς ἑορτὰς νηστεύων, οὐδ' αὐτὸ τὸ Πάσχα ἠπίστατο πότε ἐστίν; Ὅθεν γνωστέον, ὅτι πᾶν πρᾶγμα διὰ Θεὸν γενόμενον καλὸν καὶ οὐδὲν ἀπόβλητον, οὐδ' αὐτὸ τὸ φονεῦσαι, ὡς ὁ Φινεὲς καὶ ὁ Σαμουὴλ ἔδειξαν. Καὶ ἡμεῖς τοίνυν

everything for the glory of God, whether it be eating on our part or fasting on yours.

"If you reproach us because we do not fast during the ₂ Sabbath, be careful that you do not find yourselves in conflict with the holy fathers and pillars of the Church, Athanasios, Basil, Gregory, John Chrysostom, and myriad others, and with the sacred councils, none of which passed any legislation that they did not practice. This is without mention of Ambrose, your teacher, of whom it is written in his *Life* that he fasted the whole week, except for Saturday and Sunday. I do not even think that the holy Sylvester prescribed this fast in conflict with the holy fathers, for you cannot adduce any sermon or rule of his as witness to this, except for the author of his *Life,* which no one readily trusts, as there is no proof of its authenticity. Nonetheless, leaving aside idle discussions—for fasting is in no way evil—let us speak the words of the apostle, *'Food will not commend us to God,'* and the rest of the verse. If only the wretched Jews were to worship the crucified Lord, it would not concern me at all if they fasted on Sundays."

They said to him, "Is it not a sin to fast on holy Sunday?" ₃ He responded, "If it were a sin, how did Saint Benedict, who fasted every Sunday and feast day, not know when it was Easter? From this it must be understood that every deed done for the sake of God is good and not to be rejected, not even murder itself, as Phineas and Samuel demonstrated.

235

καλῶς ποιοῦμεν τὸ Σάββατον μὴ νηστεύοντες, ἐναντιούμενοι τοῖς βδελυκτοῖς Μανιχαίοις, πενθοῦσιν ἐν τούτῳ
καὶ διαβάλλουσι τὴν Παλαιὰν Διαθήκην, ὡς παρὰ τοῦ
Θεοῦ μὴ δοθεῖσαν, οὐ σχολάζομεν δὲ πάλιν ἀπὸ τῶν
ἔργων, ἵνα μὴ ἐξομοιωθῶμεν τοῖς θεοκτόνοις καὶ ἀσεβέσιν
Ἰουδαίοις, καὶ ὑμεῖς ἀναγκαίως νηστεύετε, προκαθαίρον-
τες ἑαυτοὺς τῇ ἀναστασίμῳ καὶ ἁγίᾳ ἡμέρᾳ."

78

Ἐν τούτοις καὶ πλείοσιν ἄλλοις οἱ μοναχοὶ ὠφεληθέντες
καὶ ἡδυνθέντες, ἐξίσταντο πάντες καὶ ἐθαύμαζον ἐπὶ τοῖς
λόγοις τῆς χάριτος τοῖς ἐκπορευομένοις ἐκ τοῦ στόματος
αὐτοῦ, καὶ ἔλεγον, ὅτι· "Οὐδέποτε εἴδομεν ἄνθρωπον τὰς
Γραφὰς ἑρμηνεύοντα ὡς τοῦτον τὸν ὅσιον." Καί γε ἀληθῶς
ὑπελάμβανον καὶ ὀρθότατα ἔλεγον. Πάντων γὰρ τῶν
παθῶν τὸν νοῦν καθαρώτατον κεκτημένος καὶ τῷ οὐρανίῳ
φωτὶ λελαμπρυσμένον, ὁ λόγος αὐτοῦ ἦν πάντοτε ἐν χάριτι,
ἅλατι ἠρτυμένος, τοῖς μὲν ῥαθύμοις καὶ ἀσθενέσι κέντρον
καὶ βοηθὸς χρηματίζων, τοῖς δὲ θρασέσι καὶ ὑπεραλ-
λομένοις χαλινὸς καὶ φορβέα, τοῖς δ' ἀμφοτέρωθεν ἀπο-
κλινομένοις, εὐρύθμως τε βαδίζουσι καὶ δικαίως, ζυγὸς
ἀγαθὸς καὶ εὔχρηστος ὁδηγία. Ἅπαντας τοὺς πρὸς αὐτὸν
ἐρχομένους βλέπων μακρόθεν, ἐνενόει καὶ προύλεγε τὴν
αἰτίαν τῆς τούτων ἀφίξεως, καὶ ἡ ἔκβασις τῶν πραγμάτων
ἐβεβαίου τὴν πρόρρησιν.

Indeed we do well not to fast on the Sabbath, acting contrary to the abominable Manicheans, who mourn on that day and reject the Old Testament, because, in their opinion, it was not given by God. On the other hand we do not rest from our labors on the Sabbath lest we be likened to the God-killing and impious Jews; likewise it is appropriate that you fast on the Sabbath, purifying yourselves in advance for the holy day of the resurrection."

Chapter 78

The monks were edified by and took pleasure in these and many other teachings, and they all were astounded and marveled at the words of grace proceeding from his mouth. They said, "Never have we seen anyone explaining the Scriptures as well as this holy man." They understood truly and spoke rightly, for Neilos possessed a mind fully cleansed of all passions, illuminated by the light of heaven. *His speech was always gracious, seasoned with salt;* for the idle and weak he served as a goad and helper, for the reckless and restive as a bit and halter, and for those desisting from either extreme and proceeding rightly and justly, his yoke was good and he was a most useful guide. He saw from afar all who came to visit him, and intuited and predicted the reason for their arrival; and the outcome of events confirmed his prediction.

79

Οἶδα καὶ πέπεισμαι τοῦτο, ὅτι εἴγε συνήρχοντο πάντες οἱ ζῶντες ὑπὸ τὸν ἥλιον, αἰτούμενοι παρ' αὐτοῦ συμβουλίαν τὴν πρόσφορον, οὐκ ἂν τοῦ συμφέροντος ἠμοίρησαν. Ἦν γὰρ ἡ βουλὴ αὐτοῦ ὡς βουλὴ Θεοῦ, μεστὴ πάσης συνέσεως καὶ ὠφελείας, φυλαττομένη μέν, εἰς τέλος εὐκλεὲς καταντῶσα, παραλογιζομένη δέ, κίνδυνον ψυχῆς καὶ ζημίαν σωματικὴν προξενοῦσα. Καὶ εἶχον πάμπολλα κεφάλαια περὶ τούτου συντάξαι, εἴγε μὴ εἰς ἄπειρον τέλος ἐπεκτείνετο ὁ λόγος καὶ φορτικὸς ἐγεγόνει. Ἓν δὲ τῶν πολλῶν ὑπάρχει καὶ τοῦτο.

2 Τοῦ προρρηθέντος τελευτήσαντος Πανδούλφου, ὃς ἦν ἄρχων Καπούης, ἡ τούτου γαμετή, καλουμένη Ἀβάρα, οὐκ ἔλαττον ἢ μετὰ τοῦ ἀνδρὸς πάσης τῆς χώρας ἐκείνης ἦρξε καὶ κατεκράτησεν. Αὕτη ζηλοτυπίᾳ τῆς ἀρχῆς, μᾶλλον δὲ φθόνῳ σατανικῷ κρατουμένη, ὑποβάλλει τοὺς καταλειφθέντας αὐτῇ δύο υἱοὺς δόλῳ φονεῦσαι ἕνα τῶν κομήτων ἀνεψιὸν αὐτῆς ὄντα, ὡς παρευδοκιμοῦντα τῷ κράτει καὶ παρὰ πάντων τιμώμενον· ὃ καὶ πεποίηκαν. Ἡ γὰρ τούτων ὁμαίμων μετακαλεσαμένη ἐκεῖνον εἰς συντυχίαν καὶ εἰσελθόντος πρὸς αὐτὴν ἀπονήρως, πρόφασιν εὔλογον οἱ ταύτης ἀδελφοὶ εὑρηκότες, ἐπέβησαν αὐτῷ καὶ μαχαίρᾳ κατέσφαξαν.

3 Τούτων ἡ μήτηρ μετάνοιαν ἐπίπλαστον, οὐκ ἀληθῆ, προσποιουμένη, μεταστέλλεται δεητικῶς τὸν μακάριον πατέρα πρὸς ἑαυτήν, ὡς παρ' αὐτοῦ δεξομένη τὸ ἀντίρρο-

Chapter 79

I know and I am convinced that even if all those living under the sun had come and asked him for suitable advice, they would not have failed to obtain great benefit. For Neilos's counsel was like that of God, full of all wisdom and benefit. Put into practice, it led one to attain a glorious end, but if disregarded it brought about danger for the soul and bodily harm. And I could cite numerous examples to demonstrate this, but my narrative would be stretched out to an infinite length, and become burdensome. One among the many examples is the following.

When the aforementioned Pandulf, the ruler of Capua, 2 died, his wife named Abara ruled and held sway over that entire region no less than when her husband was alive. Because of her desire to rule, or rather overcome by satanic envy, she induced her two remaining sons to murder treacherously one of the counts, a nephew of hers, because he had garnered much power and was honored by all. They then committed the deed. For their sister invited the count to a meeting, and when he entered, with no ill intentions whatsoever, her brothers used this visit as a reasonable pretext, attacked him, and murdered him with a dagger.

Their mother feigned a false regret, and then entreated 3 the blessed father to visit her so that she might receive from

πον τοῦ πταίσματος ἐπιτίμιον· εἴξαντος δὲ τοῦ ὁσίου τῇ
παρακλήσει, καὶ τὸ ἄστυ καταλαβόντος, ἔτρεχον ἅπαντες
κατὰ τὰς λεωφόρους τοῦ θεάσασθαι τὸν τίμιον αὐτοῦ χαρακτῆρα καὶ μετασχεῖν τῆς αὐτοῦ εὐλογίας. Ἐν οἷς μία
διάκονος, ἡγουμένη μοναστηρίου, σὺν τῷ ἑαυτῆς πρεσβυτέρῳ, νέῳ ὄντι καὶ σφριγῶντι τῇ ἡλικίᾳ, συναγαγοῦσα δὲ
καὶ τὰς ὑπ᾽ αὐτὴν παρθένους, ἐξῆλθεν εἰς ἀπάντησιν τοῦ
ὁσίου. Ὁ δὲ μακάριος προορατικῷ ὄμματι θεασάμενος τὰ
κατ᾽ αὐτάς, οὐκ ἠδέσθη τὴν ἀπάντησιν αὐτῶν, ἀλλ᾽
ὑπήντησεν αὐταῖς ὡς φλογίνη ῥομφαία, αὐστηρᾷ τῇ φωνῇ
καὶ δριμαίῳ βλέμματι λέγων πρὸς αὐτάς· "Τί ὑμῖν καὶ τῷ
νέῳ τούτῳ, ὑμεῖς αἱ δοκοῦσαι εἶναι παρθένοι τοῦ συνδυάζειν μετ᾽ αὐτοῦ; Οὐ γινώσκετε ὅτι ἀνὴρ αὐτός ἐστιν;
Καὶ αὐτὸς οὐκ οἶδεν ὅτι γυναῖκες ὑμεῖς ἐστε; Τὸν Θεὸν
μὴ φοβούμεναι, κἂν τοὺς ἀνθρώπους οὐκ αἰσχύνεσθε;
Ὄντως οὐχ ὁρῶ ἐν ὑμῖν καρπὸν δικαιοσύνης."

4   Ταῦτα ἐκεῖναι ἀκούσασαι, δέον ἐντραπῆναι καὶ κατα-
πτῆξαι τοῦ δικαίου τὴν παρρησίαν, ἀνεχώρησαν λέγουσαι,
"Ὁ τοιοῦτος οὐκ ἔστι δοῦλος Θεοῦ, ἀλλὰ διάβολος." Καὶ
εὐθέως τῇ ἐπαύριον ἐκρατήθη ὁ πρεσβύτερος κοιμώμενος
μετὰ τῆς τῆς διακόνου ὁμαίμονος καὶ ἠκούσθη ἐν ὅλῃ τῇ
πόλει ἐκείνῃ.

him a penance appropriate to her sin. The holy man agreed to her request and, when he entered the city, everyone ran through the streets to see his venerable countenance and receive his benediction. Among them was a deaconess, the superior of a convent, together with her priest, who was young and in the full vigor of youth. The mother superior also brought along the nuns who were under her supervision, and went out to meet the holy man. The blessed Neilos, foreseeing with a prophetic eye their situation, was not pleased about the meeting, but went to meet them like a *fiery sword,* saying, with a harsh voice and angry gaze, "What connection do you have with this young man? How is it that you, who claim to be virgins, are consorting with him? Do you not realize that he is a man, and does he not know that you are women? Even if you do not fear God, would you not at least be ashamed before mankind? Truly I do not see in you the *fruits of righteousness.*"

When the women heard this, instead of feeling ashamed and subdued by the frank speech of the righteous one, they departed, saying, "This man is not a servant of God, but a devil." Immediately thereafter on the next day the priest was caught sleeping with the deaconess's sister, and word of this spread throughout the entire city. 4

80

Κατέλαβεν οὖν ὁ ὅσιος τὸ παλάτιον τῆς Ἀβάρας, ἥτις θεασαμένη αὐτὸν καὶ σύντρομος γενομένη, προσέπεσε τοῖς ποσὶν αὐτοῦ ἐξομολογουμένη καὶ συγχώρησιν λαβεῖν αἰτουμένη. Ὁ δὲ ἀναστήσας αὐτὴν εἶπεν· "Μὴ οὕτω ποίει, ὅτι κἀγὼ ἄνθρωπός εἰμι ἁμαρτωλός, οὔπω λαβὼν ἐξουσίαν τοῦ δεσμεῖν καὶ λύειν· πορεύου δὲ πρὸς τοὺς ἐπισκόπους, τοὺς τὰ τοιαῦτα κρίνειν πεπιστευμένους, καὶ ὡς ἄν σοι εἴπωσι, ποίησον." Ἡ δὲ ἀπεκρίθη· "Τοῖς μὲν ἐπισκόποις ἐξηγόρευσα τὴν ἐμὴν ἁμαρτίαν καὶ δέδωκάν μοι ἐντολὰς τοῦ πληρεῖν τὸ Ψαλτήριον τρίτον τῆς ἑβδομάδος καὶ ποιεῖν ἔλεος εἰς τοὺς δεομένους. Παρακαλῶ δὲ τὴν σὴν ἁγιωσύνην, δοῦλε Κυρίου, τοῦ καὶ παρὰ σοῦ τὸ συμφέρον ἀκοῦσαι, καὶ τὴν ἄφεσιν λαβεῖν τοῦ ἡμαρτημένου."

2   Ὁ δὲ ὅσιος ἔφη· "Τὸ μὲν εἰπεῖν τὸ Ψαλτήριον καὶ δοῦναι ἐλεημοσύνην σοὶ καὶ τοῖς δεομένοις ἐστὶν ὄφελος, τῷ δὲ ἀδίκως σφαγέντι σωτηρίαν οὐκ ἄγει, οὔτε τῶν ἐκεῖνον πενθούντων τὴν λύπην διασκεδάσει. Τί γάρ, τοσοῦτον δίδως, ὅσον ἀφείλω; Εἰ δὲ ὅλως βούλῃ καὶ παρ' ἐμοῦ τοῦ εὐτελοῦς δέξασθαι βουλὴν καὶ ποιῆσαι τὸ θέλημα τοῦ Θεοῦ, ἰδοὺ λέγω σοι· παράδος ἕνα τῶν σῶν υἱῶν τοῖς ἰδίοις τοῦ τελευτήσαντος τοῦ ποιῆσαι ἐν αὐτῷ εἴ τι ἂν θέλωσιν, καὶ τότε ἀπαλλαγήσῃ τοῦ ἁμαρτήματος. Εἶπεν γὰρ ὁ Θεὸς ὅτι· Ἐκ χειρὸς ἀνθρώπου ἀδελφοῦ αὐτοῦ ἐκζητήσω τὴν ψυχὴν αὐτοῦ δὴ τοῦ ἀνθρώπου. Ὁ ἐκχέων αἷμα ἀνθρώπου, ἀντὶ τοῦ αἵματος αὐτοῦ τὸ αὐτοῦ ἐκχυθήσεται·

Chapter 80

Then the holy man went to the palace of Abara who, upon seeing him, began to tremble and threw herself at his feet, confessing and asking to receive his pardon. He made her stand up and said, "Do not abase yourself, as I too am a sinful human, and I have never received the authority to bind and to loose. Go to the bishops who are entrusted with adjudication in such matters, and do as they say." She responded, "I did confess my sin to the bishops and they gave me as penance to recite the Psalter three times a week and to give alms to the needy. But I beg your holiness, O servant of the Lord, that I may hear a beneficial word from you and receive pardon for my sin."

The holy man said, "Recitation of the Psalter and alms- 2 giving is beneficial for you and for the needy, but it does not save the man who was unjustly slain, nor does it alleviate the sorrow of those grieving for him. How does what you offer equal what you have taken away? If you really wish to receive counsel from my humble self and do God's bidding, then I say to you: hand over one of your sons to the relatives of the deceased, so they may do with him as they wish, and then you will be absolved of your sin. For God said, '*I will require the life of man at the hand of* his *brother man. He that sheds man's blood, instead of that blood shall* his own *be shed*,' and elsewhere,

243

καὶ πάλιν· 'Πᾶς ὁ λαβὼν μάχαιραν, ἐν μαχαίρᾳ ἀποθανεῖται.'
Οὐ γὰρ εἶ σὺ ἀσθενεστέρα Σαοὺλ τοῦ βασιλέως καὶ τοῦ
κριτοῦ Ἰεφθάε, οἵτινες δι' οἰκείαν ἐντολὴν τὰ ἴδια τέκνα
εἰς θάνατον προὔδωκαν." Ἡ δὲ ἀπεκρίθη· "Οὐ δύναμαι
τοῦτο ποιῆσαι· φοβοῦμαι γὰρ μήπως αὐτὸν ἀποκτείνω-
σιν."

81

Τότε ὁ μακάριος, ζήλου θείου πλησθείς, ἀπεκρίνατο·
"Τάδε λέγει τὸ Πνεῦμα τὸ Ἅγιον· Τὸ αἷμα τοῦ υἱοῦ σου
ἐκχυθήσεται ἀντὶ τοῦ αἵματος οὗ ἀδίκως ἐξέχεας, καὶ ἡ
ἁμαρτία αὕτη οὐκ ἐξαλειφθήσεται ἐκ τοῦ οἴκου σου ἕως
αἰῶνος. Ἄρξει δ' οὐδεὶς ἀπὸ τοῦ σοῦ σπέρματος ἐν ταύτῃ
τῇ πόλει, ἀλλ' ἔσται ἐκδιωκόμενον καὶ νικώμενον ἀπὸ τῶν
ἐχθρῶν αὐτοῦ, ἀνθ' ὧν πέποιθας ἐπὶ τῇ σῇ δυναστείᾳ καὶ
οὐκ ἔμαθες ὅτι· Κύριος πτωχίζει καὶ πλουτίζει, ταπεινοῖ καὶ
ἀνυψοῖ.'"

2 Ταῦτα ἀκούσασα ἐκείνη ἤρξατο κλαίειν καὶ ἀποδύρε-
σθαι· πλήσασά τε τὰς χεῖρας χρυσίου προσέφερε τῷ δικαίῳ, νομίζουσα διὰ τούτων αὐτὸν ἐξιλεώσασθαι. Ὁ δὲ
ὄντως ἀπαθὴς ἐκεῖνος, μήτε τοῖς δάκρυσι τοῦ γυναίου
κατακαμφθείς, μήτε τῷ πλήθει τοῦ χρυσίου δελεασθείς,
μήτε τὴν ἐξουσίαν αὐτῆς αἰδεσθείς, διαρρήξας τὸ κατα-
πέτασμα τοῦ κοιτῶνος, καὶ ὡς δορκὰς ἐκπηδήσας, ᾤχετο,

'*All who take the sword will perish by the sword.*' For you are not weaker than Saul the king or Jephthah the judge, who, as the result of a command they themselves issued, had to hand over their own children to death." She replied, "I cannot do this, as I fear that they will kill him."

Chapter 81

Then the blessed man, filled with divine fervor, responded, "The Holy Spirit says this: 'Your son's blood will be shed in exchange for the blood which you unjustly shed; and this sin will not be removed from your house until the end of time. No one from your lineage will rule in this city. Instead, they will suffer persecution and defeat at the hands of their enemies, because you trusted in your power and did not learn that *the Lord makes poor and makes rich; He brings low and lifts up.*'"

Upon hearing this, the woman began to weep and mourn, 2 and then filling her hands with gold, she offered it to the just man, expecting to win him over through these gifts. However, the truly passionless Neilos, neither moved to pity by the woman's tears, nor tempted by the abundant gold, nor awed by her power, tore open the curtain of the bed chamber and, leaping out like a deer, went away. All the while he

τοῦτο λογισάμενος, ὡς αὐτὸς εἴρηκεν, ὅτι· "Εἶπεν," φησίν, "ὁ Διάβολος· 'οὗτος ὁ μοναχὸς χοῦς ἐστιν· ἐπιβρέξω αὐτὸν ὕδατι, τοῖς τῆς γυναικὸς δάκρυσιν, καὶ ἤδη ποιῶ αὐτὸν πηλὸν τοῦ τυποῦσθαι ὡς ἂν ἐγὼ βούλωμαι.'" Οὕτως ἔργῳ ἐπλήρου τό· "Γίνεσθε φρόνιμοι ὡσεὶ ὄφεις, καὶ ἀκέραιοι ὡς αἱ περιστεραί," ὁμοίως δὲ καὶ τὸ ἀποστολικὸν παράγγελμα τό· "Μὴ κοινώνει ἁμαρτίαις ἀλλοτρίαις." Καὶ τότε μὲν ὁ ὅσιος ὑπεχώρησεν εἰς τὸ μοναστήριον αὐτοῦ.

3   Οὐ πολὺ δὲ τὸ ἐν μέσῳ, καὶ εἰς τέλος ἐξήγετο ἡ αὐτοῦ πρόρρησις. Ὁ γὰρ μικρότερος υἱὸς τῆς λεχθείσης ζήλῳ τῆς ἀρχῆς τὸν μειζότερον ἐν τῇ ἐκκλησίᾳ προσευχόμενον μαχαίρᾳ κατέσφαξεν· ἐκεῖνος δὲ πάλιν ὑπὸ τοῦ τῶν Φράγγων ῥηγὸς διὰ τὴν αὐτὴν αἰτίαν δεδεμένος ἀπήγετο. Καὶ λοιπὸν ἐντὸς ὀλίγου χρόνου πᾶς ὁ κόμπος αὐτῶν ἐξέλιπεν καὶ ἡ ἐξουσία ἀπώλετο. Καὶ μή τις τῶν πάντα εὐτόλμων ἀπήνειαν τοῦ πατρὸς εἰς τοὺς ἁμαρτάνοντας καταγινωσκέτω. Ζηλωτὴς γὰρ ἦν εἰς τὸ ἐκδικῆσαι τὸν νόμον Κυρίου, καθάπερ Ἠλίας ὁ προφήτης, οὗτινος καὶ τὸν χαρακτῆρα τῆς ὄψεως ἐπεφέρετο. Καὶ τοῦτο οὐ μόνον ἐν τοῖς ἔξωθεν καὶ μηδόλως προσήκουσιν, ἀλλὰ καὶ ἐν τοῖς δοκοῦσιν ἰδιάζειν αὐτῷ κατὰ σάρκα καὶ ἐν τοῖς αὐτοῦ μέλεσιν· ἀπροσπάθειαν γὰρ πρὸς τοὺς οἰκείους ἑαυτῷ τοσαύτην ἐκέκτητο, ὅσην ἀποδείξει τὸ λεχθησόμενον. Ἐρῶ δὲ καὶ τοῦτο πρὸς ἀσφάλειαν τῶν ἐντυγχανόντων καὶ διόρθωσιν τῶν τὸν Ἠλεὶ μιμουμένων.

was thinking to himself, as he himself said, "The Devil must have said, 'This monk is dust. I shall moisten him with water, that is, the woman's tears, and soon make him clay to mold as I wish.'" Thus Neilos fulfilled in deed the scriptural verse, *"Be wise as serpents and innocent as doves,"* and likewise the apostolic precept, *"Do not participate in another man's sins."* Then the holy man returned to his monastery at Valleloukion.

Shortly afterward his prophecy came to pass, for her 3 younger son, because of his ambition for rule, slew his older brother with a sword as he was praying in church. On account of this murder the younger brother was placed in fetters by the ruler of the Franks and led away. So within a short time all their grandeur vanished, and the family's power was destroyed. Let no one be so bold as to condemn the father's severity toward sinners, for he was a zealot in the administration of the law of the Lord, just like Elijah the prophet, whose facial features he bore upon his own visage. He displayed this behavior not only with strangers and people entirely unrelated to him, but also toward those who appeared to be blood relatives, and with regard to his own limbs. His lack of attachment to his relatives will become evident in the next episode. I will tell this story also for the assurance of my readers, and as instruction for those who emulate Elijah.

82

Υἱὸς τῆς τὸν μακάριον ἀναθρεψάσης ἀδελφῆς αὐτοῦ ὑπῆρχεν ἐν τῇ μονῇ, τῇ ἀδελφότητι συνασκούμενος, λίαν εὐφυής, καὶ κατ' ἀμφότερα ἐπιτήδειος. Οὗτος, ὁδεύων ποτὲ μετὰ ἀδελφῶν καὶ ἀργυροῦν βαστάζων δισκοποτή-ριον, ἐνέτυχε διειδεστάτῃ πηγῇ. Βουληθέντων τοίνυν πιεῖν ἐκ τοῦ ὕδατος, αὐτὸς ἐκβαλὼν τὸ ἅγιον ποτήριον καὶ λιμβισθεὶς τῇ τοῦ μετάλλου καθαρότητι, ἔπιον μετ' αὐτοῦ πάντες. Τοῦτο γνοὺς ὁ μακάριος καὶ σφόδρα θυμωθεὶς κατ' αὐτοῦ καὶ πολλὰ ἐπιτιμήσας αὐτῷ, ἀπεστράφη αὐτὸν μέχρι καὶ συντυχίας αὐτῆς. Ἡ δὲ ἀποστροφὴ αὐτοῦ ἦν ὡς ἀπαλλοτρίωσις Θεοῦ, ὑπὲρ ῥάβδον καὶ μάστιγα σωφρο-νίζουσα τοὺς ἐχέφρονας. Ὁ δὲ ἀδελφὸς τῇ λύπῃ τῆς ἐπι-τιμήσεως συσχεθεὶς καὶ τῇ ἀποστροφῇ τοῦ πατρὸς κατα-πονηθείς, ἀρρωστίᾳ περιέπεσε δεινῇ ἐν ᾗ καὶ ἐτελεύτησε.

2   Ὁ δὲ μακάριος ἐν πάσαις ταῖς τῆς ἀρρωστίας αὐτοῦ ἡμέραις εἰσερχόμενος καὶ ἐξερχόμενος ἐν τῇ ἐκκλησίᾳ καὶ τῆς διόδου οὔσης ἔμπροσθεν τοῦ κελλίου τοῦ ἀδελφοῦ, οὐδέποτε ἐπέβλεψεν εἰς αὐτόν, ἢ τῆς αὐτοῦ ἐλεύσεως ἠξίωσε μέχρι τῆς αὐτοῦ τελευτῆς. Καίτοι γε σεσημείωτο παρὰ πᾶσι τοῖς ἀδελφοῖς ὅτι, ἡνίκα ἠρρώστει ἀδελφὸς καὶ ἐσύχαζε πρὸς αὐτὸν ὁ πατήρ, οὐκ ἠγείρετο ἐκ τῆς ἀσθε-νείας ἐκείνης. Τότε τοίνυν τις τῶν γερόντων, ἰδὼν τὸν πατέρα δακρύοντα μετὰ θάνατον τὸν ἀδελφὸν καὶ θρη-νοῦντα τὴν στέρησιν αὐτοῦ, προσελθὼν κατὰ μόνας δι-ελέγετο αὐτῷ, ὡς ψυχοπονούμενος περὶ τῆς θλίψεως τοῦ

Chapter 82

A son of the sister who had raised the blessed man was residing in the monastery, practicing asceticism together with the brethren; he was very bright and adept at both practical matters and the contemplative life. Once, while he was traveling with some brethren and carrying a silver chalice and paten, the young man came upon a spring of very clear water. Since the brethren wished to drink of the water, he took out the holy chalice, and enchanted by the purity of the metal, he drank from it, along with all the others. When the blessed Neilos was informed of this, he grew very angry, severely rebuked the young man, and avoided even talking with him. This rejection was like an alienation from God, which chastens the prudent more than even a rod or a whip. Overwhelmed with sorrow at his censure and crushed by the father's rejection of him, the brother fell into a grave illness from which he died.

During all the days of the youth's illness, as the blessed 2 Neilos entered and exited the church, he never looked in on him or deigned to visit him until his death, although the passageway was right in front of the brother's cell. Neilos did this even though, as all the monks had noticed, whenever a monk fell ill and the father went to visit him, the monk would not recover from that illness. Sometime after his nephew's death one of the elders saw the father weeping for the monk and lamenting his loss. He approached Neilos and spoke with him in private, since he was grief-stricken on account of the sorrow-induced death of the monk, which

ἀδελφοῦ, μεθ᾽ ἧς ἐξῆλθε τοῦ σώματος διὰ τὴν ἀποστροφὴν
τοῦ πατρός. Ὁ δὲ ἔφη· "Εἰ μὴ ἐγὼ αὐτὸν ἀπεστράφην, οὐκ
ἂν ὁ Θεὸς προσελάβετο. Πεπληροφόρημαι δὲ ὅτι διὰ
ταύτης τῆς μικρᾶς θλίψεως μεγίστης χαρᾶς καταξιωθήσε-
ται ἡ ψυχὴ αὐτοῦ, εἴπερ οὐκ ἄδικος ὁ Θεός, ἀπὸ φυλακῆς
ἆραι καὶ εἰς φυλακὴν θεῖναι."

3   Αὕτη ἡ διάκρισις τοῦ εὐδιακριτικωτάτου καὶ σοφωτάτου
πατρὸς ἡμῶν Νείλου παρὰ πολλοὺς τῶν ἁγίων πατέρων.
Ὑπερέβαλλε γὰρ τοὺς ἀσκητικωτάτους τῇ διακρίσει, τοὺς
δὲ διακριτικωτάτους ἐν τῇ ἀσκήσει καὶ τοὺς ἐν ἁπλότητι
ἐν τῇ γνώσει καὶ τοὺς γνωστικοὺς ἐν τῇ ἀκακίᾳ, τοὺς ἐν
βίῳ τῷ λόγῳ, τοὺς δὲ ἐν λόγῳ τῷ βίῳ, καὶ τοὺς κατ᾽
ἀμφότερα ἐν τῇ ἐν ἄμφω ἀκρότητι· ξένος τοῖς ἤθεσιν,
ἀλλότριος πάντη τῷ κόσμῳ, ἀταπείνωτος τοῖς πάθεσιν,
ὑψηλὸς τοῖς νοήμασιν, ἀκαμπὴς τοῖς ὑψηλοῖς, συμπαθὴς
δὲ τοῖς ταπεινοῖς.

83

Ἔκλεψέ τίς ποτε τῶν Λογγιβάρδων ἵππον τῆς μονῆς,
καὶ προσελθόντες δύο τῶν ἀδελφῶν ἠτήσαντο τὸν μακάριον τοῦ καταδιῶξαι καὶ ἀνευρεῖν τὸν αὐτὸν ἵππον, ὅτι
χρήσιμος ἦν πάνυ ἐν τῷ μοναστηρίῳ, ὃ καὶ πεποίηκαν.
Φθασάντων γὰρ τῶν ἀδελφῶν κόπῳ πολλῷ τὸ κάστρον,

came about as a result of Neilos's aversion. Neilos said, "If only I hadn't rejected him, God would not have taken him away. I have been informed, however, that because of this minor grief his soul will be deemed worthy of the greatest joy, since God is not so unjust as to remove someone from a prison and place him in another."

This was the power of discernment of our father Neilos, the most discerning and most wise among many holy fathers. For he surpassed in discernment those who excelled in asceticism, and surpassed in asceticism those excelling in discernment; he surpassed the simple ones in knowledge and the knowledgeable in his innocence; he surpassed in his words those who excelled in their way of life, and in his way of life those famous for their eloquence, and he surpassed those superior in both through his excellence in both his words and deeds. As if a stranger in his habits, he was altogether estranged from the world, unyielding to passions, lofty in his thoughts, unbending to the mighty, and compassionate toward the humble.

Chapter 83

Once a Lombard stole a horse from the monastery, and two of the brethren approached the blessed Neilos and asked to give chase and find the horse, as it was very useful to the monastery. They then set out. After an arduous journey the brethren arrived at the fortified city where the thief

ἐν ᾧ ὁ κλέπτης ὑπῆρχεν, ἡνίκα τὸ τοῦ πατρὸς ὄνομα καὶ μόνον ὁ ἐκεῖσε ἄρχων ἀκηκόει, εὐθέως ἀγαγὼν τὸν ἵππον καὶ τὸν κλέπτην δεδεμένον παρέδωκε τοῖς ἀδελφοῖς. Ὑπο-στρεψάντων τοίνυν αὐτῶν ἐν τῷ μοναστηρίῳ καὶ τῷ πατρὶ μετὰ χαρᾶς προσπιπτόντων καὶ λεγόντων, ὅτι· "Δι᾽ εὐχῶν σου, πάτερ, ἠγάγομεν τὸν ἵππον καὶ τὸν κλέψαντα," καλεῖ ὁ μακάριος τὸν Λογγίβαρδον καὶ λέγει αὐτῷ· "Ὄντως σύ, ἀδελφέ, ἀγαπᾷς τὸν ἵππον τοῦτον;" Καὶ λέγει ἐκεῖνος· "Εἰ μὴ ἠγάπων, οὐκ ἂν ἔκλεψα τοῦτον." Τότε λαβὼν ὁ πατὴρ τὸν ἵππον δέδωκεν αὐτῷ, προσθεὶς αὐτῷ μετὰ τῆς σέλλας καὶ τὸ χαλινάριον, λέγων· "Εἰ ἀγαπᾷς αὐτόν, λάβε καὶ πορεύου." Ὁ δὲ ἀπῆλθε χαίρων καὶ ἀγαλλόμενος.

2   Ἀρξαμένων δὲ τῶν ἀδελφῶν καταγογγύζειν τοῦ μακα-ρίου, καλέσας αὐτοὺς ὁ πατὴρ ἐνουθέτει λέγων· "Μάθετε, ἀδελφοί, τοῦτο, ὅτι ἡ τῶν πραγμάτων ὁπωσδήποτε στέρη-σις, ἁμαρτημάτων ἐστὶν ἀφαίρεσις· εἶτα οὔκ ἐσμεν ἄξιοι τοῦ Γεροντικοῦ ποιῆσαι ἓν κεφάλαιον; Εἰ ὁ Θεὸς θέλει ἐλεῆσαι ἡμᾶς, ἡμεῖς αὐτῷ μὴ ἀντιτασσώμεθα." Οἱ δὲ εἶπον· "Τοῦτο θλιβόμεθα, πάτερ, ὅτι μετὰ τὸ κοπιᾶσαι ἡμᾶς πάνυ πολλὰ περιπατήσαντας καὶ εὑρεῖν τὸ ἀπολωλός, τότε αὐτῷ ἐδωρήσω τῷ κλέψαντι." Καὶ ὁ πατὴρ ἔφη· "Τοῦτο πε-ποίηκα ὑμῖν, ἵνα διδάξω ὑμᾶς *ἀγαπᾶν ἔργῳ τοὺς ἐχθροὺς* καὶ *καλῶς ποιεῖν τοῖς ἐπηρεάζουσιν ὑμᾶς* καὶ τὸ *πάντα κατέχειν ὡς μηδὲν ἔχοντες*, καθὼς τὸ Εὐαγγέλιον καὶ ὁ ἀπόστολος ἡμᾶς ἐκδιδάσκουσιν." Ὁ μὲν οὖν μακαρίτης πατὴρ ἡμῶν Νεῖλος ταῦτα ἐφρόνει τε καὶ ἐδίδασκεν, ἀεὶ ἐπὶ στόματος φέρων τὰς χρήσεις τῶν μακαρίων καὶ σοφῶν

was; as soon as the ruler of that place heard the father's name, he immediately had the horse and the shackled thief brought out and handed over to the brethren. When they returned to the monastery, they prostrated themselves at the father's feet with much joy, and said, "Through your prayers, father, we have brought back the horse and the thief." The blessed one summoned the Lombard and said to him, "Brother, do you truly want this horse?" He responded, "If I did not want it, I would not have stolen it." Then Neilos took the horse and gave it to him, also adding the saddle and bridle, saying, "If you want it, take it and go." The man departed joyful and rejoicing.

When the two brethren began to grumble against the blessed father about this, he summoned them to him and gave them the following advice: "Learn this, brethren, that the deprivation of any sort of material possessions is a release from sins; are we not able to practice even a single chapter of the *Gerontikon*? If God wishes to have mercy on us, let us not resist Him." They said, "We are distressed, father, because after we went to the trouble of walking so far to find the lost horse, you then gave it to the thief." The father said, "I did this for you, to teach you *to love your enemies* in deed and *to treat well those who have done you harm,* and *to possess everything and yet have nothing,* just as the Gospel and the apostle teach us." In this way our blessed father Neilos both believed and taught, always carrying upon his lips the sayings of the blessed and wise teachers, and striving

διδασκάλων, παντοίῳ τε τρόπῳ ἀγωνιζόμενος ἔργον ἀποδεῖξαι τὸν λόγον καὶ τὴν μάθησιν φρόνησιν καὶ τὴν πρᾶξιν κατὰ τὴν δίδαξιν.

84

Οὐ μόνον δὲ ἑαυτόν, ἀλλὰ καὶ τοὺς μετ᾽ αὐτοῦ οὕτως ἐφωταγώγει καὶ ἥλιζεν, ἀκούων παρὰ τοῦ Σωτῆρος, ὅτι· "Ὑμεῖς ἐστε τὸ φῶς καὶ ἅλας τῆς γῆς." Πολλάκις γὰρ εἴ που ηὕρισκε χρῆσιν ἢ γνώμην, εἴτε τροπάριν ἐκ τῶν κανόνων, κατόρθωσιν ἤθους διδάσκοντα, προσκαλούμενος τοὺς ἀδελφούς, ὥσπερ τινὰ κλῆρον διεδίδου αὐτοῖς τοῦ ἀποστηθίζειν αὐτά, τοῖς μὲν ἰσχύουσι τὰ ὑψηλά, τοῖς δὲ ἀφελεστέροις τὰ ἐλαφρά, καὶ ἑκάστῳ πρὸς τὸ πάθος ᾧ ἐπλεονεκτεῖτο, καὶ τὸ ἔμπλαστρον τοῦ μαθήματος ἐπετίθει. Οἷον, εἴ τις γαστρίμαργος, τὰ περὶ ἐγκρατείας· εἴ τις λάγνος, τὰ περὶ ἁγνείας· εἴ τις κενόδοξος, τὰ περὶ ταπεινοφροσύνης· εἴ τις γλωσσώδης καὶ μάχιμος, τὴν ἐπιστολὴν Ἰακώβου τοῦ ἀποστόλου. Εἰ δέ τις ἦν δυσμαθὴς καὶ μὴ δυνάμενος μνημονεύειν, γράφων τὴν γνώμην ἐν τμήματι χαρτίου, ἐκρέμνα αὐτῷ ἐπὶ τὸν τράχηλον, ἢ περὶ τὸν βραχίονα αὐτοῦ, μέχρις ὅτου αὐτὴν ἀπεστήθιζεν.

2   Οὕτως ἐποίει ὁ τρισμακάριστος τοὺς ἀλάλους λαλεῖν καὶ τοὺς κωφοὺς ἀκούειν καὶ τοὺς τυφλοὺς βλέπειν, τοὺς βαρβάρους εἰργάζετο θεολόγους καὶ τούς ποτε κτη-

in every way to demonstrate their words in deed, so that learning is wisdom, and deeds are in accordance with the teaching.

Chapter 84

In this way Neilos illuminated and seasoned not only himself, but also his companions, hearing the words of the Savior, "*You are the light and the salt of the earth.*" For often if he found somewhere a patristic saying or maxim, or a *troparion* from the canons, that taught the improvement of one's conduct, Neilos would summon the brethren and share it with them, as a kind of bequest, so that they could learn it by heart; to those with natural aptitude he would give the more sublime citations, to the simpler the easier ones. And he applied to each the salve of learning in accordance with the passion which overcame him. For example, if someone was a glutton, Neilos taught precepts of moderation; if one was lustful, precepts of chastity; if one was vain, precepts of humility; if talkative and quarrelsome, the epistle of the apostle James. And if someone was unable to learn and incapable of memorizing, Neilos would write the maxim on a piece of paper and hang it on his neck or around his arm until he learned it by heart.

In this manner the thrice-blessed man made the mute to 2 speak, *the deaf to hear, the blind to see,* the illiterate to become theologians, and former herdsmen to become teachers of

νοτρόφους ἀνθρώπων διδασκάλους· καὶ πολλοὺς μὲν
ἀπήλλαξε δεινῶν δαιμονίων, πλείονας δὲ παθῶν ἀκαθάρτων
καὶ συνηθείας ἀτόπου· μεῖζον δὲ τοῦ προτέρου τὸ δεύτε-
ρον. Πολλὰ ἔχω τοῦ λέγειν περὶ αὐτοῦ, ἀλλ᾽ οὐκ ἐᾷ με ὁ
χρόνος, ἐπείγομαι γὰρ πρὸς τὸ τέλος.

85

Mετὰ τὸ τελευτῆσαι τὸν ἀοίδιμον Ἀλιγέρνον, τὸν
καλῶς καὶ ὁσίως ποιμάναντα τὴν μονὴν τοῦ ἐν ἁγίοις Βενεδίκτου, ἀνέστη ἐπ᾽ αὐτὴν ἡγούμενος, ὃς οὐκ ᾔδει τὸν
ὅσιον Νεῖλον, ὅστις ἦν, ἀληθῶς δὲ εἰπεῖν, οὐδὲ τὸν Θεόν·
ὅμως γνωρίσει τὰ περὶ αὐτὸν τοῦτο, ὅπερ συντόμως ἐρῶ.

2   Παραβαλόντος τοῦ μακαρίου μιᾷ τῶν ἡμερῶν πρὸς
αὐτόν, ἔτυχεν αὐτὸν εὑρεῖν ἐν τῷ κάτω μοναστηρίῳ, ἐν ᾧ
ἵδρυται πάντερπνος ναὸς τοῦ ἁγιωτάτου Γερμανοῦ,
ὑδάτων πλήθει καὶ κάλλει περιαντλούμενος. Εὗρε δὲ τὸν
αὐτὸν ἡγούμενον σὺν τοῖς πρώτοις τοῦ μεγάλου μοναστηρίου λελουσμένον καὶ ἐν τῷ ἀριστηρίῳ ἐσθίοντα. Ὡς
οὖν περιέμενεν αὐτὸν ὁ ὅσιος ἐν τῇ ἐκκλησίᾳ μετὰ τῶν
σὺν αὐτῷ ἀδελφῶν, ἀκούει ὅτι κιθαριστὴς εἰσῆλθε κι-
θαρίζων ἐν τῷ ἀριστηρίῳ. Τότε ὁ μακαρίτης Νεῖλος ἔφη
πρὸς τοὺς συνόντας· "Μέμνησθέ μου τοῦ ῥήματος, ἀδελφοί, ὅτι οὐ βραδύνει τοῦ ἐλθεῖν τὴν ὀργὴν Κυρίου ἐπὶ τοὺς
ἀνθρώπους τούτους. Ἐγείρεσθε, ἄγωμεν ἐντεῦθεν." Καὶ
τοῦτο εἰπὼν ἀνεχώρησεν.

men. Also he delivered many from terrible demons, and even more from impure passions and improper habits, this second deed being more significant than the first. I have much more to say about him, but time does not permit me, as I hasten to conclude.

Chapter 85

After the death of the celebrated abbot Aligernus, who had shepherded well and in holy fashion the monastery of Saint Benedict, a superior was installed who did not know who the holy Neilos was and, to speak truly, did not even know God, as will be made clear by the account of him I shall briefly narrate.

One day the blessed Neilos went to visit him, and happened to meet him at the lower monastery, where was built a most splendid church in honor of the most holy Germanus, surrounded by an abundance of beautiful waters. Neilos found the abbot freshly bathed and eating in the refectory together with the leaders of the great monastery. While the holy man was awaiting him in the church along with the brethren, he heard that a musician had entered the refectory playing a lute. Then the blessed Neilos said to those around him, "Remember my words, brethren, that the Lord's wrath will not be slow to come upon these people. *Rise, and let us depart* from here." After saying this, he departed.

3   Οὔπω διῆλθεν ὁ χρόνος, καὶ ὁ μὲν ἡγούμενος, κρατηθεὶς ὑπὸ τοῦ πρίγκιπος δι᾽ ἀνταρσίαν, τοὺς ὀφθαλμοὺς
ἐξωρύχθη, οἱ δὲ μοναχοὶ ἀρρωστίᾳ χαλεπῇ περιπεσόντες
ἐβασανίσθησαν ἕως θανάτου, τινὲς δὲ ἐξ αὐτῶν καὶ ἀπέθα-
νον· ὁ δὲ κιθαριστὴς ἐκεῖνος ἀπελθὼν εἰς τὸ κλέψαι καὶ
πιασθείς, μετὰ πολλὰς τὰς βασάνους καὶ αὐτὸς τοὺς
ὀφθαλμοὺς ἐξωρύχθη, καὶ πάντες ἔπιον τῆς τοῦ Θεοῦ
ὀργῆς τὸ ποτήριον κατὰ τὴν τοῦ γέροντος πρόρρησιν.
Ἀλλὰ ταῦτα μὲν ὕστερον.

86

Ὁ τοίνυν μακαρίτης Νεῖλος ποιήσας ἐν τῇ μονῇ τοῦ
λεγομένου Βαλλελουκίου περὶ τὰ πέντε καὶ δέκα ἔτη καὶ
τῶν ἀδελφῶν πληθυνθέντων καὶ πάντων τῶν τῆς χρείας
ὑπερεκχυνομένων καὶ τοῦ μοναστηρίου μεγαλυνθέντος
καὶ ὀνομαστοῦ γενομένου τῇ αὐτοῦ συνεργείᾳ, οὐ πρότερον ὄντος τοιούτου, ἑώρα τοὺς ἀδελφοὺς οὐ πάνυ
φροντίζοντας τῆς πνευματικῆς λειτουργίας καὶ τῆς τοῦ
κανόνος ἀκριβείας, ἐν ᾗ τετύπωντο ἀρχῆθεν, ἀλλὰ τῇ
πλατείᾳ ὁδῷ ἡδομένους, καὶ ἀμφιβολίᾳ περιβαλλομένους,
τίς μείζων· συνήργει δὲ αὐτοῖς καὶ ἡ κουφότης τοῦ προ-
λεχθέντος ἡγουμένου, ἅτε δωρολήπτου καὶ μισευλαβοῦς
τυγχάνοντος.

2   Ταῦτα ἰδὼν ὁ μακάριος καὶ γνοὺς ὡς ἡ τῶν ὑλῶν

Not even a year had passed when the abbot was arrested 3
by the prince of Capua on charges of rebellion, and his eyes
were gouged out. The monks fell gravely ill and were tormented by illness nearly to the point of death; some of them
in fact died. Meanwhile the musician was apprehended
while committing a robbery, and after many tortures he also
was blinded. So all drank the cup of God's wrath in accordance with the prediction of the venerable Neilos; but these
events occurred later.

Chapter 86

Thus the blessed Neilos spent about fifteen years in the
so-called monastery of Valleloukion; during this period as
a result of his activity the number of brethren increased,
all the necessities were provided for in abundance, and the
monastery grew in size and fame, to a greater extent than
before. Still Neilos could see that the brethren were not
strictly observing the spiritual service and the scrupulous
monastic rule according to which they had originally been
tonsured, but they indulged in following the wide way and
quarreled over who was superior in rank. The frivolity of
the aforementioned abbot, who did not reject bribes and
scorned piety, also contributed to this.

When the blessed Neilos observed this, and understood 2

ἀφθονία αἰτία καθίσταται τοῖς πολλοῖς ἀταξίας καὶ παντε-
λοῦς ἀνευλαβείας, ἀναστὰς ἀπῆρεν ἐκεῖθεν καὶ διήρχετο
ζητῶν τόπον ὅπου εὕρῃ στενὸν καὶ κόπῳ χορηγοῦντα τὴν
τοῦ σώματος χρείαν, ἵνα κἂν τῇ ἐνδείᾳ τῶν ἀναγκαίων,
ὥσπερ χαλινῷ οἱ πολλοὶ πρὸς τὸ τῆς ἀσκήσεως στάδιον
ἑλκυσθῶσιν. Ὅθεν καὶ πολλῶν ἀπὸ τῶν πέριξ πόλεων
προστρεχόντων καὶ προσκαλουμένων καὶ τὰς οἰκείας
ὑποστάσεις τῷ μακαρίῳ προσφερόντων, τινῶν δὲ καὶ μοναστήρια προητοιμασμένα χαριζομένων, οὐδ᾽ ὅλως αὐτὸς
κατεδέξατο· οὐ γὰρ εὕρισκεν ἐν αὐτοῖς ὃ ἐπεζήτει, ἐρημίαν
καὶ ἡσυχίαν καὶ τῶν πολλῶν ἀποικίαν.

3   Ἔλεγε γάρ, ὅτι· "Οὐ συμφέρει τοῖς ἐν τῇ γενεᾷ ταύτῃ
μοναχοῖς ἄνεσις καὶ ἀφροντησία· οὐ γάρ ἐστιν ἡ σχολὴ
αὐτῶν ἐν προσευχῇ καὶ θεωρίᾳ καὶ τῇ τῶν Γραφῶν
ἀναπτύξει, ἀλλ᾽ ἐν ματαιολογίᾳ καὶ κακενθυμησίᾳ καὶ τῇ
τῶν ματαίων περιεργίᾳ. Διόπερ εὑρίσκονται τὸν ἐν κόπῳ
περισπασμὸν ἀποτροπὴν πονηρῶν λογισμῶν καὶ πολλῶν
κακῶν, προτιμητέον τό· Ἐν ἱδρώτητι τοῦ προσώπου ἐσθίειν
τὸν ἄρτον.᾽ Οὕτω καὶ ἡ ἀποστολικὴ ἐντολὴ πληρωθήσεται
καὶ οἱ πυκνῶς παρερχόμενοι συμμέτρως ἀναπαυόμενοι,
στεφάνων ἡμῖν αἴτιοι ἀξίως γενήσονται."

that the profusion of material goods had become for many the cause of disorder and utter impiety, he departed from there, and wandered about in search of a small plot of land that would provide for their bodily needs through hard labor, so that notwithstanding the lack of necessities many might be attracted to the arena of ascetic life as if pulled by reins. Therefore, although many people came from the surrounding cities and issued invitations to him, offering their own properties to the blessed one, and some of them even donated completely furnished monasteries, Neilos in no way accepted these offers, for he could not find in them what he was seeking, namely, solitude, spiritual tranquility, and an abode far from the multitude.

He used to say, "For the monks of this generation ease 3 and freedom from care are not appropriate, for their attention is not focused on prayer and contemplation and study of Scripture, but in idle talk, wicked-mindedness, and pursuit of vanities. For this reason, they find in the diversion of work a means to repel many wicked and evil thoughts. So one should favor the verse, '*To eat bread by the sweat of your brow.*' Thus the commandment of the apostle will be fulfilled, and those who frequently visit us, after resting in a fitting manner, would become the cause of our worthy garlands of victory."

87

Τ αύτης τῆς συνέσεως τοῦ δικαίου τινὲς τῶν ἀδελφῶν μηδαμῶς αἰσθανθέντες, τοὐναντίον μὲν οὖν τὴν εὐρύχωρον ὁδὸν τῆς στενῆς προτιμῶντες, ἐναπέμειναν τῷ προλεχθέντι μοναστηρίῳ, προσδεθέντες τῇ τοῦ τόπου διαναπαύσει καὶ ἀχθεσθέντες τῇ στρυφνότητι τοῦ ἁγίου· οὐ μέντοι εὗρον ἀνάπαυσιν πάσας τὰς ἡμέρας τῆς ἐκεῖσε αὐτῶν οἰκήσεως, οὔτε διέλειψεν αὐτοῖς ἀκαταστασία καὶ ἀταξία, θλίψις τε καὶ λογολεσχία· τέλος δὲ καὶ παντελῶς ἐξεώθησαν καὶ ἀπηλάθησαν.

2   Ὁ δὲ μακάριος μετὰ τῶν συνελθόντων αὐτῷ ἀδελφῶν καὶ τοῦ ἀοιδίμου Στεφάνου, εὑρὼν ἐν τοῖς τῆς Γαΐτας μέρεσι τοπάριον, ἀληθῶς δὲ εἰπεῖν σπανύδριον, καὶ ἀρεσθεὶς ἐπὶ τῇ αὐτοῦ στενότητι καὶ ξηρότητι, κατῴκησεν αὐτοῦ, ἐν ἀρχῇ μὲν ἐν ἐνδείᾳ καὶ λείψει τῶν σωματικῶν, μετ᾽ οὐ πολὺ δὲ πλειόνων ἀδελφῶν καὶ πάντων θεοφιλῶν συνελθόντων, ἅπαντα ἐν εὐθηνίᾳ κατέστη, ἀπερίσπαστός τε ἦν ἐργασία καὶ ἀδιάλειπτος ψαλμῳδία, ψαλμολογίαι συχναὶ καὶ γονυκλισίαι πυκναί, ἐγκράτεια ἑκούσιος καὶ ὑπακοὴ ἀβίαστος. Καὶ λοιπὸν ἅπαντες ἤνθουν καὶ ἐκαρποφόρουν τῇ ἀρδείᾳ τῶν λόγων καὶ ἀπαύστῳ διδασκαλίᾳ τοῦ θεοφόρου πατρὸς ἡμῶν Νείλου.

3   Ἀλλ᾽ οὐδ᾽ αὐτὸς ὁ ἀήττητος ἐν ἀγῶσιν ἀπέκοπτε τῆς συνήθους αὐτοῦ ἐγκρατείας καὶ τῶν ἐνθέων κατορθωμάτων, ἀλλ᾽ ὅσον τῷ σώματι ἐγήρα καὶ ἐξησθένει, τοσοῦτον τῷ πνεύματι ἀνέθαλλε καὶ ἐδυναμοῦτο. Οὐδέποτε

Chapter 87

Some of the brethren did not understand the prudence of the just Neilos; instead, preferring *the wide way to the narrow*, they remained in the aforementioned monastery of Valleloukion, because they were attached to the amenities of the place and annoyed by the holy man's stern character. But they did not find any repose during the entire period of their stay there, as instability and disorder, distress and idle chatter were a constant presence among them. In the end they were completely evicted from there and forced to leave.

The blessed Neilos, however, along with the brothers 2 who followed him, including the praiseworthy Stephen, found in the region of Gaeta a small plot of land or, to speak truly, a small desert. As he was pleased by its small size and aridity, he made it his abode. In the beginning they lived in poverty and lack of the vital necessities, but after a short time more brethren joined them, all lovers of God, and everything became abundant. Their labor was uninterrupted, and there was constant singing of hymns, frequent recitation of the psalms, incessant genuflections, voluntary moderation, and unconstrained obedience. In brief, everyone was flourishing, bearing fruit as a result of being watered by the words and unceasing instruction of our divinely inspired father Neilos.

Nor did he, invincible in his ascetic practices, cease from 3 his customary restraint and godly deeds; rather the older he grew and weaker in body, the more did he flourish and become stronger in spirit. It was impossible for him ever to

ἦν αὐτὸν παραλῦσαι νηστείαν, ἢ γεύσασθαι, ἢ πιεῖν καιρῷ μὴ νενομισμένῳ, ὡς ἔθος τῶν γηρασκόντων. Οὐδέποτε ἐγεύσατο κρέατος, ἢ τὸ σῶμα ἐλούσατο μέχρι τῆς τελευτῆς αὐτοῦ, καὶ ταῦτα ἐν βαθεῖ γήρᾳ—ἑκατοστὸς γὰρ ἀποθνῄσκει πέντε δεόντων—καὶ νόσοις μεγάλαις καὶ ποικίλαις πυκτεύων, οὐ μόνον διὰ τὸ γῆρας, ἀλλὰ καὶ διὰ τὴν πολλὴν κακουχίαν καὶ ἄφατον σκληραγωγίαν. Εἰς τοιαύτην γὰρ ἕξιν ἠγωνίσατο καὶ ἤγαγεν ἑαυτόν, ὅτι, καὶ εἰ ἤθελε φαγεῖν ἢ πιεῖν πρὸς τὸ ἀνακτήσασθαι ἑαυτόν, οὐκ εἴα αὐτὸν ἡ συνήθεια, ἀλλ᾽ οὐδὲ ὕπνου ἠδύνατο μετασχεῖν τὸ ἀρκοῦν.

88

Πολλάκις δὲ καὶ ἑαυτοῦ ἐξίστατο καὶ ἐπὶ πλεῖστον διέμενεν ἄφωνος καὶ τῶν παρόντων μὴ αἰσθανόμενος. Πλὴν ὅτι καὶ ἐν αὐτῇ τῇ ἐκστάσει εἴ ποτέ τι ἐλάλησεν, ἐκ τῶν τῆς θείας λειτουργίας ἀποκρίσεων ἀπεφθέγγετο, οἷον τό· "Παράσχου, Κύριε," ἢ τό· "Ἅγιος, ἅγιος, ἅγιος Κύριος," καὶ τὰ ὅμοια· ἄλλοτε δὲ καὶ τὸν Ἄμωμον στιχολογῶν ηὑρίσκετο. Εἰ δέ τις μετὰ ταῦτα τῶν ἀδελφῶν ἠρώτα αὐτόν, "Τί σοι γέγονε, πάτερ, καὶ ποῦ ἦς ἕως ἄρτι;", ἀπεκρίνετο ὅτι· "Ἐγήρασα, τέκνον, καὶ ἐλήρησα καὶ ἐδαιμονίσθην καὶ τί πάσχω οὐκ οἶδα." Ἀλλὰ καὶ τοῖς παραβάλλουσιν ἀκαίρως καὶ ἀπασχολοῦσιν αὐτὸν ἐκ τῆς κατὰ

break the fast, or eat or drink anything at a time that was not prescribed, as is usual for those growing old. Never did he taste meat, or wash his body until his death, and he maintained these habits in extreme old age, for he died at the age of ninety-five years. Also he contended with many grave and varied maladies, not only because of old age, but also because of his frequent abuse of his body and his ineffable asceticism. He strove for and attained such a state that even if he wished to eat or drink in order to refresh himself, his customary habits did not allow him to do so, nor was he even able to have sufficient sleep.

Chapter 88

Often he would fall into ecstasy and remain speechless for a long time, without even being aware of those around him; however, if he ever uttered any words while in this ecstasy, they would be from the choral responses of the divine liturgy, namely, "Grant this, Lord," or, "Holy, holy, holy is the Lord," and other similar acclamations. Other times he would be heard reciting the Amomos psalm. If afterward one of the brethren asked him, "What happened to you, father? Where were you just now?," he would respond, "I have grown old, my child, and I was delirious, and beset by demons, and I do not know what happened to me." To those who visited Neilos at an inopportune time and distracted

νοῦν θεωρίας, ἐκέλευε λέγειν, ὅτι· "Ἐδαιμονίσθη ὁ γέρων, καὶ οὐ δύναταί τινι ἀπαντῆσαι." Ὅσον δὲ αὐτὸς ἐξουδένει καὶ ἐταπείνου ἑαυτόν, τοσοῦτον διήρχετο καὶ ἐμεγαλύνετο ἡ φήμη αὐτοῦ καὶ πάντες ἔτρεχον τοῦ θεάσασθαι αὐτὸν καὶ ἀκοῦσαι τῆς συντυχίας αὐτοῦ.

2 Ἐν μιᾷ γοῦν παρακαλεῖ τὸν τῆς Γαΐτας ἄρχοντα ἡ σύμβιος αὐτοῦ τοῦ ἀπελθεῖν εἰς προσκύνησιν τοῦ δούλου τοῦ Θεοῦ. Καὶ λέγει αὐτῇ ὁ ἀνήρ· "Δηλώσωμεν πρῶτον αὐτῷ, μήπως φανῇ αὐτῷ βαρὺ καὶ ἀχθεσθεὶς φύγῃ ἀπὸ τῆς χώρας ἡμῶν καὶ ζημιωθῶμεν τὸν δοῦλον τοῦ Θεοῦ." Τότε μηνύουσιν αὐτῷ περὶ τούτου, πολλὰ παρακαλοῦντες αὐτόν· ἐγίνωσκον γὰρ ὅτι σφόδρα ἀποστρέφεται τὴν συντυχίαν τῶν γυναικῶν καὶ ὅτι οὐδέποτε εἰσέρχεται γυνὴ ἐν τῷ μοναστηρίῳ αὐτοῦ.

3 Ἀντιδηλοῖ οὖν αὐτῇ ὁ ὅσιος λέγων· "Συμπάθησόν μοι διὰ τὸν Κύριον, ὅτι ἡνίκα ἤμην κοσμικός, ἐδαιμονιζόμην καὶ διὰ τοῦ Θεοῦ, ἀφ' οὗ γέγονα μοναχός, ἐξιάθην· νυνὶ δὲ ἐὰν ἴδω γυναῖκα, παράυτα ὁ δαίμων ὑποστρέφεται καὶ κολάζει με." Ταῦτα ἡ γυνὴ ἀκούσασα καὶ νοήσασα, πλέον ἀνεπτερώθη πρὸς τὸ αὐτὸν θεάσασθαι καὶ τοσοῦτον ἐπύκτευσεν, ἕως ὅτε ἦλθε καὶ ἠξιώθη τῆς αὐτοῦ προσκυνήσεως· παρήγγειλε μέντοι μηδεμίαν τῶν γυναικῶν τοῦ ἄστεως ἀκολουθῆσαι, ἀλλὰ πάντας ἄνδρας συμπορευθῆναι αὐτῇ. Ὁ δὲ μακάριος ὀλίγα περὶ σωφροσύνης καὶ ἐλεημοσύνης καὶ φόβου Θεοῦ νουθετήσας αὐτήν, ἀπέλυσε μετὰ χαρᾶς εἰς τὸν οἶκον αὐτῆς.

him from his spiritual contemplation, he instructed that they be told, "The old man is beset by demons, and is not able to meet with anyone." Yet the more he disparaged and humbled himself, the more his reputation spread and grew, and everyone hastened to see him and to hear his words.

One day the wife of the duke of Gaeta begged her hus- 2 band that they should go and venerate the servant of God. Her husband replied to her, "First we should make our intention known to him, lest our visit should seem burdensome to him and in his vexation he flee from this land of ours, and we end up being deprived of the servant of God." Then they informed him about their wish, sending him many entreaties, for they knew that he fervently avoided the company of women, and that not a single woman had ever entered his monastery.

The holy man responded to her by saying, "Have compas- 3 sion on me for the sake of the Lord, because when I was a layman I was beset by demons; but ever since I became a monk, through God I was freed of them. Now whenever I see a woman, immediately the demon returns and torments me." When the woman heard this response and understood it, she became even more eager to see him. She insisted so much that finally she came and was deemed worthy of venerating him. Nonetheless he commanded that no woman from the city accompany her, but that only men journey with her. The blessed Neilos gave her some brief advice about prudence, works of charity, and the fear of God, and sent her back to her house full of joy.

89

Αὐτὸς μὲν οὖν ἄχθος μέγα ἡγεῖτο καὶ σφόδρα ἀπεστρέφετο τὴν τῶν ἐνδόξων τῆς γῆς συντυχίαν, ὥσπερ πρόξενον κενοδοξίας καὶ ψυχικὴν ζημίαν. Ἠνάγκαζε δὲ τοῦτο καταδέχεσθαι ἡ τῶν παρ᾽ αὐτῶν ἀδικουμένων καὶ πλεονεκτουμένων ἐνόχλησις, οὓς πολλοὺς πολλάκις διὰ γραφῆς αὐτοῦ μόνης ἐκ τῶν φαρύγγων αὐτῶν ἀνέσπασεν. Καὶ εἴ τις ἂν τὰς τοιαύτας ἐπιστολὰς αὐτοῦ συνελέξατο, πάνυ ὠφέλιμον καὶ χρησιμωτάτην βίβλον ἐξ αὐτῶν συστῆσαι ἠδύνατο.

2   Οὕτω δὲ πεποίηκεν καὶ εἰς τὸν συμπολίτην αὐτοῦ Φιλάγαθον τὸν ἀρχιεπίσκοπον. Ἡνίκα γὰρ ὁ ῥηθεὶς ἐπέβη τῷ Ῥώμης ἀπλήστως θρόνῳ, μὴ ἀρκεσθεὶς τῇ τοῦ κόσμου μεγαλειότητι, ᾗ Θεὸς αὐτὸν παραδόξως ὑπερύψωσεν—ἐν ἄμφω γὰρ τοῖς βασιλείοις δεδόξαστο—, ὁ μέν, οἷα γινώσκων τὸ μέλλον, ἐπέστελλεν αὐτῷ δυσωπῶν παραχωρῆσαι τῇ ἀνθρωπίνῃ δόξῃ, ἅτε ταύτης εἰς κόρον χρησαμένῳ, καὶ ἐν ἡσυχίᾳ πρὸς τὴν μοναχικὴν κατάστασιν ἀνακάμψαι. Ἐκεῖνος δὲ οὐ διέλειπε συντασσόμενος, ἕως ὅτου ἐξῆλθεν ὁ βασιλεὺς σὺν τῷ ἐκδιωχθέντι προέδρῳ καὶ τῆς αὐτῶν ἀφορήτου ὀργῆς ἔργον ἐγένετο. Στερηθεὶς γὰρ παρ᾽ αὐτῶν τῶν χρειωδεστέρων μελῶν, ὀφθαλμῶν λέγω καὶ γλώττης καὶ ῥινός, ἔρριπτο εἰς φυλακὴν ἐλεεινός τε καὶ ἀπροστάτευτος.

3   Ταῦτα ἀκούσας ὁ θεοφόρος πατήρ, καὶ τὴν καρδίαν τῇ θλίψει καταπιεσθείς, ἠναγκάσθη ἐν τοιούτῳ γήρει καὶ

Chapter 89

Neilos considered interaction with the powerful of the world a great burden and strenuously avoided it, as a cause of vainglory and spiritual harm. However, the appeals of those who were wronged and oppressed would force him to condescend to this practice. Often through his letters alone he would snatch many of them from their oppressors' jaws. If someone were to collect his letters of this sort, he could compile from them a very helpful and most useful book.

This he had done for his fellow citizen, the archbishop 2 Philagathos. For when the aforesaid man, not satisfied with the worldly grandeur to which God had unexpectedly raised him—for he was honored in both realms—ascended through insatiable greed to the throne of Rome, Neilos, as if knowing the future, kept writing letters to Philagathos, entreating him to renounce human glory, since he had enjoyed it to excess, and to return to monastic life in spiritual tranquility. Philagathos, however, kept on promising to leave the throne until the emperor arrived together with the deposed pontiff, and subjected him to their horrific wrath. For Philagathos was deprived of his most useful parts, I mean his eyes, tongue, and nose, and thrown into prison, pitiful and without defenders.

When the divinely inspired father heard this, his heart 3 was oppressed by sorrow, and he was forced to journey to

νόσῳ καὶ καιρῷ—Τεσσαρακοστὴ γὰρ ἦν—τὴν Ῥώμην καταλαβεῖν, καὶ τῷ βασιλεῖ μετὰ παρακλήσεως προσελθεῖν. Ὁ δὲ βασιλεὺς σὺν τῷ πατριάρχῃ, ἀκούσαντες τὴν ἔλευσιν αὐτοῦ, προϋπήντησαν αὐτῷ καὶ κρατήσαντες αὐτὸν ἀμφοτέρωθεν τῶν χειρῶν, ἀνήγαγον εἰς τὸ πατριαρχεῖον, καθίσαντές τε αὐτὸν μέσον κἀκεῖνοι ἐκ δεξιῶν καὶ ἀριστερῶν κατεφίλουν τὰς χεῖρας αὐτοῦ.

90

Ὁ δὲ ὅσιος, εἰ καὶ σφόδρα ἐβαρεῖτο καὶ ἔστενεν οὕτω τοῖς γινομένοις, ὅμως πάντα ὑπέμενεν, εἴ πως ἐπιτύχοι τοῦ αἰτήματος, καί φησι πρὸς αὐτούς· "Συγχωρήσατέ μοι διὰ τὸν Κύριον τῷ ἁμαρτωλῷ παρὰ πάντας ἀνθρώπους καὶ ἡμιθνήτῳ γέροντι, ὅτι ἀνάξιος ὑπάρχω τῆς τοιαύτης τιμῆς· μᾶλλον ἐμόν ἐστι τὸ προσκυνεῖν τοὺς τιμίους πόδας ὑμῶν καὶ σέβεσθαι τὰς τοιαύτας ἀξίας ὑμῶν. Πλὴν ἐλήλυθα πρὸς τὴν ἐνδοξότητα ὑμῶν, οὐ δόξης ὀρεγόμενος, ἢ δωρεῶν, ἢ προσόδων μεγίστων, ἀλλὰ χάριν τοῦ πολλὰ δουλεύσαντος ὑμῖν καὶ κακῶς διοικηθέντος παρ' ὑμῶν, τοῦ ὑμᾶς ἀμφοτέρους ἀπὸ τοῦ βαπτίσματος ἀναδεδεγμένου καὶ παρ' ὑμῶν τοὺς ὀφθαλμοὺς ἐξορωρυγμένου. Δέομαι τῆς φιλευσεβείας ὑμῶν δωρήσασθαί μοι αὐτόν, ἵνα, καθίσας μετ' ἐμοῦ, κλαύσωμεν ἀμφότεροι τὰς ἁμαρτίας ἡμῶν."

Rome, despite his advanced age, poor health, and the inopportune season (for it was Lent), and approach the emperor with his plea for Philagathos. When the emperor along with the patriarch heard about his arrival, they went out to greet him, and taking hold of his arms on either side, they led him to the patriarchal palace and sat him in the middle, while they themselves, seated on his right and left side, were kissing his hands.

Chapter 90

Although the holy man was burdened and oppressed by these honors, he nevertheless endured it all, in the hope of somehow obtaining his request; and he said to them, "For the sake of the Lord, forgive me, the most sinful of all men, and a half-dead old man, because I am unworthy of such honor. Rather it is I who should prostrate myself at your honorable feet and revere your great dignities. Indeed, I have come to your glorious presence, not seeking glory, or gifts, or great rewards, but for the sake of the one who offered you great services, and was harshly treated by you. He sponsored you both at baptism, but now you have gouged out his eyes. I beseech your piety to give him to me, so that he may sit with me, and we both may weep for our sins."

2   Τότε ὁ βασιλεύς, ἐπιδακρύσας μικρόν—οὐ γὰρ ἦν ἀληθῶς τὸ πᾶν τῆς αὐτοῦ βουλῆς—, ἀπεκρίθη τῷ μακαρίῳ· "Πάντα ἐσμὲν ἕτοιμοι τοῦ πληρῶσαι τὰ δοκοῦντα τῇ σῇ ἁγιωσύνῃ, εἴγε καὶ σὺ ἐπακούσῃ τῆς ἡμῶν παρακλήσεως καὶ καταδέξῃ τοῦ λαβεῖν μοναστήριον ἐν ταύτῃ τῇ πόλει, οἷον ἂν βούλῃ, καὶ εἶναι μεθ᾽ ἡμῶν διὰ παντός." Τοῦ δὲ γέροντος ἀπαναινομένου τὴν ἐν τῇ πόλει διατριβήν, προέτειναν αὐτῷ τὸν Ἅγιον Ἀναστάσιον, ὡς ἔξω θορύβου ὑπάρχοντος καὶ ἀεὶ τῷ ἡμετέρῳ γένει προσαναφέροντος. Καὶ δὴ κατεδέξατο σπουδάζων τοῦ ζητουμένου τυχεῖν δωρήματος. Ὁ δὲ ἄγριος πάπας ἐκεῖνος, μὴ χορτασθεὶς ἐφ᾽ οἷς ἔδρασεν εἰς τὸν προρρηθέντα Φιλάγαθον, ἀγαγών τε αὐτὸν καὶ τὴν ἱερατικὴν στολὴν διαρρήξας ἐπ᾽ αὐτῷ, περιήγαγεν αὐτὸν πᾶσαν τὴν Ῥώμην.

91

Ὅπερ ἀκούσας ὁ ἅγιος γέρων καὶ πάνυ λυπηθείς, οὐκέτι ἠτήσατο παρὰ τοῦ βασιλέως τὸν ἀρχιεπίσκοπον. Ὡς δὲ ἔγνω τοῦτο ὁ βασιλεύς, ἀποστέλλει ἕνα τῶν αὐτοῦ ἀρχιεπισκόπων λίαν στωμύλον πρὸς τὸ δυσωπῆσαι τὸν γέροντα. Πρὸς ὃν εἶπεν ὁ ὅσιος· "Ἄπελθε, εἶπον τῷ βασιλεῖ καὶ τῷ πάπᾳ· Τάδε λέγει ὁ ἔξηχος γέρων· ἐχαρίσασθέ μοι τὸν τυφλὸν τοῦτον, οὔτε διὰ τὸν ἐμὸν φόβον, οὔτε διὰ τὴν μεγάλην μου δυναστείαν, ἀλλὰ διὰ μόνην τὴν τοῦ

Then the emperor shed a few tears—for the fate of Phila- 2
gathos was not entirely the result of his decision—and responded to the blessed Neilos, "We are prepared to fulfill
all that your holiness desires, on condition that you heed
this request of ours, and agree to accept a monastery in this
city, whichever one you wish, and to remain with us always."
When the old man refused to stay in the city, they offered
him the monastery of Saint Anastasios, as it was removed
from any commotion and had always been associated with
our people. Neilos accepted, eager to obtain his desired gift.
Yet that savage pope, not satisfied by the punishments he
had already inflicted upon the aforementioned Philagathos,
brought him out, tore off his priestly vestments, and pa-
raded him all around Rome.

Chapter 91

When the holy old man heard this, he was sorely grieved
and no longer made any plea to the emperor for the archbishop. When the emperor Otto was informed what had
happened, he sent one of his archbishops, who was extremely eloquent, to entreat the old man. To this archbishop
the holy Neilos said, "Go and tell the emperor and the pope,
'These are the words of a crazy old man: you gave me this
blind man, neither out of fear of me, nor because of my great
power, but only for the sake of God's love. Now all the

Θεοῦ ἀγάπην. Νῦν οὖν ὅσα αὐτῷ προσεθήκατε, οὐκ αὐτῷ, ἀλλ᾿ ἐμοὶ ἐποιήσατε, μᾶλλον δὲ εἰς αὐτὸν τὸν Θεὸν ἐνυβρίσατε. Ἔστε τοίνυν γινώσκοντες, ὅτι, καθὼς ὑμεῖς οὐ συνεπαθήσατε, οὔτε ἐνεδείξασθε ἔλεος εἰς τὸν ὑπὸ τοῦ Θεοῦ παραδοθέντα εἰς τὰς χεῖρας ὑμῶν, οὕτως οὐδὲ ὁ Πατὴρ ὑμῶν ὁ οὐράνιος συμπαθήσει ταῖς ἁμαρτίαις ὑμῶν."

2   Ὁ δὲ πολυλόγος ἐκεῖνος ἀρχιεπίσκοπος περιλαλῶν τὸν ὅσιον οὐκ ἐπαύετο, ἀπολογούμενος ὑπὲρ τοῦ βασιλέως καὶ τοῦ πάπα. Καὶ ὁ γέρων, κλίνας τὴν κεφαλὴν ἔμπροσθεν αὐτοῦ, προσεποιήσατο τοῦ νυστάζειν. Ὡς οὖν εἶδεν αὐτὸν ἐκεῖνος μηδ᾿ ὅλως προσέχοντα τοῖς αὐτοῦ λόγοις, ἀναστὰς ἐπορεύθη. Ὁ δὲ ὅσιος παρευθὺ σὺν τοῖς συνοῦσιν αὐτῷ ἀδελφοῖς, ἐπιβὰς τοῖς κτήνεσι, δι᾿ ὅλης τῆς νυκτὸς ἐκείνης κατέλαβε τὸ ἴδιον μοναστήριον, τῇ προσευχῇ καὶ ἑαυτῷ προσανέχων καὶ τὸν Θεὸν ἀπαύστως ἐξιλεούμενος.

3   Μετ᾿ οὐ πολλὰς οὖν ἡμέρας, ὁ μὲν πάπας ὥσπερ τις τύραννος βιαίως τῶν ἔνθεν ἀπήγετο, ὥς τινων λεγόντων ἀκήκοα, τοὺς ὀφθαλμοὺς ἐκβρασθεὶς καὶ ἐπὶ τῶν παρειῶν αὐτοὺς περιφέρων οὕτω τῷ τάφῳ προὐδίδοτο. Ὁ δὲ βασιλεὺς μετανοεῖν ἐπαγγελλόμενος, πεζοπορῶν ἀπὸ Ῥώμης πρὸς τὸν τοῦ Γαργάνου ἀπήει ἀσώματον Ἀρχιστράτηγον καὶ ἡ αὐτοῦ ὑποστροφὴ διὰ τῆς ξενίας τοῦ μακαρίου ἐγίγνετο.

injuries you have inflicted were not upon him, but upon me, and, even more, you have insulted God Himself. Therefore you should know that, just as you did not show compassion or mercy to the one delivered into your hands by God, so neither will your Father, who is in heaven, forgive your sins.'"

When that verbose archbishop continued to ramble on 2 to the holy Neilos, apologizing on behalf of the emperor and the pope, the old man bent his head down in front of him and pretended to sleep. When he saw that Neilos was not paying attention to his words, the archbishop rose and departed. Meanwhile the holy one and the brethren who accompanied him mounted their mules. After journeying throughout the whole night, he reached his own monastery, and there he kept propitiating God, by devoting himself to ceaseless prayer and meditation.

A few days later, the pope met a violent death, just like a 3 tyrant, as I have heard from certain people. His eyes were gouged out and he was buried with them still dangling on his cheeks. The emperor then promised to repent, and walked on foot from Rome to the sanctuary of the incorporeal Archangel Michael at Gargano. His return was by way of the abode of the blessed father.

92

Ἐλθὼν γοῦν ἐπάνωθεν τοῦ μοναστηρίου καὶ θεασάμενος τὰς καλύβας τῶν ἀδελφῶν περὶ τὸ εὐκτήριον πεπηγμένας, ἔφη· "Ἰδοὺ αἱ σκηναὶ τοῦ Ἰσραὴλ ἐν τῇ ἐρήμῳ· ἰδοὺ οἱ πολῖται τῆς τῶν οὐρανῶν βασιλείας· οὗτοι οὐχ ὡς κάτοικοι, ἀλλ' ὡς παροδῖται ἐνθάδε μένουσιν." Ὁ δὲ μακάριος κελεύσας θυμιατὸν γενέσθαι, ὑπήντησεν αὐτῷ σὺν πάσῃ τῇ ἀδελφότητι καὶ μετὰ πάσης ταπεινοφροσύνης καὶ εὐλαβείας προσεκύνησεν αὐτῷ. Ὁ δὲ βασιλεὺς ὑποθεὶς τὴν χεῖρα καὶ ὑποστηρίζων τὸν γέροντα, εἰσῄεσαν ἅμα εἰς τὸ εὐκτήριον.

2   Εἶτα εὐχῆς γενομένης, εἶπεν ὁ βασιλεὺς τῷ ἁγίῳ· "Ὁ Κύριος ἡμῶν Ἰησοῦς Χριστὸς ἕως συμπαρῆν τοῖς ἀποστόλοις, ἐκέλευεν αὐτοῖς *μὴ πήραν, μὴ ῥάβδον, μήτε δύο χιτῶνας κεκτῆσθαι. Ἐρχόμενος δὲ πρὸς τὸ πάθος, πάλιν εἶπεν αὐτοῖς· Ἀλλὰ νῦν ὁ ἔχων βαλάντιον, ἀράτω καὶ πήραν.* Καὶ αὐτὸς τοίνυν, γηράσας καὶ μέλλων ἀπιέναι πρὸς τὴν τῶν οὐρανῶν βασιλείαν, φρόντισον τῶν σῶν γεννημάτων, μήπως στενοχωρηθέντες μετά σε τῇ δυσκολίᾳ τοῦ τόπου, ἀναχωρήσαντες σκορπισθῶσιν. Ἡμεῖς δώσομεν μοναστήριον καὶ προσόδους, ὅπου ἂν κελεύσῃς ἐν ὅλῳ τῷ ἡμετέρῳ κράτει." Καὶ ὁ ὅσιος ἀπεκρίθη· "Τοῦ Δαβὶδ ἤκουσα λέγοντος· *Σῶσόν με, Κύριε, ὅτι ἐκλέλοιπεν ὅσιος, ὅτι ὠλιγώθησαν αἱ ἀλήθειαι ἀπὸ τῶν υἱῶν τῶν ἀνθρώπων·* καὶ πάλιν· *Οὐκ ἔστι ποιῶν χρηστότητα, οὐκ ἔστιν ἕως ἑνός.* Εἰ δὲ καὶ ὅλως εἰσὶ μοναχοὶ οἱ μετ' ἐμοῦ ἀδελφοὶ καὶ φυλάξουσι κατὰ

Chapter 92

When the emperor arrived at a place above the monastery and saw the brothers' cells set around the chapel, he said, "Behold, *the tents of Israel* in the desert; behold, the citizens of the kingdom of heaven. These men stay here not as residents, but as passersby." The blessed father ordered incense to be burned and went out to meet the emperor with the entire brotherhood, and bowed before him with complete humility and reverence. The emperor, however, placed his hand under the old man's arm to support him, and together they entered into the chapel.

When the prayers were completed, the emperor said to the holy man, "While our Lord Jesus Christ was with the apostles, He commanded them *not to possess a bag, a staff, or two cloaks.* When approaching His passion, He again told them, *'But now, let him who has a purse take it, and likewise a bag.'* Since you in fact have grown old and are about to depart for the kingdom of heaven, you should take care of your offspring, lest after your death they be hard pressed by the hardships of the place and so leave the monastery and disperse. We shall give you a monastery and the income to maintain it anywhere you wish in our entire empire." The holy man responded, "I heard David say this, *'Save me, O Lord, for the godly man has failed; for truth is diminished among the children of men,'* and later, *'There is none that does good, no not one.'* If the brethren who are with me are truly monks,

δύναμιν τὰς ἐντολὰς τοῦ Χριστοῦ, αὐτὸς ὁ οἰκονομήσας αὐτοὺς ἕως τοῦ νῦν μετ᾽ ἐμοῦ, πολλῷ μᾶλλον φροντίσει αὐτοῖς καὶ ἄνευ ἐμοῦ, ὃς οὐκ ἐν τῇ δυναστείᾳ τοῦ δυνατοῦ, οὐδὲ ἐν ταῖς κνήμαις τοῦ ἀνδρὸς εὐδοκεῖ, ἀλλ᾽ ἐν τοῖς ἐλπίζουσιν ἐπὶ τὸ ἔλεος αὐτοῦ."

93

Τούτων καὶ ἑτέρων πολλῶν λαληθέντων, ἀνέστη ὁ βασιλεὺς τοῦ ἀναχωρῆσαι. Καὶ πάλιν ἐπιστραφεὶς πρὸς τὸν γέροντα εἶπεν· "Αἴτησόν με ὡς τέκνον σου, εἴ τι ἂν βούλῃ, καὶ μετὰ πάσης προθυμίας πληρώσω σοι." Ὁ δὲ μακάριος, ἐκτείνας τὴν χεῖρα πρὸς τῷ στήθει τοῦ βασιλέως, εἶπεν· "Οὐδὲν ἄλλο δέομαι τῆς σῆς βασιλείας, ἀλλ᾽ ἢ τὴν σωτηρίαν τῆς ψυχῆς σου· κἂν γὰρ βασιλεὺς τυγχάνῃς, ἀλλ᾽ ὡς εἷς τῶν ἀνθρώπων τελευτῆσαι ἔχεις καὶ εἰς κρίσιν παρασταθῆναι καὶ λόγον δοῦναι, ὧν ἔπραξας πονηρῶν τε καὶ καλῶν ἔργων." Καὶ ὁ βασιλεὺς ταῦτα ἀκούων σταγόνας δακρύων προέχεεν ἀπὸ τῶν ὀμμάτων. Εἶτα τὸν στέφανον κλίνας ἐν ταῖς χερσὶ τοῦ ἁγίου καὶ εὐλογηθεὶς παρ᾽ αὐτοῦ σὺν πᾶσι τοῖς μετ᾽ αὐτοῦ, ἐπορεύετο τὴν ὁδὸν αὐτοῦ.

2   Ἀλλ᾽ οὐδ᾽ οὕτως ἐξέφυγε τῶν τοῦ Θεοῦ κριμάτων τὸ πέρας. Εὐθέως γὰρ ἐλθὼν ἐν τῇ Ῥώμῃ καὶ στάσεως αὐτῷ γενομένης, ἀνεχώρησε φεύγων καὶ κατὰ τὴν ὁδὸν ἐτελεύτησεν. Οἱ δὲ πατέρες διεγόγγυζον κατὰ τοῦ γέροντος

and keep to the best of their ability the commandments of Christ, He who cared for them up to now, together with me, will take even greater care of them without me. *He does not take pleasure in the strength* of the powerful, *nor in the legs of man,* but *in those that hope in His mercy.*"

Chapter 93

After these and many other words were spoken, the emperor rose to depart, and turning again to the old man he said, "Ask me, as if I were your son, for whatever you wish, and I will eagerly fulfill your request." The blessed man extended his hand toward the emperor's chest and said, "I ask for nothing else from your majesty except for the salvation of your soul. Even if you happen to be an emperor, nevertheless as a human you have to die and stand for judgment and give an accounting for all your deeds, both wicked and good." At these words the emperor shed tears from his eyes. Then he bent his crowned head down into the hands of the holy man, and so after he and all his attendants were blessed by Neilos, the emperor continued his journey.

But not even in this way did he flee the fulfillment of 2
God's judgment; for as soon as he came to Rome, there was an uprising against him, and he was forced to flee, and died during the journey. The fathers grumbled against the old

ὡς μὴ δεξαμένου τὴν πρὸς τοῦ βασιλέως χάριν, μοναστήριον αὐτοῖς δωρήσασθαι βουλομένου. Ὁ δὲ πατὴρ
πρὸς αὐτοὺς ἔφη· "Ἐγὼ μὲν ὥσπερ ἄφρων ἐλάλησα ἅπερ
εἶπον, ὑμεῖς δὲ μετ᾽ ὀλίγον γνώσεσθε ἃ φρονεῖτε." Μετὰ
ταῦτα γοῦν ἀκούσαντες τὴν τελευτὴν τοῦ βασιλέως,
ἐθαύμασαν τὴν τοῦ μεγάλου οἰκονομίαν.

94

Ἐν δὲ ταῖς ἡμέραις ἐκείναις ἠρρώστησεν ὁ μακάριος
Στέφανος τὴν ἐπιθανάτιον ἀρρωστίαν· ψυχορραγοῦντος
οὖν αὐτοῦ καὶ τοῦ γέροντος αὐτῷ παρακαθημένου,
συνήχθησαν οἱ ἀδελφοὶ ἅπαντες κύκλῳ, καὶ λέγει ὁ μέγας·
"Ἀδελφὲ Στέφανε!" Ὁ δὲ εὐθέως ἀνακαθίσας ἔδησε τὰς
χεῖρας καὶ προσεῖχε τῷ μακαρίῳ. Εἶτα λέγει πρὸς αὐτόν·
"Εὐλόγησον τοὺς ἀδελφούς, ὅτι ἐκλείπεις." Ὁ δέ, ἁπλώσας
τὰς χεῖρας καὶ ἐπευξάμενος, τὸ κελευσθὲν αὐτῷ ἐποίει.
Καὶ πάλιν λέγει αὐτῷ ὁ μέγας· "Ἀναπαύου λοιπόν, ὅτι
οὐκέτι ἰσχύεις·" καὶ ἀνακλιθεὶς ἀνεπάη, πληρώσας τὸν τῆς
ὑπακοῆς ὅρον ἐν τῷ θανάτῳ.

2   Μετὰ δὲ τὸ αὐτὸν ἀποπνεῦσαι ἐθρήνει ὁ γέρων ἐπ᾽
αὐτῷ λέγων· "Ὦ καλέ μου συναγωνιστὰ καὶ σύμπονε
Στέφανε, μετὰ τοσαῦτα ἔτη χωριζόμεθα καὶ ἀλλήλων ἀπο-
στερούμεθα. Καὶ σὺ μὲν ἀπέρχῃ πρὸς τὴν ἀνάπαυσιν, ἣν
σεαυτῷ ἡτοίμασας, ἐγὼ δὲ ἐναπέμεινα εἰς τὴν κόλασιν. Σὺ

man because he had refused the favor from the emperor, who wanted to give a monastery to them. But the father said to them, "I said what I said as a foolish man, but you will soon realize the error of your thoughts." Afterward, when they heard of the emperor's death, they were amazed at the great man's prudent discretion.

Chapter 94

During that time, the blessed Stephen fell ill with a mortal sickness. When he was breathing his last, the old man was sitting beside him, with all the brethren gathered around them, whereupon the great Neilos said, "Brother Stephen!" Immediately he sat up, clasped his hands, and gazed at the blessed man. Then Neilos said to him, "Bless the brethren, because you are departing." Stephen extended his hands and blessed them, carrying out his command. Again the great one said to him, "Now rest, since you no longer have any strength." So he lay down and rested, fulfilling the precept of obedience at the moment of death.

After Stephen breathed his last breath, the old man lamented for him, saying, "O Stephen, my good companion in struggle and toil, after so many years we are separated and deprived of each other's company. While you depart to the repose which you prepared for yourself, I remain here in

ἀθλητὴς καὶ μάρτυς τυγχάνεις· ἐγὼ γάρ σοι γέγονα δήμιος."

3 Τοῦτο δὲ ἐλάλει ὁ γέρων, ἐπειδὴ μέχρι γήρως οὐ διέλειπεν αὐτὸν κολαφίζων, ἀγωνιστὴν αὐτὸν ἐπιστάμενος καὶ πύκτην. Καθάπερ γὰρ ξυστῆρα αὐτὸν εἶχεν ἢ ἄλλο τι ἐργαλεῖον πρὸς τοὺς ἀβαστάγους καὶ ἀνυπομονήτους. Ὁπηνίκα γοῦν εἰς τὴν ἐκκλησίαν τις τῶν ἀδελφῶν κοιμώμενος ἔρρεγχεν ἐν τῇ ἀναγνώσει, τοῦ μεγάλου διερμηνεύοντος, ἔλεγεν αὐτὸς ὁ μακάριος ὡς ἀγνοῶν· "Οὐδείς ἐστιν ὁ ῥέγχων, εἰ μὴ ὁ Στέφανος· ἐκβάλετε αὐτὸν ἔξω, μήπως διδάξει ἡμᾶς κακὴν συνήθειαν." Πολλάκις δὲ καὶ ἐκ τῆς τραπέζης αὐτὸν μετὰ ὕβρεων καὶ ὀνειδισμῶν ἐξήγαγεν, ὡς ἀπαιδεύτως ἐσθίοντα, διορθούμενος τοὺς αὐτὸ πράττοντας.

4 Καὶ ἁπλῶς, εἴ τι ἂν πταῖσμα ἐγίνετο ἐν πάσῃ τῇ ἀδελφότητι, ὁ Στέφανος ἐπετιμᾶτο ὡς τῶν πάντων ὑπαίτιος. Καὶ οὐκ ἤρκει αὐτῷ τοῦτο, ἀλλὰ καὶ μετὰ τῶν ἀδελφῶν ἐργαζόμενος γέρων ὢν πλείω περὶ τὰ ἑβδομήκοντα ἔτη καὶ πάνυ κυρτωθεὶς ἐκ τοῦ γήρως καὶ τῶν πολλῶν νοσημάτων, οὐκ ἀνένευεν ἐν τῷ θέρει ἢ ἐν τῇ ἅλῳ ὅλην τὴν ἡμέραν. Καὶ ὅπου δ' ἂν ἦν ῥυπαρώτερον ἔργον ἢ κοπωδέστερον, ἐκεῖ εὑρίσκετο. Ὅλως δὲ οὐκ οἶδεν ἀνάπαυσιν ἢ ἄνεσιν πάσας τὰς ἡμέρας τῆς ζωῆς αὐτοῦ ἐν οἰῳδήποτε πράγματι.

torment. You are an athlete and martyr, for I was your tormentor."

The old man said this, since right up to his old age he had 3 not stopped slapping him, understanding that Stephen was a warrior and fighter. For he used Stephen like a scraper or some other such tool on annoying and insufferable monks. In fact, whenever one of the brethren fell asleep in church and was snoring during the reading of Scripture, while Neilos was giving an explanation, the blessed one would say, feigning ignorance, "The one snoring could be no one but Stephen; throw him out, lest he teach us bad habits." Often he would expel him from the refectory with insults and reproaches, on the grounds that Stephen was eating in an ill-mannered way, thus correcting those who did in fact act this way.

To put it simply, if there were any faults among the entire 4 brotherhood, Stephen was punished, as if he were responsible for them all. Nor did this suffice, but he even continued to labor with the brethren while an old man of more than seventy years. Although wholly bent over by old age and his many infirmities, he did not stop working the whole day long, either harvesting or on the threshing floor. Indeed, wherever the work was most filthy or laborious, there was Stephen to be found. Truly he did not know repose or rest all the days of his life in any circumstance.

95

Ὅτε οὖν ἀνεπάη τὴν μακαρίαν καὶ αἰωνίαν ἀνάπαυσιν, διετάξατο ὁ πατὴρ τὸν τάφον διπλοῦν γενέσθαι, ἵν᾽ εἰ καὶ αὐτὸς τελειώσας τὸν δρόμον συνταφῇ τῷ μακαρίτῃ Στεφάνῳ. Ὁ δὲ ἄρχων Γαΐτας, λίαν φιλόθεος ὢν καὶ πίστιν πολλὴν ἔχων εἰς τὸν ὅσιον πατέρα, ἐρωτήσας καὶ μαθὼν τὴν αἰτίαν τοῦ τάφου, εἶπεν πρὸς τοὺς παρόντας· "Λοιπὸν ἐὰν ὁ πατὴρ τελευτήσῃ, ὧδε αὐτὸν καταλείψω, ἀλλ᾽ οὐκ ἀπαγαγὼν ἐν τῇ πόλει μου καταθήσω, ἵν᾽ ἔχῃ αὐτὸν καθάπερ ἄσειστον πύργον;" Τοῦτο τοίνυν μαθὼν ὁ μακάριος γέρων καὶ σφόδρα λυπηθείς, ἐβουλεύσατο πάλιν μετοικῆσαι ἐκεῖθεν καὶ ἀπελθεῖν, ὅπου οὐδείς ἐστιν ὁ γινώσκων.

2   Προῃρεῖτο γὰρ ἀποθανεῖν κακῶς ἢ ὑπόληψιν σχεῖν ἁγίου παρά τινος τῶν ἀνθρώπων· τοὐναντίον μὲν οὖν ἠγωνίζετο παρὰ τοῖς πολλοῖς θυμώδη καὶ ὑβριστὴν καὶ πάντων τῶν ἄλλων παθῶν μέτοχον ἀποδεῖξαι. Πολλοὶ δὲ ἀνόητοι καὶ ἐσκανδαλίσθησαν, ἡμεῖς δέ, οἵτινες συνεφάγομεν καὶ συνεπίομεν αὐτῷ ἀναξίως, πεπείσμεθα καὶ πεπληροφορήμεθα—ἐνώπιον Θεοῦ καὶ ἀγγέλων ὁμολογήσομεν—ὅτι ἅγιός ἐστιν ὁ μακάριος Νεῖλος, ὡς εἷς τῶν θεοφόρων πατέρων καὶ ὑπερβάλλων πάντας τοὺς ἐν τῇ γενεᾷ ταύτῃ ἀνθρώπους, ἄν τε σημεῖα ποιήσῃ, ἄν τε καὶ μή· ὅπερ οἱ πολλοὶ τῶν ἀσυνέτων ἐπερωτῶσι, τοῦ αὐτῶν βίου μηδένα ποιούμενοι λόγον, ὅπερ καὶ ἐν πολλοῖς τῶν κακοδόξων εὑρέθη. Τοῦτο δὲ εἶπον, οὐχ ἵνα τὴν αὐτοῦ

Chapter 95

When Stephen took his rest in his blessed and eternal repose, the father gave orders to prepare a double tomb, so that when he himself would come to the end of his course, he might be buried together with the blessed Stephen. When the duke of Gaeta, a very God-loving man, who had great faith in the holy father, inquired and learned the reason for the tomb, he said to those present, "When the father dies, should I leave him there, or rather bring him into my city for burial, so that it might have him as an unshakable bulwark?" Upon learning of this the blessed old man was very much saddened and decided to move again from there and go to a place where no one would know him.

For he preferred to die a miserable death rather than to gain the reputation of a holy man among mankind. He thus strove to present himself to people as a short-tempered, arrogant man, possessed of all the other vices. Many foolish people were scandalized by his behavior, but we, who undeservedly shared his food and drink, are convinced and assured—and this we will confess in the presence of God and the angels—that the blessed Neilos is a saint, one of the divinely inspired fathers, who surpasses all the people of this generation, whether he performs miracles or not; this performance of miracles is something about which many foolish people inquire, paying no attention to actual lives of the saints, and despite the fact that miracles are credited to many people who do not possess the right faith. I say this,

χάριν ἄπορον θαυμάτων ἐλέγξω—βλέπουσι γὰρ ἀεὶ τὴν
αὐτῆς δύναμιν οἱ τοὺς ὀφθαλμοὺς ἐν τῇ κεφαλῇ ἔχοντες—
ἀλλ' ἵνα τὴν ἄκαιρον καὶ ἀνόητον ἐρώτησιν ἀνατρέψω.
Πᾶν γὰρ τὸ ζητούμενον ὁ βίος τυγχάνει· θαυμάτων δὲ
πλῆθος καὶ δύναμις στεργομένη μὲν συνεκλάμπουσα,
περιφρονουμένη δὲ μὴ συνάδουσα.

3   Ἐπὶ τὴν νύσσαν τοίνυν ἐπανακάμψωμεν. Βουληθεὶς οὖν
ὁ μισόδοξος πατὴρ ἡμῶν Νεῖλος καταλιπεῖν τὸ μοναστήριον, ὅπερ λέγεται Σέρπερις, ἐν ᾧ ἤσκησε περὶ τὸν
δέκατον χρόνον, μόλις ἐπικαθίσας διὰ τὸ γῆρας ἵππῳ,
ᾤχετο ἐπὶ τὴν Ῥώμην. Ἔλεγε δὲ τοῖς ἀδελφοῖς ἐποδυ-
ρομένοις τῷ χωρισμῷ αὐτοῦ· "Μὴ λυπεῖσθε, ὦ πατέρες καὶ
ἀδελφοί, πορεύομαι γὰρ ἑτοιμάσαι τόπον καὶ μοναστήριον,
ἔνθα συναγάγω πάντας τοὺς ἀδελφοὺς καὶ τὰ διεσκορ-
πισμένα τέκνα μου."

96

Ἐκεῖνοι δὲ μὴ νοοῦντες τίνα ἦν ἃ ἐλάλει αὐτοῖς παρ-
εμυθοῦντο. Τοῦ τοίνυν Θεοῦ καθοδηγοῦντος αὐτὸν ἐπὶ
τὸν προωρισμένον τῆς ταφῆς αὐτοῦ τόπον κατὰ τὸν προ-
εγνωσμένον θεϊκῶς αὐτῷ τρόπον, καταλαμβάνει κώμην
τινὰ καλουμένην Τουσχολάναν, ἀπέχουσαν δώδεκα μίλια
ἀπὸ Ῥώμης, περὶ ἣν ἵδρυται μοναστήριον ὀλίγων ἀδελφῶν
ὁμοφύλων ἐπ' ὀνόματι τῆς Ἁγίας Ἀγάθης.

not to criticize his grace as bereft of miracles—for those who have eyes in their head always see the power of his grace—but so that I may refute this inopportune and foolish question. For the life must be examined in its entirety; the extent and the power of miracles are praised when they shine out together with the life, but are despised if they are not equally praiseworthy.

But let us return to the course of our narrative. Our father Neilos, who despised glory, decided to leave the monastery, which is called Serperi, where he had practiced asceticism for a decade. So with great difficulty—on account of his old age—he mounted a horse and headed for Rome. He said to the brethren who were lamenting at their separation from him, "Do not be saddened, fathers and brothers, for I journey to prepare a place for a monastery. There I shall gather together all the brethren and my dispersed children." 3

Chapter 96

They were consoled, because they did not understand the meaning of his words. As God was guiding him to the preordained place of his burial, which he had known in advance through divine revelation, he arrived at a town called Tusculum, which was twelve miles from Rome; nearby was a monastery of a few of our fellow Greek brethren, dedicated to Saint Agatha.

2 Κἀκεῖσε καταλύσας ὁ ἅγιος γέρων καὶ τό· "Αὕτη ἡ κατάπαυσίς μου," εἰρηκώς, "εἰς αἰῶνα αἰῶνος," οὐκέτι τοῦ λοιποῦ ἴσχυσέ τις αὐτὸν ἀνασπάσαι ἐκεῖθεν, καίτοι καὶ τῶν συνόντων αὐτῷ ἀδελφῶν ἐνοχλούντων καὶ τῶν τῆς Ῥώμης μεγιστάνων πρὸς αὐτὸν παραγενομένων καὶ δυσωπούντων τοῦ εἰσελθεῖν ἐν τῇ Ῥώμῃ κἂν διὰ τοὺς πρώτους τῶν ἀποστόλων. Ἀπεκρίνατο πᾶσι καὶ ἔλεγεν, ὅτι· "Τοὺς πανευφήμους καὶ ὄντως τρισμακαρίστους καὶ κορυφαίους τῶν ἀποστόλων καὶ ἐντεῦθεν δυνατὸν τοῖς *πίστιν ὡς κόκκον σινάπεως* κεκτημένοις αὐτοὺς προσκυνῆσαι, εἰ καὶ ἐγὼ ἀνάξιος πέλω καὶ τοῦ μόνον αὐτοὺς ὀνομάσαι· ἐν μέντοι τῷ εὐτελεῖ τόπῳ τούτῳ δι' οὐδὲν ἄλλο ἐλήλυθα, εἰ μὴ μόνον διὰ τὸ τελευτῆσαι."

3 Ὁ δὲ ἄρχων τῆς κώμης ἐκείνης, Γρηγόριος τῷ ὀνόματι, περιβόητος ἐν τυραννίδι καὶ ἀδικίᾳ τυγχάνων, λίαν δὲ ἀγχίνους καὶ συνέσει κεκοσμημένος, κατελθὼν καὶ προσπεσὼν τοῖς ποσὶ τοῦ ἁγίου ἔλεγε ταῦτα· "'Εγὼ μέν, δοῦλε τοῦ Θεοῦ τοῦ Ὑψίστου, διὰ τὰς πολλάς μου ἁμαρτίας *οὔκ εἰμι ἱκανὸς ἵνα μου ὑπὸ τὴν στέγην εἰσέλθῃς·* καὶ *πόθεν μοι τοῦτο, ἵνα ἔλθῃς* ὁ ἅγιος τοῦ Κυρίου μου *πρός με;* Ἐπεὶ δὲ μιμούμενος τὸν σὸν Διδάσκαλον καὶ Δεσπότην προετίμησώ με τὸν ἁμαρτωλὸν τῶν δικαίων, ἰδοὺ ὁ οἶκός μου καὶ ἅπαν σὺν τοῖς περιχώροις αὐτοῦ τὸ καστέλλιον πρὸ προσώπου σου· εἴ τι κελεύεις περὶ αὐτῶν, πρόσταξον."

There the holy old man took up residence, and ex- 2
claimed, *"This is my resting place for ever."* From then on, no
one could move Neilos from there, even though the brethren with him were insisting on this, and dignitaries were
coming to him from Rome, imploring him to enter into
Rome in order to venerate the chiefs of the apostles. Neilos
responded to them all, saying, "It is possible to venerate the
all-praiseworthy and truly thrice-blessed chiefs of the apostles from here, for those who have *faith as a grain of mustard
seed,* although I myself am unworthy even to name them.
However, I have come to this humble place for no other reason than to die."

The ruler of that town, named Gregory, well known for 3
tyranny and injustice, but also very shrewd and adorned
with intelligence, came down and prostrated himself at the
holy man's feet, saying, "O servant of God the Most High,
because of my many sins *I am not worthy to have you come under my roof. And why is this granted me, that* you, the holy man
of my Lord, should come to me? Since in imitation of your
Teacher and Lord you have given preference to my sinful
self over the righteous ones, behold, my home and all my
castle together with its environs are at your disposal. If you
have any wish concerning them, we are at your command!"

97

Ὁ δὲ μακάριος πρὸς αὐτὸν ἀπεκρίνατο· "Εὐλογήσαι Κύριος καὶ σὲ καὶ τοὺς σοὺς σὺν τῷ οἴκῳ σου καὶ τῇ κώμῃ σου. Μέρος δὲ ὀλίγον ἐν τῷ κράτει σου ἡμῖν διαχώρισον, ὅπως ἐν αὐτῷ ἡσυχάσαντες τὸν Θεὸν ὑπὲρ τῶν ἁμαρτιῶν ἡμῶν ἐξιλεωσώμεθα καὶ ὑπὲρ τῆς σῆς σωτηρίας εὐξώμεθα." Τότε ὁ Γρηγόριος μετὰ πολλῆς προθυμίας ἐξεπλήρου τὸ κελευόμενον. Οἱ δὲ ἐναπομείναντες ἐν τῇ μονῇ ἀδελφοί, μετὰ δύο ἡμέρας μηνῶν μαθόντες ὅτι οὐχ ὑποστρέφει πρὸς αὐτοὺς ὁ πατήρ, ἀπάραντες σὺν μηλωταρίοις καὶ περιβολαίοις καὶ τοῖς λοιποῖς, κατέλαβον τὸν ὑπὸ τοῦ ἄρχοντος ἀφιερωθέντα τόπον αὐτοῖς ἐν λόγῳ μονῆς· μαθὼν τοίνυν ὁ παμμακάριστος πατὴρ τὴν ἄφιξιν αὐτῶν, ἠγαλλιάσατο τῷ πνεύματι καὶ δεδήλωκεν αὐτοῖς· "Ἀρκετόν μοι, ὦ πατέρες καὶ ἀδελφοί, ὅτι διὰ τὴν τοῦ Θεοῦ ἀγάπην καὶ τὴν ἐμὴν ἐσκύλητε ἕως αὐτοῦ. Νῦν οὖν παρακαλῶ τὴν ἀγάπην ὑμῶν, ἵνα περιμείνητε μέχρις ἂν καὶ αὐτὸς ἐλεύσομαι πρὸς ὑμᾶς."

2   Ἐν τῷ οὖν ἑτοιμάζεσθαι αὐτὸν τοῦ ἀποπληρῶσαι αὐτομάτοις ποσὶ τὴν οἰκείαν σύνταξιν—ἦσαν γὰρ οἱ ἀδελφοὶ ὡς ἀπὸ μιλίων τριῶν—συγκαλεσάμενος τοὺς προσκαρτεροῦντας αὐτῷ ἀδελφοὺς σὺν τῷ ἡγουμένῳ Παύλῳ, ᾧ ἦν πρὸ πολλῶν προκεχειρημένος ἡμερῶν τὴν ἡγεμονίαν, ἀνδρὶ παλαιῷ καὶ τὴν φρόνησιν καὶ τὴν ἡλικίαν καὶ τὴν ἄσκησιν καὶ τὴν φιλοσοφίαν, τούτοις διαμερίσας τὰ μικρὰ ῥάκια αὐτοῦ—οὐ γὰρ ἄλλο τί ποτε ἦν αὐτῷ τοῦ

Chapter 97

The blessed one replied to him, "May the Lord bless you and your people along with your household and town. Allot a small portion of your dominion to us, where we may live in spiritual tranquility and propitiate God for our sins and pray for your salvation." Then Gregory fulfilled his request with great joy. When the brethren who remained in the monastery at Serperi learned after two months that the father was not returning to them, they set forth with their sheepskin garments, cloaks, and the rest of their goods and arrived at the place that the ruler had granted them for the construction of a monastery. Once the all-blessed father learned of their arrival, he rejoiced in his spirit and declared to them, "For me it is enough, O fathers and brothers, that for the sake of your love for God and for me you have arrived there. Now I beseech you, my beloved, to wait until I shall come to you."

While preparing to fulfill his promise by visiting them 2 on foot—for the brethren were staying some three miles away—Neilos called together the brethren who were living with him, together with the superior Paul, a mature man in all respects, wisdom, years, asceticism, and spiritual discipline, whom he had entrusted with the abbacy of the monastery many days before. Neilos distributed to them his tattered garments—for he had no other worldly possessions,

κόσμου, ἕως καὶ τοῦ ἐσχάτου λεπτοῦ—ἐκέλευσε μεταλαβεῖν τῶν ζωοποιῶν Χριστοῦ μυστηρίων.

3   Ἔπειτα λέγει τῷ ἡγουμένῳ καὶ τοῖς ἀδελφοῖς· "Δέομαι
ὑμῶν, ἐὰν ἀποθάνω, μὴ βραδύνητε τοῦ κατακρύψαι τῇ γῇ
τὸ σῶμά μου· μήτε ἐν οἴκῳ κυριακῷ κατάθησθε, μηδὲ
θελήσητε ποιῆσαι καμάραν ἐπάνω μου, ἢ ἄλλον τινὰ
κόσμον οἱονδήποτε. Εἰ δὲ ὅλως βούλεσθε ποιῆσαί τι σημεῖον διὰ τὸ γνωρίζειν ποῦ τέθημαι, ὁμαλὸν ἔστω ἐπάνωθεν, ἵνα οἱ ξένοι ἐκεῖ ἐπαναπαύονται—καὶ γὰρ κἀγὼ ξένος
ἐγενόμην πάσας τὰς ἡμέρας ἃς ἔζησα—, καὶ μνημονεύετέ
μου ἐν ταῖς ἁγίαις ὑμῶν εὐχαῖς."

98

Ταῦτα εἰπὼν καὶ εὐλογήσας αὐτούς, ἐπευξάμενός τε
πᾶσι τοῖς ἀδελφοῖς, ἐξῆρε τοὺς πόδας αὐτοῦ καὶ ἥπλωσεν
ἑαυτὸν ἐν τῷ κοιταρίῳ αὐτοῦ. Ἐποίησεν οὖν δύο ἡμέρας
μὴ συντυγχάνων, μήτε ἀνοίγων τοὺς ὀφθαλμοὺς αὐτοῦ,
καὶ ἐθαύμαζον οἱ ὁρῶντες αὐτόν, ὅτι οὐκ ἦν ὡς ψυχορ-
ραγῶν, ἀλλ᾽ ὡς ἀναπαυόμενος· μόνον δὲ τὰ χείλη κινῶν
καὶ τῇ δεξιᾷ χειρὶ κατασφραγιζόμενος, ἐγνωρίζετο τοῖς
παροῦσιν ὡς προσευχόμενος. Καί τις τῶν ἀδελφῶν προσ-
εγγίσας τῷ ὠτίῳ πρὸς τῷ στόματι αὐτοῦ, τοῦτον μόνον
τὸν στίχον ἐνόησε λέγοντος· "Τότε οὐ μὴ αἰσχυνθῶ, ἐν τῷ
με ἐπιβλέπειν ἐπὶ πάσας τὰς ἐντολάς Σου."

not even a copper coin—and bade them partake of the life-giving mysteries of Christ.

Then he said to the superior and the brethren, "I beg of 3 you, when I die, do not delay in burying my body in the earth, nor should you bury it in a church, nor decide to build a vault over me, or any other such adornment whatsoever. But if you really wish to make some sign to indicate where I am buried, let it be on level ground, so that the pilgrims may rest there—for I too have been a pilgrim all the days of my life—and remember me in your holy prayers."

Chapter 98

Having said this, Neilos blessed them and prayed for all the brethren. He then *lifted up his feet,* stretched himself out on his bed, and spent two days not speaking to anyone, nor opening his eyes. Those who saw him were amazed that he did not seem to be in death throes, but as if he were resting, and only because he was moving his lips and making the sign of the cross with his right hand did those around him realize that he was praying. One of the brethren placed his ear next to Neilos's mouth and so heard that he was saying this one verse alone, *"Then I shall not be ashamed, as I regard all Your commandments."*

2 Ἀκούσας δὲ καὶ ὁ ἄρχων Γρηγόριος τὰ περὶ αὐτοῦ, δρομαίως κατῆλθεν ἀπὸ τοῦ καστελλίου αὐτοῦ, φέρων καὶ τὸν
ἰατρὸν Μιχαὴλ μετ᾽ αὐτοῦ, ὃς ἦν ἐμπειρότατος. Καὶ ἐπι-
πεσὼν τῷ μακαρίῳ, ἔκλαιε πικρῶς καὶ ἔλεγε· "Ὦ πάτερ,
πάτερ, διατί οὕτω ταχέως με ἐγκατέλιπες; Διατί ἐβδελύξω
τὰς ἁμαρτίας μου, καὶ ἀφίεις με;" Καταφιλῶν δὲ τὰς χεῖρας
αὐτοῦ ἔλεγεν· "Ἰδοὺ οὐκέτι κωλύεις με τοῦ φιλῆσαι τὰς
χεῖράς σου, καθὼς ἐποίεις τὸ πρότερον, λέγων, ὅτι· Οὐκ
εἰμι ἐπίσκοπος, ἢ πρεσβύτερος, οὔτε διάκονος, ἀλλὰ μόνον
καλογήριον μικρόν· διατί οὖν θέλεις φιλῆσαι τὴν χεῖρά
μου;" Ταῦτα δὲ λέγων τοσοῦτον ἐδάκρυεν, ὥστε πάντας
τοὺς παρεστῶτας διεγεῖραι πρὸς δάκρυα. Κρατήσας δὲ καὶ
ὁ ἰατρὸς τοῦ σφυγμοῦ αὐτοῦ, διϊσχυρίζετο, λέγων ὅτι·
"Οὗτος οὐκ ἀποθνήσκει· οὐ γάρ ἐστιν ἐν αὐτῷ πυρετός,
οὔτε ἄλλον τι σημεῖον θανάτου." καὶ γὰρ οὕτως εἶχεν.

3 Ἀναχωρησάντων τοίνυν ἐκείνων καὶ τῆς ὥρας τοῦ λυχ-
νικοῦ καταλαβούσης—ἦν δὲ καὶ ἡ μνήμη τοῦ ἀποστόλου
Ἰωάννου καὶ θεολόγου—, ἔδοξε τοῖς ἀδελφοῖς ἀπαγάγαι
τὸν ὅσιον ἐν τῇ ἐκκλησίᾳ· ἐμνήσθησαν γὰρ τοῦ πόθου καὶ
τοῦ φίλτρου αὐτοῦ, οὗπερ εἰς τὰς μνείας τῶν ἁγίων
ἐδείκνυτο, καὶ ὡς ἀεὶ ἔλεγεν, ὅτι δεῖ τὸν μοναχόν, ἐκτὸς
πάσης ἀνάγκης, ἐν τῷ εὐκτηρίῳ τελευτῆσαι.

When the ruler Gregory heard this news, he came rush- 2
ing down from his castle, bringing with him the physician
Michael, who was very experienced. Prostrating himself before the blessed one, Gregory wept bitterly and said, "O father, father, why have you abandoned me so soon? Why did
you feel loathing at my sins, and leave me?" Kissing Neilos's
hands he then said, "Behold, no longer can you forbid me to
kiss your hands, as you did before, saying, 'I am not a bishop
or a priest, or a deacon, but only an insignificant monk. Why
then do you wish to kiss my hand?'" Upon saying this Gregory wept so much that he roused all those standing around
him to tears. The physician took his pulse and said, "He is
not dying, for he has no fever or any other sign of death."
This was, in fact, Neilos's condition.

After they had departed, as the hour of vespers arrived— 3
it was the feast day of John the apostle and theologian—the
brethren decided to carry the holy man into the church; for
they remembered the desire and love Neilos showed for the
commemoration of the saints, and how he had always said
that a monk should die in the church, except under special
circumstances.

99

Τούτου δὲ γενομένου, καὶ τοῦ ἑσπερινοῦ ὕμνου τέλος λαβόντος, ὁ ἥλιος ἔγνω τὴν δύσιν αὐτοῦ καὶ αὐτὸς παρέδωκε τὸ πνεῦμα· καὶ ἔδυ, ἀληθῶς εἰπεῖν, ὁ ἥλιος μετὰ τοῦ ἡλίου, καὶ ἐξέλιπε φῶς ἀπὸ τῆς γῆς ἐν τῇ ἡμέρᾳ ἐκείνῃ καὶ λύχνος ἀπὸ προσώπου ὁρώντων. Ἦ γὰρ καὶ αὐτὸς οὐ προέγνω τὴν παροῦσαν σκοτόμαιναν καὶ ἀπόλειψιν τῶν φωτιζόντων ἁγίων καὶ διδασκόντων τοὺς ἄλλους; Καὶ ποῦ εὕρατο ἄλλην παραμυθίαν ὁ κόσμος, τῶν καθ᾽ ἡμᾶς λέγω, οἵαν ἀπώλεσεν ἐν τῇ ἡμέρᾳ ἐκείνῃ;

2   Πολλοὺς μὲν γὰρ εὑρήσεις ἐγκράτειαν ἀσκοῦντας, οἳ μέχρις αὐτῆς τὴν ὠφέλειαν διϊστῶσι, λόγου δὲ ἀμοιροῦσι, πλείστους δὲ πάλιν τῶν λόγου μὲν ἐπιμελουμένων, ἔργου δὲ ἀμελούντων· ὧν ἐκεῖνος ἀμφοτέρων πλεονεκτῶν κατὰ πάντα, περιδέξιος ὄντως ὑπῆρχε καὶ ἀμφοτερόφθαλμος. Καὶ ταῦτα ἵνα μὴ λέγω τὴν καθ᾽ ἡμᾶς γενεάν, ὁλότυφλον, μᾶλλον ἤπερ μονότυφλον οὖσαν, καὶ ἐν σκοτομήνῃ διάγουσαν, ὅπερ καὶ αὐτῷ τῷ προβλεπτικωτάτῳ ὡς ἐν ἐκστάσει ἀπεκαλύφθη· ἑώρα γὰρ ὡς πάντες οἱ ἄνθρωποι καὶ πάντα τὰ ζῷα καὶ πᾶν ἑρπετὸν κινούμενον ἐπὶ τῆς γῆς τυφλώσει καὶ ἀβλεψίᾳ κατείχοντο, ζόφος δὲ βαθύτατος καὶ γνόφος ἀμύθητος ἐπὶ πᾶσαν τὴν γῆν περιεκέχυτο. Καὶ τοῦτο μὲν πρότερον, νῦν δὲ ὅτε καταλιπὼν τὰ ἐπίγεια, τῷ πνεύματι τοὺς οὐρανοὺς ἐνεβάτευεν ὁ ἀείμνηστος, πᾶσαν μὲν τὴν νύκτα ἐκείνην ἐν ψαλμοῖς καὶ ὕμνοις ἐπιταφίοις διήλθομεν, πρωΐας δὲ γενομένης, διαβαστάσαντες τὴν

Chapter 99

After this happened, at the conclusion of the vespers hymn, *the sun knew its going down,* and then Neilos *gave up his spirit.* To speak truly, the sun set along with the sun, a light left the earth on that day, and a lamp has gone out from the face of those who see. For truly, did he not foresee the present darkness and the lack of saints who illuminate and teach others? Where will the world—I mean our generation—find another consolation such as it lost on that day?

For you will find many practicing continence, who con- 2 sider this alone to be beneficial, but get no benefit from teaching, and many more who place great importance on teaching, but neglect good works. Neilos was superior to both in all respects, as he was truly ambidextrous and could see with both eyes. Let me not refer to our present generation, which is totally blind, rather than one-eyed, and lives in absolute darkness. This was revealed as if in ecstasy to this most prophetic father, for he saw that all men and all animals, as well as every reptile that crawls upon the earth, also dwelt in blindness and sightlessness, and that a most profound gloom and an ineffable darkness were shed over the entire earth. This he saw before his death; but now that the man of eternal memory had left behind earthly matters, and ascended with his spirit to heaven, we spent that entire night in singing psalms and funerary hymns. When day

κλίνην μετὰ κηρῶν καὶ θυμιαμάτων καὶ ψαλμῳδίας ἀπηγάγομεν τὸ λείψανον ἔνθα οἱ ἀδελφοὶ ἀπεκδέχοντο τὸν μακάριον.

100

Ὅτε δὲ ἐξ ἐναντίας αὐτῶν ἐγενήθημεν καὶ τῆς ψαλμῳδίας ἀκήκοαν, ἐξῆλθον καὶ ὑπήντησαν ἡμῖν ἅπαντες, νέοι τε καὶ γέροντες, μικροὶ καὶ μεγάλοι, ὅλοι συμπεφυρμένοι τοῖς δάκρυσι καὶ πικρῶς ὀδυρόμενοι. Θέντες τοίνυν ἐπὶ τὴν γῆν τὸ κλινίδιον καὶ τὸ ψάλλειν ἐάσαντες, πάντες ὁμοῦ ἐθρηνοῦμεν τὴν κοινὴν ζημίαν καὶ ὀρφανίαν καὶ τὴν τοῦ πατρὸς στέρησιν.

2   Οὐδὲν δὲ ἄλλο ἦν ἰδεῖν καὶ εἰκάσαι, ἢ ὅπερ περὶ τοῦ Ἰακὼβ γέγραπται, ὅτε παρεγένοντο οἱ υἱοὶ αὐτοῦ ἐφ᾽ ἅλωνα Ἀτάδ, ἥ ἐστι πέραν τοῦ Ἰορδάνου, καὶ ἐκόψαντο κοπετὸν μέγαν καὶ ἰσχυρὸν σφόδρα· καὶ γὰρ καὶ ἡμᾶς μικρὸν ἁλώνιον περιεῖχε καὶ ὁ νέος Ἰακὼβ νεκρὸς ἔκειτο ἐν τῷ σκιμποδίῳ καὶ οἱ υἱοὶ Ἰσραὴλ ἐπεθρήνουν. Καὶ οἱ κάτοικοι τῆς χώρας, ὅσοι εὑρέθησαν σὺν τῷ ἄρχοντι Γρηγορίῳ, οὐ μόνον τὰ γινόμενα ἐθεώρουν, ἀλλὰ καὶ συνεπένθουν ἀκολουθοῦντες καὶ οὐ πρότερον ἀνεχώρησαν, ἕως ὅτου τὸ λείψανον ἀπηγάγομεν καὶ ἐν τῷ προωρισμένῳ αὐτῷ τόπῳ κατεθέμεθα, καθὼς αὐτὸς ὁ τρισόσιος διετάξατο.

3   Παρέμεινε δὲ τῷ τάφῳ πᾶσα ἡ ἀδελφότης σὺν τῷ

broke we carried his bier accompanied by candles, incense, and psalmody, and we brought his body to the place where the brethren awaited the blessed one.

Chapter 100

When we arrived across from them and they heard the psalmody, they all came out to meet us, young and old, small and great, all in tears and bitterly lamenting. Then we placed the bier on the ground and ceased our psalmody, all of us mourning our common loss, orphanhood, and separation from our father.

To see this was to see nothing other than what is written 2 about Jacob, when his sons *came to the threshing floor of Atad, which is beyond the Jordan, and they bewailed him with a great and very sore lamentation.* For in fact a small threshing floor surrounded us, and the new Jacob lay there dead on the bier, while the sons of Israel were mourning. *And the inhabitants* of the region, who were there with the ruler Gregory, not only observed the events, but also grieved together with us, following the funeral procession. Nor did they depart, until we took away the corpse and buried it in the assigned place, just as the thrice-blessed Neilos had ordained.

The whole brotherhood remained at the tomb together 3

ἡγουμένῳ τῷ προλεχθέντι, ἐργαζομένη καὶ ἐν ὑπομονῇ κοπιῶσα διὰ τὸ ἀκατάσκευον εἶναι τὸν τόπον τὸν ἐπιούσιον ἄρτον, τόν τε τῇ ψυχῇ ἁρμόδιον καὶ τὸν τῇ σαρκὶ αὐτάρκη. Πολλοὶ δὲ καὶ τῶν τέκνων τοῦ ἁγίου τῶν διεσκορπισμένων συνήχθησαν τῇ ἐκείνου πρεσβείᾳ καὶ κεκοίμηνται περὶ τὸ μνῆμα αὐτοῦ, ἄνδρες, ἀληθῶς εἰπεῖν, ἐπιθυμιῶντες τοῦ Πνεύματος καὶ πλήρεις χάριτος καὶ δυνάμεως. Ὧν πάντων πρεσβείαις ἀξιωθείημεν καὶ ἡμεῖς, οἵ τε ἀναγινώσκοντες καὶ ἀκροώμενοι τῶν ἐνθέων καὶ ἐναρέτων πόνων αὐτῶν, κοινωνοὶ γενέσθαι αὐτῶν καὶ ἐν τῇ βασιλείᾳ τῶν οὐρανῶν, ἐν Χριστῷ Ἰησοῦ τῷ Κυρίῳ ἡμῶν· ᾧ ἡ δόξα σὺν τῷ Πατρὶ καὶ τῷ Ἁγίῳ Πνεύματι, νῦν καὶ ἀεί, καὶ εἰς τοὺς αἰῶνας τῶν αἰώνων. Ἀμήν.

with the aforementioned superior, working and toiling patiently since the place was not fit to provide for their daily bread, which was both appropriate for the soul and sufficient for the body. And many of the holy man's spiritual children, who had been dispersed, assembled at the monastery through his divine intercession, and they died near his tomb. These *men were* truly *desirous* of the Spirit, and full of grace and power. Through the intercessions of them all, may we, who read and hear about their godly and virtuous toils, also be deemed worthy to become their associates in the kingdom of heaven, in Jesus Christ, our Lord, to whom, along with the Father and the Holy Spirit, may there be glory now and always, and unto the ages of ages. Amen.

Abbreviations

CPG = Ernst L. von Leutsch and Friedrich G. Schneidewin, eds., *Corpus Paroemiographorum Graecorum,* 2 vols. (Göttingen, 1839–1851); repr., 3 vols. (Hildesheim, 1958–1961)

CSEL = *Corpus scriptorum ecclesiasticorum Latinorum* (Vienna-Berlin, 1866–)

EEC = Angelo Di Berardino, ed., *Encyclopedia of the Early Church,* trans. Adrian Walford, 2 vols. (Cambridge, 1992)

LbG = Erich Trapp et al., eds., *Lexikon zur byzantinischen Gräzität, besonders des 9.–12. Jahrhunderts,* 7 fasc. (Vienna, 1994–)

ODB = Alexander P. Kazhdan et al., eds., *Oxford Dictionary of Byzantium,* 3 vols. (New York, 1991)

ODP = John N. D. Kelly, ed., *The Oxford Dictionary of Popes* (Oxford, 1986)

PG = Jacques-Paul Migne, ed., *Patrologiae cursus completus, series Graeca,* 161 vols. (Paris, 1857–1866)

PL = Jacques-Paul Migne, ed., *Patrologiae cursus completus, series Latina,* 221 vols. (Paris, 1844–1864)

PmbZ = Ralph-Johannes Lilie et al., eds., *Prosopographie der mittelbyzantinischen Zeit,* 2 parts, 14 vols. (Berlin, 1998–2013)

Note on the Text

The edition of the Greek text is based on the 1972 edition of Germano Giovanelli,[1] with the kind permission of Fr. Emiliano, the abbot of the Grottaferrata monastery. We have made some modifications as a result of collation of the printed text with the Grottaferrata manuscript, Crypt. gr. B. β II (430), ff. 12–155, of which we obtained a digital file through the courtesy and generosity of Stefano Parenti and Elena Velkovska, whom we thank warmly. We have added some emendations suggested by Sister Maxime of the Ormylia convent in her 1991 edition of the Greek text,[2] and by Alexander Alexakis, who thoroughly reviewed the Greek text at a late stage in its preparation and revised the notes to the text. We have also adopted most of the corrections suggested by Enrica Follieri in her two articles proposing a new edition of the text furnished by Giovanelli.[3] With rare exceptions we have not taken into consideration the variant readings of two witnesses of the sixteenth century, Vaticanus gr. 1205, ff. 1–56v, and Paris, suppl. gr. 106, ff. 1–118, since they are much later apographs of the Grottaferrata version. We have noted, but rarely accepted, variant readings from the 1624 edition of Matthaeus Caryophilus (Matthaios Karyophylles),[4] which was reproduced with

only a few changes by the *Acta Sanctorum* and *Patrologia Graeca*.[5]

Crypt. gr. B β II is a parchment manuscript that has been dated to the eleventh century by Nadezhda Kavrus Hoffmann; at an unknown date (but prior to the sixteenth century) it lost four folios (25–28), the text of which was replaced in the Greek editions by the relevant passage of a Latin translation (carried out before 1565 by Guglielmus Sirletus and published for the first time by Edmond Martène).[6] The subsequent folios were renumbered, with the new numbering to be found in the lower right-hand corner of the recto. The manuscript is distinguished by the use of iota adscripts, enlarged red majuscules to start new sections of the narrative, and large raised dots, outlined in red, to mark the end of sentences. The entire manuscript is devoted to the cult of Saint Neilos; ff. 12–155v contain his biography, while the remaining folios contain hymns and other materials for the perpetuation of his memory.

Despite its handsome appearance, the text of the Grottaferrata manuscript is marred by numerous mistakes in orthography. To avoid excessive annotation we have tacitly corrected iotacisms, dittography, haplography, and the confusion of similar sounding letters such as *o* and *ω, αι* and *ε,* and the like, and some errors of accentuation. It should be especially noted that we have systematically normalized the spelling of Σαρακινός in the manuscript to Σαρακηνός. We have also omitted the breathings over double rhos employed by Giovanelli. Finally, we have retained much of Giovanelli's system of chapter divisions, but modified it where necessary.

AA = Alexakis

C = *Crypt. gr.* B. β II

F = Follieri

G = Giovanelli

K = Karyophylles (Caryophilus)

M = Maxime

V = *Cod. Vat. gr.* 1205

add. = added

corr. = corrected

om. = omitted

<...> = editorial insertion

NOTES

1 Giovanelli, *Βίος καὶ πολιτεία τοῦ ὁσίου πατρὸς ἡμῶν Νείλου τοῦ Νέου.*

2 Sister Maxime, *Ὁ ὅσιος Νεῖλος ὁ Καλαβρός.*

3 Enrica Follieri, "Per una nuova edizione della Vita di san Nilo da Rossano," 71–92; eadem, "Per il testo della vita di San Nilo da Rossano," *Byzantino-Sicula III. Miscellanea di scritti in memoria di Bruno Lavagnini* (Palermo, 2000), 123–33. Two of Follieri's students, Andrea Luzzi and Francesco d'Aiuto, are currently preparing a new critical edition of the vita for which she laid the groundwork.

4 Caryophilus, *Vita s. patris Nili Junioris.*

5 *AASS* Sept. VII (3rd ed.), 259–319; PG 120:15–165.

6 Sirletus, "Vita Sancti Nili confessoris, a B. Bartholomæo cryptæ ferratæ abbate græce conscripta," col. 887–956. The passage in question (a large part of chapter 9 in the present volume) is found in ibid., col. 895B–96D. For the possible reason why the missing folios were removed from the Grottaferrata manuscript, see Follieri, "Per una nuova edizione della Vita di san Nilo da Rossano," 86–89, esp. 89.

Notes to the Text

1.1   ζητοῦντές <τε>: τε *add.* M

        μέτρα κρίνειν CF: μετακρίνειν KGM

2.1   ἅμα τῷ: KGM: ἅμα τὸ C

2.2   πολλοῦ πόθου: πόθου KGM, C *add. in margin*

4.1   λεῖπον *corr.* KM: λοῖπον CG

        Συνείπετο *corr.* KM: συνήπετο CG

5.1   Ἄθρει δὴ τότε πάλην ἀγγέλου καὶ διαβόλου C: ἄθρη δεὶ δὲ
        τότε ἥν ὁρᾶν πάλην ἀγγέλου καὶ Cᶦ *add. in margin*; Ἄθρει δὴ
        καὶ τότε ἥν ὁρᾶν πάλην ἀγγέλου καὶ διαβόλου GM

        προσῳκειώσῃ *corr.* F: προσῳκειώσηι C; προσοικειώσῃ KGM

5.2   ἔχιδνα *corr.* KM: ἐχίδνη CG

        οἴχοντο *corr.* M: ἤχοντο C; εἴχοντο KG

        δαιμόνων CF: δαίμοσι KGM

5.3   εὐθάρσως CF: εὐθαρσῶς KGM

6.1   ἀναγγείλαντος KGM: ἀναγγείλοντος CF

7.1   ὀνειδίζειν αὐτοῦ: αὐτοῦ *corr.* AA: αὐτόν CGM; αὐτῷ K

7.3   λεῖπον *corr.* G: λοῖπον CM; λοιπὸν K

        ὑπάγῃς CM: ὑπάγεις G; ὑπάγεις K

        ἥπερ εἰσερχόμενος: ἥπερ *corr.* GM: εἴπερ C; περ *om.* K

8.1   εὔξονται C: εὔξωνται KGM

        σφριγῶσι *corr.* KG: σφρίγουσι CM

        ἐπήλειψαν *corr.* AA: ἀπήλειψαν CKG; ὑπήλειψαν M

8.2   τὸ ἐν τῇ τάξει *corr.* KGM: τῶι ἐν τῇ τάξει C

9.1   ἀντιτεῖνον *corr.* KGM: ἀντιτείνων C

9.4   circumierunt *corr.* Zaleski: circuierunt GM

9.7–8   λόγοις παρακλητικοῖς . . . ἀναισθησίᾳ πολλῇ *add.* V

9.9 ἀνήγγελε CG: ἀνήγγειλε M; ἀπήγγειλε K

10.2 μέγιστον *corr.* M: μεγίστου CKG
κατὰ πάντα CF: κατὰ πάντων KGM

11.1 προσθήσωμεν CM: προθήσωμεν KG

11.3 ἀκμὴν *corr.* KGM: ἀγμὴν, κ *above the line in* C

13.1 πλανωμένοις *corr.* KM: πλανομένοις CG

13.2 βουλῆς αὐτῶν KGM: βουλῆς αὐτὸν C

13.3 ἰσχύσει C: ἰσχύσῃ GM; ἰσχύσαι K
τεκμήραιτο *corr.* M: τεκμήροιτο CKG

14.1 Ἐχέγγυα CF: Ἔλεγχος KGM

14.2 ὅσα ἡμῖν . . . ἡ ἀψευδὴς αὐτοῦ εἴρηκε γλῶσσα: ὅρα ὅτι ἐκ
στόματος τοῦ ἁγίου [. . .] ὁ συγγράψας τὸν ὅσιον βίον τοῦτον
C *add. in margin*
ἐγκαυχώμενον *corr.* GM: ἐκκαυχόμενον C; ἐουκαυχώμενον K
δόξουσιν *corr.* K: δόξουσι M: δόξωσι CG

15.2 ἐλλείψει *corr.* M: ἐλλείψει C; ἐλλείψῃ KG
ὑποβάλλει *corr.* M: ὑποβάλλῃ CKG

16.2 τρὶς *corr.* KM: τρεὶς CG
μόνον *corr.* AA: μόνος C; μόναις K; μόνως GM

17.1 διῄει *corr.* KGM: δῖει C

17.2 μεσονυκτινῶν CF: μεσονυκτικῶν KGM

17.3 εἰ μὴ *corr.* KGM: εἰμὶ C
δι' ὧν CKG: δι' ἃ M

18.1 ἐννοῆσαι *corr.* KM: ἐννοήσῃ CG
ἃς αὐτῷ F: ἃς αὐτῶι C; ἃς αὐτὸς KGM
ἰσχύσας C: ἰσχύσαι KGM
φράσαιτο CG: φράσαι KM

18.2 ἐποίει αὐτῷ AA: ἐποίει αὐτῶι C; ἐποίει αὐτὸ KGM

19.1 προστρίψει CKM: προτρίψει G

19.2 ἀνερευνήσεως *corr.* M *in note*: ἀνερευνήσει CKGM
ἀλαμάναν C: Ἀλεμάναν KGM

19.3 βῆλον *corr.* KM: βίλον CG

20.1 διεγείρει C: διεγείρῃ KG; διεγερεῖ M

20.2 βούλευμα CF: βούλημα KGM

21.2 τὸν ἐντὸς ἄνθρωπον C: τοῦ ἐντὸς ἀνθρώπου KGM

22.1 ἀντεσηκοῦτο *corr.* KM *(in note)*: ἀντεισηκοῦτο C; ἀντισηκοῦτο
GM

22.3   παραγενάμενος CF: παραγενόμενος KGM

23.4   εὐχαρίστει CF: εὐχαριστεῖ KGM

        προσανατίθων CG: προσανατιθεὶς Μ; προσανετίθει Κ

24.1   ἀγῶνα CKGM: C¹ added nu at end of word above the line

24.2   ὅμως CG: ὁμοίως ΚΜ

25.2   τὸ τῷ Θεῷ CF: τὸ Θεῷ KGM

26.1   Στεφάνου τοῦ μάκαρος: περὶ τοῦ ὁσίου πατρὸς ἡμῶν στεφάνου C add. in margin

        γνωρίζεται CF: γνωρίζηται KGM

        θαυμάζεται CF: θαυμάζηται KGM

26.2   οὐκ <ἂν>: ἂν add. Μ

27.1   παροικησίας F: παροικησείας C; παροικίας KGM

        Ἀκμὴν corr. KGM: ἀγμὴν C

        ᾔδει corr. KGM: εἴδει C

27.2   ἐδίδει CG: ἐδίδου ΚΜ

28.1   τίθων CG: τιθεὶς ΚΜ

        ἐξομολογεῖ CM: ἐξομολογῇ KG

28.3   σπαράγγια corr. ΚΜ: σπαράγια CG

        παρὰ τοῦ πατρὸς CK: παρ᾿ αὐτοῦ πατρὸς G; παρ᾿ αὐτοῦ τοῦ πατρὸς Μ

        γλυκεῖα corr. F: γλυκεία C; γλυκέα KGM

31.1   αὐτό, οὕτως: οὕτως CF; οὕτω KGM

31.2   τέθηκεν C: τέθεικεν KGM

32.1   ἐθέλη corr. GM: ἐθέλει C; θέλη Κ

33.1   ἀναπαήσῃ corr. F: ἀναπαείσῃ C; ἀναπαύσῃ KGM

33.2   κύρι CM: Κύριε GK

35.1   Βισινιάνῳ: βισινιάνῳ CK; Βυσινιάνῳ GM

35.2   νομοθετημένα CF: νενομοθετημένα KGM

        Βισινιάνον corr. ΑΑ: βισιννιάνον C; Βυσινιάνον KGM

37.2   φθόνον αὐτῶν KGM: φθόνον αὐτὸν C

        δι᾿ αὐτῶν CGM: περὶ αὐτῶν Κ; δι᾿ αὐτούς suggested by Μ in note

37.3   μαχόμεθα C: μαχώμεθα KGM

38.1   ἐργάσονται C: ἐργάσωνται KGM

38.2   ἀνεκομβώσατο corr. ΚΜ: ἀνεκομμώσατο CG

        μαχαίρης CG: μαχαίρας ΚΜ

        δώσωμεν corr. ΑΑ: δόσωμεν C; δώσομεν KGM

38.3   γευσόμεθα C: γευσώμεθα KGM

38.4	ἐσθίετε CF: ἐσθίητε KGM
40.1	τῆς ἐγκυκλίου παιδεύσεως: ἑρμ(ηνεία): τῆς τοῦ κόσμ(ου) παιδ(εύ)σε(ως) C *add. in margin*
40.3	μοναχικὸν CM: μοναδικὸν KG
	ἀποδιδοῦντι CKG: ἀποδιδόντι M
	ἀνακάμψωμεν *corr.* KGM: ἀναγκάμψωμεν C
41.1	μόνον CM: μόνην KG
41.2	Βούλγαρι F: βούλγαρη C; Βούλγαρε KGM
	ὠφελήσεις CF: ὠφελήσῃ KGM
42.3	καθαρπάξας *corr.* KGM: κατ ἁρπάξας C
43.1	Ἀπόδοτε *corr.* KGM: ἀπόδετε CF
43.2	καταπίει C: καταπίῃ KGM
44.1	προσπαθείας ἑαυτοὺς CM: προσπαθείας αὐτοὺς KG
44.2	ἀντεισῆκτο *corr.* M: ἀντεΐσηκτο C; ἀντείσηκτο G; ἀντισήγετο K
44.3	ταύτην οὖν: οὖν CKM; *om.* G
47.2	ἐρωτήσει CM: ἐρωτήσῃ KG
48.1	ψυχροῦν CF: ψυχρὸν KGM; K *reverses the order* τὸ ποτήριον τὸ ψυχρὸν
48.3	<αἱ> ἐντολαί: αἱ *add.* KM
49.1	καὶ σὺ *corr.* KM: καὶ σοὶ CG
50.1	κελεύεις *corr.* KM: κελεύῃς CG
50.2	ἀκεραίους *corr.* KGM: ἀκαιρέους C
	εἰ μὴ *corr.* KGM: εἰμί C
	οὐδὲν ἔτι πρὸς τὸν ἅγιον ἀπεκρίνατο GM, C *add. in margin*
51.2	γενόμεθα C: γενώμεθα F; γινόμεθα KGM
	μᾶλλον ἤπερ: ἤπερ *corr.* KGM: εἴπερ, ἢ C *add. in margin*
53.1	νοσφισάμενον *corr.* KGM: νοσφισάμενος C
	ἀξιώσει CM: ἀξιώσειέ KG
53.3	<οὐκ>: οὐκ *add.* AA
54.1	εἰσεπράττετο *corr.* KAA: εἰσπράττετο CGM
54.2	ἐπιτύχει C: ἐπιτύχῃ KGM
54.3	οἰκτροτάταις *corr.* KGM: οἰκτοτάταις CF
55.2	ἔχων CM: ἔχον KG
55.4	μεσάζομαι C: μεσάζωμαι KGM
	καθορκίζων *corr.* KGM: κατορκίζων C
	Θεὸν αὐτὸν *corr.* M: Θεὸν αὐτὸ C; Θεὸν αὐτῷ KG

56.2	τῆς τοῦ ὁσίου: τῆς C: τῇ GM; ταῖς K
57.1	ἀποδώσοντα C: ἀποδώσοντι KGM
58.2	δυναίμην corr. KGM: ἐδυναίμην C
58.3	κακοχούμενος C: κακουχούμενος KGM
	ἐπιτύχει C: ἐπιτύχῃ KGM
58.4	ἐσπλαγχνίσθη C: σπλαγχνισθεὶς K; εὐσπλαγχνίσθη GM
	ἐλαίῳ corr. KGM: ἔλαιον CF
59.1	καπνοῦ Cᶦ: καπνὸς CKGM
59.2	ἀλλά γε CF: γε om. KGM
60.1	νυττόμενος CF: νικώμενος KGM
60.2	χελάνδια CKGM: C add. τὰ κάτεργα in margin
61.1	κατοιδαίνοντα corr. KGM: καθ᾽ ὑδαίνοντα C
61.3	μαχαίρῃ CG: μαχαίρᾳ KM
	ἐγχειρῆσαι KGM: ἐγχειρίσαι C
	τελέσωμεν C: τελέσομεν KGM
62.1	ἐπόψεως corr. KG: ὑπόψεως CM
63.1	ἐκπρίω corr. AA: ἐκπριῶι C; ἐκπριοῦν KG; ἐκπρίου M
63.3	τίθων CG: τιθεὶς KM
	πλήρους corr. KM: πλήρης CG
	οὔσης πολλῆς om. K
64.1	προεβάλλοντο corr. KM: προεβάλοντο CG
	φάγονται CM: φάγωνται KG
	κοινωνήσουσιν CM: κοινωνήσωσιν KG
	κατέχουσιν CF: κατεχόντων KGM
64.3	<ὁ> add. AA
	ἀγάγαι CG: ἀγαγεῖν KM
65.3	εἰ μὴ corr. KGM: εἰμὶ C
	ἐνεδυσάμεθα CK: ἐνδυσώμεθα G; ἐνεδυόμεθα M
66.1	ἐξέλιπεν KM: ἐξέλειπεν CG
68.2	ἀπευχαριστήσας C: ἐπευχαριστήσας KGM
68.3	ἐβδελύξατο corr. KGM: ἐβδελλύγξατο C
	πλείους corr. M: πλείω CKG
	συγκλείει corr. KM: συγκλείῃ C; συγκλείῃ G
70.2	ἵνα ἔχῃ corr. GM: ἵνα ἔχει C; ἵν᾽ ἔχῃ K
70.3	φαράγγοις CG: φάραγξι KM
	γεναμένης CF: γενομένης KGM

71.1	τοῦ τῶν *corr.* AA: τοῦ τὸν C; τοῦ K; τὸν τοῦ GM
71.2	ἀμμηρᾷ CG: ἀμιρᾷ M; Ἀμηρᾷ K
	ἠξίους *corr.* KGM: ἠξίοις C
71.3	ἐφθέγξατο *corr.* KGM: ἐφθέξατο C
72.1	ἀκμὴν *corr.* KGM: ἀγμὴν C
72.2	ἔνθεν *corr.* GM: ἔθεν C; ἐκεῖθεν K
	Ὥρα CKM: ὄρα G
73.1	Πανδούλφου *corr.* AA *(see below, 79.2)*: Πανδόλφου CKGM
73.2	τὸ λεχθὲν περίδοξον μοναστήριον: περὶ τοῦ βενεδίκτου μοναστηρίου *in margin of* C; *om.* KGM
74.1	κασίνῳ C: Κασσίνου K; Κασίνου GM
74.2	δεῖ *corr.* KGMF: δὲ C
75.2	ἀμβακοὺμ C: Ἀββακοὺμ GM; Ἀββακοὺκ K
76.1	ἡμεῖς *corr.* KGM: ὑμεῖς C
	ἡμῶν *corr.* GM: ὑμῶν CK
77.2	τῆς ἐκκλησίας *corr.* KGM: τοῖς ἐκκλησίας C
78.1	θρασέσι *corr.* KM: θρασέοις CG
79.2	πανδούλφου C: Πανδόλφου KGM
79.3	δριμαίῳ CG: δριμεῖ KM
79.4	ὁ τοιοῦτος CM: ὅτι οὗτος KG
81.2	ὡσεὶ ὄφεις CF: ὡς οἱ ὄφεις KGM
81.3	ἐν μέσῳ *corr.* KGM: ἐμμέσω C
	ἀποδείξει *corr.* KGM: ἀποδείξῃ C
82.2	ἔμπροσθεν *corr.* KGM: ἔνπροσθεν C
83.1	τὸν αὐτὸν ἵππον: αὐτὸν CG: αὐτῶν M; *om.* K
83.2	ἐπηρεάζουσιν KGM: ἐπερεάζουσιν CF
	ἔργον CM: ἔργῳ KG
84.1	μετ' αὐτοῦ KG: μετ' αὐτὸν CM
	τροπάριν C: τροπάριον KGM
	ὅτου αὐτὴν: αὐτὴν *corr.* KGM; αὐτὸν C
84.2	μεῖζον *corr.* KM: μείζω CG
85.3	ἀρρωστίᾳ *corr.* KGM: ἀρρωστεία C
86.3	ἱδρώτητι *corr.* G: ἱδρότητι C; ἱδρῶτι KM
87.1	τῷ προλεχθέντι μοναστηρίῳ: Βαλλ(ε)λούκι(ον) ἡ μονὴ ἣν ἐποίησεν ὁ ἅγιος νεῖλων εἰς τ(ὸν) ἅγι(ον) γερμαν(όν) *in margin of* C, *fol. 136v*

88.2 ἀχθεσθεὶς *corr.* KGM: ἀχθωθεὶς C

90.1 ἐβαρεῖτο *corr.* AA: ἐβαροῦτο CGM; ἐβαρύνετο K

90.2 τῷ ἡμετέρῳ γένει: τῶν γραικῶν C *add. in margin*

91.2 παρευθὺ CF: παρευθὺς KGM

94.1 ἐκλείπεις *corr.* KGM: ἐκλύπης C

94.3 διδάξει C: διδάξῃ KGM

94.4 πάσῃ *corr.* KGM: πᾶσι CF

ἤρκει αὐτῷ: αὐτῷ *corr.* KGM; αὐτὸ C

95.3 τὸ μοναστήριον, ὅπερ λέγεται Σέρπερις: ἡ εν γαϊμον σερπερις
ωνομαζετο . . . . . δὲ ἡ εν τῷ ἁγίῳ γερμ(α)ν(ῷ) C *add. in upper
margin*; Σέρπερις ἡ ἐ<ν> γαϊταν C *add. in right margin*

96.3 ἔλθῃς CMF: ἔλθῃ KG

97.1 ἐλεύσομαι CF: ἐλεύσωμαι KGM

97.2 προκεχειρημένος CK: προκεχειρισμένος *corr.* GM

ἡγεμονίαν CKG: ἡγουμενίαν M

Χριστοῦ: *before* Χριστοῦ KGM *add.* τοῦ

97.3 ἐπαναπαύονται C: ἐπαναπαύωνται KGM

98.3 ἀπαγάγαι CKG: ἀπαγάγειν M

99.1 ἐξέλιπε *corr.* KM: ἐξέλειπε CG

100.1 ἀκήκοαν CGM: ἀκηκόασιν KM *(in note)*

100.3 ἐπιθυμιῶντες *corr.* Talbot: ἐπιθυμιῶντων C; ἐπιθυμιῶν τῶν
KGM

Notes to the Translation

1.1 *may the grace . . . be with all:* 2 Corinthians 13:13. Neilos's biographer opens his narrative with an invocation to God, echoing the language and usage of the liturgy, and concludes it in the same fashion. See below, chapter 100.

 Neilos the Younger: At baptism he was given the name Nicholas. He took the name Neilos at the time of his monastic profession in memory of Neilos the Elder, also called the Ascetic, who died circa 430 CE. A more complete identification of the earlier Neilos seems impossible, since it is based upon a body of writings under that name, but which may in fact be the works of two individuals, one possibly from Ancyra, the other possibly from Sinai. See *EEC* 2:597 and *ODB* 2:1450.

 last times of the last centuries: Toward the end of the tenth century, expectations had spread that the world would end one thousand years after the coming of Christ. Such expectations continued into the early eleventh century—the likely time for the composition of Neilos's life—as the starting date for this millennial period was shifted from the birth to the resurrection of Christ. See Paul Magdalino, "The Year 1000 in Byzantium," in *Byzantium in the Year 1000,* ed. idem (Leiden, 2003), 233–70, esp. 241; and Paul Magdalino, "The End of Time in Byzantium," *Endzeiten: Eschatologie in den monotheistischen Weltreligionen* (Berlin, 2008), 119–34.

 the beneficial paths: The benefit that will come to them through reading of the lives of saints.

 judge by their own standards . . . suspecting that it is essentially false: The hagiographer introduces his subject in a manner that echoes Gregory of Nyssa's conclusion to his *Life* of his sister,

Makrina the Younger. See Gregory of Nyssa, *Vita Sanctae Macrinae,* PG 46:997D–1000A.

1.2   *it will be for us monks who study this account:* The hagiographer intended this *Life* to be read by the monastic community to which he belonged, thus indicating those whom he believes will probably be his principal audience.

2.1   *Rossano:* A southern Italian port city and bishopric, one of the major centers of Byzantine Calabria.

Calabria: A theme (province) of the Byzantine Empire, established in the tenth century.

the great threat of the Saracens: Saracens was a Greek ethnonym for Arabs that was used to refer more generally to Muslims. In the early tenth century, Calabria suffered a series of attacks led by Arab and Berber Muslim forces from North Africa and Sicily. While such incursions were often temporary or intended to collect tribute, Muslims also gained pockets of territory and established strongholds in southern Italy. Early raids upon Calabria were led by the Aghlabid dynasty, which dissolved around the year of Neilos's birth (910). During Neilos's life, Muslim attacks upon southern Italy were either individual or joint efforts led by the forces of the emergent Ismai'li Shi'i Fatimid caliphate, local rulers in Sicily, or the Fatimid-friendly Kalbid dynasty, established in Sicily in 948.

Hagarenes: Like the terms Saracen and Ishmaelite, Hagarene/Hagarite was a Byzantine ethnonym for Arabs, who were believed to be descended from Hagar, the slave of Abraham and mother of Ishmael. See Genesis 16:15.

2.2   *the church of the Mother of God:* That is, the cathedral of Rossano, now known as the church of the Most Holy Mary Acheiropoieta.

his understanding and his answers: Luke 2:47.

Anthony: Anthony of Egypt (ca. 251–356), called the Great, from Heracleopolis Magna in Lower Egypt, lived a life of primarily eremitic asceticism in the Egyptian desert. The *Life* of Anthony, written by Athanasios of Alexandria, became the principal model for monastic hagiography, and as a result of the *Life,* Anthony was the single most influential figure in the spread of

Christian monasticism, venerated in both the Christian East and West.

Sabas: Sabas (439–532) founded the Great Lavra (483) in the Judean desert near Jerusalem, as well as other monastic centers, which spread the ascetical life throughout Palestine. He, too, is venerated in both East and West.

Hilarion: Hilarion of Gaza (291–371), a convert from paganism, practiced an anchoritic form of monasticism. His search for solitude is said to have taken him to Libya, Sicily, Dalmatia, and Cyprus, where he died.

whose images were painted in the cathedral: This passage is ambiguous and could also be translated as "the others who were members of the Catholic Church."

3.1　　　*no bishop, or priest, or abbot or monk:* Although at first sight this statement might sound paradoxical, the monks were in search of solitude and were not to be found inside the city walls. The paucity of bishops and priests is apparently the hagiographer's way of emphasizing the spiritually impoverished state of Rossano at that time.

4.1　　　*Gregory:* Probably a monk from Rossano. See *PmbZ* 2, no. 22396.

the monastery: A monastery in the region of Mount Merkourion (Eparchy of Merkourion), located approximately fifty-seven miles from the city of Rossano. See *ODB* 2:1345.

I ran the way of Your commandments . . . my heart: Psalms 118(119):32.

4.2　　　*Mount Merkourion:* The monastic Eparchy of Merkourion was located at the border between Calabria and Lucania. Beginning in the tenth century, it was one of the most flourishing monastic provinces of southern Italy, known as a "new Thebaid" (a reference to the early Christian monastic center in the vicinity of Egyptian Thebes) because of its great concentration of monasteries and monks who practiced both solitary-contemplative and communal lifestyles.

the great John: The abbot John was renowned for his learning, being called "the Great" and "the Theologian" among the monks of Merkourion. See *PmbZ* 2, no. 22946, Giovanelli, *Vita di S. Nilo,* 128, and Giovanni Saladino, *Ascetismo calabro. Mille anni di santitá bizantina* (Rome, 2012), 50.

the renowned Phantinos: Phantinos the Younger (ca. 900–974) was perhaps the most famous of the Calabrian ascetics. In the face of Saracen destruction, he left Merkourion and Italy for Greece, where he died at Thessalonike. See *PmbZ* 2, no. 26576, and *ODB* 3:1646.

the angelic Zacharias: Little more is known of Zacharias than his reputation for exceptional asceticism. See *PmbZ* 2, no. 28481.

4.3   *horrible threats from the governor:* This is the *strategos* of the theme of Calabria. Both Sister Maxime (Ὁ ὅσιος Νεῖλος ὁ Καλαβρός, 321n31) and *PmbZ* 2, no. 25503, suggest that either Neilos's abandoned family or the local ecclesiastical authorities had petitioned the governor not to allow Neilos to disregard his obligations and take the monastic habit.

a cleric of this sort: As a reader, Neilos belonged to a minor order of the clergy.

5.1   *monastery named for Saint Nazarios:* Nazarios was a martyr for whom there is little reliable historical information. The monastery named for him was situated about a day's journey from the Merkourion but within Lombard lands, in the modern-day region of Salerno. See *EEC* 2:584, and Giovanelli, *Vita di S. Nilo,* 129–36.

5.2   *just like Paul's viper:* This is an allusion to Acts 28:3–5, which tells how Paul suffered no harm when bitten by a viper.

black Ethiopians . . . appearing like demons: This language is shaped by a trope in monastic literature—the appearance to monks of demons in the form of Ethiopians or people with black skin. See chapter 23.1, in which the Devil appears to Neilos in the guise of an Ethiopian. The trope dates back to Athanasios's *Life of Anthony.*

6.1   *not yet reached the age of thirty:* Neilos became a monk in 940.

at his understanding and his answers: Luke 2:47.

6.2   *in the midst of a fiery furnace:* See Daniel 3:21.

in the midst of lions: This is an allusion to Daniel 6:23, in which Daniel is rescued from the den of lions.

of serpents and scorpions . . . from the power of every enemy: See Luke 10:19.

neither bread nor bag: Luke 9:3.

7.2   *to lift up his eyes to heaven:* See Luke 18:13.

"What shall I render to You, Lord, . . . with which You have rewarded me?": See Psalms 115:12.

You . . . have helped me from my mother's womb: Psalms 138(139):13.

and You did not shut me up into the hands of enemies: See Psalms 30(31):8.

Bless the Lord, O my soul . . . and forget not all His gifts: See Psalms 102(103):1–2.

7.4   *the laborer deserves his food:* Matthew 10:10.

stopping his ears . . . like an asp: See Psalms 57(58):5.

that holy monastery: That is, the monastery of Saint Nazarios mentioned in chapter 5.1.

8.2   *think of himself more highly than he ought:* Romans 12:3.

the love of money, the root of all evils: See 1 Timothy 6:10.

9.1   *In the very way wherein I was walking, they hid a snare for me:* Psalms 141(142):3. The Latin text starts here. There are four folios (25–28) missing from the eleventh-century cod. gr. Crypt. B. β. II (430), which is preserved at the monastery of Grottaferrata.

9.2   *beautiful calligraphy:* Neilos and his disciples worked as scribes, employing a distinctive Greek minuscule. See the description of Neilos's calligraphic practice in chapter 15.3. For further reading on Neilos and his calligraphic "school," see Lucà, "Scritture e libri della 'scuola niliana'"; and Santo Lucà, "San Nilo e la 'scuola' calligrafica niliana," in *San Nilo di Rossano e l'Abbazia greca di Grottaferrata: Storia e immagini,* ed. Filippo Burgarella (Rome, 2009), 101–16.

and not be denounced as a man who ate bread in idleness: This is an allusion to Paul's exhortation to work for one's bread in 2 Thessalonians 3:6–12. The language also reflects the description in Proverbs 31:27 of the good wife who "eats not the bread of idleness."

9.3   *he chose the good part which shall not be taken from him:* See Luke 10:42.

9.4   *spotted hide:* This is a translation of the Latin phrase "pellem . . .

variam," perhaps a rendering of the Greek δέρμα ποικίλον, meaning a "speckled or spotted skin/hide." The allusion may be to an ancient breed of sheep called a "Jacob sheep," after a passage in Genesis 30:31–43, which describes Jacob's cross-breeding of sheep, resulting in sheep with spotted black and white skins.

"They wandered about in sheepskins and goatskins.": Hebrews 11:37.

9.5   *He kept his head uncovered . . . the rule of the apostle:* This is a reference to 1 Corinthians 11:7.

he wore only one coat . . . following the words of the Gospel: This is a reference to Matthew 10:10.

because in this way his feet were admired by the prophet: This is an allusion to Isaiah 20:3, in which Isaiah's bare feet are approved by God, and to Isaiah 52:7, in which Isaiah praises the feet of those who announce salvation.

there remain these three: hope, faith, and charity: 1 Corinthians 13:13.

9.6   *There was a petty king, whom they call a count in those regions:* The Latin term used for "petty king" is *regulus,* possibly the equivalent of the Greek δυνάστης. The identity of the man in this episode is unknown. He was probably a local Lombard count, a *comes* as the text also calls him, who exercised an almost absolute power over his territory. The presence of such powerful local lords underscores the instability of a region caught between the Eastern and the Western Empires alongside Arab Sicily.

a certain domestic servant: The Latin translation makes the servant male, but in chapter 9.9 it becomes clear that she was female.

to fulfill his carnal desire: Literally, "to fill his belly."

fearless speech: The Latin *eloquendi libertas* is likely a translation of παρρησία *(parrhesia),* a term that recurs in chapter 9.9. Παρρησία, the virtue of fearless and uninhibited speech in the presence of the powerful, was a technical term in hagiographic literature and one of the signs of a holy man.

9.7   *words of exhortation:* The Greek text resumes with "words of exhortation."

10.1   *Peter and John:* The apostles Peter and John are repeatedly paired

at critical events in the New Testament, with Peter typically shown as the senior of the two, as at the Last Supper (John 13:23–24), the High Priest's house (John 18:16), the empty tomb (John 20:2–6), and the cure of the crippled beggar (Acts 3:1–7). The implication is that the role of Peter corresponds to Phantinos, and John to Neilos.

Basil and Gregory: The intimate friendship between the Cappadocian Fathers Basil of Caesarea (ca. 330–379) and Gregory of Nazianzos (ca. 330–ca. 383) is not the only relevant factor in the Neilos-Phantinos comparison. Gregory became known in Greek Christianity as simply "the Theologian," and his thought heavily influenced Neilos. Similarly, Basil, called "the Great," laid the foundations for much of Greek, or Eastern, monasticism. Basil was the "senior" of the two and would predecease Gregory, as Phantinos did Neilos.

the great father John: Likely the same as the "great John" introduced in chapter 4.2.

11.2   *Saint Gregory the Theologian:* That is, Gregory of Nazianzos. See the note on Gregory in chapter 10.1.

11.3   *Saint John the Baptist:* Neilos's regard for Abbot John as another John the Baptist operates on several levels: the Baptist was the proto-ascetic/monk of the Gospel age (see Matthew 3:1–4), he was the prophet announcing and preparing the way for the Messiah (see Matthew 11:13–14; Luke 1:41, 44, 76), and he was called by Christ the greatest of those "born of women" (Matthew 11:11; Luke 7:28). Thus, John the Baptist uniquely served to show Neilos the way to Christ at the start of his monastic life.

12.1   *spiritual tranquility:* This is the Greek term ἡσυχία *(hesychia),* which the translation has rendered consistently as "spiritual tranquility." Ἡσυχία referred to the inner "quiet" that monks sought to achieve through solitude and prayer, a stillness not only of their bodily movements but of their thoughts and passions as well.

     a thought occurred to him: The term for "thought" is λογισμός *(logismos).* This was a technical term in monastic literature, which

usually referred to the sinful, passionate, or heretical thoughts that hindered the monk's ascetic practice and disturbed his spiritual tranquility. Such thoughts could arise either from the monk's own mind or from his demonic adversaries.

13.1 *Be of good courage . . . let your heart be strengthened and endure:* Psalms 26(27):14.

light and salt: This is an allusion to Matthew 5:13–14.

to be gladdened by the pain I have caused: See 2 Corinthians 2:2.

13.2 *his ascent toward God and deification:* With the appearance of the term *theosis* (deification), the hagiographer expresses the very heart of his purpose. The belief in the ultimate perfection of human nature and intimate union with God by virtue of the Incarnate Son is an extremely rich strain of patristic theology and a fundamental part of the thinking of the Fathers of both the Greek East and the Latin West. See *EEC* 1:242–43, under "Divinization," and *ODB* 3:2069–70, under "Theosis."

the zeal of Elijah: The prophet Elijah exhibited extraordinary courage in the face of his own people's apostasy and the evil machinations of the rulers of his day. See 3 Kings 18:1–19:18.

the perseverance of Elisha: Elisha, the successor to Elijah, fulfilled his office amid famine, war, drought, plague, and the labyrinthine politics of the Holy Land's multiple kingdoms. Notably, he often preferred a life of seclusion, becoming for Christians an archetypal monk. See 4 Kings 3:11–13:21.

13.3 *In this cave:* In fact, Neilos dug his own cave (see chap. 23.1) near the shrine to the archangel just mentioned, but close enough for the two to be considered the same location. See Giovanelli, *Vita di S. Nilo,* 140.

"Your Father who sees in secret will reward you openly": Matthew 6:4, 6.

"for I will only honor them that honor me": 1 Kings 2:30.

14.2 *not those deeds which demonstrate his great miracles or portents:* See Gregory of Nazianzos, *Or.* 8.1–2, PG 35:789D–92C. Not a direct citation; rather, a parallel is being drawn between the hagiographer and Neilos's theological mentor, who insists here on his preference for factual data about his subject rather than

more fantastic tales that can be easily dismissed and scorned. The hagiographer expressed similar concerns in chapter 1.

labors and toils . . . the apostle was made proud: This is an allusion to Paul's declaration of his labor among the Thessalonians in 1 Thessalonians 2:9.

burning desire for recollection: Gregory of Nazianzos, *Or.* 8.22, PG 35:813C.

15.1   *the law of the Spirit:* See Romans 8:2

until it was obedient and responsive to the nod of the One who governs: See Athanasios, *Contra Gentes,* 44.1, PG 25:88. The hagiographer uses the same language for Neilos's harmony with the will of God as Athanasios uses to describe God's governance of creation in all its details. This idea of perfect harmony among creature, creation, and Creator is a common feature of hagiographic literature.

15.3   *the third hour:* The Divine Office, which formed the rhythm of the monastic day, consisted of prayers based upon the Psalms and other biblical readings, along with prayers and litanies, that varied according to the liturgical calendar. The monks would have followed the cycle of *orthros*/matins (at daybreak), *prime* (approx. 6 A.M.), *terce* (approx. 9 A.M.), *sext* (midday), *none* (approx. 3 P.M.), vespers (at sunset), *apodeipnon*/compline (before bedtime), and *mesonyktikon*/nocturns (midnight). In the Constantinopolitan Rite, *terce* (the "third hour") is composed of two parts, each made up of Psalms 17 and 25 for the first part and Psalms 30, 32, and 61 for the second part, with invitatory, *troparia,* and final prayer.

he would rapidly copy manuscripts: The phrase ὀξέως καλλιγραφεῖν implies his copying in longhand, though with the rapidity of someone writing in shorthand.

his own minute and compact handwriting: Neilos used a small-lettered writing style with no spaces between letters, handwriting unlike that of other Italo-Greek scribes, who wrote in large and well-spaced letters; see Lucà, "Scrittura e libri della 'scuola niliana.'"

quire: A sheaf consisting of four folded sheets *(bifolia)* of parch-

ment, stacked on top of one another and folded in the middle, yielding sixteen pages, was the most common form of a quire; this was called a *tetradion* in Greek or a *quaternio* in Latin.

commandment that bids one occupy himself with work: This is a reference to Paul's command in 1 Thessalonians 4:11.

in the company of Mary and John: That is, Mary the Mother of Jesus, and John the Evangelist. This is an allusion to John 19:25–27, which describes Mary standing beside the cross along with the "beloved disciple."

the commandment exhorting us to pray constantly: This is a reference to Paul's command in 1 Thessalonians 5:17.

"Attend to the reading of scripture": 1 Timothy 4:13.

the service of the ninth hour: In Italo-Greek monasteries, the ninth hour of the day (the mid-afternoon prayer held around 3 P.M.) was immediately followed by vespers. See *ODB* 1:133, 2:947, 3:1539, and 3:2161–62, under "Apodeipnon," "Horologion," "Orthros," and "Vespers," respectively.

as incense: Psalms 140(141):2.

"Ever since the creation of the world . . . the things that have been made": Romans 1:20.

"We comprehend the Creator from His creations": Gregory of Nazianzos, *Or.* 43.11.2, PG 36:508C.

16.1   *many of the Theologian's orations:* That is, the orations of Gregory of Nazianzos. This remark is a reference to the quotation immediately above from Gregory's funeral oration for Basil of Caesarea.

wild acorns: The Greek term κεράτια usually means carob pods, but in this context it must mean acorns; see *LbG* under κεράτιον.

became as a wineskin in the frost: See Psalms 118(119):83. This probably means "shriveled up."

16.2   *forty days without food:* Some early ascetics were said to fast for periods of forty days, in imitation of Moses (Exodus 34:28), Elijah (3 Kings 19:8), and Christ (Matthew 4:2).

to crush . . . horn of conceit: See Methodios, *Encomium and vita of Theophanes,* ed. Demetrios Spyridonos, "Βίος τοῦ ὁσίου

πατρὸς ἡμῶν καὶ ὁμολογητοῦ Θεοφάνους. Ποίημα Μεθοδίου
πατριάρχου Κωνσταντινουπόλεως," Ἐκκλησιαστικὸς Φάρος
12 (1913): sec. 7, l. 56.

from the example of a pious woman in the Practical History of Theodoret: The hagiographer refers to the episode concerning Marana
of Berroia, who imitated biblical figures in her fasting habits.
See Theodoret of Cyrrhus, *Religiosa Historia seu Ascetica Vivendi
Ratio* 29, PG 82:1492BC.

16.3   *one of the four virtues, moderation:* The other three are typically
given as justice (δικαιοσύνη), courage (ἀνδρεία), and prudence
(φρόνησις). The set of four virtues derives ultimately from
Plato and was adopted in early Christian texts.

*he aspired to free his body from the natural flow ... the saints had also
tried to accomplish:* The author suggests that Neilos wished to
eliminate the nocturnal emission of semen. Early and medieval monks (both Greek and Latin) often saw nocturnal emission as a sign of imperfect chastity and sought, by restricting
their food and water intake, to "dry up" the excessive liquid
that caused emission of semen. See David Brakke, "The Problematization of Nocturnal Emissions in Early Christian Syria,
Egypt, and Gaul," *Journal of Early Christian Studies* 3 (1995):
419–60.

the avoidance of water ... profitable: This phrase occurs in Evagrios
of Pontos, *Praktikos* 17, *Traité pratique, ou, Le moine,* ed. Antoine
Guillaumont and Claire Guillaumont, vol. 2 (Paris, 1971), 542,
and is quoted in Mark the Hermit, *Opuscula V: Praecepta Salutaria,* 7, PG 65:1041A. Both Evagrios and Mark describe the
avoidance of water as helping the monk develop "moderation"
(sophrosyne), the virtue mentioned by the author earlier in the
paragraph; elsewhere, Evagrios suggests that restricting one's
drinking of water can lead to freedom from sexual lust (*To
Monks* 102, *Ad Monachos; Ad Virginem; Institutio ad Monachos =
Der Mönchsspiegel; Der Nonnenspiegel; Ermahnung an Mönche,* ed.
Christoph Joest [Freiburg, 2012], 202).

the monk who spent three years tending the oven: See John Moschos,
Pratum Spirituale 184, PG 87:3057BC.

17.1   *"My soul has cleaved . . . according to Your word"*: Psalms 118(119):25.

        "You have revived my breath, and I am comforted and live": Isaiah 38:16.

        "Thirst cures thirst . . . hunger": See John Klimax, *Scala Paradisi,* Logos 14, PG 88:868B.

        partaking of nothing else except the blessed bread: That is, the *antidoron,* or remains of the loaves from which the various portions are cut for consecration in the Divine Liturgy.

        daily bread: This is an allusion to the Lord's Prayer; the phrase "daily bread" occurs in both Matthew 6:11 and Luke 11:3.

17.2   *the singing of the midnight and matins hymns:* After the midnight office, cenobitic monks returned to their cells to rest until four o'clock in the morning, when they came back to the church for the *orthros,* or matins service. Neilos, although a solitary at the time, followed the canonical hours.

17.3   *But he fixed wax onto a wooden tablet and upon this he copied most of his books:* This is a puzzling statement since it is extremely unlikely that Neilos would have used wooden tablets to make copies of books (personal communication of October 28, 2016 from Prof. Santo Lucà). See chapter 15.3, where it is implied that Neilos is writing on parchment, since he produces one quire a day.

18.1   *image and likeness:* See Genesis 1:26.

18.2   *"I would rather die . . . my ground for boasting"*: 1 Corinthians 9:15.

19.2   *he went to Rome for the sake of prayer:* The founders of Grottaferrata, Neilos and Bartholomew, like other Italo-Greek holy men, regularly visited the tombs of the apostles Peter and Paul in Rome in the tenth and eleventh centuries. See Enrico Morini, "The Orient and Rome: Pilgrimages and Pious Visits between the Ninth and Eleventh Century," *Harvard Ukrainian Studies* 12–13 (1988–89): 849–69.

19.3   *the divine vision:* This vision was depicted by Domenico Zampieri (Domenichino) in a fresco commissioned by Cardinal Farnese in 1602. The fresco still adorns the founders' Farnesian Chapel in Grottaferrata.

20.1   *to employ pretexts for sin:* Psalms 140(141):4.

20.2   *insults his brother shall be liable to the hell of fire:* See Matthew 5:22 (the author has combined direct quotations of two parts of this verse).

God has called us . . . to peace: 1 Corinthians 7:15.

21.1   *obol:* A reference to a large bronze coin, more usually termed a *follis.* See *ODB* 2:794–95.

monastery of Kastellion: This is probably the town of Laino Castello bordering Merkourion. The hagiographer preferred to refer to the monastery with the same name as the town. See Giovanelli, *Vita di S. Nilo,* 145–46. It is unclear whether this monastery is the same as the one referred to in chapter 33.2 as the monastery of Kastellanos. Giovanelli considered Kastellion and Kastellanos to be two names for the same foundation, but, as Enrico Morini has argued, the textual evidence to confirm such a claim is lacking (Enrico Morini, "Eremo e cenobio nel monachesimo greco dell'Italia meridionale nei secoli IX e X," *Rivista di Storia della Chiesa in Italia* 31 [1977]: 358n149).

22.1   *his weekly allotment of bread:* Usually this meant three loaves of bread a week, with Neilos consuming half a loaf each day.

the labor of his own hands: That is, the books that Neilos copied.

22.2   *among those who fear God so that He would fulfill my desire:* See Psalms 144(145):19.

'You shall not covet': See Exodus 20:17 and Deuteronomy 5:21.

the Lord lives: Psalms 17(18):46.

22.3   *A monk who came from the upper region of the mountain:* The monks from the numerous monasteries in the mountainous region not far from Rossano were in frequent contact with Merkourion.

23.1   *the Devil appeared to him in the guise of an Ethiopian:* On this hagiographic trope, see the note on chapter 5.2.

23.2   *"Draw near, O God, to my help . . . that seek my soul":* See Psalms 69(70): 2–3.

23.3   *the feast day of the holy apostles:* The feast of the apostles Peter and Paul, celebrated on June 29.

the encomium for the apostles composed by Saint John of Damascus:

Probably a panegyric in prose adorned with iambics and metrical verses was read; canons were usually sung. Niccolò Balducci translates it as panegyric; see Balducci, *Vita di S. Nilo,* 51. John of Damascus (ca. 650–ca. 750) was an Arab Christian who lived his life under Muslim rule. A powerful advocate for the veneration of icons and master synthesizer of theological learning, which he saw as serving monastic life, his influence on Eastern and Western Christianity is substantial.

24.1   *I know not ... His servant:* The author seems to be referring to himself here.

24.2   *a state of ecstasy:* For more on Phantinos's state of ecstasy and living naked for four years in the mountains, see Enrica Follieri, *La vita di San Fantino il Giovane: Introduzione, testo greco, traduzione, commentario e indici* (Brussels, 1993), chaps. 27 and 28, pp. 430 and 432.

change ... most High: Psalms 76(77):10.

Jeremiah ... with lamentations: This is an allusion to Jeremiah 7:29. The Book of Lamentations was traditionally ascribed to this prophet.

the same thing also happened with regard to ... Phantinos: Phantinos exhibits some of the traits of a "holy fool." Such individuals typically comported themselves with such extreme humility as to seem "foolish"; however, their behavior also demonstrated a radical freedom from the conventions of this world. See *ODB* 2:795.

24.3   *I shall go to the upper land:* This must refer to Greece, where he died in Thessalonike circa 974.

25.1   *the narrow gate and along the hard way found by few:* See Matthew 7:14.

the monastery of the holy Phantinos: This is the monastery of Saint Zacharias at Merkourion; see *PmbZ* 2, no. 24763.

Loukas by name: Loukas would follow Neilos in his wanderings, until finally dying on November 20, 991, at the monastery of Valleloukion near Monte Cassino, where he was buried in the narthex of the monastery church. See *PmbZ* 2, no. 24763, and Giovanelli, *Vita di S. Nilo,* 149–50.

26.1   *the blessed Stephen:* Stephen of Rossano (ca. 920–ca. 1002) was the
        first among Neilos's disciples and was known for his simplicity
        and innocence. See *PmbZ* 2, no. 27257.

        also be marveled at for its holy fruit and branches: This is an allusion
        to Matthew 12:33–35; Luke 6:43–45.

26.2   *patriarch Jacob:* The Bible describes the young Jacob, son of
        Isaac, as "a simple man" (Genesis 25:27), not unlike the youthful
        Stephen. Moreover, Jacob would soon undergo twenty years of
        labor and patient discipline, often seemingly unfair (Genesis
        29:1–30, 31:38–41), so that the comparison here foreshadows
        the rigors Stephen will endure.

        Paul the Simple: A fourth-century Egyptian monk, Paul the Sim-
        ple was subjected by Anthony the Great to rigorous training,
        especially in the ways of humility, obedience, and faith, very
        similar to Stephen's training under Neilos. See Palladios, *Histo-
        ria Lausiaca* 28, PG 34:1076–84.

        Anthony: Anthony the Great, see note on chapter 2.2.

26.3   *in accordance with the Gospel loved Christ . . . more than himself:* This
        is a reference to Matthew 10:37.

27.1   *during the second year:* This would be around 945.

        the commandments of the Gospels: This is perhaps a reference to
        Matthew 5:22.

28.1   *potbreakers:* The Greek word *chytroklastes* is a neologism and
        likely a play on the word iconoclast.

28.4   *Theodora . . . the place called Arinarion:* Theodora was a tenth-
        century nun and abbess; see *PmbZ* 2, no. 27603. For her con-
        vent location at Arinarion, also known as Arienarium or Are-
        nario, see Kirsopp Lake, "The Greek Monasteries in Southern
        Italy," *Journal of Theological Studies* 4 (1902–3): 539–40.

29.1   *the godless Hagarenes . . . sacked everything:* This is probably a ref-
        erence to the incursion of Sicilian Arabs in 950/51; see Sister
        Maxime, Ὁ ὅσιος Νεῖλος ὁ Καλαβρός, 333n98.

29.3   *completely compassed me about, but . . . I repulsed them:* Psalms
        117(118):11.

30.1   *to lay down his life for his friend:* See John 15:12–13.

31.1   *as the great Basil says:* Monks were not to seek work or activity

beyond what was enjoined upon them for fear that doing so would allow personal willfulness and self-pleasing to take root. See Basil of Caesarea, *Regulae Brevius Tractatae,* 117–19, PG 31:1161B–64B.

32.1   *an old man named George:* George became the second follower of Neilos. See *PmbZ* 2, no. 22131.

   city's noble families: The Greek term for "city" is *kastron,* denoting a fortified city, but often meaning just "city." See *ODB* 2:1112.

   the city near which stands the house of the holy apostles: Rome, where the apostles Peter and Paul are buried in their respective basilicas.

   the entire sanctuary: The sanctuary *(bema)* is the area around the altar that was reserved for the clergy and choir in Byzantine churches.

   dressed in white like angels: In dream visions, angels customarily appear as eunuchs dressed in white.

33.2   *the monastery of Kastellanos:* On the possible identity of this foundation with the monastery of Kastellion, see the note on chapter 21.1.

34.2   *"How sweet are Your words . . . honey in my mouth":* Psalms 118(119):103.

34.3   *canons:* The canons are elaborate verse paraphrases of the biblical canticles that were chanted in the *orthros.* During the eighth century, the canons gradually replaced those canticles and the verse sermon *(kontakion)* sung in the service. See *ODB* 2:1102 and 2:1148, under "Kanon" and "Kontakion."

35.1   *the fortified city called Bisignano:* An important Byzantine city in the vicinity of Sant' Adriano, Rossano, and the Eparchy of Merkourion where Neilos and his brethren were living at that time.

   delivered him . . . to be crucified: See Matthew 27:26 and John 19:16.

35.2   *"the law that prescribes . . . the killing of seven Jews":* There is no evidence of such a law. Nino Tamassia, *Studi sulla storia giuridica dell'Italia meridionale* (Bari, 1957), 158–60, argues that in all probability Neilos's hagiographer referred to the Italo-

Byzantine custom that a Jew needed to present seven co-religionists in any case against a Christian.

36.1   *a small chapel in honor of Saint Adrianos:* Adrianos of Nikomedia was a martyr of the fourth century. The chapel mentioned here and the subsequent monastery were very near San Demetrio Corone, a town lying fourteen miles from Rossano across rugged terrain.

36.2   *poor in spirit, whom the Lord had invited to His supper:* This is an allusion to the parable in Matthew 22:2–14 and Luke 14:16–24; the phrase "poor in spirit" comes from Matthew 5:3.

      the wide way to the narrow one: See Matthew 7:13–14.

      for the sake of the kingdom of heaven: Matthew 19:12.

37.2   *keeping the words of David on his lips:* This is a reference to Psalms 119(120): 6–7: "My soul has long been a sojourner. I was peaceable among them that hated peace; when I spoke to them, they warred against me without a cause."

38.2   *distribute them to the poor:* Luke 18:22.

      a soul like that of Abraham: An allusion to Abraham's willingness to kill his son Isaac. See Genesis 22:1–13.

38.4   *"Why did you listen . . . against your will.":* Eating apart from the community at the established times was forbidden, although a superior could make allowances for brothers absent for legitimate reasons. The infraction, therefore, goes beyond the question of willfulness and implies a lack of trust in the superior's good judgment and goodwill. See Basil of Caesarea, *Regulae Brevius Tractatae,* 136, PG 31:1172CD.

39.1   *"What sort of monks . . . severe penance.":* In some male monasteries it was strictly prohibited for women to enter the church or *katholikon.*

40.1   *"You are not to be called rabbi, neither be called masters,":* Matthew 23:8, 10.

      Proklos: No *Life* of the monk Proklos survives, and this account is the only testimony to his life and deeds. See *PmbZ* 2, no. 26756.

40.2   *the city:* Probably Rossano, according to Sister Maxime (Ὁ ὅσιος Νεῖλος ὁ Καλαβρός, 338n123) and *PmbZ* (2, no. 26756).

40.3   *he mortified his earthly limbs:* See Colossians 3:5.

   in accordance with their toil: 1 Corinthians 3:8.

41.1   *a great earthquake struck Rossano:* The terrible earthquake that struck Rossano, accompanied by vast landslides reported by the hagiographer, probably occurred between 973 and 975.

   church of Saint Irene: This church in Rossano dedicated to the martyr Irene seems to be otherwise unknown.

41.2   *Others called him a Frank and yet others an Armenian:* The point seems to be that Neilos's disguise made him look like a foreigner.

   The custodian, who was called Kaniskas: The custodian *(prosmonarios)* was a steward of church property. He might or might not be a member of the ordained clergy. On the office of *prosmonarios,* see *ODB* 3:1739. For Kaniskas, who is otherwise unknown, see *PmbZ* 2, no. 23668.

42.1   *latrines:* For the translation of ὑπηρεσίοις as latrines, see Sister Maxime, Ὁ ὅσιος Νεῖλος ὁ Καλαβρός, 340n133.

42.2   *employed pretexts for his sins:* See Psalms 140(141):4.

43.1   *Render to Caesar . . . and to God the things that are God's:* Matthew 22:21.

43.2   *the Devil is afoot, seeking someone to devour:* See 1 Peter 5:8.

43.3   *pray not to enter into temptation:* See Matthew 26:41.

   'The angel of the Lord will encamp . . . and will deliver them': Psalms 33(34):7.

44.1   *With these words . . . to pray always:* The ideal of constant or unceasing prayer is expressed in several New Testament texts: Luke 18:1; 1 Thessalonians 5:17; Ephesians 6:18.

44.2   *Anthony:* For Anthony the Great see note on chapter 2.2.

   Arsenios: Arsenios the Great (ca. 350–ca. 445) was a Roman noble who had been tutor to the sons of Emperor Theodosios I (r. 379–395), before abandoning everything to lead an ascetic life in Egypt. See *EEC* 1:83, and *ODB* 1:187–88.

   John Kolobos: John Kolobos (ca. 339–409) lived an ascetic life in the Egyptian desert, both in a monastery and as a hermit.

   "Let no one seek his own good . . . may be saved": 1 Corinthians 10:24, 33.

45.1   *until the third hour:* That is, until about nine o'clock in the morning.

45.2   *the Holy Mountain of Athos and Sicily:* The promontory of Mount Athos in northern Greece became a center of monasticism in the Byzantine period, attracting both numerous hermits (from the ninth century on) and cenobitic monks (from the tenth century on). For more information, see the recent DOML volume, *Holy Men of Mount Athos,* ed. and trans. Richard Greenfield and Alice-Mary Talbot (Cambridge, Mass., 2016). Before the Muslim conquest, Sicily was the center of Greek-speaking monasticism in the central Mediterranean, with close ties to Calabrian monasticism. While the ecclesiastical and monastic infrastructure in most parts of Sicily suffered near total collapse under Muslim rule, communication between the island, including its Christian population, and Calabria remained unbroken.

45.3   *their long and intensive fast and abstinence:* A reference to the strict forty-day Lenten fast of the Eastern Church.

         all my desire is before You: Psalms 37(38):9.

         "You are my portion, Lord, and my desired inheritance": Although the first part of this phrase is based on Psalms 118(119):57, the whole verse comes from a *troparion* in Ode 4 of the Tone 3 Canon to the Theotokos for Sunday Orthros. See Παρακλητικὴ ἤτοι ὀκτώηχος ἡ μεγάλη (Rome, 1885), 195 (Μερίς μου εἶ ὁ Κύριος) and 282 (Μερίς μου εἶ Κύριε, as a model melody). We thank Daniel Galadza for his assistance with this note.

46.1   *Saint Anastasia:* Anastasia was martyred in the fourth century at Sirmium in Pannonia; her cult spread to Constantinople and then to Rome. The church mentioned here is no longer extant. See *EEC* 1:35.

         Eupraxios, who was imperial judge: See *PmbZ* 2, no. 21807, and chapter 53.1.

         a monk named Anthony: The monk Anthony is also mentioned in chapter 53.1. See *PmbZ* 2, no. 20495.

47.1   *the metropolitan of Calabria, Theophylaktos:* Theophylaktos, archbishop of Reggio from 959 to 980, also held the title of metro-

politan of Calabria. There were two metropolitan sees in Calabria at that time, Reggio and Saint Severina. See *PmbZ* 2, no. 28225.

the domestikos Leo: The title *domestikos* pertained to a wide range of Byzantine civil, ecclesiastical, and military dignitaries over the course of Byzantine history, but here most probably refers to a military official. See *ODB* 1:646, and *PmbZ* 2, no. 24420.

the church of the desert-loving John the Baptist: The church is in one of the monasteries in the territory of Rossano. See Giovanelli, *Vita di S. Nilo,* 162n123.

47.3   *Saint Symeon of the Wondrous Mountain:* Symeon Stylites the Younger (521–597) practiced one of the most extreme forms of anchoritic life on a mountain near Antioch, dwelling atop a pillar for nearly seventy years. See *ODB* 3:1946–47.

"From the thousands . . . in the hands of the holy angels": Symeon Stylites the Younger, Logos 22, ed. Giuseppe Cozza-Luzi, *Novae Patrum Bibliothecae,* vol. 8 (Rome, 1871), part 3, p. 112. It is most likely that the book in which Neilos found this passage from Symeon was a florilegium of monastic literature.

47.4   *Chrysostom:* John Chrysostom (ca. 349–407), priest of Antioch and bishop of Constantinople, was a devoted practitioner of the ascetic life who preached tirelessly for Christians to transform their world rather than be transformed by it. He was also one of the most revered patristic authors.

the most holy Ephraim: Ephraim (ca. 307–ca. 373) was the greatest composer of hymns and poetry in early Christianity. Whether or not he truly was the great ascetic he was held to be in Neilos's time, his writings hold in high regard central aspects of monasticism, such as celibacy and community life.

Theodore the Stoudite: Theodore the Stoudite (759–826), so-called from the Stoudios monastery in Constantinople, which he directed, was a strenuous opponent of iconoclasm and of the emperors' laxity in marital practice.

even the holy Gospel: The New Testament contains numerous warnings against spiritual complacency and carelessly following "another Gospel" (see Matthew 3:9, 8:11–12, 22:14, 25:41–46;

Luke 3:8, 13:23–30, 14:24; John 8:39–40; 1 Corinthians 10:1–12; 2 Corinthians 11:4, 13:5; Galatians 1:8). Key to the narrative, however, is that this scene shows how Neilos is becoming an *alter Christus,* who likewise was presented with questions to trip Him up (see Matthew 19:3, 22:15; Luke 10:25). The questions posed to Neilos concern obscure scriptural passages and mimic the types of questions and answers recorded in monastic literature. Compare the questions on scripture and monastic practice posed to Neilos by the monks of Monte Cassino in chapters 74.2–77.3.

resist the Holy Spirit: See Acts 7:51.

48.1   *Nicholas the protospatharios: Protospatharios* was a dignity of the imperial hierarchy, which usually conferred membership in the senate. In this period, the office was fundamentally one of military command. Like the *domestikos,* it was a position of influence at court. See *PmbZ* 2, no. 25955, and *ODB* 3:1748.

'Whoever gives . . . shall not lose his reward': Matthew 10:42.

48.2   *'Everyone who looks . . . has already committed adultery with her':* See Matthew 5:28.

'If anyone destroys God's temple, God will destroy him.': 1 Corinthians 3:17.

With regard to Solomon . . . repented after his sin: Because of his many foreign wives, Solomon permitted the worship of other gods in his realm, in contrast to his father, David, resulting in a turbulent end to his reign and leading to the division of the tribes of Israel into the rival Kingdoms of Israel and Judah. See 3 Kings 11:1–42.

as is found for Manasses: Manasses, king of Judah, was also guilty of promoting idolatry in the Kingdom of Judah. However, unlike Solomon, he repented and ended his reign in divine favor. See 2 Chronicles 33:11–20.

48.3   *"Holy father, what was the tree . . . was condemned?":* This is a reference to Genesis 3:6.

49.1   *'How will an unfamiliar woman . . . his own wife has destroyed?':* Gregory of Nazianzos, *Or.* 44.6, PG 36:613B. Gregory's oration was delivered on "New Sunday," that is, the Sunday that fol-

lows Easter. He uses the opportunity to call for a renewal of all things in light of the Paschal mystery; the specific text cited here refers to Adam's yielding to Eve. Neilos's interpretation of it as a general teaching about women is a quite unsupportable stretch.

'Wife, how do you know whether you will save your husband?': 1 Corinthians 7:16.

If that woman who came from the flesh of Adam: This is a reference to Genesis 2:22–23.

49.2   *'What God has joined together, let not man put asunder':* Matthew 19:6.

is not worthy of me: Matthew 10:37.

'Because of the temptation . . . each man should have his own wife': 1 Corinthians 7:2.

marveling at the blessed man's virtue and wisdom: This question-and-answer exchange about the permanence of marriage and the demand of the call to follow Christ apart from family may well shed important light upon the nature of Neilos's own marriage, which he was permitted to dissolve. See chapters 3.1 and 4.3.

50.1   *a Jew by the name of Domnoulos:* Shabbetai ben Abraham, called Domnoulos in Greek, was born in 913 in Oria, one of the most important cities of Byzantine Apulia, and died after 982, possibly in Rome. He was a renowned Jewish scholar and author of *The Book of Remedies,* a physician, and a theologian. See *PmbZ* 2, no. 26949. For more see Francesca Lagana Luzzati, "La figura di Donnolo nello specchio della Vita di S. Nilo di Rossano," in *Sabbetay Donnolo: scienza e cultura ebraica nell' Italia del secolo X,* ed. Giancarlo Lacerenza (Naples, 2004), 69–103.

very learned in the law: Probably a reference to his knowledge of the Torah.

50.2   *'It is better to trust in the Lord, than to trust in man.':* Psalms 117(118):8.

51.1   *take your prophets along with the law:* A reference to the Pentateuch and prophetic books of the Old Testament.

'Be still and know that I am God.': Psalms 45(46):10.

51.2 *'Many of the authorities believed in Jesus . . . praise of God.'*: See John 12:42–43. The Gospel text shows the cause of tension to be "the Pharisees" and not "the Jews," as the hagiographer has Neilos render the verse.

53.1 *appropriated the property of Anthony:* For the story of Anthony, see chapter 46.1.

53.2 *appointed judge of both Italy and Calabria by the emperors:* A Byzantine bureaucrat (*PmbZ* 2, no. 21807), Eupraxios was named judge in 968 (Giovanelli, *Vita di S. Nilo,* 167n145). His appointment was related to the reform of the civil and military administration of the Byzantine territories in Italy by Emperor Nikephoros II Phokas (r. 963–969; *PmbZ* 2, no. 25535). Eupraxios continued at his post into the reign of John I Tzimiskes (r. 969–976; *PmbZ* 2, no. 22778). It is not clear whether the phrase "by the emperors" refers to Nikephoros II and John I, or to Basil II and Constantine VIII, who had been proclaimed nominal co-emperors in the early 960s. Subsequently in the vita (chaps. 60.1, 65.3, and 72.3), the text always uses "emperors" in the plural to refer to the co-emperors Constantine and Basil.

   in princes . . . the children of men in whom there is no safety: Psalms 145(146):3.

53.3 *track of a serpent on a rock:* See Proverbs 30:19.

54.1 *the prayer of the venerable father anticipated it:* This refers back to Neilos's prayer for Eupraxios's spiritual salvation at the end of chapter 53.2. In chapter 56 we learn that Eupraxios asks forgiveness, is tonsured as a monk, immediately recovers from his affliction, and dies three days later, repentant and with hope in his salvation.

54.3 *prostitute . . . asking forgiveness for her transgressions:* This is an allusion to Luke 7:36–50.

55.3 *this blessed baptism:* Monastic tonsure was viewed as a second baptism.

   like the youth of the eagle: Psalms 102(103):5.

55.4 *at that time the metropolitan of Saint Severina was there:* The ecclesiastical district of Saint Severina was elevated to a diocese and metropolis for chiefly political—rather than religious—rea-

sons under Emperor Leo VI (r. 886–912; *PmbZ* 2, no. 24311), following the conquests of his general Nikephoros Phokas (*PmbZ* 2, no. 25545) in Italy; see Francesco Russo, "La metropolia di S. Severina," *Archivio storico per la Calabria e la Lucania* 16 (1947): 1–20.

56.1   *the bishop of the city of Rossano:* The hagiographer does not name the bishop of Rossano, though he appears in the narrative once more (see chap. 68.1). The records for the episcopate of Rossano are incomplete for this period, so it is difficult to determine his identity.

    Daniel taming the lions: This is an allusion to Daniel 6:6–28.

56.3   *"I do not desire the death of the sinner . . . live forever.":* See Ezekiel 18:23, 32; 33:11.

57.1   *the monastery of the holy virgin Anastasia:* For the convent of Saint Anastasia, see note on chapter 46.1.

    "Flee to the mountains as a sparrow . . . the upright in heart.": Psalms 10(11):2–3.

58.1   *devoted themselves to prayer and to the ministry of the word:* See Acts 6:4.

    a military officer named Polyeuktos: Polyeuktos (*PmbZ* 2, no. 26713) held the rank of *stratelates,* a title whose origin lies in the Greek translation for the late Roman *magister militum.* The importance of the rank varied over time. Polyeuktos himself was probably a lower-ranking officer. See *ODB* 3:1965.

    the region of Mesoubianon in Calabria: It corresponds to Mesiano, which was a flourishing city at the time of Neilos and a vicariate of the diocese of Mileto.

58.4   *a brother who was invested with the priestly rank:* That is, a hieromonk. In the Italo-Greek monasteries of Calabria, as elsewhere in the Christian East, most monks were not ordained.

59.1   *the young man was immediately healed:* This episode of miraculous healing is depicted by Domenichino in the founders' chapel at Grottaferrata. Miraculous healings in Byzantium were often effected by oil from an icon lamp or the lamp hanging over a saint's tomb.

59.2   *as the blessed father appeared before their very eyes:* An ability rarely found among holy men, the gift of bilocation—that is, the ability to appear suddenly in distant locations—was attributed to Neilos. See Giovanelli, *Vita di S. Nilo,* 176n156.

as the lion is recognized by his claws: A Greek proverb. See, for example, Diogenes, V.15, *CPG* 1:252.

60.1   *magistros Nikephoros . . . the governor of both Italy and our Calabria:* Nikephoros Hexakionites (*PmbZ* 2, no. 25608) was in charge of the two administrative provinces of Longobardia and Calabria in southern Italy. He received this distinction from John I Tzimiskes and continued in the position into the reign of Basil II (r. 976–1025; *PmbZ* 2, no. 20838). It was against Basil II that the people of Rossano rebelled. Before his Italian assignment, Nikephoros was *anthypatos,* patrician, and *strategos* of Thessalonike. The high-ranking dignity of *magistros,* which he received, was conferred only rarely in this period. See *ODB* 2:1267.

60.2   *the so-called chelandia:* Also referred to as *dromones, skelandria,* or *salandria.* The term *chelandia* was sometimes used synonymously with *dromones* to refer to oar-and sail-powered warships of varying sizes and speeds, but other sources indicate that *chelandion* generally meant a transport ship. Here it seems to refer to warships. See *ODB* 1:417–18 and 662. For more on *dromones,* see John H. Pryor and Elizabeth M. Jeffreys, *The Age of the Dromon: The Byzantine Navy ca. 500–1204* (Leiden, 2006), 188–203.

bring destruction to their hostile neighbor Sicily: Since Sicily was the springboard for the Arab incursions afflicting Calabria, the frustration of the *magistros* with the opposition at Rossano, even had it been without intense violence, might be understandable.

61.4   *the collection of the penalty:* This was for the murder of the captains and damage to the ships.

62.1   *the man serving as praktor . . . Gregory, surnamed Maleinos:* Little beyond this episode is known about Gregory (*PmbZ* 2, no. 22426);

the Maleinos family, however, was one of great wealth and influence in the empire, serving in both civil and ecclesiastical positions; see *ODB* 2:1276. The *praktor* was a tax collector and property assessor of the Byzantine state; see *ODB* 3:1711–12.

62.3   *the one truly worthy of the blessedness of the peacemakers:* This is an allusion to Matthew 5:9.

       giving his prayers to God: See Psalms 49(50):14.

       to associate with workers of lawlessness: See Psalms 58 (59):2 and 140 (141):4.

63.1   *"Deliver them . . . that are appointed to be slain":* Proverbs 24:11.

63.2   *a small book, an anthology of the New Testament:* The reference is to a so-called gospel amulet, containing excerpts from the New Testament. It could take the form of a miniature booklet on a tightly rolled scroll. See Thomas J. Kraus, "Miniature Codices in Late Antiquity: Preliminary Remarks and Tendencies about a Specific Book Format," *Early Christianity* 7 (2016): 134–52. We thank Ivan Drpić for his assistance with this note.

       into Your hands I commit my spirit: See Psalms 30(31):5 and Luke 23:46.

63.3   *in his mouth . . . sweet as honey:* Ezekiel 3:3. While the wording follows that in Ezekiel 3:3, this is a conflation of several biblical episodes: (1) the prophet Elijah being strengthened by the angel's food when he had given up on his life (see 3 Kings 19:4–8), and (2) the prophet Ezekiel (see Ezekiel 3:1–4) and the seer John (see Revelation 10:9–10), who were each given a scroll to consume that was sweet as honey.

       'When he falls . . . pleasure in his way.': See Psalms 36(37):23–24.

64.1   *they shall eat . . . hands:* See Psalms 127(128): 2.

       do not participate in another man's sins: See 1 Timothy 5:22.

       since I have nothing and yet possess everything: See 2 Corinthians 6:10.

64.2   *The koitonites, who was a eunuch:* The *koitonites* was a courtier who served within the imperial bedchamber and thus had some responsibility for the emperor's safety. See *ODB* 2:1137.

64.3   *This man is an independent being, like the unicorn:* The comparison of Neilos to the unicorn is another indication of his assump-

tion of a Christ-like stature. In medieval lore, the mythical creature, which could not be trapped by any hunter, was identified with Christ, who could not be caught by any temptation.

65.2 *'I say to you, Do not swear at all . . . from the Evil One.':* Matthew 5:34, 37.

65.3 *the holy emperors:* That is, the co-emperors Basil II and his younger brother Constantine VIII. For Constantine VIII, see *PmbZ* 2, no. 23735.

66.1 *'The kingdom of heaven . . . buys that field.':* Matthew 13:44.

66.2 *hard way:* This is an allusion to Matthew 7:14.
poor in spirit: This is an allusion to Matthew 5:3.
Arsenios: This is a reference to Arsenios the Great. See chapter 44.2.
'Mine is the gold and the silver': Haggai 2:9.
'Whoever does not renounce . . . be my disciple': Luke 14:33.

67.1 *"In the very way wherein I was walking they hid a snare for me":* Psalms 141(142):4.
in accordance with the proverb: This is an allusion to Proverbs 4:14, *"The path of the wicked enter not . . ."*
two are better than one: Ecclesiastes 4:9.
"Woe to him . . . no one to lift him up": See Ecclesiastes 4:10.

67.2 *against the temptation of making bread out of stones:* This is an allusion to Matthew 4:3 and Luke 4:3.
man falls down and worships the Tempter: This is an allusion to Matthew 4:9.
the pinnacle of the temple: This is an allusion to Matthew 4:5 and Luke 4:9.

68.2 *"Perceiving that they were about to come . . . withdrew to the mountain by Himself":* John 6:15.

68.3 *"You took hold of my right hand . . . upon the earth beside You?":* Psalms 72(73):23–25.
"All my desire is before You, Lord": Psalms 37(38):10.
"You know that I have not desired the day of man": Jeremiah 17:16.
over ten cities: Luke 19:17. The term "talent" comes from the version of the same parable in Matthew 25:15–28.

69.1 *the metropolitan Blatton:* Blatton of Otranto, who became the

first archbishop of that city in 968. Hoping to secure peace with the Arab rulers of North Africa by various means, which included offering his sister in marriage to the Fatimid caliph Al-Muʿizz (r. 953–975), he returned from Africa with freed Christian prisoners in 970/71. Neilos's warnings against the venture went unheeded, and the unfortunate archbishop met the fate prophesied by the saint. See *PmbZ* 2, no. 21184.

for at that time the king of the Saracens: This is Al-Muʿizz (r. 953–975), the fourth Fatimid caliph of North Africa, who in 969 extended his rule to Egypt, where he reigned at Cairo until his death. See *PmbZ* 2, no. 25444.

69.2   *brood of vipers:* Matthew 3:7.

70.2   *"It is not right to punish a righteous man":* Proverbs 17:26

"Let the thief no longer steal . . . give to those in need.": See Ephesians 4:28.

70.3   *the work of darkness:* This is an allusion to Romans 13:12.

71.1   *At that time, when the godless Hagarenes invaded . . . Calabria:* Around 976 Calabria was subjected to Arab raids carried out under the Emir of Sicily Abūʾl-Qāsim ʿAlī b. al-Ḥasan al-Kalbī (r. 975–982; see *PmbZ* 2, no. 20072).

who remained in the monastery, following their own individual regimen: This may be an allusion to idiorrhythmic monasticism, a more individualized form of ascetic life. In this period, it tended to be viewed negatively in Byzantine sources on account of its inevitable weakening of the communal bonds of cenobitic life. See *ODB* 2:981–82.

Basil, the strategos of Calabria: The eunuch Basil Lekapenos (see *PmbZ* 2, no. 20977) was the indispensable confidant of Emperor Nikephoros II Phokas in political and military matters; he was made *strategos* of Calabria in 970.

71.2   *This notary . . . translated that wonderful letter for the emir:* The emir is Abūʾl-Qāsim (see chapter 71 above). Like other Muslim rulers of Sicily, Abūʾl-Qāsim employed Christian court officials and secretaries (often called *kuttāb,* sing. *kātib*) due to their multiple linguistic competences.

coins paid in ransom: The Greek term is *tarion,* the name given in

southern Italy and Sicily to the Muslim gold quarter dinar. See *ODB* 3:2012.

71.3   *meat came forth:* See Judges 14:14.

"All these things I will give to you, if you will fall down and worship me.": Matthew 4:9.

72.1   *as the centurion had for the Savior:* This is an allusion to Luke 7:1–10.

For when we conquered Crete with the most blessed Nikephoros who was not yet emperor: After almost 140 years of domination by an Arab dynasty of Spanish origin, Crete was reconquered in the spring of 961 in a campaign led by Nikephoros Phokas, a victory that set him on the path to the imperial throne.

camel's hair: Matthew 3:4. The garment's bloodied neck is a reference to the beheading of John the Baptist under Herod (Matthew 14:10).

72.2   *"Then allow me at least to enlarge and beautify the chapel":* This is the chapel at the monastery of Saint Adrian, in the province of Cosenza, where Neilos established his first monastery and stayed for twenty-five years; see Minasi, *S. Nilo di Calabria,* n. 16, pp. 299–302.

72.3   *refused to leave for the east:* That is, to Constantinople, where he had been invited to go by the *koitonites.* See chapter 65.3.

our Christ-loving emperors: This is a reference to Basil II and Constantine VIII; see note on chapter 65.3.

73.1   *prince Pandulf:* Pandulf I (d. 981), surnamed Ironhead, was a Lombard ruler whom Otto I made Prince of Capua and Benevento in 961. He was also Duke of Spoleto (966/67–981), Camerino, and Salerno (977–981). Neilos arrived in this territory around 980. See *PmbZ* 2, no. 26228.

the abbot of the monastery of Saint Benedict of Monte Cassino: The monastery of Saint Benedict of Monte Cassino was founded circa 529 by Benedict of Nursia (480–ca. 550), an enormously influential figure in early monasticism. Aligernus was the twenty-seventh abbot of Monte Cassino, a position he held from 948 to 985. It was Aligernus who led the permanent return of the Benedictines to Monte Cassino after their long ab-

sence in the wake of the abbey's destruction by the Arabs in 883, earning him remembrance as the Benedictine order's third founder (after the reformer Benedict of Aniane, circa 745/50– 821). Aligernus also undertook an internal reform of the community's life, the results of which were much admired by Neilos. See *PmbZ* 2, no. 20258.

73.2   *The holy man then journeyed to see the . . . monastery:* That is, Monte Cassino. For more on the visit of Neilos to Monte Cassino, see Sansterre, "Saint Nil de Rossano et le monachisme latin," 339– 86; and Rousseau, "La visite de Nil de Rossano au Mont-Cassin," 1118.

73.3   *just as once among the Israelites manna was transformed . . . temperament and appetite:* This is an allusion to the divine feeding of the Israelites in Exodus 16:4–36; the description of the manna as suiting each one's temperament and appetite reflects Wisdom 16:20 and Psalms 77(78):29 and 104(105):40.

    there was not a feeble one among their tribes: Psalms 104(105):37.

73.4   *the so-called Valleloukion:* The monastery's name was derived from its geographical location in a valley full of light (Valleluce). The monastery was founded probably by the end of the eighth century by Abbot Gisulf (abbot from 796 to 817). It was located approximately six miles north of Monte Cassino.

    the great monastery: That is, the monastery of Monte Cassino.

    so that . . . God would be everything to everyone: 1 Corinthians 15:28; see also Colossians 3:11.

    "the lion and the ox . . . their young shall be together.": See Isaiah 11:7 and 65:25.

74.1   *"How should we sing the Lord's song in a strange land":* Psalms 136(137):4.

    from the fruits of his lips: Proverbs 18:20.

    a hymn of praise for our blessed father Benedict: The hymn, which is still used at Grottaferrata, was based on Gregory the Great's *Dialogues,* II, which contains the most extensive biographical information on Benedict. For an edition of the hymn, see Sofronio Gassisi, *Poesie di San Nilo Iuniore e di Paolo Monaco, abbati di Grottaferrata* (Rome, 1906), 12–14.

74.2   *in the Roman tongue:* That is, in Latin.

         in his spiritual father: That is, the superior.

         Yet in your case . . . belong to salvation: See Hebrews 6:9.

75.1   *'With the holy . . . You will pervert':* Psalms 17(18):26–27.

         'You will save the lowly people and will humble the eyes of the proud.':
         Psalms 17(18): 27.

         'I your Lord live . . . I shall rightly journey with you.': We cannot lo-
         cate this quotation in the Psalms.

         'sends crooked ways': Proverbs 21:8.

         to love your enemy and to do well to those who hate: See Matthew
         5:44.

         not to repay evil for evil: See Romans 12:17.

75.2   *'I will rest . . . from going up to the people of my sojourning':* Habak-
         kuk 3:16.

         'all these things happened to them . . . for our instruction': See 1 Corin-
         thians 10:11.

         For when I hear about Adam, Cain, Lamech: This is an allusion to
         Genesis 3:6–19; 4:8, 23.

         'I watched . . . the prayer from my lips': See Habakkuk 3:16.

         'If I have requited with evil those who requited me with good': Psalms
         7:4.

         'Judge me, Lord . . . according to my innocence': Psalms 7:9.

         'God shall come manifestly . . . a fire shall be kindled before Him':
         Psalms 49(50):2–3.

         'and burn up His enemies round about': Psalms 96(97):3.

75.3   *On this day of my affliction:* See Habakkuk 3:16.

         strangers and exiles: Hebrews 11:13.

         commonwealth is in heaven: Philippians 3:20.

         They have nothing . . . and yet possess everything: 2 Corinthians 6:10.

         Wherefore my fig tree, . . . in God, my Savior: See Habakkuk 3:16–
         18.

76.1   *'Obey your superiors and submit to them . . . have to give an account.':*
         Hebrews 13:17.

77.1   *the Sabbath fast:* Fasting on Saturdays was an early tradition of
         the Church in Rome that spread gradually in the Latin-
         speaking world. It appeared as a novelty in fourth-century

North Africa, as Augustine attests in *Epistulae* 36.13.31, and 82.14, *CSEL* 34, pp. 60–61, 363–64. Byzantine canons, however, banned Sabbath fasting, and the Quinisext Council held under Justinian II in 692 explicitly condemned the Roman practice of fasting on Saturdays during Lent. The author thus presents Neilos as speaking to Latin monks about a divergence in Greek and Latin ascetic practice. For further reading on Neilos's exchange with the monks of Monte Cassino on fasting, see Sansterre, "Saint Nil de Rossano et le monachisme latin," 361–63.

'Let not him who eats despise him who abstains . . . for God has welcomed both': Romans 14:3.

'Why do you pass judgment on your brother?': Romans 14:10.

77.2   *Athanasios:* Athanasios of Alexandria (ca. 295–373) endured five exiles from his see rather than compromise the Nicene faith, thus becoming the supreme champion of orthodoxy in the early Church. Moreover, the *Life of Saint Anthony,* attributed to him, contributed incalculably to the spread of the monastic ideal in the fourth century.

Athanasios, Basil, Gregory, John Chrysostom: Athanasios, Basil of Caesarea, Gregory of Nazianzos, and John Chrysostom were considered great Fathers of the Eastern Church in its formative period; all of them were major proponents of asceticism and monasticism.

Ambrose, your teacher: Ambrose (ca. 340–397), bishop of Milan, was one of the last of the Latin Fathers fluent in Greek and was deeply influenced by the theology of the Cappadocians Basil and Gregory of Nazianzos. He was venerated in the Christian East to a degree uncommon for a Westerner.

it is written in his Life that he fasted the whole week, except for Saturday and Sunday: See Paulinus, *Vita Sancti Ambrosii* 38, PL 14:42CD.

the holy Sylvester: Sylvester I was bishop of Rome from 314 to 335 during one of the most decisive periods for Christianity, but little is known about him. As the hagiographer notes, his *Vita* was viewed with suspicion.

'Food will not commend us to God': 1 Corinthians 8:8.

77.3   *how did Saint Benedict . . . not know when it was Easter:* This is an allusion to the account in Gregory the Great's *Dialogues* II.I (PL 66:130B), in which a priest brings food to Benedict while he has been fasting in solitude, unaware that it is Easter Sunday. Gregory's Latin *Dialogues* was introduced to Byzantine Christians through a translation attributed to Pope Zacharias (pope from 741–752; *PmbZ* 1, no. 8614), a Greek-speaking native of Calabria.

    as Phineas and Samuel demonstrated: Phineas checked the plague afflicting the Israelites by slaying the unnamed Israelite man and Midianite woman who had submitted to the rites of Baal of Peor; see Numbers 25:7–8. Samuel the prophet slew Agag, the king of Amalek, for his cruelty, which "has made women childless"; see 1 Kings 15:33.

    Manicheans: Followers of Manicheism, a form of religious dualism founded by the Persian Mani in the latter half of the third century.

    the holy day of the resurrection: That is, Sunday. Neilos's position on fasting falls in line with the teachings of the Fathers mentioned above who saw ascetic works as subordinated to the building up of charity and community; these works are means, not ends in themselves. See Basil of Caesarea, *Regulae Brevius Tractatae* 129–40, PG 31:1169–76.

78.1   *His speech was always gracious, seasoned with salt:* See Colossians 4:6.

    his yoke was good: This is an allusion to Matthew 11:30.

79.2   *his wife named Abara:* Also known as Aloara of Capua (*PmbZ* 2, no. 20261), the regent of Benevento, Abara began to reign in 982, one year after her husband's death. For Pandulf see chapter 73.1.

    she induced her two remaining sons: These were Landonulph (*PmbZ* 2, no. 24271) and Laidulph (*PmbZ* 2, no. 24263).

79.3   *fiery sword:* See Genesis 3:24.

    fruits of righteousness: Philippians 1:11.

80.1   *the authority to bind and to loose:* This is an allusion to Matthew 16:19.

80.2   *'I will require the life of man . . . instead of that blood shall his own be shed':* Genesis 9:5–6.

        'All who take the sword will perish by the sword.': See Matthew 26:52.

        who, as the result of a command . . . hand over their own children to death: Jephthah rashly vowed that if he were granted victory over the Ammonites he would offer as a burned sacrifice whoever should first come out of his house. His daughter would fall victim to that vow. See Judges 11:29–40. Saul swore death to anyone in his army who ate before the king had carried out his wrath against the Philistines, not realizing that his own son Jonathan would break his command by eating a drop of honey. Saul insisted that Jonathan must die that day according to his oath; however, the army's intervention prevented this from taking place, and Jonathan ultimately died as divine punishment for Saul's failure to exact God's wrath upon the king of Amalek. See 1 Kings 14:23–45 and 28:17–19.

81.1   *the Lord makes poor and makes rich; He brings low and lifts up:* 1 Kings 2:7.

81.2   *passionless:* The author presents Neilos as having attained the monastic ideal of *apatheia,* or "freedom from the passions." Generally, monks did not conceive of *apatheia* as entailing the elimination of emotions and affects; rather, the passionless monk was one who was no longer disturbed by spiritually harmful thoughts and emotions, because he had oriented the passionate aspects of his self toward love of God and hatred of sin.

        "Be wise as serpents and innocent as doves": Matthew 10:16.

        "Do not participate in another man's sins.": 1 Timothy 5:22.

81.3   *On account of this murder . . . the ruler of the Franks:* Landonulph was murdered in the church of Saint Marcellus at Capua on Thursday of Easter week in 993, with the complicity of his brother Laidulph. Laidulph was eventually taken prisoner and exiled to Germany in 999 by "the ruler of the Franks," Emperor Otto III (r. 996–1002; *PmbZ* 2, no. 26213). See also *ODB* 3:1542, under "Otto III."

82.2   *he was grief-stricken:* I.e., the elder.

83.1   *a Lombard:* A Lombard was a member of a west Germanic tribe

that invaded Italy in the sixth century; they held much of southern Italy by the late seventh century and established an independent principality after 774. In the ninth century they held the principalities of Salerno and Capua. Lombard regions in Italy developed important cultural and economic ties with Byzantium, while retaining political independence. Lombard rule in Italy ended with the Norman conquest of the peninsula in the eleventh century. See *ODB* 2:1249.

83.2   *a single chapter of the Gerontikon:* A *Gerontikon* (literally, a "book of the elders") was a collection of anecdotes and sayings drawn from the experiences of men and women who practiced asceticism in the Egyptian desert in the fourth century. Such collections, known also as *Apophthegmata Patrum,* were compiled in the fifth and sixth centuries. Widely diffused in multiple languages, they were a practical reference guide for monks throughout Christendom. The principal alphabetic anthology became perhaps the single most influential text in the formation of Christian monasticism. See *EEC* 1:60–61, and *ODB* 1:139.

    to love your enemies . . . who have done you harm: See Luke 6:27–28.

    to possess everything and yet have nothing: See 2 Corinthians 6:10.

84.1   *"You are the light and the salt of the earth.":* See Matthew 5:13–14.

    a troparion from the canons: The *troparion* was a set of stanzas inserted into the psalms sung at *orthros* and vespers. See *ODB* 3:2124. On the canons, see the note on chapter 34.3.

    the epistle of the apostle James: See James 1:19, 26; 3:1–12; 4:1–12.

84.2   *the deaf to hear, the blind to see:* See Matthew 11:5.

85.1   *a superior was installed:* Abbot Manso led Monte Cassino from 986 to 996. He was a relative of the Lombard prince of Capua, Pandulf the Ironhead, whose widow Abara (see chaps. 79.2–81.3) was instrumental in Manso's selection. His tenure marked a retreat from his predecessor's reforms, and, tellingly, his name is not mentioned in Neilos's *Life.* See *PmbZ* 2, no. 24862.

85.2   *in honor of the most holy Germanus:* Germanus was a sixth-century bishop of Capua.

    a musician had entered the refectory playing a lute: Both David Hester (*Monasticism and Spirituality,* 217) and Herbert Bloch (*Monte-*

cassino in the Middle Ages [Cambridge, Mass., 1986], 1:11) interpret the Greek term *kitharizo* (play the lyre) to mean playing a
lute. Neilos objected to the musician both because he was pre-
sumably playing nonliturgical music and because instruments
played no part in liturgical music at this time. In both East and
West the liturgy relied on the unaccompanied voice alone. See
ODB 2:1424–27.

Rise, and let us depart: Matthew 26:46.

85.3 *the prince of Capua:* This is Laidulph, youngest son of Pandulf I
and Abara. See chapters 79.2 and 81.3.

but these events occurred later: The downfall of the abbot and musician, predicted by Neilos, occurred in 995/96.

86.1 *the blessed Neilos spent about fifteen years:* That is, from about 979
to 994.

they indulged in following the wide way: This is an allusion to Matthew 7:13.

86.3 *'To eat bread by the sweat of your brow.':* See Genesis 3:20.

the commandment of the apostle: This is a reference to Ephesians
4:28: "Let the thief no longer steal, but rather let him labor, doing honest work with his hands, so that he may be able to give
to those in need."

87.1 *the wide way to the narrow:* See Matthew 7:13–14.

87.2 *Gaeta:* a city in central Italy approximately forty-four miles
northwest of Naples. At this time (around 994) Gaeta was an
independent duchy ruled by Duke John III (*PmbZ* 2, no.
23492), with his son John IV as co-ruler from 991. See *ODB*
2:813, and Patricia Skinner, *Family Power in Southern Italy: The
Duchy of Gaeta and Its Neighbours, 850–1139* (Cambridge, 1995).

he made it his abode: The monastery of Serperi was founded circa
994. Its name derives from the locality where it was believed a
temple to the Egyptian-Greek god Serapis once stood. See
Giovanelli, *Vita di S. Nilo,* 209–10.

88.1 *the Amomos psalm:* Psalms 118(119), the longest psalm in the Septuagint; it is sung at a variety of services including *orthros,* but it
is most often associated with the funeral service. Monks recited it often as a reminder of death. Its name, Amomos

(blameless), comes from the first verse, "Blessed are the blameless in the way, who walk in the law of the Lord."

88.2   *the wife of the duke of Gaeta:* Emily of Gaeta (*PmbZ* 2, no. 21685), the wife of John III, who visited Neilos in 998. After the death of John III (d. 1008) and his son John IV (d. ca. 1011 or 1012), Emily was regent of Gaeta on behalf of her grandson John V. On John III and the duchy of Gaeta, see the note to chapter 87.2.

89.1   *he would snatch many of them from their oppressors' jaws:* This is an allusion to Job 29:17.

    If someone were to collect his letters of this sort: Unfortunately, no such collection of Neilos's letters has been preserved, despite allusions to his extensive epistolary output.

89.2   *the archbishop Philagathos:* John Philagathos (antipope 997–998; *PmbZ* 2, no. 23486) was a native of Rossano, abbot of Nonantola in 982, and archbishop of Piacenza in 988. Though close to the Ottonian dynasty, he unwisely allowed himself to be elected pope amid the confusion caused by Crescentius II Nomentanus's (*PmbZ* 2, no. 21352) uprising against Pope Gregory V (*PmbZ* 2, no. 22324), taking the title of John XVI. See *ODP* 135–36.

    for he was honored in both realms: That is, in both the Eastern (Byzantine) empire and the Western (Holy Roman) empire.

    the emperor arrived together with the deposed pontiff: Emperor Otto III and Pope Gregory V, who entered Rome in February 998. Pope Gregory V (May 3, 996–February 18, 999) was son of the Salian Otto I, Duke of Carinthia, who was a grandson of the emperor Otto I the Great (936–973). Gregory V succeeded Pope John XV (985–996) when only twenty-four years of age. See *ODB* 2:877 and *ODP* 134–35.

89.3   *despite his advanced age:* In 998, Neilos was probably eighty-eight years old.

    the patriarch: Here the term "patriarch" refers to the pope.

    the patriarchal palace: The Lateran Palace in Rome, which was the principal papal residence until the fourteenth century.

90.2   *the monastery of Saint Anastasios:* The monastery of Saint Anastasios *ad Aquas Salvias,* the present Trappist complex of the

Three Fountains located near Rome, and the traditional location of Saint Paul's martyrdom. Anastasios was a convert from Zoroastrianism, martyred by the Sasanians in 628.

had always been associated with our people: The monastery belonged to a Greek community shortly after its foundation in the early seventh century as a refuge for Eastern monks fleeing the pressures of Arab and Persian invasions as well as persecution by Monothelites, supporters of the doctrine of a single will in Christ. See Andrew J. Ekonomou, *Byzantine Rome and the Greek Popes. Eastern Influences on Rome and the Papacy from Gregory the Great to Zacharius, A.D. 590–752* (Lanham, Md., 2007), 163, 205–6.

91.1   *the holy old man:* Although in the previous chapters γέρων *(geron)* has been rendered as "elder," from here to the end it seems appropriate to render it as "old man," since Neilos is indeed very elderly at this point.

'so neither will your Father . . . forgive your sins.': This is an allusion to Matthew 18:35.

91.2   *he reached his own monastery:* This is a reference to the monastery of Serperi, which is first mentioned by name in chapter 95.3. See also chapter 87.2 with note.

91.3   *A few days later, the pope met a violent death:* Gregory V died in February 999.

the sanctuary of the incorporeal Archangel Michael at Gargano: The pilgrimage to the famed sanctuary in northern Apulia on Italy's eastern coast was said to have been imposed upon the emperor by Saint Romuald (ca. 950–1027) as a penance for his cruelty to John Philagathos. See Giovanelli, *Vita di S. Nilo,* 221–23.

92.1   *"Behold, the tents of Israel in the desert; behold, the citizens of the kingdom of heaven":* The penitent emperor's spontaneous exclamation echoes the chastened prophet Balaam's uncontrolled blessing on the tents of Israel in Numbers 24:5.

92.2   *not to possess a bag, a staff, or two cloaks:* See Matthew 10:10.

'But now, let him who has a purse take it, and likewise a bag.': Luke 22:36.

'Save me, O Lord, for the godly man has failed . . . among the children of men': Psalms 11(12):2.

'There is none that does good, no not one.': Psalms 13(14):3.

He does not take pleasure, . . . but in those that hope in His mercy: See Psalms 146(147):10–11.

93.2 *the emperor's death:* Otto III died on January 23, 1002, near Viterbo, Italy.

94.2 *Stephen breathed his last breath:* Stephen died in Serperi, Gaeta, in 1001. His feast day is the same as that of Neilos (September 26).

95.2 *whether he performs miracles or not:* Here the hagiographer attempts to deal with the awkward fact that he will not record any posthumous miracles performed by Neilos, as would be typical of most saints' lives. As for Neilos's reluctance to perform miracles during his lifetime, but rather delegate his healing powers to others, see chapters 58 to 59.

96.1 *a town called Tusculum:* Modern Frascati in Latium, approximately fifteen miles southeast of Rome.

a monastery of a few . . . dedicated to Saint Agatha: Very little is known about this Greek monastery of Saint Agatha, except that the foundation was quite ancient, perhaps as early as the fourth century. See Giovanelli, *Vita di S. Nilo,* 226.

96.2 *"This is my resting place for ever":* Psalms 131(132):14.

the chiefs of the apostles: That is, the apostles Peter and Paul.

faith as a grain of mustard seed: Matthew 17:20.

96.3 *The ruler of that town, named Gregory:* Gregory I (*PmbZ* 2, no. 22494), Count of Tusculum (d. before 1012), was the father of Popes Benedict VIII (1012–1024; *PmbZ* 2, no. 21143) and John XIX (1024–1032; *PmbZ* 2, no. 23503).

I am not worthy . . . the holy man of my Lord, should come to me?: Count Gregory's words of greeting deliberately echo those of the Roman centurion to Christ, Elizabeth's greeting to Mary and the unborn Jesus, and Christ's own description of His purpose. With them, the hagiographer illustrates that Neilos has indeed become a second Christ and that his path to perfection/deification is complete.

I am not worthy to have you come under my roof: Matthew 8:8; Luke 7:6.

And why is this granted me, that you . . . should come to me?: See Luke 1:43.

> *Since in imitation of your Teacher and Lord . . . over the righteous ones:* This is an allusion to Matthew 9:13.

97.1   *the construction of a monastery:* This would become the monastery of Grottaferrata.

97.2   *the superior Paul:* Although previously unmentioned in the *Life,* Paul had been a disciple of Neilos for some forty years. A native of Rossano like his mentor, Paul also composed hymns and produced calligraphy of high quality, examples of which still exist. He was the second abbot of Grottaferrata. See *PmbZ* 2, no. 26366.

> *the life-giving mysteries of Christ:* The Eucharist.

97.3   *the pilgrims:* The Greek *hoi xenoi* may also mean strangers and wanderers, but here implies those who will travel to visit Neilos's tomb.

98.1   *lifted up his feet:* See Genesis 49:33. This verse alludes to the death of Jacob.

> *"Then I shall not be ashamed . . . all Your commandments.":* Psalms 118(119):6. Neilos's last words are from the psalm associated with monastic funeral services. See note to chapter 88.1.

98.2   *the physician Michael:* See *PmbZ* 2, no. 25351.

98.3   *it was the feast day of John the apostle and theologian:* The feast of the Dormition of Saint John the Evangelist and Theologian is celebrated on September 26 in the Greek calendar.

99.1   *the sun knew its going down:* Psalms 103(104):19.

> *then Neilos gave up his spirit:* John 19:30. Neilos died on September 26, 1004.

100.2 *came to the threshing floor of Atad . . . sore lamentation:* Genesis 50:10.

> *And the inhabitants:* Genesis 50:11.

> *men were truly desirous:* The emendation of the Greek text to ἄνδρες ἐπιθυμῶντες is based on the phrase ἀνὴρ ἐπιθυμῶν, found in the Theodotion version of Daniel 10:11; see the Rahlfs edition of the Septuagint.

Bibliography

EDITIONS AND TRANSLATIONS

Balducci, Niccolò, trans. *Vita di S. Nilo, fondatore del monasterio di Grotta Ferrata.* Rome, 1628.

Caryophilus (Karyophylles), Joannes Matthaeus, ed. and trans. *Vita s. patris Nili Junioris.* Rome, 1624.

Giovanelli, Germano, ed. *Βίος καὶ πολιτεία τοῦ ὁσίου πατρὸς ἡμῶν Νείλου τοῦ Νέου.* Grottaferrata, 1972.

———, trans. *Vita di S. Nilo, fondatore e patrono di Grottaferrata.* Grottaferrata, 1966.

Minasi, Giovanni, trans. *S. Nilo di Calabria, monaco basiliano nel decimo secolo, con annotazioni storiche.* Naples, 1892.

Rocchi, Antonio, trans. *Vita di San Nilo abate, fondatore della Badia in Grottaferrata, scritta da San Bartolomeo suo discepolo.* Rome, 1904.

Sirletus, Guglielmus, trans. "Vita Sancti Nili confessoris, a B. Bartholomæo cryptæ ferratæ abbate græce conscripta." In *Veterum scriptorum et monumentorum amplissima collectio,* vol. 6, edited by Edmundus Martène, col. 887–956. Paris, 1729.

Sister Maxime, ed. and trans. *Ὁ ὅσιος Νεῖλος ὁ Καλαβρός. Ὁ Βίος τοῦ ὁσίου Νείλου τοῦ Νέου (910–1004). Εἰσαγωγὴ - Κριτικὴ ἔκδοσις τοῦ κειμένου - Μετάφρασις - Σχόλια - Ὑμνογραφικὸ ἔργο τοῦ ὁσίου.* Ormylia, 1991.

SECONDARY SOURCES

Cappelli, Biagio. *Il monachesimo basiliano ai confini calabro-lucani, studi e ricerche.* Naples, 1963.

Falkenhausen, Vera von. "Il percorso geo-biografico di san Nilo di Ros-

sano." In *San Nilo di Rossano e l'Abbazia greca di Grottaferrata: Storia e immagini,* edited by Filippo Burgarella, 87–100. Rome, 2009.

————. "La Vita di S. Nilo come fonte storica per la Calabria bizantina." In *Atti del congresso internazionale su S. Nilo di Rossano, 28 settembre–1° ottobre 1986,* 271–305. Rossano, 1989.

Follieri, Enrica. "Per una nuova edizione della Vita di san Nilo da Rossano." *Bolletino della Badia greca di Grottaferrata,* n.s. 51 (1997): 71–92.

Hester, David Paul. *Monasticism and Spirituality of the Italo-Greeks.* Thessalonike, 1992.

Lucà, Santo. "Scrittura e libri della 'scuola niliana'." In *Scritture, libri e testi nelle aree provinciali di Bisanzio: Atti del seminario di Erice (18–25 settembre 1988),* edited by Guglielmo Cavallo, Giuseppe de Gregorio, and Marilena Maniaci, vol. 1, 319–87. Spoleto, 1994.

Morini, Enrico. "Greek Monasticism in Southern Italy." In *Monastic Tradition in Eastern Christianity and the Outside World: A Call for Dialogue,* edited by Ines Angeli Murzaku, 69–101. Leuven, 2013.

Peters-Custot, Annick. "Le monachisme italo-grec entre Byzance et l'Occident (VIIIe–XIIe siècles): Autorité de l'higoumène, autorité du charisme, autorité de la règle." In *Les personnes d'autorité en milieu régulier: des origines de la vie régulière au XVIIIe siècle. Actes du septième colloque international du CERCOR, Strasbourg, 18–20 juin 2009,* edited by Jean-François Cottier, Daniel-Odon Hurel, and Benoît-Michel Tock, 251–66. Saint-Étienne, 2012.

Rousseau, Olivier. "La visite de Nil de Rossano au Mont-Cassin." In *La chiesa greca in Italia dall'VIII al XVI secolo: Atti del convegno storico interecclesiale (Bari, 30 apr.–4 magg. 1969),* vol. 3, 1111–37. Padua, 1973.

Russo, Francesco. *Monachesimo greco e cultura in Calabria, conferenza tenuta il 16–12–1976 e dibattito.* Reggio Calabria, 1977.

Sansterre, Jean-Marie. "Saint Nil de Rossano et le monachisme latin." *Bollettino della Badia greca di Grottaferrata,* n.s. 45 (1991): 339–86.

Index